Impact!

Coaching *Successful* Youth Football

Volume One: The Program

By Derek A. "Coach" Wade

Coach_Wade@hotmail.com

http://forums.delphiforums.com/dwingers

Bloomington, IN Milton Keynes, UK

authorHOUSE™

AuthorHouse™
1663 Liberty Drive, Suite 200
Bloomington, IN 47403
www.authorhouse.com
Phone: 1-800-839-8640

AuthorHouse™ UK Ltd.
500 Avebury Boulevard
Central Milton Keynes, MK9 2BE
www.authorhouse.co.uk
Phone: 08001974150

First published by AuthorHouse 01/23/06

ISBN: 1-4208-9210-X (sc)

Library of Congress Control Number: 2005909168

Printed in the United States of America
Bloomington, Indiana

This book is printed on acid-free paper..

Special Thanks To...

...John T. "Jack" Reed. For his incredible books.

...Hugh Wyatt. Coach, you have done more for the sport of football than anyone else I have ever met. I can never put into words my gratitude for the time you've spent making me better, as a coach and as a man. You're my mentor as a coach, and I'm very proud to consider you a friend as well. Best of wishes to you and Connie, always.

...Steve "Dipper" Popovich. Steve, I don't know anyone that works harder to make his kids successful. Someday you and I are going to coach together, and God help the opposing teams!

...The rest of the forum at Dipper's Message Board. (forums.delphiforums.com/dwingers) I'm very proud to be a part of such a fantastic group of coaches that work so hard.

...The 1999 Kodiak Lions Football Team (Undefeated Senior Division Champions!) You were the first team I was ever fully responsible for, and I am so proud of you. Thanks for teaching me how to win.

...Leon Feliciano, Head Coach, Tomales High School. Coach, you took me under your wing. You trusted me with your defensive backs, and then with your Junior Varsity players. What can I say that could possibly tell you how much your trust means to me?

...Darren Burbank. You left us far too soon. What you left behind was an inspiration, and a 6'2" hole in our hearts.

...Mitch, Jerry, Bob, Bill, Chris, and Frank. Guys, working with you at Tomales has been a dream come true. Every day I learn something new from you. Thanks.

...Steve Calande, Steve De Marino, JJ Lawson, Ted Seay, and Jack Gregory, for their invaluable assistance in proofreading the final version.

...My mom, Kathy Hart. Hey, I didn't turn out *that* bad, did I?

...My grandmother and grandfather. You did most of the work of raising me. I hope I've made you proud. I still miss you every day, Papa.

...My wife, Anna. My love, a coach is only as good as his wife. If you're any indication then I'm a damn fine coach. I know you cringe in March when I start trying to talk about pass coverages, but without you on my sidelines, I couldn't do this.

...My brothers and sisters of the American Armed Forces. You stand on the decks of ships, patrol the sands of far away countries, and risk your lives every day to keep us safe here at home. Thank you, and Semper Paratus!

...You, the coach holding this text in his hands. Without you, there is no football. You're the best thing that will ever happen to a whole bunch of kids. They will never forget you.

...The kids. Every year brings a new group. From the big and powerful to the small and quick and everything in between, they are what makes this sport great. Keep working hard, keep playing hard, and above all, keep living hard. You're the future, and from what I've seen so far, the future is in good hands.

~D.

On The Issue of Gender

The astute reader will be quick to ascertain that the pronouns and possessives used in this text are of a gender-specific nature. In no way is this meant to be any form of insult to any female, living, dead, or walking the earth as a flesh-eating zombie (especially not those). It is simply a genuflection to eight hundred years of textual consistency within the English language. If your world is so empty that you really must be offended because an author somewhere used the word "his" instead of taking the time to type "his or her," or failed to randomly switch from he to she to satisfy a deep-seated need for fairness, well, there really isn't much more that can be said to you.

Sorry.

Not a Joke!

Football is a rough sport. No amount of padding, protective equipment, or preparation can completely eliminate all dangers. The methods advocated within this book are designed to reduce danger to young athletes as much as possible. Use of these techniques, drills, and methods in any way constitutes acceptance of a certain amount of risk and is considered agreement that you indemnify and hold the author and publisher of this work not responsible for any injuries that may occur.

ALWAYS TEACH YOUR PLAYERS TO BLOCK AND TACKLE WITH THEIR **HEADS UP!**

Hey Mom, *I did it!*

"The physical benefits of football playing, as of every other outdoor sport, have been retailed so often I need not stop for them. But their valuable mental and moral efforts have not yet, it seems to me, been set forth as they deserve. I shall make a lame attempt." *~John Heisman, 'Principles of Football' - 1922*

"Football might be the best taught subject in American High Schools because it may be the only subject that we haven't tried to make easy." *~Dorothy Farnan, English Department Chairman, Erasmus Hall HS, Brooklyn, NY. (Borrowed from Hugh Wyatt's web site,* www.coachwyatt.com.*)*

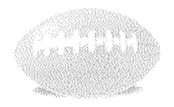

TABLE O' CONTENTS

FOREWORD

By Steve "Dipper" Popovich

Creator: *Delphi Double Wing Coach's Forum*

I'm honored to claim that Coach Derek Wade is my friend. No better friend could there be and no more intelligent, talented and passionate coach have I ever encountered. Coach Wade has a true calling for coaching young football players. In the simplest terms, he is the kind of the man that I would want to coach my own kids from the first day they decided to step onto a football field.

Impact! is a superb coaching resource that I wish had been available when I began coaching. From green coaches to old veterans, every coach who wants to provide their players and themselves with the tools to succeed at football, regardless of the system they run, will find what they need in these pages, delivered with the wit, attention to detail, and no-nonsense attitude that has become Coach Wade's hallmark.

Steve Popovich

Lathrop Titans Varsity Football
Creator: Delphi Double Wing Coaches' Forum
http://forums.delphiforums.com/dwingers

WELCOME TO COACHING

Why Coach Football?

Introduction

Before you do anything on a football field, including step on one, before you purchase a whistle, or a hat that says "Coach," you absolutely *must* have a solid understanding of why you are there and what you're going to do.

Read the above sentence again. I'll wait.

Football, bar none, is the absolutely most complex sport played in America. It is also one of the most dangerous. While not as dangerous as some people think, the potential for a lethal or crippling injury is higher in football than in many other sports.

The National Youth Sports Coaching Association, in a 2002 poll of sports-related injuries, ranked football tenth in per capita injuries. Leading the pack was gymnastics, with a severe injury per child percentage of 6%. While that's not as dangerous as some things a young person could be doing, it's dangerous enough that it should make you scared if you don't know what you're doing.

Teamwork

Football also requires teamwork above and beyond that of any other sport. Basketball is a team sport, but only five players compete at a time. Soccer offers an eleven on eleven competition, but only a very few players can cross the entire field.

Wrestling, martial arts, track and field, these are all team sports that involve competition as an individual. Baseball offers nine on, well, *one*. Think about it: how many men are at bat at one time?

It is only football that offers cooperation on such a large scale. Unfortunately, it is this very teamwork in which the most dangerous vipers lurk. The loss-of-self necessary to be a functioning part of a team, the selflessness that leads one to "hold the fort" in your area when the ball appears to be going somewhere else, or execute a perfect fake and absorb a bruising tackle to distract the defense, requires an emotional openness that can lead to powerful feelings of loss and hurt if the team goals are not successful.

I will use myself as an example. In 1988 I was the defensive captain of the Sumner Junior High Bobcats varsity football team. I was the middle linebacker in a 5-3 front that set records for yards and points allowed. We were *horrible*.

I remember very few things about that season. The number one most vivid is the third play from scrimmage against our rivals, Lakeridge Junior High. That play is indelibly inked into my mind, and I carry the memory in more than that as well, because during an open field tackle on the Lakeridge tailback, Tim Burleigh, I mistimed my approach and heard a sickening crunch as my shoulder was torn apart.

The Pain of Self

As I lay on the field, biting my lip hard enough to draw blood, and watched Tim streak thirty yards to score, my only thought was how badly I had let my teammates down.

I refused to leave the game. We lost 40-0, and as the time ticked from the game clock I remember thinking, *God I wish my mom wasn't here.* Mom was a schoolteacher that had worked her way through college the hard way. Ninety-hour weeks were the norm for her, and it was rare that she could, or would, break away from her difficult job to attend one of my sporting events.

But she'd made this one, and we'd gotten our asses kicked right in front of her.

Most of the rest of that season sits dimly in my memory. The crunch of my shoulder and watching the time tick off the clock are two of the real recollections I have of that season.

The third memory I have of that season is the day we scored our first touchdown of the year. It was a cold, blustery October afternoon, and it was the last game of the season against the Ballou Junior High Bruins.

In six games we were outscored 174-6. Our defense allowed an average of twenty-nine points per game.

Unable to lift my arm, I learned to tackle exclusively with my left shoulder, and spent the season in a fugue of pain. I am no hero. Heroes sleep in foxholes and risk their lives.

Coaches' Promise - *Broken*

Unfortunately, and it pains me greatly to say this, my football coaches didn't uphold their end of the deal. The men I idolized understood less of football than of nuclear physics. They were unable to adapt or modify their ways, and consequently, they continued to use ineffective and often brutal methods.

Teamwork requires open honesty and commitment from all involved. Whether your team is designing a better airplane, trying to score the winning hockey goal, or fighting to defend America in a Middle Eastern sand dune, the emotional attachment remains the same. Teamwork requires a lowering of defenses that you typically keep up to protect yourself from emotional harm.

It is this, football's greatest triumph, which is also its greatest potential defeat. Being part of a team can open a young man or woman up for emotional anguish if their teammates do not uphold their end of the bargain, and the *coach* is one of their teammates.

I know, because I still have trouble putting on tight undershirts, that teamwork can leave indelible scars upon the body as well as the heart.

Commitment

If you are reading this book in preparation for your first season on the field as a football coach, then you need to understand that you are making a commitment to your players. Your age or experience does not matter. One of the best football coaches I have ever met was nineteen years old when he first began coaching eleven and twelve-year-olds. Another coach I have been privileged to learn from had his knee replaced, at age 79, in 2003. His response when asked about it was, "I think I've got ten more years of good coaching in me."

They are both outstanding examples of coaches because they understand the commitment coaching is. They know that, to the players, there is no more exalted title than that of "Coach."

As you read further in this book, you're going to come across times when I say things like, "You need to," and "You must." My reasoning comes from a term coined by Jack Reed in his book, *Coaching Youth Football: Defense 2nd Edition.*

"Coach Hustle"

In this book, Reed makes reference to something he calls 'Coach Hustle.' We all know what "hustle" is. "Hustle" is something you yell at players when they're dogging it during sprints. "Hustle" is something you bellow when you've given two minutes for water and the kids take five.

"Hustle!" is what you shriek when you're down by five with three minutes left in the game and your offensive line is walking to the line of scrimmage.

"Hustle," in my opinion, is the most overused and worthless word in football. Hustle won't teach your players to tackle safely and effectively. Hustle won't teach your players to block the right man. Hustle won't even keep score for you.

"Hustle!" is something that poor coaches yell when they're out of ideas and have no idea how to coach. It ranks there with lines such as "You've gotta hit somebody!" and "You don't *want* to win!" and all of the other choice phrases my coaches humiliated us with as we went, in five years, 1-36-1.

Coach hustle, on the other hand, is something you need to have. *Coach* hustle is answering a promise with one of your own.

Coach hustle is scouting. It's attending clinics. It's communicating online with other coaches. It's searching continuously for ways to improve everything you do, from how you block your plays, to how you teach tackling. These are tasks that poor coaches will find to be "too much work," and hustling, i.e. "Good," coaches will find absolutely necessary.

Football is the most difficult sport to coach of all the traditionally "American" sports. Why on earth would anyone want this responsibility?

There are a lot of reasons. I'm going to detail a few, but the most important thing I can tell you right now is that they are *all* good reasons.

Reasons to Coach

Here are a few examples of why people may choose to coach football:

- Their own kids decide to play.
- They love the game.

- They want the challenge.
- They want to win.
- They want to develop young men (and women).

None of these are bad reasons to coach. Some people, particularly those who can't see past the end of their own noses, think that wanting to win is a horrible thing. Football coaches are always accused of wanting to win at the expense of their players. For some reason soccer and basketball coaches, typically the only sports allowed to practice year-round, are never blamed for only wanting to win. I'm not sure why.

You need to understand something if you plan to coach football: winning isn't the *only* thing, as Vince Lombardi is often misquoted, but it is far more important than you may think.

Winning at the Game of Life

Life is a competition. Self-esteem is based on accomplishments. Those individuals who say otherwise are sadly out of touch with reality.

When I decided to coach, the first thing I thought about was looking at that scoreboard and thinking about my mother. I'll never forget how much it hurt, and I made a promise to myself that I would never, *ever* let that happen to a team I coached. I swore that I would work harder than any coach alive to study my sport, and be able to teach my players to be winners.

I've been accused of only caring about winning, and charged with trying to relive my past 'days of glory' through my players. These are both accurate and inaccurate indictments. The truth is that I don't really care if my teams win or lose. I care only that my players learn the lessons about life that football can teach, and that we are always competitive. It's one thing to lose. It's something completely different to be crushed. Defeats like we endured when I was a player can sap your spirit; make you forget your own worth. I also love to see the world through my player's eyes. What coach doesn't? Isn't that part of why we bought a whistle?

The Importance of Winning

Winning really is important. Currently, there's a wide expanse of wishful thinking that runs through American culture. It's a misplaced belief that if we just want something bad enough, it will happen. Nothing could be further from the truth. The most important goals take time, and you've got to work hard to achieve them. We've slowly come to take our freedoms for granted here in America, and begun to forget that they were bought and paid for with blood by people that understood how important winning really is. They knew that if they lost, it would mean more than getting knocked out of the playoffs. That's the closest you'll ever hear to me making a comparison between football and war.

This is what football teaches. It doesn't surprise me that the best leaders and heroes of the last century of American history have been football players in their youth. I was saddened, but not shocked in the least to hear that the events of

September 11th, 2001 took a horrible toll of the New York City Police and Fire Department football teams. Football players that truly learn the lessons of the game grow up to be heroes.

Life is About Competing

Everything in life is a competition. From job interviews to the dating scene, winning is important. There are some people that feel we place too much emphasis on winning at the youngest levels, but generally these are people that have never played the sport, and don't understand how it fits into life. During discussions online and at coaching clinics the odd parent, and the odder coach, that felt I place too much emphasis on winning, has confronted me. I have generally reacted with a smile and described a situation:

> *'Your son is eight years old and has just completed his first season of football when you discover that he has contracted leukemia. Now, as he lays in a hospital bed fighting for his life, would you rather he have been coached by me, with my emphasis on winning, or by someone that only cared about having fun?'*

What About Having Fun?

This does not mean that I don't think having fun is important, and I do not place all my emphasis on winning alone. There are times when it is just as vital to lose because of what it teaches you. Losing uncovers a lot about a person; like the Chinese yin/yang you must have both to be balanced. Football absolutely should be fun. I want my players to count the minutes before practice begins every day. I want the young men and women that share the field with me to be like our 2002 Black Lion award winner, Neil Spalletta, still suiting up for varsity practices two weeks after the junior varsity season has ended, because, in his words, "I'm not ready for the season to be over, Coach."

Be the Coach You Wish You'd Had

My goal, really, is to create a love for the sport in my players like the men that coached me long ago did in me. I think of how my life would be different if Pat Kelly, my wrestling coach, hadn't approached me in the hallway at Sumner Junior High and said, "You should go out for football. I think you'd like it." Almost twenty years later I'm still indebted to him for that, and the best way I know how to repay him is to give that same joy and love of the game to my players.

What I hope this book will do is give you a few more of the tools you'll need to reach the right balance. Football is the greatest sport in the world, but it is also the most complex, and it can be extremely dangerous to its participants if the coaches do not approach their task with the right amount of caution and a sincere desire to protect their players.

It's <u>Not</u> Me, It's the <u>Kids</u>!

What I hope this book won't give you is a sense that I'm in any way special or responsible for the success my players have had on the field. I am no more extraordinary or important than you are, although I'm probably shorter. I have simply been privileged to coach some of the finest young men and women alive, and our on-field success came about as the result of their efforts, not mine. They executed the blocks and tackles that made us successful, and in many cases it was despite my coaching, rather than because of it. I look at the kids I've coached over my career—Mike McGowan, Juan Ruiz, Jeff Holden, Jon Venezia, Alex Patterson, Ryan Pipkin, Neil Spalletta, Alexandria Hill, Joshua Perrucci— and I wonder how it could be possible to *not* be successful in football with them at your side.

I hope everyone that reads this book gets the chance to coach players just like them.

~D.

CHAPTER ONE
Basic Football Information

Introduction

It has been my experience that assumptions don't do anyone any good. This chapter is here for those few readers that don't really have a frame of reference to the game of football. Its purpose is to establish a common ground between me, the author and an experienced football coach, and you, the reader and inexperienced football coach.

There's no shame in not knowing the game of football. I didn't learn to throw a football until I was eleven years old, and I was playing in my second season at the age of fourteen before I understood the four down system. My coaches assumed that everyone on the team knew as much about football as they thought they did, and they simply forgot to teach important parts of the game.

If you understand football already, feel free to skip this chapter. If you have basic questions about terminology, game play, rules, history or the like, this chapter is here to get you started.

I was astonished at how little I really knew about football when I decided to coach it. Other than the absolute basics (There's grass involved. The ball's pointy), I was pretty much lost. After a season spent fumbling my way around the league, I found some excellent resources online for coaching the sport, but most of them assumed that the reader already knew the basic rules and techniques. It's taken many years of more or less constant study to learn as much about football as I know now, which is less than half what I *thought* I knew when I first started coaching.

When talking about the rules, my reference is the 2004-2005 National Federation of State High School Athletics rulebook. This book is used by 95% of high school leagues, and probably a greater number of youth leagues. Massachusetts and Texas use separate rulebooks and play by NCAA rulings. Make sure that you know the ruling affiliation your league uses, and be aware of any special rules within your organization. Many youth leagues have added changes to the rules for whatever reason that may include restrictions on blocking techniques and alignments. It's your responsibility to look into these changes and be familiar with them.

We're going to start from ground zero here, and build our way up from there, including a play-by-play description of the first half of a high school football game, so if you have never seen the game played before, you should have a pretty good idea how it works by the time you move on.

~D.

What the heck is Football?

Football is much older than most people assume. The ancient Greeks played a form of soccer that they called *harpaston*, and the Romans played another version called *harpastum*. In medieval times a form of football known as *calcio* flourished in Italy. Natives of Polynesia are known to have played a variety of the game with a football made of bamboo fibers, and the Inuit played a form of football with a leather ball filled with moss.

The modern game of football, however, originated in England, where soccer in its first easily recognizable form made an appearance in the 12th century. In later years, soccer became so popular that various English monarchs, including Edward II and Henry VI, actually banned the game because it was distracting their soldiers from the military sport of archery.

Despite this, or maybe even because of it, the game grew in popularity. By the beginning of the 19th century several different versions of the game, all permitting the players to kick—but not to carry—the ball were being played across England, usually in schools such as Eton, Harrow, and Rugby.

The First Time Someone Gets His *Hands* on the Ball—We Change the Name to *Foot*ball!

In 1823 a major rules modification was made when one player, frustrated at his lack of ability to accurately kick the ball, tucked it under his arm and bolted for the goal line.

Soon after, a number of football groups and clubs began to spring up across Britain, playing both versions of the game. In 1863 a bunch of the clubs that played the kicking version of the game sent representatives to London, where they codified a uniform set of rules and created the London Football Association. The kicking game began to slowly be known as "association football," and later, "soccer," a word derived from "association."

In 1871 an association of ball carriers organized the Rugby Football Union, and adopted the rules that were currently in vogue at Rugby School. It wasn't much longer before the game began to be known as rugby football. Both organizations are still around, and still operate as rules bodies for their respective games on both the national and international levels.

In about the middle of the 19th century a new game was developed in Australia that comprised elements from rugby, soccer, and Gaelic football. Australian Rules Football, or "Footie," is a fast-paced game played on an oval field between teams of 18 players. The ball cannot be thrown, but can be caught, and overhand catching, known as "marking" and long kicking are two very distinctive features of the game.

In America, a form of football using an inflated bladder was played in the colony of Virginia as far back as 1609. In 1820, students at what is now Princeton played a soccer-like game called "ballown" in which the ball was advanced by punching it with their fists.

Rule Changes in History

Constant rule changes have been a characteristic of the game of football since its inception. Changes have been implemented to bolster the excitement of the game of football and to increase the game's safety.

By 1906 the game was extremely rough, and many serious injuries and even some deaths had occurred. Educators considered dropping the sport despite its popularity on campuses. Football leaders were forced to revamp the game, and many of the rougher tactics were outlawed.

At the professional level, modern football is a fan's game. In a constant attempt to maintain public interest in the game, NFL rule makers review trends in their sport and make adjustments to the rules as necessary. For example, in the early 1970s, the rule makers brought the hash marks in closer to the center of the field to give offenses more room to throw wide.

The move, which increased scoring and made the game more exciting, also helped bolster the running game. Ten NFL runners gained more than 1000 yards in one season (1972) for the first time in history. During the next season, Buffalo Bills' running back O.J. Simpson rushed for more than 2000 yards, the first time a player had gained that many yards in a single season.

However, the passing game eventually suffered as defenses quickly adjusted. The Pittsburgh Steelers had a stranglehold on the NFL during the 1970s, with four Super Bowl victories. The dominant defensive athletes the Steelers put on the field shut down the wide-open passing attacks that had developed in the previous era. By 1977 scoring was the lowest it had been since 1942, while offensive touchdowns had fallen to their lowest levels since 1938.

Since the offenses were unable to cope with the suffocating defenses, the rule makers felt that the game had to be amended, fearing a loss of public interest in the defense-dominated game. They established a zone of only five yards from the line of scrimmage in which a bump by a pass defender was permitted, and offensive linemen could extend their arms and open their hands on pass blocks. Offenses responded slowly, but by the 1980s they began to score again, and a renewed spirit of defensive innovation began.

To counter the improved passing game, a new breed of defensive player emerged. While speedy defensive backs covered equally fast wide receivers, a player called the rush-linebacker emerged with one specialized duty: pressuring the quarterback. With no pass-coverage responsibilities, the fast and strong rush-linebacker focused his attention on the quarterback or the running backs. The New York Giants' Lawrence Taylor, perhaps the best player of all time at this position, demonstrated the importance of the role by leading New York to a Super Bowl victory in 1987.

Soon, the pressure of the pass rush made longer passes more difficult to complete. Defenses choked off the short pass and defied the quarterback to throw long, assuming that their rush would get to the quarterback first. Additionally, zone defenses, which had been sporadically used since the 1920s, became more complex and harder to read. Offenses stalled. Additional adjustments to the rules have slowly begun to move offensive production back to an upward trend.

The game of football has always been distinguished by constant adjustment to the rules. As the game has progressed, the types of athletes needed to play have also gradually changed. The adjustments and systems in use at the professional level have a way of trickling down to the college, high school, and youth levels, little by little.

The First College Football Game

Intercollegiate football competition began on November 6, 1869, with a game between Rutgers and Princeton. The game was more similar to soccer than modern day football, but it was the start of America's passion.

Columbia, Cornell, and other eastern American colleges began to develop teams soon after and petitioned to be allowed to compete interscholastically.

Harvard University preferred its own rules, and abstained from this competition. In 1874, however, Harvard faced off against McGill University of Montreal, Canada in a game played following McGill's rules, which were very similar to the modern game of rugby. The Harvard players, impressed, altered their own rules to match those of McGill, with some of their original ideas tossed in for flavor.

In 1875, on November 13th, Harvard and Yale played a football game for the first time using Harvard's new rules.

In 1876 representatives from Harvard, Yale, and Columbia met with representatives from Princeton in Springfield, Massachusetts. The end result of this convention was a new set of rules for the sport of football, and the creation of the Intercollegiate Football Association. Although Harvard's rugby-like rules set the standard, certain soccer rules were also incorporated. The resulting marriage was hugely popular with players and spectators alike, and as time went on the rules were continuously adapted until a new game evolved.

The Intercollegiate Football Association was disbanded in 1894, and later that same year a rules committee, dominated by Yale graduate and football pioneer, Walter Chauncey Camp, was formed by the eastern schools. In 1905 an independent association of colleges also formed a rules committee, and within two years the committees merged. Since that time, they have governed American collegiate football.

In 1895 the first professional football game was played in the United States. Sadly, most people in America and abroad today think that professional football is the epitome of football, not realizing that fewer than one half of one percent of all football players play professionally or even semi-professionally.

The Forward Pass

The forward pass that has become the staple of the National Football League's offensive attack has been credited to several different inventors in several different time periods, among them John Heisman, after whom the Heisman Trophy is named. The most common information suggests that legendary Notre Dame coach, Knute Rockne may be responsible for its integration when he was a player at Notre Dame.

In 1913 Rockne was an All-American end, and worked with an excellent quarterback named Gus Dorais. Against Army that year, the duo performed the first ever passing-based attack that set the cadets back onto their heels from the get-go. When the dust had settled, Dorais had completed 12 of 14 for 243 yards with two touchdown passes and only one interception, on their way to a 35-14 romp over the hapless cadets.

Dorais orchestrated a passing attack that kept the Army defense confused and prevented the Cadets from crowding the line. After the game, the press was full of praise for Harper's squad and his revolutionary style of play.

"Coach Harper undoubtedly has put together the best 11 which ever wore the Gold and Blue," Lamber G. Sullivan wrote in the Nov. 2 edition of the Chicago Daily News. "The team is almost perfect in every detail of technical play."

It has been said that Dorais and Rockne invented the forward pass for the game against Army. The pass, however, was not created in 1913; it had been around at least since 1906 when St. Louis University head coach Eddie Cochems began using it.

The Gridiron

Football at the turn of the century was a totally different animal almost indistinguishable from the modern-day game. The field was marked with lines drawn in a graph pattern at five-yard intervals. The referees spotted the ball the nearest intersection after each play, and the ball could not be run forward until it had moved laterally outside these lines. It was this formation of lines that led to the term "gridiron."

The rule against direct forward movement was added in an attempt to make football safer. Theodore Roosevelt, President of the United States and a former football player himself, acted to ban the game in 1905-06 because of the number of serious injuries and even fatalities that resulted from interlocked formations charging downfield and trampling defenders. The most notable and commonly remembered formation of these was the "Flying Wedge." Unfortunately for the game at the time, the gridiron pattern did little to make the game safer, and ultimately, interlocking formations ended up being banned by the end of the 1906 season. (Scrimmage kick formations, such as punt and field goal, allow interlocking ankles at the professional level, but NCAA and NFSHSA rules prohibit interlocking prior to the snap in college and high school games.)

Developing the Football *Play*

There were other rules that made the game appear different. The concept of the football "play" was not introduced until President Roosevelt's potential ban altered the sport. Teams would gain possession of the ball and line up, snap, and try to run one another over. The ball would be spotted, and the teams would immediately line back up for another try. It was a game of brute force. Consequently, tightly bunched formations like the single wing and Glenn "Pop" Warner's "A" formation (a precursor to the modern Double Wing), were in wide use. These offensive formations maximized power, and in some cases allowed for a great deal of misdirection as well.

Substitutions were mostly limited. A player could come out of the game, but not return until the next quarter, so the modern rules of situational substituting were impossible to use. Players needed to play both offense and defense, which led to many of the positions being given the same title, such as offensive and defensive "halfbacks," "tackles," and "guards."

Strategy and Tactics

As the game evolved, more and more emphasis began to be placed on the idea of both strategic decisions made before the game started, based on the scouting reports and common game situations, and tactical decisions based on the ebb and flow of the game.

It was therefore surprising that college football outlawed communications from the sideline to the huddle in the mid fifties. Coaches were forbidden to signal in plays in any way, shape, or form. Some coaches got away with unobtrusive hand signals, but it wasn't until the rule was changed in the late fifties that coaches began to really have a significant impact on playcalling and situational responses to the game.

It was during this same time period that the rules regarding substitutions were relaxed, and the concept of the situational substitution began to come into vogue. Coaches began dividing their teams into offensive and defensive units, called "platoons."

Development of Offensive Football

The offensive techniques and formations prevalent in the contemporary game were developed from the foundation of ideas and concepts used by early and mid-20th century coaches such as Walter Camp, Alonzo Stagg, Pop Warner, Fielding "Hurry Up" Yost, Bob Zuppke, Knute Rockne, and Paul Brown. Without the advantages modern newcomer coaches have, such as mentors, years of successful coaching to study, and modern video and print libraries of coaching materials, these men operated on a wing and a prayer and developed unique strategies that changed the nature of football forever.

Stagg, for example, operating out of the early T-formation, invented the between-the-legs snap from center to quarterback and put a player in motion in the backfield before the snap of the ball.

The Single Wing: 101 Years Young and Still Winning Games!

In 1906 Warner placed four offensive linemen on one side of the center and two on the other side, while shifting the backfield into a wing formation. The quarterback functioned as a blocker, set close behind the line and a yard wide of the center. At the same depth, but outside the line, was the wingback. Deep in the backfield was the tailback, who received most of the snaps, and in front and to the side was the fullback. This formation became known as the "Single-Wing," and it remained football's basic formation until the 1940s. Even today, the single wing is still winning games at the youth, high school, and even small college level.

Warner's "Double-Wing," emerged from the Single-Wing. Both wingbacks were set wide on either side of the line. This forced the defense to spread itself across the field in order to protect against the pass, and to defend against potential running threats to each of the ten gaps.

The modern Double Wing uses this formation for similar reasons, forcing the defense to remain balanced and then using the compressed power of the formation to overload one side or another with pulling offensive linemen after the ball has been snapped. The compressed formation also allows for a bunch passing attack that, by virtue of alignment, interferes with defenders' ability to cover receivers man-to-man, forcing them into zone coverages that can be overloaded.

The Winged-T

Another invention that came about from the natural shift towards wing offenses was the development of the most successful offensive system in the history of football: the Wing-T.

The Wing-T first appeared in a book published in 1940 as an alternate formation to the straight T-Formation that was in vogue. At the time, it was called the "Winged-T." Shifting one of the halfbacks to an alignment just outside the tight end, and splitting the opposite end out approximately seven to twelve yards from the tackle created an immediate running and passing threat. Defensive ends were placed in conflict of alignment. Any time they aligned head up on the tight end, the wingback would block down on them, and the ball carrier would run outside. If they aligned outside the wingback to stop this, the fullback would attack them with a kickout block and the ball would run inside them.

On the other side, the split end forced the defense to a horizontal stretch, and placed the opposite defensive end in another poor position. The split end was located in a prime place to block down at full speed (called a "crack" block) on them, while at the same time they had to be alert to counters and quarterback rollouts. Eddie Robinson of Grambling University developed the offense, and used it to win 408 games throughout his career, a record that stood until 2004 when St. John's University head coach John Gagliardi reached 409.

Despite Coach Robinson's success, the real development of the Wing-T came about at Delaware University, under the able eye of Harold "Tubby" Raymond. Coach Raymond codified a playcalling terminology that numbered each formation, 100-900, and each specific series of backfield actions 10-90. By numbering the offensive holes 1-9 across the formation, the plays could be called with simple three digit codes such as "929," or 900 formation, 20 series, 9 hole.

Even today, the Wing-T is commonly referred to as the "Delaware Wing-T," and thousands of high schools and youth programs use it, many quite successfully.

Evolution of the Passing Attack

Although talented, the quarterbacks of the 1930s and parts of the 1940s seldom completed 50 percent of their passes, while many were even less successful. To begin with, the emphasis was largely upon the running game. The conservative nature of most football coaches prevented more than a very few passes in each game.

Another major cause of these low percentages was the primitive nature of pass-blocking schemes. With little protection, passers always had to throw while avoiding incoming rushers, and it was rare to find a quarterback capable of making the split second decisions necessary to successfully locate the open receiver and deliver a catchable ball while under that kind of pressure.

In the 1940s, the coach of the Cleveland Browns, Paul Brown, installed a blocking system that altered passing forever. Brown changed the system by arranging the linemen in the form of a cup. They pushed most incoming pass-rushers to the outside. A fullback named Marion Motley would meet—at high speed—anyone who penetrated the line to the inside.

From that point on, the passing game achieved a new significance. Other teams implemented strong blocking lines, providing the quarterback with more time to release the ball. The decline of rushing attacks in professional football and the rise of the modern "pocket passer" came about largely as a result of these adjustments to the passing game.

Option Football

In the late fifties and early sixties another advance to the game of football began to change the way offenses attacked the defense. This new concept was the *Option*.

In 1964, Bill Yeoman was the head coach at the University of Houston. He began toying with the concept of using two split backs behind the offensive guards, and placing the third back out wide. The idea of the double option (sometimes called the *speed option*) had been in wide use at least since the 1940s when Doug Faurot of Missouri used the play with a called fake to a diving back. In the double option the quarterback takes the snap and immediately sprints to the off-tackle hole, attacking the inside shoulder of the defensive end, who is left unblocked.

A running back generally gets to a four yard deep and four yard outside angle (called a "pitch" relationship) with the quarterback. This places him far enough outside that the same defender cannot threaten both the quarterback and the pitchman.

The player that would have blocked the defensive end in other offensive systems instead assists with the defensive tackle, preventing him from taking the inside angle to the ball carrier. The defensive end is allowed to come across the line of scrimmage untouched.

If the end commits to tackling the quarterback, this triggers a "pitch" call, in which the quarterback makes a basketball-style toss of the football to the pitch-back.

Properly run, this double option places the defender responsible for outside contain into a conflict on every play. If he squeezes down to defend the off-tackle, the quarterback will pitch the ball to the running back, who will go outside him. If he instead tries to play contain to prevent the outside action, the quarterback will cut inside him for a gain of several yards.

Bill Yeoman and the Veer Option

Coach Yeoman developed the concept of the *Veer*. To start with, no one on the play side is blocked, not even the defensive tackle that is sitting at ground zero for the dive. All offensive linemen avoid the defensive line and instead attack the second level, double-teaming or angle blocking the linebackers. The split back formation of Yeoman's team allowed one back to dive immediately to either side, and forced defenses to respect the dive threat at all times.

At the snap, the quarterback turns and places the ball into the belly of the diving back while looking at the defensive tackle. The dive hits very quickly, and the defensive tackle only has an instant to decide what to do. If he jumps to make the tackle on the diving back, the quarterback will pull the ball back and execute a double option on the defensive end, using the second running back in the offense as a pitchman. If the defensive tackle is caught flatfooted, or moves in another direction, the quarterback will hand off the football and execute a double option fake, further freezing the linebackers and defensive backs.

The near handoff between the quarterback and diving back is called the *mesh*. It is a skillful part of the option offense requiring many repetitions to get correct. When properly executed, however, it remains an extremely deceptive attack in which the defenders simply can't do anything right. This was the birth of the triple option that went on to win thousands of football games.

Houston's Veer attack won an astounding number of games in the late sixties, and led to the invention of the Wishbone Triple Option in the summer of 1968 thanks to Emery Bellard of Ingleside and Breckenridge High Schools in Texas. Coach Bellard had always liked option football and the advantages three back formations such as the tee formation gave an offense.

Coach Bellard felt to be successful on offense, one needed to:

- Have a blocker on a defender with a ball carrier behind.

- Have two blockers on one defender with an option play.

- Create one-on-one match-ups in the passing game.

That summer Coach Bellard, his sons, and some former Texas players ran through the option from a variety of sets and came upon the wishbone. Coach Bellard never called his formations the wishbone. He simply called the formations right and left. The originator of the wishbone nickname was Mickey Herskowitz of the Houston Chronicle.

After Coach Bellard developed the idea he gave his material to his head coach, Texas legend Darryl Royal. Texas tied their first game, lost their second, then won thirty straight games and two national championships while using the wishbone.

The Veer Triple Option attack is so versatile and effective that it is still in use today at a number of levels. De La Salle High School won 151 straight games from 1991 to 2004 using the system, and outscored their opponents by an average of 46-7 during that thirteen-year span.

The offense is simple enough and effective enough to be used even at the youth levels, provided it is competently taught.

Run and Shoot   At the professional level, offenses such as the run and shoot began to take advantage of the passing protection schemes developed by Paul Brown in the 40s, and the game of football continued to advance. Characterized by a two split end, two wingback set, the run and shoot depends on a smart, talented receiver corps and a smart, talented quarterback reading the defense in tandem.

The standard rules developed for the run and shoot were for the receiver, and allowed him to change his pass route at the line of scrimmage. The basic rules were designed to place the defender in conflict no matter what he did or where he was aligned, in much the same way as the triple option was doing in the ground game.

The most basic form for the rules was: "He near, me far." This meant that if the defender were aligned closely to the receiver, the receiver would burst past him on a deep pattern. A second rule was "He in, me out." If the defender took an inside shade alignment to the receiver, the receiver would attempt to release from the line towards the outside, and so on. A well-coached receiver/quarterback tandem needed little, if any, direct communication with each other to execute the correct pattern against the type of coverage shown by the defense.

A modern day version of the run and shoot offense has evolved at the high school and college levels to incorporate aspects of the option passing game as well as the triple option running attack. Using a motion back to achieve a pitch relationship, the fullback can be used to dive, and all the principles of the Houston Veer can be brought into play, while also using an extraordinarily effective passing attack. The downside to this system is the personnel intensive nature of the offense, and the time required to train and develop each position. Air Force, in particular, is achieving fame for their "flexbone" triple option offense that has led to several bowl appearances and victories for the Falcons.

The West Coast Offense

In the 1980's the San Francisco 49ers, under the tutelage of Bill Walsh, developed an offensive attack that was based around the defensive thinking at the time. For decades teams had used a standard offensive style that used two wide receivers (a flanker and split end) and also a pair of running backs in the backfield. Typically, defenses would cover the split receivers with defensive halfbacks (called "cornerbacks" in modern football), and the linebackers were responsible for coverage on the running backs.

Under Walsh, the concept began to evolve of using more three and four receiver sets, forcing the defense into mismatches in which linebackers tried to cover receivers much faster than they were. When the defense began to make adjustments to the offense, substituting extra defensive backs for linebackers, the offense was free to exploit this with the inside running game. Formation, motion, and personnel became more important than the specific play called, and it was not uncommon to see five and six yard passes taken eighty or ninety yards for touchdowns by speedy receivers such as Jerry Rice and John Taylor.

The shortened passing distance increased the likelihood of a successful completion as well, further forcing the defense to react quicker. In 1990, 49er quarterback Joe Montana completed an amazing 91% of his passes throughout the postseason, an NFL record that still stands unbroken. In the playoffs, he took the team to an astonishing fourth Super Bowl win over the hapless Denver Broncos, crushing Denver 55-10.

At a Price...

Sadly, the success of the San Francisco 49ers and other teams that emulated them, such as the 1999 and 2000 St. Louis Rams, has led to a widespread abandonment of the running game at the NFL level. The West Coast Offense is now run by twenty-eight of the thirty-two NFL teams. Purists miss the days of high rushing numbers and Swiss-watch blocking execution, and it is unfortunately not uncommon to see teams in a short yardage position, traditionally thought of as a running situation, decide to spread the field with no backs at all and throw the ball.

Evolution of Defensive Football

An important feature of modern football is the emphasis on defense as well as offense. NFL Hall of Fame Coach Vince Lombardi was once quoted as saying, "A good offense will win you many games, but it takes a good defense to win a championship."

Subsequent to World War II (1939-1945), the adjustment to the rules permitting free substitution of players—that is, a player could enter and leave the game an unlimited number of times, as long as the ball was not in play during the substitution—led to the modern two-platoon system, in which one group of eleven players enters the game to play offense and a second group enters to play defense. This rule change, effected to reduce fatigue, made an enormous impact upon the game of football by fostering the development of individual skills and position specialization among players.

The Early Years of Defense

At the turn of the century offensive football was a game of brute force. Consequently, defenses had to match that force. Defensive strategies revolved around large bodies on the line of scrimmage.

As the game evolved, specific defensive formations began to emerge to counter the offensive techniques and systems that were being used. For example, the 7-Diamond defense used seven down linemen and one linebacker in an attempt to clog the running lanes and pressure the rare pass. Coverages were usually man-to-man since the passing attacks were relatively unsophisticated.

As passing began to take hold upon the offensive strategies, defenses were forced to counter by removing more and more of the larger "power" players they had used in bygone times to stop up the running lanes. In their place they began to use smaller, faster players that could cover offensive receivers as well as travel to the hole and make the tackle on the run. The first true linebacker, as we understand the term, was born.

It was a natural evolution to progress from the eight man fronts of the 10s and 20s, to the seven man fronts of the 30s, to the six and five man fronts of the 40s.

The 5-3, possibly the most common defensive front in football today, in use throughout high school and youth ball, was designed as a hybrid between the necessary run-stopping formation, and the pass coverage that was becoming more and more important to successful defense. Oklahoma coach Bud Wilkinson adapted another version of the 5-3 into an option-stopping defense called the "Oklahoma 5-2." By placing the corners at linebacker depth and assigning zone pass coverage responsibilities, the defense became very effective at stopping the most successful threats of that era.

Tom Landry and the 4-3

In the 1950s, the New York Giants had two things that changed the game of football forever, especially at the professional level. The first of these was a defensive genius named Tom Landry. The second was an outstanding middle linebacker named Sam Huff.

Coach Landry hit upon the idea of removing one more defensive lineman from the field, and using the incredible athlete he had in Sam Huff to play "sideline to sideline." His defense became known as the 4-3, and is such a commanding mixture of power and flexibility that it is still in use today.

The basic principle of the 4-3 is the concept of four powerful and fast defensive linemen that can engage the offensive linemen and keep them from blocking the linebackers. Outside linebackers are responsible for preventing sweeps and squeezing down to assist against the off-tackle run, and defensive ends are usually responsible for rushing the passer.

The middle linebacker is the key to the defense. Much as Sam Huff did, forty years ago, he must play from sideline to sideline, making tackles and stopping the run.

Against the pass, linebackers may either blitz through an assigned gap to overload the offensive blockers, or they may drop back into pass coverage, depending on assignment.

Defensive football has acquired an extensive terminology of its own. In some ways defense is more complicated than offense, because defensive teams have fewer restrictions on their manner of lining up.

The 3-4

The next evolution of defensive football was the 3-4, which is primarily in use at the professional level. While you will find many versions of the 4-3 played even at the high school echelons, the 3-4 is extremely rare. Essentially, the defense is designed to sacrifice a defensive lineman in favor of an additional linebacker who is primarily charged as a pass rusher. NFL teams have toyed with the 3-4, but it has never really achieved the same rate of success or acceptance that the 4-3 has.

Buddy Ryan and the "46"

In the early eighties the stage was set for the next great evolution in defensive football when the Chicago Bears drafted a dominating strong safety named Doug Plank. The Bears defensive coordinator was the highly intelligent Buddy Ryan, who developed the concept of using Plank as a combination lineman/safety/linebacker.

From a normal "TNT" alignment across the front the defense started out looking very similar to a compressed 50 front. However, Coach Ryan assigned a defensive end that was more outside linebacker to play on the outside shade of the tight end, and placed Doug Plank on the inside shade. This became a modified 60 front that put tremendous pressure on the passer, and also could switch coverages easily, assigning that tight end to either Plank or the defensive end/outside linebacker.

The result was the fewest points allowed in the history of the NFL, both in the regular season and in the playoffs, and a Super Bowl win for the Bears It was not until the 2000 Baltimore Ravens, another 46 team, that the Bears defense was bettered.

Most of the innovative thinking by coaches in the NFL during the last fifty years has come on defense. Offensive statistics plummeted in the seventies and early eighties as defenses dominated. Offenses, unable to cope, were forced to amend the game in order to keep up. This led to rule changes such as the 1975 ruling that made it illegal to make contact with receivers downfield, and the 1977 ruling that allowed offensive blockers to use their hands as long as they didn't hold the defensive players.

Zone Pass Coverage

Another huge advance to defensive football came about when a rival league to the NFL was formed in the 1960s. Called the American Football League, this upstart group was unable to attract the talented players that the NFL had acquired, particularly on defense.

Since they were unable to procure a good corner for each side of the field, the AFL teams began trying different types of pass coverages in which defenders covered a particular area of the field, rather than a specific man.

Zone pass coverage had been around for some time, but rarely had it been used so effectively. The preponderance of talent as athletes returned from World War II had led to a reliance on man coverage, and zone became an entirely new way to confuse a quarterback and effectively stop the passing attack. Additionally, because zone pass defenders were watching the ball instead of a man they were able to react quicker to the run and be more successful against the rushing attack.

The Popularity of Football

Teams representing colleges and universities popularized football in America. For the first one hundred years of American football these teams were the dominant force behind it. Rule changes, uniform and safety gear requirements, even strategies and tactics were the result of collegiate decisions.

Today, most fans seem to be attracted to the professional game, but more than 35 million spectators attend intercollegiate contests—played by some 640 teams—each year. Many college stadiums hold more than 50,000 spectators; one stadium, at the University of Michigan, holds more than 100,000.

Ranked among the greatest United States sports heroes of the 20th century are such student athletes as Jim Thorpe of Carlisle Institute; George Gipp of the University of Notre Dame; Red Grange of the University of Illinois; Tom Harmon of the University of Michigan; Doak Walker of Southern Methodist University; Glenn Davis and Doc Blanchard, the "Touchdown Twins" of Army (the U.S. Military Academy); Joe Namath of the University of Alabama; and O. J. Simpson of the University of Southern California.

The Heisman Trophy

In 1935 the Downtown Athletic Club of New York City established an award honoring one of the outstanding college football coaches in the country, John William Heisman. Heisman is credited with legalizing the forward pass in 1906. The John W. Heisman Memorial Trophy, called the "Heisman" for short, is awarded annually to the outstanding college player of the year, as decided by a national poll of sportswriters. Unfortunately, this relatively unsophisticated method of selection has led to an overwhelming selection of offensive players instead of defensive ones. It is also sad to see that this award has never recognized the offensive line.

After World War II ended in 1945, college athletes began to receive football scholarships, often paying the player's room, board, tuition, and incidental expenses while enrolled in college.

The Bowl Game

College teams generally play about eleven games during the fall. The best college teams are awarded trips to bowl games, matching outstanding teams in games that conclude the season's competition.

The tradition began in 1902 at Pasadena, California, when Stanford University invited the University of Michigan to come to California for a New Year's Day contest. This event soon became the celebrated Rose Bowl game.

Bowl games now represent the climax of the college season. Other notable bowl games include the Cotton Bowl in Dallas, Texas; the Orange Bowl in Miami, Florida; and the Sugar Bowl in New Orleans, Louisiana.

The National Championship

The huge number of colleges made a playoff prohibitive throughout much of the history of college football. The result was a national poll of coaches and sportswriters that annually selects the national champion based on a largely arbitrary system of points and opinion.

In modern times, a playoff system is far more feasible than it was eighty years ago, but traditionalists tend to prefer the bowl structure. It must be noted that in a playoff, only one team ends the season on a positive note, with all others being eliminated by a loss.

Critics of a playoff system also argue that with such a system, the popular bowl games would lose their identity. In addition, players' seasons would extend by one or two months, cutting into academic time. However, advocates for a playoff point to the controversial 1993 season in which the Florida State Seminoles won the number-one ranking over Notre Dame, a team that beat the Seminoles convincingly earlier in the season.

Playing Field

The football field is rectangular in shape, measuring 100 yards long and 53.5 yards wide. At both ends of the 100-yard rectangle, white lines called goal lines mark off the entrances to the end zones. Each team defends one end zone. A team must carry, or pass the ball into the 10-yard end zone on the opponents' half of the field to score. Lines parallel to the end zones cross the field at 5-yard intervals.

Another set of lines, known as the sidelines, runs along both sides of the field. In addition, two rows of lines, called hash marks, run parallel to the sidelines. The hash marks are 53 ft 4 in from each sideline in college and high school football, and 70 ft 9 in from each sideline in the National Football League (NFL). Youth teams typically use the high school sized hash marks.

Each play must begin on or between the hash marks. Before each play, the officials place the ball either between the hash marks or on the hash mark closest to the end of the previous play. Situated in the middle of the rear line of each end zone are goalposts, consisting of a 10-ft vertical pole topped by a horizontal crossbar from which two vertical upright posts extend. In college and professional football, the posts are 18 ft 6 in apart. At the high school and youth level the goal posts are 23 ft 5 in wide.

The Ball

The football consists of an inflated rubber bladder encased in a leather or rubber cover. The ball is an extended spheroid, having a circumference of 28.5 in around the long axis and 21.25 in around the short axis. It weighs between 14 and 15 oz. Youth footballs are comparatively smaller.

Scoring in Football

The object of the game is to score more points than the opposing team within the regulation playing time. In case of a tie in an exhibition or regular-season professional game, the teams play an overtime period, known as sudden death, in which the first team to score is declared the winner. If neither team has scored at the end of this 15-minute overtime period, then the tie is allowed to stand.

In professional playoff games no ties are allowed, and the teams play until one scores.

At the college level ties are broken by the use of offensive series. The ball is placed at the twenty-yard line, heading into the end zone, and each team is given four downs in which to advance the ball ten yards or score. If the ball is advanced ten yards, a new series of downs is awarded. If a team scores a touchdown, they are allowed a point after attempt as if the score was awarded in the regulation time period.

The game ends when one team successfully defends the field after scoring more points than their opponents.

At the youth and high school level, ties may be decided in the same fashion, except that the ball is usually placed on the ten-yard line instead of the twenty.

Touchdowns

A team scores a touchdown when one of its players carries the ball into the opposing team's end zone or catches a pass in the end zone. A touchdown is worth 6 points. After a team has scored a touchdown, it tries for an extra-point conversion. This is an opportunity to score an additional one or two points with no time elapsing off the game clock. In college and high school football, the offensive team lines up three yards from the goal line of the opponents and passes, kicks, or runs with the ball. A running or passing conversion in which the ball crosses the goal line counts for 2 points. A conversion by placekick that propels the ball between the goalposts and over the crossbar counts for 1 point.

In professional football, the offensive team lines up 2 yards from the goal line. A conversion attempted by placekicking the ball is worth 1 point.

In some youth leagues, the kicking game is encouraged by awarding two points for a successful placekick after touchdown.

In 1994 the NFL introduced the running or passing 2-point conversion. The ball is still placed at the two-yard line, and the offensive team is given one attempt to run or pass the ball across the goal line and gain an additional two points. High school, college, and youth teams had been using that scoring rule for decades.

Field Goals

On offense, teams may also attempt to score by kicking a field goal, which counts for three points. A field goal is scored by means of a placekick, in which one player holds the ball upright on the ground (youth and high school players are allowed the use of a kicking tee) for a teammate to kick. For a successful field goal, the ball must be kicked between the goalposts and over the crossbar.

After each successful field goal and extra-point conversion attempt, whether successful or not, the scoring team must kick off to its opponents. This ensures that both teams receive a chance to score.

Safeties

Finally, a defensive team earns two points for a safety when it causes the team on offense to end a play in possession of the ball in its own end zone. Safeties are relatively rare.

In certain situations the offensive team may down the ball behind its goal line intentionally. This is done only after a change of possession such as an interception or kickoff into the end zone. This play is known as a touchback and does not count in the scoring.

When the offensive team suffers a safety, it must kick the ball to the opponents from the twenty-yard line to restart play. Teams are given the choice to either punt or free kick (kick off from a tee), and usually choose to punt because the ball is in the air longer, allowing the kicking team to get downfield and make a secure tackle on the returner.

Playing Time

A game of football is divided into four periods, known as quarters, each consisting of fifteen minutes of playing time at the college and NFL level, twelve minutes at the varsity high school level, ten minutes at the junior varsity high school level, and eight minutes or less at the youth level.

The first two periods constitute the first half; the second two comprise the second half. Between the halves, a rest period, usually lasting about 15 minutes, is permitted the players, who may leave the field. The teams change halves of the field at the end of each quarter. The clocks stop at the end of each quarter and at certain other times, when particular events occur or when designated by the officials.

The Positions

Two opposing teams, each fielding eleven players, play football. Each team tries to move the ball down the field to score in the end zone defended by its opponents. During a game the teams are referred to as the offensive team (the team in possession of the ball) and the defensive team (the team defending a goal line against the offensive team).

The kicking situations, punt, punt return, kickoff, kickoff return, field goal, and field goal block or return, are known as the special teams.

The eleven positions of the offensive team are divided into two groups: seven linemen, who play on the line of scrimmage (an imaginary line designating the position of the ball) and a backfield of four players, referred to as backs, who stand in various positions behind the linemen.

Offensive Linemen

Typically, the lineman whose position is in the middle of the line is called the center and is relegated the snapping duties. On his left is the left guard and on his right is the right guard. Outside the guards on either side are the tackles, also called left and right, respectively. On either side of the line are the ends, who are the only eligible receivers on the line of scrimmage.

Offensive Ends

Many teams use two tight ends, but some formations split one end out wide and keep the other tight, and some split *both* ends out wide. Doing so is usually a function of the offensive play called, and it typically has a specific purpose, such as isolating an effective split end on a solitary cornerback, or using a tight end to compress the defense and help block on the line.

Offensive Backfield Positions

The position usually aligned directly behind the center and directing the play of the offensive team is known as the quarterback. In a balanced backfield formation, or "T-formation," the fullback stands behind the quarterback, and the left and right halfbacks stand to either side of the fullback.

Teams may shift the backfield to any possible alignment, and may take any size splits that they choose between offensive linemen. They may also choose to place one or more of the backfield players on the line of scrimmage, for a total of eight linemen, or even more. Doing so does not change the eligible receiver rules; only the *last* man on each side of the line is eligible to catch passes. At least seven members of the offense must be on the line of scrimmage when the ball is snapped.

Defensive Positions

The defensive team consists of a row of linemen, who comprise the defensive line, a row of linebackers, and a collection of defensive backs, known as the secondary.

Defensive Line

The defensive line can use any number of players, though most teams use three to five linemen. Defensive linemen are chiefly responsible for stopping the rushing attack and, in passing situations, rushing the quarterback and trying to tackle him before he throws the football, called a "sack."

Linebackers and Secondary

The linebackers line up behind the defensive line and, depending on the situation, are used to stop runners, pressure the quarterback, or cover receivers. Teams usually employ three or four linebackers. The secondary is comprised of cornerbacks, who cover wide receivers, and safeties, who cover receivers, and offer support in stopping the rushing attack. The secondary commonly consists of two cornerbacks and two safeties at the NFL and college level.

Protective Gear

To protect themselves from the violent bodily contact and impact that characterizes football, players wear elaborate equipment, including lightweight plastic padding covering the thighs, hips, shoulders, knees, and often the forearms and hands. Players also wear plastic helmets with guards that cover most of the face. Helmets and mouth guards are especially important for concussion safety.

Officiating

Theoretically impartial officials supervise play. Professional and major college football programs use seven officials: a referee, an umpire, a linesman, a field judge, a back judge, a line judge, and a side judge. Lower levels of football may use some or all of these positions, depending on league requirements and monetary solvency. Since officials are typically the only persons on the field that are paid for their effort at the youth levels, youth teams tend to have the fewest number of officials.

The officials carry whistles and yellow penalty flags. They blow the whistles or throw the flags to indicate that an infraction of the rules has been committed. The flag is used to mark the specific spot of the foul, since many penalties are enforced from the location the infraction occurred.

Penalties are generally assessed in terms of yardage. Since the objective of the game is to move the ball across the opposing team's goal line, a punishment that moves the offensive team backwards ten yards can have a hugely detrimental impact on its success.

Officials are designated as part of the field by the rulebook, and it is their responsibility to avoid the play. It is not uncommon to see officials trampled by running plays or hit by passes, although some effort is usually made by the players to avoid them.

The Referee

The referee is in charge of the game at all levels of play. The referee supervises the other officials, decides on all matters not under other officials' specific jurisdiction, and enforces penalties. The referee indicates when the ball is dead (out of play) and when it may again be put into play, and uses hand signals to indicate specific decisions and penalties. A white hat designates the referee.

Prior to the snap, the referee takes up a position behind the offensive formation where he will watch for holding within the line, and the safety of the quarterback during passing plays.

The Umpire

The umpire makes decisions on questions concerning the players' equipment, their conduct, and their positioning. The umpire typically aligns just behind the linebackers on the defensive side of the ball, and watches for illegal play in the interior of the line. Since many offensive plays are designed to target this area of the defense, the umpire must be swift of foot to avoid the press of bodies.

Linesmen

The principal duty of the linesman is to mark the position of the ball at the end of each play. The linesman has assistants who measure distances gained or lost, using a device consisting of two vertical markers connected by a chain or cord 10 yards long. The linesman must particularly watch for violations of the rule requiring players to remain in certain positions before the ball is put into play. An officiating crew may use one or two linesmen, placing the side judge on the home side and the line judge on the visitor side of the field.

Judges

The field judge times the game, using a stopwatch for this purpose. In some cases, the stadium scoreboard has a clock that is considered official. The field judge also watches for illegal play downfield, especially on passing plays where his primary concern is pass interference. He is aided in this by the back judge, who also watches for illegal play on passes to the intermediate areas of the field.

The Game

At the beginning of each game, the referee tosses a coin in the presence of the two team captains to determine which team gets to choose whether to kick off or receive the kickoff. The winner of the toss may choose to receive the ball, kick the ball away, or defer the choice to the second half.

At the start of the second half, these conditions are *not* reversed—that is, the team that kicks off in the first half will not automatically receive the kickoff to start the second half. It is the *choice* that is reversed, i.e., the team that chose in the first half must allow the other team to choose for the second half.

Kickoff

During the kickoff, the ball is put in play by a placekick from the kicking team's 35-yard line at the college level, or the 30-yard line in the National Football League (NFL). High school players usually kickoff from the 40-yard line, and youth players may kick off from as close as the fifty.

The NFL kickoff was moved from the 35-yard line in 1994 because the leg strength of kickers was beginning to make the kickoff return a thing of the past. It was not unusual to see kickers putting the ball in the back of the end zone in three of five attempts from the opposite 35.

Onside Kicks

Unfortunately, the corresponding change in field position has made the surprise onside kick an anachronism. The onside kick takes advantage of the rule that once the ball has gone ten yards and touched the ground; it belongs to *either* team, and may be recovered by anyone (although the kicking team cannot advance the ball.) When the NFL kickoff was closer to midfield, onside kicks were far more frequent. Unfortunately, now teams tend to ignore them until the end of the game, when they are behind and need to get the ball back quickly to score.

For a normal kickoff, the kicking team lines up at or behind the ball, while the opponents spread out over their territory in a formation calculated to help them to catch the ball and run it back effectively. If the kick stays within the boundaries of the field, any player on the receiving team may catch the ball, or pick it up on a bounce, and run with it.

Downing

As the player runs, he may be tackled by any opposing player and stopped, known as being downed. The player carrying the ball is considered downed when one knee, shoulder, or any part of the body other than the hand touches the ground.

After the ball carrier is stopped, the referee blows a whistle to stop play and places the ball on the spot where the runner was downed. Play also stops when the ball carrier runs out of bounds.

Calling Plays

A scrimmage (action while the ball is in play) then takes place. Before scrimmage begins, the team on offense usually gathers in a circle, called a huddle, and discusses the next play it will use to try to advance the ball. A coach either signals the play choice to the team from the sidelines, or the team's quarterback chooses from among the rehearsed plays in the team's repertoire.

The defensive team also forms a huddle and discusses its next attempt to slow the offense. Code numbers or words, called signals, designate each play. The offensive signals describe the formation, pre-snap motion, blocking schemes, point of attack, ball carriers, or pass patterns. Defensive signals describe the alignment, gap control responsibilities, stunts and blitzes, and pass coverage responsibilities for each player.

After the teams come out of their respective huddles, they line up opposite each other on the line of scrimmage. If the quarterback analyzes the defensive alignment and decides that the chosen play should be changed, he can shout the coded directions for a new play, known as an audible. Play begins when the center crouches over the ball and, on a spoken signal, snaps it—generally to the quarterback—by handing it between his legs.

Based upon the chosen play, the quarterback can pass the ball, hand it off to a teammate, or run with it. During the scrimmage, the players on the offensive team may check the defenders using their bodies, known as blocking, but they are constrained by specific rules regarding the use of their hands or arms.

Blocking

Loosely, these rules allow the use of the hand in a striking motion into the frame of the defender's body only. The hands may be closed, provided that impact is not made with the knuckles. The defender's "frame" is a box drawn from shoulder to shoulder and hip to hip from the front only. Blows to the face are not allowed, and blocking below the waist is prohibited except in certain locations and circumstances. Good blocking is considered a fundamental technique in football.

Passing

Perhaps the most spectacular offensive play is the forward pass, in which the ball is thrown in a forward direction to an eligible player. The ball is nearly always thrown by the quarterback, and those who may catch it include the other three backs and the two ends. A forward pass may be made only during scrimmage, and then only from behind the line of scrimmage. A lateral (backward) pass may be made anywhere on the field anytime the ball is in play. (Note: Offensive linemen are prohibited from touching forward passes at all unless they are tipped by an eligible receiver or defender first.)

The defending team tries to prevent the attacking team from advancing the ball. The defending players may use their arms and hands in their attempt to break through the opponents' line to reach the player with the ball.

Downs and Distance

The offense must advance the ball at least 10 yards in four tries, called downs. After each play, the teams line up again and a new scrimmage takes place. If the team on offense fails to travel 10 yards in four downs, it must surrender the ball to its opponent after the fourth down. A team will often punt on fourth down if it hasn't gained at least ten yards in its previous three tries. In punting, the ball is snapped from the center to a kicker, who drops the ball and kicks it before it touches the ground. By punting, a team can send the ball farther away from its own end zone before surrendering it, thus weakening the opponent's field position.

The Game

Let's talk through a couple of series of a football game, to give you an idea of what goes on. We'll assume this is a high school game.

To start with, we'll need two football teams. Team "A" is the Albertson Angels. They have a very good offensive line when it comes to run blocking, but they're not very adept at pass blocking. They also don't have any really fast receivers. On offense, they run a Wing-T, and tend to use a sweep series called the "20" or "buck sweep" as their main group of plays. Right now, their fullback is averaging about 5.4 yards per carry. Their quarterback, #7, has a great arm, but doesn't place the ball well on long throws. #21, halfback, breaks a lot of tackles, but is slow for the position.

Defensively, Team "A" runs a 5-3. Those huge, run blocking offensive linemen also play on the defense, since the team doesn't have enough players to platoon. This means that fatigue can be a factor late in the game. They're about average at stopping the run, but they really excel at pressuring the passer. The best two athletes on the defense are middle linebacker #44, who is also that fullback, and cornerback #23, who has already intercepted four passes this season thanks to the pass rush from the defensive line.

Team "B" is the Bravetown Brawlers. The Brawlers are a passing team all the way. They like to spread the field out and even make their linemen take huge, four foot, splits. They have a great receiver in #80, and a quarterback, #12, that's pure magic on his throws. The problem is, the offensive line isn't very good at run blocking, and those huge splits are tough to defend while pass blocking. The result of this is that #12 has been hit a lot this season, and is nursing some bruised ribs. Running back #33 has good moves, but he can't seem to break tackles very well, so the first person to touch him usually brings him down.

Defensively, the Brawlers like to run a 4-4, which gives them a bunch of different blitzes and ways to confuse offensive linemen. They like to pressure passers from all different angles, and stunt linebackers into the gaps to clog up the running lanes. #80 plays free safety on defense, but the rest of the Brawlers are platooned. #51 is at the strong inside linebacker position, and he's averaging fifteen tackles and three sacks per game.

The Coin Toss

Both teams send their captains out to the fifty-yard line. Since the Brawlers are the visiting team, the referee selects the Brawler captain to call heads or tails while the coin is in the air. The Brawler selects tails, but it comes up heads.

The Angel captain decides he wants to get the ball first and try to put some points on the board from the first possession. He elects to receive the kickoff. The Brawler captain is then asked which side of the field he wants to defend. Since there's a light breeze blowing from the West, he elects to kickoff towards the East.

Kickoff

The officials place the ball on the forty-yard line as both teams take the field. The Angels are spread out across the field so they have the best possible chance to recover the football and block their opponents. The Brawlers take their positions behind the kicker, who raises his hand to show that he is ready to kick the ball. In acknowledgement of this, the referee blows a whistle, signaling that the ball is ready for play.

The kicker begins his approach and boots a high, arcing kick that comes down on the Angel's ten-yard line. #23, cornerback and kickoff returner, catches the ball and starts forward behind a screen of Angel blockers. He makes it to the twenty-eight before a Brawler is able to wrap him up with a tackle. As soon as he hits the ground the referee blows the play dead, and the kicking teams leave the field so the offense and defense can come on.

The referee spots the ball on the field at the location where #23 was tackled. When he's finished with that, he blows a short blast on his whistle to let both teams know the ball is ready for play. The Angels have twenty-five seconds after that whistle to get lined up and snap the ball or they will be called for delay of game. If this were an NFL game they would have 45 seconds.

Playing From Scrimmage, Team "A" on Offense

Both teams line up on the ball, the Angels in their Wing-T, with the tight end and wingback to the right, and the Brawlers in their 4-4. As soon as the Angels start to line up, the Brawlers start to point towards #81, the Angels tight end while calling out, "Strong *left*!" Once they've determined which side has more offensive players on it, the defense arranges itself to put their strongest players against it.

They don't have a lot of time to make that read and get into position, because the Angels are lining up in a hurry. They've been well trained, though, so they manage to get there a few seconds before #7 calls for the ball.

As expected, the first play the Angels run is the buck sweep look, but instead of handing the ball to the sweeping back, the quarterback hands off to the fullback, #44, who charges into the line. The Brawlers' defensive line engages the blockers, and #51 comes up hard to make the tackle. He does, but #44 falls forward, adding to the play. He gains four yards. The referee blows the play dead as soon as #44 goes down, and the teams unpile and go back to their huddles.

It's now second down and six yards to go. The Angels' coach signals in a new play, and they begin to line up again. This time the wingback and tight end are on the left, and the defense calls out "Strong *right*!" as they line up.

#7 takes the snap, but instead of handing off the ball, he sprints towards the sidelines to the left. #21, the halfback trails him slightly, in an option pitch relationship. The Brawlers are expecting the speed option, however, and the playside defensive end forces the quarterback to pitch early. #21 charges forward around the end, but is met by the outside linebacker after gaining only two yards to bring up third and four.

The teams head back to their huddles and the coaches send in new plays. When the Angels line back up again, they're back to the wing right, so the defense is yelling, "Strong left!" They try the buck sweep a second time, again handing to the fullback and faking the handoff to the sweeping back, but the defensive coordinator of the Brawlers decided to try a blitz, and #51 stunted right into the hole. He catches #44, the fullback, right at the line of scrimmage for no gain on the play.

The Punt

The Angels are looking at a fourth down and four yards to go from their own thirty-four yard line. This kind of field position isn't very good. They could go for it; running a fourth play in an effort to get the needed four yards, but if they don't make it, the Brawlers will take over on downs wherever the play ends. Since that would be inside their thirty-eight yard line, it would give the Brawlers a very short field to move down and score.

Better to punt the ball away. The Angels line up in a punt formation with their kicker back from the center about fourteen yards. This gives him time to kick the ball while avoiding the rush of the defenders trying to block the punt. When the ball is snapped, he makes a clean catch, and kicks a high, arcing ball that comes down on the Brawlers' thirty-yard line.

#80, the Brawlers' outstanding receiver, is also their punt returner. He catches the ball easily, and starts upfield. The high arc of the kick, however, gave the Brawlers time to get tacklers downfield, and he's swarmed under before he can make it to the thirty-five. It'll be first and ten at the thirty-four.

Since all the plays have been running plays, the game clock has continued to run, stopping only at the change of possession. From twelve minutes it's now down to 10:33 left in the first period.

Playing From Scrimmage, Team "B" on Offense

The Brawlers line up in their spread formation, with two split ends, a wingback on the left side, and a slot receiver in the middle of the large gap between the right end and the tackle. The slot receiver is back off the line of scrimmage, so he's eligible to catch passes.

Since there is no tight end, the Angels use the wingback to determine the strong side, and they yell out "Strong *right*!" as they line up.

Right from the start the Brawlers come out throwing the ball, #12 dropping back as soon as he gets the snap and firing the ball towards #80, who takes a sharp step forward and then arrows across the field at a 45-degree angle. #23, the Angels' cornerback, is ready for him, though, and hits him just as the ball touches his hands. #80 can't hold on, and the pass bounces off the ground. The field judge signals this and also signals to stop the game clock.

A Penalty

Wait! There's a yellow flag on the ground. One of the Brawler linemen grabbed the jersey of the pass rushing Angel. The official signals to the crowd that an infraction has been performed by the offense, and moves the ball backwards ten yards. First down will be repeated, but now the offense has to move *twenty* yards in four plays to get another first down.

They do it in one play. The next time they line up, they motion the wingback across the formation, giving them two slot receivers on the right hand side. When the ball is snapped, both slot receivers block down hard on the linebackers while the split end on that side, #80, runs a deep route that makes the cornerback follow him. The quarterback doesn't drop back to pass this time, but instead turns and pitches the ball backwards to #33, who uses his speed to get outside the defensive ends. He heads downfield, and makes it to the forty-eight before he's brought down, a gain of twenty-four yards.

The Brawlers are given a first down and ten yards to go at their own forty-eight yard line.

Next play they pass again, hitting #33 near the sideline for a short gain. He manages to get three yards before he's brought down to bring up second and seven to go. #12 is shaken up a little on the play, when the pass rushing Angels manage to hit him just as he throws the ball. His bruised ribs aching, he comes out for one play, and his backup, #13 comes in.

Fumble!

Unfortunately, #13 hasn't had a lot of practice taking snaps from the center. He doesn't keep his hands together, and the ball slips up between them. The loose ball bounces around on the ground before the Angels #44 dives on it from his middle linebacker position. It's now the Angels' football, and since the fumble rolled backwards slightly, they get the ball at the Brawler forty-seven.

Both teams continue to battle around midfield until the quarter ends. When the field judge signals the end of the period, both teams are given a brief rest break before they switch sides. We'll pick up the action with three minutes left in the first half and the Brawlers on offense, driving from the Angels' thirty-eight yard line after a great punt return by #80.

On first down, quarterback #12, who came back in as soon as the Brawlers got the ball back, rolls out slightly to his left, looking deep downfield for #80. With the pressure on and #23 covering #80 very well, the quarterback instead throws the ball to a shorter pass route, between the linebackers, to #18, the slot receiver. #18 catches the ball for seven yards, down to the Angels' thirty-one.

Next play, the Brawlers bunch up their receivers to one side, in a triple receiver look that draws the defense over. The Angels don't cover #89, the split end on the other side, very well, but #12's pass is too low, and bounces off the ground, incomplete.

Touchdown!

On third down and three yards to go from the thirty-one, #80 manages to get behind the defenders, and #12 lofts a high, arcing pass that he can run under. He catches it at the three, and scoots untouched into the end zone for the first touchdown of the game with just under two minutes left in the half.

For the extra point conversion, the Brawlers elect to kick a field goal, and when it's good it makes the score 7-0 in their favor.

Like they did to start the game, the teams line up for a kickoff. Angels #23 catches the ball on the fifteen, and manages to get all the way to the Angels' forty-one before being tackled.

Managing the Clock

The game clock shows 1:41 left in the half when the Angels come out on offense. They don't have a lot of time to waste, so they go into a hurry-up mode, lining up quickly and not huddling. Instead, the Angels' quarterback calls the plays at the line of scrimmage based on what he reads from the defensive alignment.

The first play aligns the team with the wingback and the tight end on the left, and this time the buck sweep isn't faked. The ball is handed off to #21, who steams as fast as he can to the outside of the defense.

Unfortunately, it's not fast enough, and the corner on that side of the field comes up and forces him out of bounds after a gain of just three yards. It's now second and seven from the forty-four. At least the clock stopped when he ran out of bounds, though.

Since the game clock isn't moving, the Angels have twenty-five seconds from the ready-to-play whistle to snap the ball. #7 gets the play signal from the coach, and calls the play in the huddle. This time it's a play action pass, faking a run to the fullback before dropping back to pass.

The linebackers aren't fooled, and drop into their pass coverages, but #44 is able to split the seams between zones, and catches a pass good for eight yards over the middle. He gets a further seven yards when he breaks a tackle and barrels over one of the linebackers. Finally, #80 brings him down from his free safety position on the Brawler forty-one.

The clock stops to move the first down markers, and the Angels have a few seconds to get a new play from their coach. As soon as the ready-to-play whistle sounds again the Angels snap the ball, and #7 throws a deep sideline pass to his split end. Unfortunately, his lack of accuracy plays against him, and the pass is badly overthrown. This brings up second down and ten from the forty-one with 1:22 left in the half.

On second down they go back to the buck sweep, giving the ball to the fullback on the dive again. The linebackers are thinking pass, and the defensive linemen are fighting upfield trying to rush the passer, so #44 is seven yards deep before they realize it's a running play. He's brought down immediately after two more yards to the thirty-two.

Using Time Outs

Since they didn't get the first down, the Angels have to use a time out to stop the clock with 1: 10 left in the first half.

This brings up third down and one yard to go, and the Angels get the necessary yardage by swinging their halfback, #21, wide to the split end side and throwing a quick pass to him. He gets five more yards after the first down, all the way to the twenty-six yard line. Again, the clock stops to move the chains, and the Angels snap the ball again with 1:03 left in the half. They try the sweep again, and #21 makes it to the twenty before being tackled. The Angels have to call their second time out with 0:49 left on the game clock.

They go back to the fullback up the middle, but this time the linebackers are waiting for it, and he only gets two yards to the eighteen. The Angels decide to save their last timeout to get their field goal unit on the field if they don't score a touchdown, so they line up quickly and snap the ball while the clock is running. The Angels' quarterback spikes the ball into the ground, recording an incomplete pass that stops the clock with 0:38 left on the game clock.

It's now third down and eight from the eighteen yard line. If they don't get the first down with their next play, they'll pretty much have to go for a field goal attempt.

The ball is snapped, and #7 drops back to pass, but #51 from the Brawlers is rushing him hard on the blitz. The quarterback manages to evade, but the receiver has to break off his pass route instead of going deep, and he catches the ball for only a six-yard gain. This is a first down, but the officials start the clock as soon as the ball is spotted. The ball is sitting at the twelve-yard line, which makes it a twenty-nine yard field goal attempt on fourth down. (Ten yards for the end zone and seven yards for the ball placement behind the line of scrimmage plus the twelve yards out from the end zone.)

The Angels don't want to give the ball back to the Brawlers with enough time to score again, so they sit and wait as long as possible before calling time out. They could run the clock completely out, since the referee blows the ready-to-play whistle with seventeen seconds left on the game clock and they have twenty-five seconds to snap the ball, but then they wouldn't be able to try their field goal.

The Angel captain waits until the clock reaches five seconds before signaling time out. It takes another two seconds for the clock to be officially stopped, leaving three seconds in the first half.

Field Goal!

The field goal unit comes on, and the Brawlers' field goal block team lines up across from them.

The center snaps the ball back to #23, who is holding it for the kicker. He catches it and places it on a rubber block, holding it with the palm of his hand. The kicker steps forward, ignoring the rush of defenders trying to block the kick, and boots it up and through the uprights.

The clock starts as soon as the ball is snapped, and runs down while the ball is in the air. The half doesn't end until the ball is blown dead, and the field goal is called good.

Halftime

The halftime score is Brawlers: 7, Angels 3. The teams are given a fifteen minute rest period in which they can leave the field and get water, talk about adjustments to their assignments, or just rest and conserve energy.

To start the second half, the Brawlers would get to choose whether to kickoff or receive, since the Angels got to pick in the first half. This is why the Angels were so frantic to score before the half ended: even if they were right on the one yard line, once the second half began they'd have to kick the ball away.

Will the Brawlers be able to hang onto their lead, or will the halftime adjustments to the defense shut down #80? Will the Angels' running attack finally get sighted in and start producing touchdowns, or will #51 keep stopping #44? Those are the questions that make football such an exciting sport to, play, watch, and coach.

The Rest of the Book

Even if you've never seen a football game before, as you read through the rest of this book, you'll start to understand more and more about how the game is played. Drop back into this chapter and reread the game summary when you get a little more knowledge.

What Big Things are Made of...

As a coach, you have to be aware of a number of different things that aren't apparent to the football fan. For example, when #13 went into the game for the Brawlers, he wasn't prepared to take the snap from center, and the resulting fumble turned the ball over to the Angels. That could have led to a touchdown, and lost the game. A well-prepared coach would have made certain that his backup quarterback had plenty of practice snaps to get used to that aspect of playing the game *before* he had to go out onto the field.

The Angels, however, did a great job of managing the clock, something that football coaches have to always be aware of. Competent football coaches work on clock management with their teams almost every day, and there's a lot more to it than just running a two-minute drill every now and then.

Both teams have to learn to tackle and block. In fact, all other things being equal, the team that performs each of these key skills the best will most likely win the game. It's the coaches' responsibility to teach these skills while keeping the safety of the players a top priority.

There are literally hundreds of additional skills that football players need to be able to perform. Football is the most complex sport played in America, and it takes a special person to coach it properly. It takes a person that can blend the motivational skills of a leader, the patience of a teacher, and the attention to detail of a dedicated anal-retentive.

I am just such a person, and hopefully, by the end of this book you will be as well.

~D.

CHAPTER TWO
Sources of Football Knowledge – Books

Introduction

My football-coaching library consists of over three hundred books. My wife constantly complains about the space they're taking up, but the one thing she admits is that she has, at one time or another, seen them on my bedside table or the toilet tank. (What? Where do *you* read?)

Many coaches will recommend that you use interlibrary searches for books that are out of print or difficult to locate. For getting an initial idea of a book's worth this is a great idea, but for serious study I recommend the same philosophy that you would have with your college textbooks: *buy* it, *keep* it, and *refer* to it.

Treat Your Football Books Like Textbooks – Because That's What They *Are*!

Every professor I've talked to, most of my high school teachers, and my mother, who earned two Master's Degrees, all agreed on one point when it came to books for college: buy them and keep them, because you never know when the answer you need for next year's exam will be in *this* year's textbook. If you coach long enough, you will eventually run into someone running a short punt offense, and it would be nice to have a copy of Lou Howard's *The Modern Short Punt: A Winning Formation* (ASIN: B0007DP83E) right there on your shelves to study.

Also, it's a good idea to read through different books on systems that you don't run. I've picked up a few neat ideas for my Double Wing offense out of such unlikely places as Dennis Creehan's *The Wing-T from A-Z*, and Bob Reade's *Coaching Football Successfully* (ISBN 087322518X). Not to mention the insight it gives you into *stopping* those systems when you see them on the field.

There are going to be a couple of books I'm going to steer you towards, and away from, in this section. My goal isn't to make you think I know everything there is to know about football, or even about writing football books, because I most certainly don't. What I want to do is show you the types of things to look for in a book, and how to apply those things to your own systems. This isn't a book of book reviews, though, so I'm only going to talk about the three best and three worst books that I own. I'll save videos for Section two.

~D.

Read Any Good Books Lately?

Any English teacher will tell you that a well-written essay about how to do something should be built on a solid foundation of common sense. Haynes™ auto repair manuals assume that you know which end of a screwdriver goes towards the screw but not much more, and there is no reason to be any different when it comes to coaching football.

Problems With Coaching Books

The problem usually comes when a football coaching author does one of two things: uses so much jargon and incomprehensible writing that the beginner can't follow his thinking, or, almost worse by comparison, writes for the level of a ten-year-old. Those guys make you wonder, are you writing for the youth *coach* or for the youth *player?*

Writing a book on coaching football for the youth level is not as easy as people may think. NFL coaches have screwed it up for years. If you're looking for an entertaining read, try the book review I posted on Amazon.com for Tom Flores and Bob O'Conners's book *Youth League Football: Coaching and Playing*. My original review was about average, and called into some question the competence of the authors to write a book about a level of football they have never coached at. Unfortunately, Mr. O'Conners read the review and had to respond. That forced me to update the review to clear up a few points—like the fact that he's never coached youth football and isn't qualified to discuss it.

Coaching in the NFL Doesn't Make a Good Youth Coach!

The problem is, youth football is not the same as the NFL. The animals are so far apart that they're barely the same species. No one with a brain would try to breed a Chihuahua with an Irish Wolfhound, so why assume that the highest and lowest levels of football are the same?

The NFL and the youth game both have a 100-yard field with goalposts at each end and eleven players from each team on the field—that's about the farthest you can take the similarities.

My Favorite Books

Okay, every single person that knows me is going to be chanting this out loud as they read it. I would say that a good 75% of my coaching philosophy, and probably 50% of my technique comes from one source: Jack Reed.

Jack Reed does an outstanding job of pointing out the fallacies most youth coaches hold and the mistakes they make. His books present a real, common sense approach to coaching football. Everything from time management to specific plays is discussed. Additionally, I have only seen *one* book on youth football that discussed the subject of clock management, and that was his.

Clock Management

You don't think clock management is important? Well, neither did I, really, although I went through the mechanics of teaching it. The 2003 football season changed that for me in game two, when the St. Helena Saints put my Tomales Braves down 19-0 by halftime. In the second half we had the ball for eighteen minutes out of twenty, and scored three touchdowns, the final one coming with just 23 seconds left in the game. That final score made the game 20-19 in our favor. The clock management principles that I had just given brief service to for the first part of my coaching career turned out to be one of the most important things we'd instilled in the players, and that game was the difference between a second year of 5-3, and improving to a record of 6-2.

Nobody's Perfect

I like Jack Reed. I've met the man personally, eaten dinners with him, and yakked his ear off for countless hours. There's a coaching clinic in my area called the

"All-Sports" clinic that my head coach sends me to every year, and Jack is always there as well. He's always fun to talk to, and always gives me excellent advice.

The problem is, there are a lot of people in this world that get offended by some pretty stupid things. Jack is, to be blunt, awfully darned snarly. One of his pet peeves is the *average* youth football coach. It drives his hair up when he sees some guy come out and 'coach' a football team to a penalty-fest and an O-Fer record because he didn't take the time to learn how to coach this sport correctly. Since I played on teams that were *coached* by people like that, I admit that I share his frustration with the youth coaches that won't learn their responsibilities properly. I more or less agree with him, and personally, nothing makes me madder than the thought of one of my players getting hurt because our opponents' daddy-coach told them to tackle by putting their "facemasks on the numbers."

It also *hurts* to leave everything you have on a football field and still come away with a crushing 40-0 loss. Try twenty or thirty of those and see what happens to your self-esteem. I don't tolerate coaching incompetence. It's your *responsibility* to learn to coach this sport properly, and if you're not going to make the effort, then you have no business being on the field.

If my saying that offends you, then you need to put this book down right now, and you really shouldn't bother purchasing the rest of the series, because you're going to find it's a recurring theme for me. When kids are counting on you, I don't feel that any adult has the right to give them less than 100% effort.

Confidence Isn't *Cockiness*

The biggest issue that people have with Jack Reed's books is what they erroneously refer to as his *arrogance*. There's a huge difference between cockiness and confidence. Jack knows his stuff; he did, after all, write several books on the subject of coaching football. He's heard from literally hundreds of coaches that have used his techniques with a great deal of success.

Jack Reed is supremely confident in his methods and techniques for coaching youth football. His common sense approach to the game should be the first thing every youth football coach reads. I begin *every* research season, typically February to May, by rereading his books *Coaching Youth Football 3rd edition* and *Coaching Youth Football: Defense.*

Common sense- *Get Some!*

In these books you will find some simple concepts that are difficult to swallow. For example, it seems like basic, elementary logic that youth football teams aren't usually exceptional at passing the football, and if you want to stop their offenses, you need to be able to stop a running game.

Duh! That's probably the first thing I ever noticed about football, unfortunately in reverse. I remember making the shift from linebacker to defensive back and asking my coach why no one ever passed against us.

I don't remember what his answer was, but I can tell you what the reason was: nobody needed to.

Youth Football is Played on the Ground

Youth football is a division of ground-pounders. If you've been to my web site, then you've seen the article written by Clark Wilkins, "Dum Coach," about how a successful passing game can win national championships even at the youth level. Folks, recent research conducted by the Youth Football Coaches Association indicates there are somewhat in excess of *300,000* youth football teams in America.

Of those, I'll bet the entire proceeds from the sales of this book that fewer than 500 of those teams can pass the ball with a better completion percentage than 40%.

$$500 \div 300,000 = 0.0016 \text{ or less than one tenth of one percent.}$$

Yes, there are exceptions to every rule. I'm not going to tell you that youth football teams *can't* pass, because I know for a fact that mine can (yours will, too, if you use the offensive principles that are coming up in the next books). What you need to realize, though, is that this ain't the NFL, and you're most likely not going to see thirty passes a game per team.

If you're watching my teams, you'll be lucky to see thirty passes a *season*. This is because I've bought into the Reed philosophy, and my teams keep the ball where Coach Wade won't get gray hair: on the ground.

Complexity vs. Precision

Gene Cox is a very well respected coach in the Southeastern part of the country. In Florida, his name is revered. His Wing-T based "Multiple Offense" has set records for most points scored and helped him win five state titles in the 70's and 80's.

Unfortunately, I don't think very much of his system, and it's certainly not one that a youth football coach could expect to use with any effectiveness. Coach Cox subscribes to the theory that you must confuse and confound the defense to be successful. His system calls for numerous formations, shifts, motion calls, adjustments, and line calls. The same play is sometimes blocked two or three different ways against the *same front!*

I don't know if this confuses the defense, but it sure as heck confuses me. I can't see the reason for it. When I was a wrestler in junior high, my coach told those of us on the varsity, "I'm going to show you every takedown I know. I want you to pick just *one*, and that's going to be *your* takedown. No matter what I tell you to practice after that, you just practice your takedown."

Instinct

What Coach Kelly wanted from us was *instinct*. When I took a stance against the wrestler from Lakeridge, he darn well knew that I was going to be firing as soon as the whistle blew for a double leg tackle, and we *both* knew that he was going to the mat.

That's the sort of instinct Jack Reed wants his players to have. That's the sort of reflex I want instilled in my players.

It's only going to get there one way, folks. You, as the coach, have to put it there.

Are *You* a Coach?

I read a book review of Jack Reed's books on Amazon.com that cracked me up. Some guy made a number of comments about Reed's systems, all the while being sure to say, "I'm not a coach, *but....*" He was also sure to point out that his son had been a great blitzing linebacker in a 6-2 defense, but then his coach had switched to the Reed "Gap-Air-Mirror" (GAM) and his son hadn't made a sack all season.

Well, I hate to tell the guy this, but the game of football involves more than just his kid. That's in the *first* place. In the second place, how about if you let the coaches make the decisions about what defenses to run, huh? If you want to make those decisions, buy a whistle and be here from 5:45 to 8:15.

I've heard from a lot of guys that tried the GAM defense, or the Single Wing offense that Reed recommends. Of course, they didn't buy into the system completely. "Can't do that in our league," they'd tell me. "We just can't put eight guys on the line of scrimmage like that." So they make a bunch of unsound changes to the system. They pull their linebackers off the line of scrimmage, or install a zone-based pass coverage scheme.

Blaming the System

Then some team shreds their defense for three hundred rushing yards off tackle because the linebackers are off the line and out of position, and suddenly it's the fault of the *defense*. Somehow Jack Reed is to blame for what happened.

Coach, Jack Reed is *never* going to be on your practice field. You are, so who is responsible for what happens? You need to run his stuff *as written*, if you want to use his system. Half-assing it is *not* going to work!

I don't use Reed's offense. I found a better one that I'll describe in detail in volume four of this series. I used the *heck* out of his defense, though, and destroyed the league. I also still use most of the coaching principles he advocates in his books, like keeping the kids moving and not wasting time talking. You'll find that my chapter on practice planning covers a lot of ground that mirrors Reed's ideas, if in more detail.

Even at the high school level, having the brains to not flap your jaw can save your season. I've seen a coach that wouldn't shut his mouth and give them a chance to practice screw his team. You need to avoid making that mistake.

Winning With the Reed System

On the other hand, I've talked with literally hundreds of coaches that use Reed's systems and are winners. I, myself, as a rookie head coach in all but name in 1999, went undefeated because I ran his *defense*. I've wondered for years how good we could have been if I'd been smart enough to order the books with his *offense* in them.

Using only the Gap-Air-Mirror defense, *very slightly* modified, our defense was able to shut out four opponents, and finished the season allowing a total of 168 offensive yards from scrimmage. That's an average of 28 offensive yards *per game*! We also scored three times on defense. Opposing parents would groan when we didn't make a first down, because they knew their offense wouldn't go anywhere but backwards against our defense.

Give credit where it's due, I made a lot of mistakes that season, but the kids triumphed, and the scheme gave them a chance to be successful despite my lack of knowledge and experience. I owe any success I had as the Lions' head coach to Jack Reed and the kids.

Review

Coaching Youth Football 3rd Edition
By Jack Reed.
(ISBN 0-939224-40-2)
★ ★ ★ ★ ★ (5.0 *Highest rating!*)
Available through: www.johntreed.com.

Get this book. Look past Jack's comments about the *average* youth coach. Understand that you aren't average because you're working hard to learn your sport better. Apply the information and concepts he has in his book to your own practices. You'll be glad you did. After you've read it, try Reed's other materials on coaching youth football.

A Good Offense

I mentioned above that I don't use Jack Reed's single wing. It's a good system, and I agree with his reasons for selecting it. In fact, I took those reasons and put my own spin on them when I finally decided to go with a slightly different approach.

I wanted power, misdirection, and explosiveness. There were some other criteria that I'll go over in more detail in the next book, but the bottom line is that I wanted a little more flexibility than the Single Wing had to offer.

Not that the Single Wing isn't flexible. My problem was that I didn't particularly care for the Reed flavoring to the offense. There are some things that he does that I would like to do differently.

I wanted a tight, compressed formation that could help me with the passing game by utilizing crossing routes and rubs to scrape my receivers clear of coverage. I also wanted power and easy-to-understand blocking schemes that I could teach at any level.

Ask Someone You Can Trust

So, I went to the one source of football coaching material that I felt I could rely on. I went to Jack Reed to ask him where I could find an offense that met those criteria.

Jack had been intrigued by the Double Wing, and although he'd run it with a couple of variations that made it a kissing cousin to his Single Wing, he'd gotten most of his ideas from one source, a book called *The Toss: A New Offensive Attack for High Scoring Football* by Jerry Vallotton.

As soon as I got the email from Jack, I leapt to the Amazon.com web site and placed an order for that book. It was one of the smartest moves I've ever made in my life.

Inside the pages of that book I found everything I was looking for. In the final volume to this coaching series I'll give you my offense and how I coach it, in fact, I'll give you my entire playbook, but to really understand the Double Wing and expand on it for yourself, you're going to need to locate copies of *The Toss*.

Ordering *The Toss*

The best place to do that is www.doublewing.org. That's Jerry Vallotton's web site, and you can place an order with him. The publisher that he was going through dropped him (dumb move), so he's now self-published.

Review

The Toss: A New Offensive Attack for High Scoring Football
By Jerry Vallotton
(ASIN 0136325483)
★ ★ ★ ★ ★ (5.0 *Highest rating!*)
Available through: www.doublewing.org.

There are a lot of sources of material out there on the Double Wing, but the first place I always send new coaches is to this book. It's not only a great playbook, but it's a manual of installation, and also gives you a frame of reference to start with when you're discussing the system with other Double Wing coaches.

Building a Successful Program

Sooner or later, if you stay in coaching, you're going to have to put together a system from scratch. I'll try to help you out with that here, but I'm also going to point you towards someone that built two incredible systems from the bottom up.

Bob Reade coached J.D. Darnall High School in Geneseo, Illinios from 0-9 to a sixty straight game winning streak, and then moved to Augustana University, where winning was something they hadn't been able to manage for even a single game in three years. There, he coached the Vikings to a seventy-five game winning streak. In his book *Coaching Football Successfully* (ISBN 087322518X), Coach Reade shows you, step by step, how he pulled that off.

If you're looking for systems, Reade has them. I'll be truthful and tell you that I don't particularly like his offense or defense for the youth level. While coaches like Clark Wilkins and Malcolm Robinson have proven time and again that the triple option is possible, and even quite effective, below the freshman level the odds of teaching it successfully remain slim.

Building a Winner

What I like the most about Reade's book is the way he takes you through the philosophy of coaching a successful program. My firm belief in a "two-up/three-down" substitution rule comes straight from part one, where Coach Reade points out the stupidity of trying to "keep a score respectable" when you have subs on the sideline that could improve your team in the future if they got experience now.

Quite often coaches get caught up in the points and forget the point. You have to think long-term, and remember that today's rookies are tomorrow's veterans. Besides, our playing days are over. We're here now to create a new generation of kids that love the sport of football, and in order to do that, they have to get on the field.

The Foundation of Success

The book is well worth the cover price based on section three by itself. This part of the book is all about preparing for game day. Building a scouting report, planning your practices, motivating your kids, everything you need to know to get your team ready to flatback your opponents is in this section.

Reade also fills his books with some pretty humorous anecdotes. My favorite is about the scout that was sent to make notes on an upcoming opponent. Apparently he got bored, because the scouting forms were blank except for the single sentence, "Check out the third cheerleader from the left. She's a fox!" Apparently that scout doesn't work with Coach Reade any more. I can't say that I'm incredibly surprised. Personally, I'd have killed him.

Review

Coaching Football Successfully
By Bob Reade
(ISBN 087322518X)
★ ★ ★ ★ ★ (5.0 *Highest rating!*)
Available through: www.amazon.com

Reade's book is about an entire program, start to finish. If you're just looking for help with line blocking or a specific defense, it's not going to be the on target volume you're looking for.

On the other hand, though, if you have any desire to take your own football team, at any level, and be successful with them, this is a great book to take you step-by-step from the foundation to the battlements of program development.

Books to Avoid

When I got the bug to coach again, I went online looking for resources, and since my favorite web site at the time was Amazon.com that was the first place I looked for materials.

That turned out to be a mistake. At the time, the American Sports Education Program (ASEP) had a rather poorly written book titled *Coaching Youth Football*. Well, as you've seen above, Jack Reed's book has the same title.

Someone, several someones in fact, had gone on Amazon and reviewed Reed's book in glowing terms. Unfortunately, the review was attached to the ASEP book because of the title.

I paid nine bucks for that book, and another nine for mouthwash to get the taste of it out of my mouth.

Problems

There were a lot of problems with the book, but the largest was that the authors simply couldn't make up their minds if they were talking about tackle football or flag football. They ended up writing a book that explained neither one very well, and definitely made my 'worst' book list.

A great deal of the information contained in the book is wrong or completely irrelevant. Explain to me why a tackle football coach needs to know the required length of flags?

Review

Coaching Youth Football
By American Sports Education Program
(ISBN 0736037926)

★ ⟩ (1.5 *Bad!*)
Available through: Why bother?

Badly put together, poorly organized, and written for a fifth grader, the book would simply insult the intelligence of the average youth coach. Worse, any dad-coach that hit the field with only this book and his good intentions would find himself either getting someone hurt, or just losing every game 40-0. I don't really like either option.

What the *Hell?*

When a person writes a book on a subject, you generally expect them to be somewhat knowledgeable on that particular subject. For example, if you read Stephen Hawking's *A Brief History of Time*, you can operate freely with the assumption that he knows a thing or two about quantum mechanics and physics. That's why you're willing to shell out $19.95 for the book, right?

So, what happens when a football coach that doesn't know the rules writes a book on coaching the sport? What if his grasp of offensive theory is abysmal? What if he lists seven defenses, but doesn't bother to show anything but alignments, and completely omits pass coverage rules and gap control responsibilities? What if several of those fronts are completely unsound against the offensive formation he's drawn them against? What if the author completely disregarded *all* special teams?

Well, then you have Ray Leiber's *For Kids' Sake: Teaching Tackle Football*. Fighting hard for the number two slot on my all-time crappiest listing, this book does a great job of making me wish that Coach Lieber were in my league.

Castrated Football

I don't want to be in *his* league, though. I got an email from a coach after I reviewed *For Kids' Sake* on my web site. This coach is in the same league that Lieber is, and he told me a little about the restrictions they have there. You'll hear my views on restrictive coaching rules later on, but before you do, answer me this: Do you really want to take advice from a guy that coaches in a league that:

- Requires a 6-2-3 defense for every team,

- Requires corners and linebackers to be five yards from the line of scrimmage,

- Restricts the defensive backfield from being in motion towards the line at the snap,

And,

- Eliminates punts, field goals, and kickoffs?

Don't Write a Book on Football Unless You Know the Rules!

I mean, come on! Let's reconnect with reality, shall we? Where does a guy get off writing a book on coaching football and leaving a third of the game out? How can this dude even look himself in the eyes in the mirror after writing a book on football in which he makes blunders like these:

- Page 7-1 "The offensive backs cannot line up on the line of scrimmage or the seven man rule will be violated." (Coach Leiber is referring to a completely *mythical* rule that requires no more than seven men on the line of scrimmage. This is a clear error. Rule 2, Section 14, Article 1 of the NFHSH Rule Book states that seven is a *minimum*; there is absolutely no *maximum!*)

- Page 8-3 "A defender can jump into the neutral zone as long as he gets back before the center snaps the ball." (*What?* Is Coach Leiber watching too much TV? This is an NFL and NCAA rule. Unless you're in Massachusetts or Texas, which use NCAA rules for high school, you're probably coaching in one of the 95% of football leagues where this is illegal!)

That's Not What I Meant by *Offensive*!

The offensive portion of the book is also poorly written. Maybe I got spoiled by Jack Reed's book in which he spends seven pages talking about *one play*, but I expected more than a diagram to teach me how to run an offense. I also was not surprised to see that the plays are shown against only one defensive front: the lone defense Coach Leiber faces, a 6-2-3 with deep linebackers and landmark zones.

The weakest part of the offense is the lack of a system. Plays don't 'interconnect' with one another. For most formations there are only one or two plays shown, which means if you scout Coach Lieber's team and see his tendencies, then you know where each play is coming as soon as he lines up. (Note: This isn't the same as challenging a defense to stop you from running the plays you run the best, like I do with my Double Wing.)

Worse, if you tried to run his system, you'd be reduced to grab-bagging your plays, hoping to find something that worked.

Misdirection in his system is very feeble, and back positioning would place the fakers in clear view of the linebackers. Not a big deal when those 'backers are five yards from the line, but a little more significant if they're in a normal alignment and scraping to a gap.

This Sucks, Want Some More?

I was vastly amused that the final section of the book didn't contain special teams information, but instead was comprised of three tear-out order forms for *more copies of the book!* (Hey coach! Maybe next time you could instead drop in some stuff on punting. We need that a lot more than we really need extra copies of a book we already have.)

Review

Coaching Youth Football
By American Sports Education Program
(ISBN 0965998509)

✴ (1.0 *Horrible!*)
Available through: Why bother?

I don't think it's too much to ask that the author of a book on football be familiar with the rules. The standard high school rulebook used by 95% of teams in the country is available through the National Federation of State High School Athletics for $4.95. If you're coaching this sport, it's a requirement that you get it and read it. Yes, it's dry and boring, but it's your *job*.

If you're going to write a book about football, *learn the rules!*

The Best of the Worst!

Now, we're finally at the all-time worst football coaching material I know of. There's only one thing worse than buying something that sucks, and that's buying something that sucks from someone that claims everyone else in the world is an idiot.

If you've been to my web site, then you're familiar with the pop-up window I installed in July of 2003. I hate pop-ups. I'm sick and tired of trying to access my 'Yahoo!' email only to have ninety-gazillion ads for nasal wart cream and ear-lengthening pills pop up and bother me. I'm ornery about it at the best of times.

I put that window on the web site because I really didn't have much of a choice. In late June of 2003 a friend of mine in the Delphi Double Wing Coaches' forum informed me that he had purchased some *very* poor coaching materials from a guy online.

Art and Dan Haege—A Fool, His Son, and Their "Manual!"

The joker he purchased from was named Dan Haege, and he ran a web site on which he sold two things: football coaching "manuals" and a workout program designed for big men. Now, I've talked to a lot of medical and strength professionals, including some strength and conditioning coaches from Div-I and professional sports teams, and my training and conditioning instructor at the

American Military University. To a man, each and every one of them has laughed at the preposterous notion that size has anything to do with the structure of a weight lifting workout.

I digress. The football coaching "manual" that my friend had ordered was a fifteen-page copy of badly typed and spelled notes. In fact, several of the pages were actually out of order and had to be put back together correctly. When he emailed the seller and politely asked for his *thirty bucks* back, the seller became abusive and threatening.

Face Tackling—Dangerous and Against the Rules!

I got involved when my buddy sent me a copy of this material. As I read through the preposterous notions of an ego-driven jackass with delusions of grandeur, I suddenly got very, very concerned. Not only did Dan Haege's 'manual' contain no practical or useful information about coaching football at the youth level, but it also advised coaches to teach "nose on the numbers" tackling. This is *dangerous, ineffective*, and <u>*illegal*</u>.

I ended up sending an email to Danny-boy in which I, rather patiently I thought, explained to him that real football coaches no longer teach hitting with the facemask, and that, in fact, a 1986 NFSHSA rule change added 9-4-2i to the books, "No player shall butt block, <u>face tackle</u> or spear an opponent." Additionally, I informed him that if I ever heard of a child becoming injured thanks to his attempts to make a buck, I'd personally lead a crusade to have him sued —or at the very least, lynched.

The email I got back doesn't bear repeating.

I must admit I got a little assed when I read Danny's response to my initial comments. Okay, I got really assed. The bottom line is that it is the responsibility of all good football coaches to protect their players and coach within the rules of the sport. Tackling with the facemask is illegal, *period*. To advocate or teach those tactics is wrong.

Imagine This

Here's my worst-case scenario: imagine a youth football coach. He's a dad, and his eight-year-old son is in his first year of playing.

Dad-coach doesn't remember much, other than his high school days from twelve years before, but he vaguely remembers a tackling method that involved the numbers and the helmet somehow. Unfortunately, since he's the head coach (no one else was interested), he's got to find some way to teach tackling.

So he goes online and runs a web search for "Football manuals." The web site he comes to is Dan Haege's.

He's not turned off by Danny's misspellings and grammatical mistakes on the web site, because he's thinking, "Hey, this guy's a coach, and he claims his dad has been coaching for forty years. I can't expect him to be a writer, too. Besides, there's a picture of Kurt Warner in a Rams uniform on the main page."

He buys the "manual." When he reads it, he doesn't know that 68 high school players were *killed* the year before face tackling was outlawed by the NFSHSA. He might even snap his fingers and say, "That's right!" when he sees the paragraph on tackling, because it jives with his faded memories.

Tomorrow he goes to practice.

What if...?

What if that was your son he's coaching? What if he's on your schedule, and your ten-year-old running back is going to be carrying the ball when his linebacker comes up and slams his facemask into the ball carrier's ribs.

Think this is farfetched? Believe me, it's not even close. There are *high school coaches* that still teach face tackling, largely because "I've always done it that way and see no reason to change." In August of 2004 I posted a message on the eTeamz message board at the website http://eteamz.active.com/football/boards/football/ about proper tackling form, and one football coach responded to me that he'd been teaching face tackling for thirty years without a problem.

Not having a problem doesn't mean that it's safe, and just because you've done it for thirty years is no reason to continue doing it after you've been told it's illegal and dangerous.

Why change? I mean, they're only someone else's kids, right?

The bottom line is that I wrangled with Dan Haege via email for a couple of weeks before I finally told him, point blank, that every obscene comment and insult he'd emailed me would be posted in loving detail on my web site. I won't bore you with a recap, but some of the things he said about youth coaches are truly vile. Now, I don't particularly care if Danny Haege thinks that I'm a good coach or not. I'm not in this business to get rich or win friends. I'm in this business to help kids. To do that, I do whatever I can to help coaches, which is why I'm steering you *away* from the Haeges'.

On a Personal Note

It goes like this: Art and Dan Haege have developed coaching materials that present no real knowledge of football, they hold nothing but contempt for the youth football coaches, and the methods they advocate can get kids hurt. I strongly recommend that every coach that reads this book avoid the Haeges and their material.

Review

Football Coaching "Manuals" by Art Haege
Published by his son, Dan Haege

☽ (.5 *Potentially lethal!*)
Available through: Who cares?

Safe and effective techniques are out there, and it is the responsibility of all good coaches to discover those techniques and learn to teach them properly. Taking shortcuts and using techniques demonstrated time and again to be illegal is only going to get kids hurt. I won't condone that.

CHAPTER THREE
Sources of Football Knowledge – Video

Introduction

Picture is worth a thousand words. Moving pictures are probably worth more. Moving pictures of a football team are priceless.

It's one thing for me to sit here and tell you how to coach football. I can write out, word-for-word, everything you need to do in order to teach the fullback dive from the Wing-T's 100 formation, but that is simply not the same as seeing it happen.

That's because writing is an *abstract*. Stephen King, David Eddings, Terry Pratchett, and David Drake are world-famous authors in several genres. What brings their writing to the forefront is the ability to write with a clarity that causes the reader to 'see' what they intend in a scene. I can remember getting ideas for stories and the frustration that comes with them; the knowledge that no matter how well I wrote, the reader would never see the landscapes searing across my mind, or be able to imagine the creatures and people precisely as I saw them in my head.

This is part of why most coaching books are so poor. Being a good coach doesn't make you a good writer. Being a good writer doesn't make you a good coach. It's the rare cat that can be good at both.

Importance of Video

Video can be amazingly helpful. I can tell you exactly how to teach a single handed bail technique for a corner to bump a receiver off his intended route, but that's not going to be nearly as effective as one single still picture, demonstrating the technique. Video demonstrating the technique can explain so much more that it's not even funny.

Special Teams

Where video is really important is with special teams play. Although special teams are extremely important (According to NFL.com, the average change of field position on punts in the NFL during the 2003 season was 31.12 yards. The average change per scrimmage play: 2.33 yards.), the relatively few number of these plays makes it hard to be familiar with them.

We all have a smattering of an idea how a drop back pass is supposed to look. We've all seen Joe Montana and Drew Bledsoe take a snap and crossover step three, five, or seven times while reading a defense. In fact, thanks to the NFL's inability to run the football any more, we're seeing a lot more of that than I'd like to. NFL teams run about fifty plays per game, and about thirty to forty of those are passes.

At best, though, you'll probably see eight to ten kickoffs in a game. That sounds like a lot, but if you figure the points on that, you're looking at 56 total points and you'll only see eight kickoffs. That's a pretty high scoring game: 56-0, 49-7, 42-14, 35-21, etc.

So, although you've seen close to a hundred offensive plays, you've probably only seen eight kickoffs, seven to twelve punts, and eight PATs.

Camera on the Ball, Not the Play

Also, because the cameraman only follows the darn ball, you won't see the blocking patterns for a punt return or kickoff return at all. In fact, although I watch about sixty NFL or college games a season, I still can't tell if a punt return team is running a wall or a standard return most of the time because the camera is never where I want it to be. It's hard enough trying to tell if they're even going for a block or a return.

The commercial breaks cause some heartache, too. Typically, the NFL and Div-I televised games cut to a commercial after a touchdown, and then cut back to the field just before the start of the PAT attempt. That means you don't get more than a few brief seconds to try and figure out the defensive alignments before the snap. About the best you can do is tape the game and try to run it back in slow motion.

Not that it's going to help you much, anyway. The NFL and Div-I games are too far removed from the youth game to be of any use. Besides, NFL players generally don't even *try* to block extra point kicks.

Where Are Your Skills the Weakest?

You're going to need some videos that give you a chance to see the skills and positions you're not familiar with. I was fortunate as a younger player, in that I started my first season at guard, moved to center, moved to fullback, drifted back to the line to play tackle, moved outside to play tight end, and ended the season at quarterback.

Defensively, I started on the inside and worked outwards on the defensive line before my coach noticed that I wasn't growing and I started moving towards the backfield. By the time I was a sophomore I'd played every possible position on both sides of the ball with the solitary exception of placekicker and punter.

What this has *not* done is improve my ability to coach any of these positions, since all that moving around gave me "jack of all trades, master of none" training. On the other hand, it's made me realize that each position has separate skills and techniques that have to be mastered.

Take long snapping, for example. I long snapped *once* in seventh grade. I know the basics, but that's not good enough. In fact, if it wasn't for Fred Guidicci of Menlo College patiently explaining to me how to teach the snap, and the excellent video by Mark Ingram I'd be in a real bind trying to teach that skill.

Videos Are Usually a Safe Investment

When I first decided to put together this chapter it was my intention to follow the same pattern as Chapter Two and present three excellent videos and three mediocre ones. Once I started thinking about it, however, I realized that there really aren't many poor videos out there; or at least if they *are* out there, I don't have any of them. Any idiot can write a book (Ahem!), but the costs of video direction and production are prohibitive to people that don't know what they're doing. Even the most boring videos I own that are nothing more than coaches standing in front of whiteboards for two hours, generally present incredibly useful information.

For that reason, here are my top four instructional video picks. If you get your hands on them, you should have a solid foundation of material for your program.

Coaches that know me are going to be wondering why I'm not adding Steve Calande's 46 Gambler DVD, Pete Noble's 4-4 Split series, or Jack Gregory's Double Wing DVDs to this mix. The reason is pretty simple. This book is supposed to be non system-specific. While I recommend the Double Wing Symposium DVDs, it's because I've heard from several coaches that don't run that offense that have purchased the DVDs and expanded their Wing-T or I-formation systems. Beyond that, the object of these videos is to increase your understanding of specific positions that usually aren't well coached or to enhance your already existing program.

~D.

Hugh Wyatt's *Safer and Surer Tackling*

Teaching proper blocking and tackling form is the most important thing you can do on a practice field. According to the National Center for Catastrophic Sports Injury Research (NCCSI), located at http://www.unc.edu/depts/nccsi/SurveyofFootballInjuries.htm, "In 2004 three fatalities occurred **while being tackled, one while tackling, and one in a tackling drill. [Emphasis mine ~D.]** Four of the injuries involved helmet-to-helmet contact." (Does everyone understand now what my beef was with Art and Dan Haege in the last chapter?)

It is crucial, therefore, for each football coach to competently instruct his players in proper tackling form. The helmet is not a weapon, and it is not there to be used as a club. It's there to protect the player's tender young melon from being deflated like a soccer ball. In appendix six, you're going to have an opportunity to see just one kind of injury associated with improper tackling and how far-reaching and life-altering the effects can be.

I've looked around for a long time to find the best tackling materials available. There are books on the subject, such as Kevin Bullis and Tom Journell's *Tackling Fundamentals and Techniques* (ISBN: 1585183180), but for the moment, we're talking about video that takes you step by step through the movements of a proper and secure form tackle, all the way to drills for reinforcement of proper technique.

Safe *AND* Successful

In my opinion, proper tackling needs to be as safe as it is efficient. While it might be effective to tackle at the hips or ankles, the risk of neck and head injuries is far too great for me to teach that form of tackling to the players.

However, the effectiveness of a tackling form cannot be forgotten, either. Arm tackles might be safer for the tackler's neck and head, but they don't do a lot of good on the field, and they have a tendency to turn into clotheslines when they're performed too high. You need a tackling system that is easy to teach, works well, and minimizes injuries as much as possible.

If you can make it dovetail with your drive blocking steps, that's even better, and that's precisely what Coach Wyatt does.

What you'll get:

1) Slow-motion and freeze frame shots from numerous angles of each step of the tackling form.

2) Drills for developing pursuit, approach, breakdown, and tackling steps safely and effectively.

3) Footage of the tackling technique used live in scrimmages and on game day.

4) Ways to integrate the tackling method with your blocking procedure so you can practice both at once.

Review

Safer and Surer Tackling
By Hugh Wyatt.
★ ★ ★ ★ ★ (5.0 *Highest rating!*)
Available through: www.coachwyatt.com.

The video won't give you a specific defensive system that you must run in order to take advantage of this technique, which is a good thing. It doesn't matter whether you're running a 4-4, 5-3, Gap-8, or whether you're lining your players up backwards; ultimately, a good tackling system will make your overall defensive play better. Remember, if you can't tackle, then you can't play defense.

Jerry Sandusky's *Linebacker Skills and Drills*

Every defense has linebackers. Improving their coaching is one of the things you can do to immediately improve your defensive success. The simplest errors in footwork can result in huge gains for the offense.

Most coaches, however, are unaware of the basics of linebacker play, such as keeping the feet within the frame and turning the hips instead of the shoulders to pursue to the sidelines. The misdirection of offenses like the Wing-T and the Double Wing depends entirely on getting linebackers just a single step out of position.

What if you could have your linebackers coached by the academic dean of "Linebacker University?" Do you think that would make them more effective?

You bet it would, and such a man exists. For years Penn State has been known as "Linebacker U," and that's due, in large part, to assistant head coach and defensive coordinator Jerry Sandusky.

In his outstanding drills-oriented video Coach Sandusky takes you step-by-step through the essential elements of linebacker play, starting with the most important fundamentals of stance and footwork. With simple, highly effective drills that build atop one another, Coach Sandusky has put together a tightly focused program for training linebackers.

Each drill is shot from multiple angles to give the inexperienced coach the best possible chance to understand the purpose and coaching points of the skills involved. The drills are also so simple in execution that dozens of reps of each skill can be obtained in a few minutes, increasing retention without sacrificing practice time.

You'll find echoes of the "Mirror drill" in appendix one, where it is known as "Defensive Backs Drill A: Punch and Goes." "Tackling Drill B: Head on Tackling" also has some roots that you'll clearly see in Coach Sandusky's "Mat Tackle" drill, although I do not like the head position Coach Sandusky advocates, which clearly uses the helmet as a contact point for the tackle, and is in violation of NFSHA rules. Instead, see Hugh Wyatt's *Safer and Surer Tackling*, reviewed above.

The tape includes a section on the most vital area of playing linebacker: playing off of blocks. Many defenses, such as the 5-3 and "46," demand that the linebackers be able to engage a lead blocker and ride him to the ball carrier by neutralizing his charge and defeating the block. Power and size have something to do with the linebacker's ability to do this, but skill and technique have much to do with it as well, and the quick and easy drills demonstrated in the video will develop this technique.

The latter part of the tape builds on the skills and drills learned previously by combining them into game-like situations.

Closing out the video is a series of drills for teaching pass coverage, both man and zone, and refining techniques for good pass defense. Somewhat hastily tacked on at the end is a fumble recovery section that is additionally useful to any coach.

Review

Linebacker Skills and Drills
By Jerry Sandusky of Penn State.
★ ★ ★ ★ ★ (5.0 *Highest rating!*)
Available through: www.coacheschoice.com.

Linebacker is a difficult position to play, and requires good athleticism and finely honed technique. In conjunction with Lou Tepper's *Complete Linebacking* (ISBN: 0-88011-797-4) the two are the lecture and text portions of a college course that can only be described as linebacking excellence.

Meadia Productions *Double Wing Symposium DVDs*

I'm recommending these DVDs not only because I'm in them, and I'm incredibly good looking, but also because the information contained in the almost forty hours of video is absolutely top notch.

The first series of DVDs contains a two and a half hour presentation from the father of the Double Wing, Don Markham himself, as well as special sections devoted to coaching "Bobbleheads," the youngest levels of youth football. Five of the best bobble coaches in the business function on one panel in a question and answer session that covers everything from discipline to bathroom breaks. (You'll have to see it.)

Yes, Even Passing

Additionally, the 2004 DVD set has noted Wild Bunch author and highly successful coach Ted Seay in a discussion of bunch attack passing that is, in my opinion, the lecture portion of a class in which Coverdale and Robinson's book, *The Bunch Attack* is the text. If you want to throw the ball, you need to see this video.

You'll even get to see my smiling face as I discuss successful defenses and how to read and attack them. Overall, the first set is about fourteen hours of film.

The 2005 Vegas Symposium

The 2005 DVD set was filmed in Las Vegas, Nevada, and contains four hours of field demonstrations and lecture from Clovis East head coach, Tim Murphy, whose 2004 team was ranked 23rd in the nation. His highly intricate offense features so much versatility that almost any coach of any system will find some kind of trick or tip to make their lives easier. Lewis and Clark College head coach Roger Vandezant delivers a lecture on coaching at the college level, and Hall of Fame coach Chuck Klausing discusses teamwork, leadership, and the rocket sweep series.

Another bobblehead panel, facilitated by highly successful youth coach Dave Potter, from Durham, North Carolina, will offer sound advice for those coaches working with the younger set, and Symposium coordinator Jack Gregory field demos wedge blocking. I even get into the act with two presentations, one on advanced passing misdirection, and another on integrating new formations into an existing offensive system.

Review

The 2004 & 2005 Double Wing Symposium DVDs
By Meadia Productions.
★ ★ ★ ★ ★ (*5.0 Highest rating!*)
Available through: www.gregorydoublewing.com.

Overall, the more than forty hours of information contained in these two DVD sets makes them one of the best football coaching aids you can buy. Think of it as a "clinic-in-a-box" for the sport of football. No matter the specific offense you run, you'll find something to help you out.

Mark Ingram's
Teaching the
Long Snap

In keeping with our understanding of the importance of special teams, the most important play in football is the punt, and the punt has to start with a snap. Watching youth football teams that have not properly focused on the importance of the long snap try to pull off a punt on game day is one of the most frustrating and bile-raising experiences I know of. (It's worse to watch at the high school level.) Almost as frustrating is watching youth football teams go for it on fourth and fifteen from their own thirty yard line because their coach never taught them how to punt.

It's something of a travesty that such little emphasis is placed on special teams in general and long snapping in particular at the youth and even high school levels. Fathers always dream that their sons will play in the NFL, and I've spoken with dozens of college and professional coaches that have recommended long snapping as the surest route to the NFL. Former New York Giants' offensive line coach Jim McNally told me point blank at the 2002 All-Sports Clinic in Northern California that, "Any player that can long snap is automatically given a second chance to make it for the Giants."

Express Lane to the 'Next Level'

If you're like me, and I know I am, you like to see your players move on to bigger and better things after leaving your program. I love to see my players suited up for the local colleges on Saturday, and now that someone has told me that teaching a successful long snap gives me the best chance to see that, you can bet I'm going to put some effort into teaching it properly.

Mark Ingram has spent many years teaching the basics of stance, grip, and spirals for speed and accuracy to long snappers at the collegiate and professional levels. Now you can take advantage of his tremendous amount of knowledge and training to help teach your special teams units.

The video begins with the grip for a proper snap, and carefully discusses the reasons for each aspect of the grip before moving on to throwing a tight spiral with a palm out motion, the same as that used by the quarterback. Included in this section are tips for troubleshooting wobbly or inaccurate snaps.

Moving to the body mechanics of the snap, Coach Ingram reinforces the importance of making the player set up to the football before each snap, and taking the proper body position with the ball far out in front of the snapper for maximum power. In this section he also discusses the importance of aiming points on the punter's body. Snaps should be made to the hip of the punter's punting foot.

Admittedly, some of the techniques Coach Ingram discusses are slightly different from the specific ones that I use. For example, I teach a level hips snapping method, rather than a lifting hips technique. Ultimately the end result is the same, and for a coach with no experience at coaching this vital skill, I definitely recommend following the video to a tee.

Moving further into the video, Coach Ingram discusses snapping for field goals, and even covers some important points for the holder, such as making sure the inside knee is down to provide a "backstop" for a poor snap.

The video also covers one of the more obscure field goal techniques, called the "tackle over." Essentially, this is an unbalanced line that is used to compensate for the extreme angle of a field goal from the hash mark inside the sixteen-yard-line. The kicker's position changes, and as a result the holder has to move as well, altering the skills the snapper has to use.

Coach Ingram does an outstanding job of explaining how to troubleshoot errant snaps, and even provides examples of incorrect snaps to use as a visual aid.

In this most crucial of skills, for the most crucial of plays, Mark Ingram's delivery, presentation, and knowledge demonstrates a clear understanding of the techniques needed, and presents them in a clear and logical manner for any coach to take and use with his team. Even the youngest players can be taught to snap quickly and accurately using the steps and techniques in this video.

Review

Teaching the Long Snap
By Mark Ingram.
★ ★ ★ ★ ★ (5.0 *Highest rating!*)
Available through: www.coacheschoice.com.

I believe that special teams are the cornerstones of a good football team. Although the announcers of the NFL and collegiate game do not trumpet the success of a team's punting unit with the same fervor and volume with which they track passing statistics, the importance of a good punting unit to a football team is undeniable. Even the undefeated 1972 Miami Dolphins and 1942 Army football teams were forced to punt on occasion.

Every punt starts with a snap. Coaching good long snaps can be the difference between a punt that pins the opponent deep in their own territory, and the blocked kick that loses you the game. Mark Ingram's video will give you everything you need to teach your long snapping properly.

CHAPTER FOUR
Film Study

Introduction

There is one tool that is absolutely invaluable to any football coach, and that's the video camera. In the last chapter I talked about instructional videos, but believe it or not, those are only going to have limited usefulness to you. Only video of your *own* football team can show you the places where you've made mistakes in your teaching. Proper film study can tell you if you're winning because of talent, or because your players are well coached. Talent varies from year-to-year, coaching doesn't.

The problem is; most people only have the vaguest idea what to look for on film. I think it begins because most youth football coaches start as fans, and the typical fan isn't very knowledgeable about the game of football. This is one of the reasons why most youth coaches tend to want to coach the offensive unit, and they also tend to want to work only with the backfield. TV producers are inclined to put inordinate emphasis on following the football, so that's what the average fan, and the average fan-turned-youth-coach, is likely to do.

The average youth football coach doesn't have the advantages you have, like this book in your hands. If you follow the ideas I present in it, you'll be able to break down film properly and swiftly. You'll also be able to take your film and make effective notes for constructing a highlight tape, which will help build interest in your program.

I'm not going to lie to you. Breaking down game film is a time-consuming process. It's arduous, and it requires a great deal of attention to detail. It can also be a painful procedure, particularly after a blowout loss, but it's at least as necessary as it is slow. You need to find the mistakes.

Once you've isolated the faults, then you can work to correct them. Speaking as an electronics technician, troubleshooting a football team is not that much different from troubleshooting a piece of electronics equipment. It all comes down to components not doing what they were supposed to be doing. The hardest thing to figure out is *why*.

This is one of the things you need to do to make your team successful. There are bunches of excuses you can make as to why you can't break down game film, and none of them are true. If coaching your players to be successful is important to you, then you'll get it done. It's part of "Coach Hustle."

~D.

Where it Starts

Like everything else in football, film study starts with a foundation. That foundation is the film itself. You need to find at least three people that can commit to taping, and one of them needs to be at each and every game for you. There are also a couple of other things you're going to need that I'll get to in a moment.

This has got to be a promise, from them to you. Whether the taper is an injured player you can trust to concentrate on the filming, or a parent, or an assistant coach is irrelevant, they need to be at every game, prepared with a blank tape and a fully charged camera, and they need to be able to do it with as little input as possible from you during the game.

The Local High School

One highly successful coach I know at the youth level contacted his local high school's photography class about seven years ago. He made a minor donation to the department, and from then on it became a class requirement for each student to tape at least one of his games every season. Since he played ten games (including the playoffs), and there were almost forty students in the photography class, this meant that he was able to get three or four camera angles on each play. The highlight tapes for his ten year olds look like NFL Films™ material with their cutting and editing jumps.

I don't necessarily recommend that you take things to that level. For one thing, you'll spend every day for the rest of your life trying to get all that film broken down, especially if you're as anal-retentive as I am. I think the idea is sound, though: talk to the photography instructor at your local high school or junior college and see if they would be willing to assign extra credit to any students that tape your games. This should give you a very competent videographer or two for each game.

Parents

I try not to use parents for taping unless I have to. It's no slight to them, but parents tend to want to focus on their own kids. Plus, they tend to forget, or not think it's really *that* important, or leave at halftime when the game is in the rain because they don't want their camera to get wet, or not show up when their kid is sick and has to miss the game. I've even had a parent tell me he wanted to keep using his crappy analog camera instead of the digital one because he was more familiar with it—even though the film was nearly unusable.

Additionally, I feel that it is somewhat unfair to the parents to make them watch their child play football on a 1.5" LCD screen. There have been times when my coaching duties have required me to tape the varsity games at Tomales High School, and it drives me nuts to not be able to see what's happening.

If you have to use a parent, though, then use one. Film is *important*. It's not something you can blow off. You *have* to have that film. If you let parents tape for you, they have to understand how important it is, and they have to make the commitment to you to be at every game, no matter what, and give you the best possible quality that you can get.

Siblings

Another possible source of videographers is older brothers and sisters of your players. If you have the older sibling of a player, especially one that you've coached before that understands how important it is, you can use them as a taper. Bear in mind, though, that many of the same problems will occur with the siblings that happen with parents.

Where you can really use the help of the siblings is at *practice*. I said above that there were other things than the games that you needed a videographer for, and practice is one of them.

In 1999 I asked a parent to videotape our games. (He was the one that bolted during a rainy halftime and only gave me six minutes of usable film.) He had purchased a brand new camera, and came to football practice to do some filming and get some practice with it.

What the Hell was I *Doing!?*

I was astonished, completely dumbfounded, when he gave me the tape of the first game. He'd taped on the same blank tape that he'd used at the practice, and I had about twenty minutes of film that showed my players goofing off, standing around, chatting, and playing grab-ass—during practice.

I watched that tape more than I watched the tape of our game. I had thought that I was coaching well, because we'd won in a 33-13 blowout, but as it turned out, my kids were spending more time standing around than they were working on learning football. Since I'd only had three days of practice before the first game thanks to a shortened season, all that time I wasted had a drastic impact on my team's readiness and preparation.

I was up all night on Saturday and Sunday with a calculator and a stopwatch. By the time I was finished, my new practice schedule had the kids working almost every second. No one stood in one place for longer than fifty seconds, and there were no water breaks—they had those fifty seconds in line to drink water.

I went to the local Wal-Mart and bought a digital cooking timer with a shoestring hole in it. This, I hung around my neck, and when I said we had five minutes for a drill, we had *five minutes*, not five minutes and three seconds.

I'll go into practice planning in more depth in chapters seven and eight, where I'll give you my basic plans and also teach you how to plan your own. For right now, take it on faith that you need someone to videotape your practices to show you where you're making mistakes *while* you teach.

Liability

There's another, sadder reason why you should have someone tape at least one practice a week. Like it or not, we live in a world today where some people feel that litigation is an easier way to get money than working for it. The current fashion is to sue McDonald's. An idiot sued McDonald's because she spilled hot coffee on herself. More idiots have tried to sue because the Golden Arches made them fat.

Two years ago, I had a blistering mediation session with a woman whose child had been bitten by my dog when he opened a locked fence gate and walked into the door of my house to try to sell me candy I didn't want. My wife and I had some real terror over that one, being new homeowners, although eventually our lawyer said the woman didn't have a case once her son opened our gate without permission. (She still lives four doors down from me, and still gives me the finger when I drive past her house. Charming soul. Her kid is a soccer player.)

Football is a rough game, and no amount of coaching, padding, or preparation is going to ever make it completely safe. As a football coach, you're going to have to teach safe and effective methods for blocking and tackling, both. My advice to you is to not only teach those methods, but also *videotape yourself teaching them.*

If you constantly admonish your players to tackle with their heads up, and someone gets hurt because they didn't listen to you, that's bad enough. If his parents somehow decide that you are at fault, that's worse, and if they decide to take it to court, that's nearly as bad as it gets.

You can avoid a lot of that agony by coaching proper and safe contact, and by obtaining video proof that you do so. In fact, one coach I know videotapes himself at the beginning of every season in front of his team, reading the warning label from the back of the helmet to his players. He then files the tape away just in case.

The Camera

After you obtain the videographer, the next step is to get your hands on a decent quality camera. In 2004 I made the switch from Hi-8 to mini-digital video, and it was one of the smartest things I've ever done. I recommend it very highly. I purchased a Sharp VL-WD450U MiniDV video camera for three hundred dollars from a private party through an online classified ads message board called *Craig's List*. (That was also where I got my motorcycle for about half the listed retail. Great website!) The site is located at www.craigslist.com. I'm so far very happy with the camera, and the fact that it interfaces seamlessly with my Macintosh PowerBook laptop.

No matter what kind of camera you purchase, try to avoid being taken in by the phrase "digital zoom." Digital zoom is a form of computer enhancement, and it gives you a blocky, pixilated image. Optical zoom is done with lenses, and gives a clear and crisp picture. Most cameras have at least a 10X optical zoom, and some go to 14X. By the time this hits print, 25X or better will probably be available. If your camera has digital zoom, it's a good idea to just turn it off if you can.

I use the laptop and camera in tandem, even while on the road. After our game is done, I grab the camera from our videographer, and set it in the back of my jeep right next to the laptop. Using an IEEE1394 connection (referred to as "firewire"), I set the game to import while I'm driving home.

By the time I get home from the game, the video is completely imported into my computer. Generally, I make a DVD copy of the video, with chapter markers set for the start of each quarter, and then I export it to a VHS tape. I use the DVD for breaking down the game film, and the VHS for the coaches' office, to show the film to the players.

Sound

Once you get the camera, I strongly recommend that you turn off the microphone, or simply don't plug in the audio cable when you're porting to tape. Occasionally people in the booth have made some comments about my team that they didn't realize were going to show up nice and clear on my game film. If your microphone doesn't shut off, you can disable it by taking an old microphone plug and cutting the cord off. Then stick this in the "external mike" port, and it should disable the built-in microphone.

Highlights

I also take the highlights from that game and import them directly into the season's highlight project. By the time the final gun sounds on the last game of the season, the only thing that should need to be done for the highlights is the addition of music. My goal is to be able to give the kids their highlight tapes (DVDs) within two weeks of the season end. (Haven't hit that goal yet, but I'm trying.)

Another *very* enterprising and technically savvy coach I know requires each of his players to purchase a DVD-RW, which is a DVD that can be copied over many,

many times. They turn these in to him on Friday, and when the game is over on Saturday he burns a copy of the game onto each one. When he gives them back to the kids, he gives them instructions based on the time codes, "Billy, watch 00:13:15 through 00:13:28, your footwork was wrong on that play."

Bear in mind that burning 26 DVDs is going to take a preposterous amount of time unless you put a lot of money into a high speed DVD burner.

Low Lights

Here's another idea I got from my mentor, Jack Reed: a low light tape. Everyone knows what a highlight tape is; those are the plays everyone wants to watch. Long runs, great tackles for losses, completed passes, interceptions, etc all seem to make it onto a highlight tape.

For the coach, though a low light tape is a lot more important, if more excruciating to watch. Start with a video clip of the play being run properly and perfectly, by your team or by someone else's that runs the same system. Then, make a short video, preferably of the same play being run over and over again and failing. Put ten or twelve of them on the same tape, and then switch to a new play, following the same pattern of a successful play and then a few bad plays. Then, watch each one in slow motion and see if you can spot what went wrong and, more importantly, *why* it went wrong. What was different between that and the play that succeeded? Break down the low lights using the same techniques you'll use to break down the game film. I'll give them out later in this chapter.

Low Budget

Now, I know that not every coach out there has disposable income for computers and cameras. Use whatever you have to use to get the job done. For years our game film at Tomales was taped on a gigantic VHS camcorder from the 1980s. The film was blocky, color washed, and difficult to deal with, but it was better than no film at all. My point is, don't make excuses. If you can't afford a high tech, $15,000 camera, there's still no excuse for not getting your hands on a $150 special and using that to break down film for your kids.

In dealing with the military, I've learned a phrase that I want to pass onto you. "Stop trying to think of reasons why it *can't* be done, and *do* it." I promise you that there's nothing in my books that can't be done. It just depends on whether or not you choose to put in the effort.

A rougher, but just as accurate version of that saying is adapted from the old Army order, "Soldier, shut up and *soldier!*"

Ahem, "Coach, shut up and *Coach!*"

What You Need

After you've obtained a videographer and a decent quality camera, your next step is to sit down with them and show them exactly what you're looking for in your film. In my years of trying to make sense of bad film, I've decided there are three key areas you *have* to have.

(1) High angle. It is impossible to see the interior of the offensive line without at least a 30-degree angle from the field. 45-degree or more is even better. Our rivals, St. Vincent's, actually rent a cherry picker and place it next to the field. From that 45-foot height they film almost straight down onto the field.

(2) Tight shots. Here is where most videographers make mistakes. Inexperienced tapers tend to zoom in too far or too quickly, or they are afraid to miss

something and they whip the zoom back so the players look like little uniformed ants. They should practice a slow, controlled zoom in and out; starting from an establishing shot that fits the offensive formation into the frame from the deepest back to the deepest linebacker. (Back up a little more on spread formations.)

(3) Timing. This is another area where tapers tend to make some errors. Either they leave the camera going through all the dead time in the game, they're late with the start, or they end too soon, leaving you to guess what formation the offense was in to start or how the play ended.

I'm going to go over each of these requirements in some detail, beginning with the angle.

High Angle Filming

When you're looking at the interior of the line, especially on misdirection plays like traps, you're mostly going to be looking at footwork. You need a high angle to see this, as well as to see missed handoffs. It will interfere with your ability to see center/quarterback exchanges, so my recommendation is that you give them so many snaps in practice that they never fumble in the game—that way you don't have to worry about trying to troubleshoot a botched snap from that high angle.

Some coaches like to see film from the end zone. I, personally, can't really make much sense out of that sort of video. I'm used to looking from a sideline view, so I'm not very good at breaking down end zone angles.

California rules also prohibit videotaping from ground level at either end zone. Make sure you know what applicable rules are in force *before* you set up your videographer.

Tight Shots

Cropping the shot is very important for football coaches. Many of the things we're looking for appear to be insignificant to the casual observer. A former semi-pro football player once described an inside trap play to me in which he, as the left guard, was to put his right foot down in the exact space vacated by the center's left foot at the snap. A deviation of six inches to either side would cause the timing of the play to fail.

With that in mind, trying to troubleshoot the film of such a play when it is zoomed way out to make the players look like bugs is an exercise in frustration. The taper should start with an establishing shot that is as tight as possible. A good rule of thumb is to start one side of the frame on the deepest offensive back, and the other on the deepest linebacker.

Take a look at the picture on the next page to get an idea of the angle and zoom your taper should use.

Adjust this slightly depending on who has the ball. I'm generally a lot more interested in my own team than in my opponents', so I have my taper shift the camera slightly to our side of the line of scrimmage. This might need the cameraman to back off the zoom slightly to still fit everyone in.

Smooth Movement

Remember in Shakespeare's *Hamlet* when Prince Hamlet is talking to the players he acquired to perform the play he had written? He tells them, "…do not saw too much at the air with your hand, thus. But rather use all gently, for in the very torrent, tempest, and (dare I say it?) whirlwind of your passion you must beget a temperance that will give it smoothness."

Okay, so you never read Shakespeare. The point is still valid. Your tapers need the same thing. To translate what Sir Willie S. was saying: be smooth. There are several mistakes rookie tapers tend to make, and they all come about from fighting the camera.

Common Mistakes

Mistake number one: too close to the action. I don't really care about the pores on my quarterback's nose. He's a quarterback. He's going to get dates whether he has acne or not. In the picture above you can see the field is set just about perfectly. It's easy to see feet, numbers, and body positioning. It's also easy for the taper to follow the ball.

Unfortunately, if you tell the taper to get close, most of the time he'll get *too* close, and you'll be able to count the ball carrier's nose hair, but not figure out where the offensive line mistake was that let him be tackled for a four yard loss.

Mistake number two: too far away. This is probably more common among rookie tapers. They don't want to miss any of the action, so they zoom out far enough to see everything. The problem is, it's almost impossible to get the information you need out of the shot if you end up doing things that way. You can't see footwork very well, and it really becomes difficult to spot the ball, especially on passes.

Mistake number three: the fire hose. You see this a lot in home movies where the cameraman is completely lost. You'll see it a lot more in video of football games that was taped by inexperienced tapers. Offensive systems that rely on misdirection to confuse the defense tend to give the cameraman nightmares.

When the cameraman loses the ball, he should slowly zoom back while panning downfield until he reestablishes the shot and finds the ball carrier. If he panics and starts waving the camera back and forth like a fireman trying to douse my mom's cooking you're going to end up with footage that is a) unusable for breaking down film, b) not viable for a highlight film, and c) going to make you seasick when you watch it.

Put the Cameraman on Headset

Probably the number one thing you can do to reduce the likelihood of this mistake is to obtain a third headset on the same frequency that the rest of your headsets are on. I'd remove the microphone, since you don't need advice from the fourteen-year-old older brother of your outside linebacker that happens to be taping for you.

Once you've obtained the extra headset, sit down with the taper and show him your offense. Have him attend a couple of practices and tape them for the experience. When he understands your terminology, he'll always know where the ball is going when you call a play. Instead of being faked out, he'll be nice and precise.

It's easy to tape my offense, if you can find the ball, because I run a Double Wing system with tight line splits, and we very rarely split an end out. Usually, our most widely split players are within five yards of the ball. Things get a little more problematical when we're on defense and the other team is running something like the spread, West Coast, or virtually any other offense that tries to cover the entire field.

For these situations, a lot has to do with the level you coach at. Bear in mind that youth football players generally don't pass the ball well, and definitely not well to wide receivers. You should be able to have your taper stick to a tightly cropped shot and still get most of the offense in. It's a good idea to talk to the taper before the game and let him know about any defensive keys he might be able to take advantage of, as well.

For example, if a team tends to pass from one formation and run from another, and you pick that out of the scouting report and give it to your players, give that to the videographer as well, so he knows where to keep the camera focused when the play starts. Or, if the other team only has one really good athlete carrying the ball, and they tend to move him around depending on where they want to run, have the taper follow him.

Use your best judgment. Obviously you can't clutter the taper's head with everything that's cluttering your own, but you can give him a few tips.

Check the Rule Book!

By the way, some leagues prohibit any form of communications from the booth. Always check with the officiating crew and make sure that they know you are on headset with the videographer, and that he doesn't have a microphone. You can always use the phrase, "We want to make a good quality highlight tape for the kids." By saying, "It's for the kids," you're more likely to get the officials to allow the communications, as long as it's one way. Getting better quality film for breaking down and improving your team is just a side bonus.

Tripods

One thing that really makes a lot of difference to the smoothness of a shot is the tripod your camera is mounted on. My first year at Tomales I used a huge, clunky tripod that must have weighed 25 pounds. On the plus side, it was gimbal-mounted, so every movement had just enough resistance to keep from being jittery, while still moving freely.

Climbing to the top of the press booth at Albany High School wasn't a lot of fun with that tripod, but at least I knew that once I was up there, it wasn't going to blow over, which was nice, because it was a 50-foot drop onto a chain link fence. I was *not* leaping after it if it fell.

You can get a decent quality tripod for under fifty bucks now at most camera supply stores. I recommend getting one that features "quick click," which is a quick release snap that mounts to the bottom of your camera. You leave the mount there, and it fits into a receiver on the top of the tripod. It's secure, and takes a just a few seconds to set in and lock down. (Nothing like missing the opening kickoff because you were wrestling with your equipment.)

Weight is an issue. A light tripod is much easier to carry around and set up/break down quickly, but a heavier one is much less likely to blow over when your taper is in the bathroom at halftime. It's also less likely to be damaged bouncing around in the back of your car with all your coaching equipment.

Kenny Mead, the outstanding videographer that has produced two incredible DVD sets from the Double Wing Coaches' Symposiums in Dallas and Las Vegas, gave me another tip that I'm going to pass on to you. Hang your camera bag from the bottom of the tripod, where the spreader legs are. This gives you a little more weight and helps keep things steady in the wind.

Timing

People who know of my adherence to the Jack Reed philosophy of coaching are going to be surprised when they read this next portion. In his book, *Coaching Youth Football, 3rd Edition* Reed advocates telling the videographer to leave the camera running between plays so you can check your clock management. Me, personally, I've found that it wastes too much tape, and makes breaking down the game film into a logistical nightmare.

Also, most video editing software out there has the ability to create its own video clips based on the input data you feed it. Every time the camera starts and stops again it logs that as a clip. Trust me on this; it makes your life much, *much* easier to have the computer do that, instead of importing the video as one long, horrendous clip and sectioning it yourself.

The cameraman should start the camera rolling when the offense breaks its huddle. If he keeps the camera on the ball, zoomed slightly in, he can then gradually expand as the offensive formation spreads across the field.

When the play unfolds, that's when the experienced taper becomes a real asset. Someone on headset with the coach calling the plays will make the right movements to follow the ball almost automatically, but it's when you're on defense and he's looking at an unfamiliar offense that he can really shine. As he gets better and better at taping, you'll find that he'll get an idea what plays are coming based on his instinctive flow of the game.

If only you could then make him play linebacker, you'd be set.

Once the play is done, the cameraman can't be too swift at shutting off the recorder. He needs to give it two or three seconds after the play is blown dead. Many cameras have the playout spool roll backwards slightly when they are stopped, to keep the tape taut. This can lose you one or two seconds on the video, and the end is usually the most important part of the play. That's where you're going to get the jersey number of the kid that made the tackle and prevented you from scoring the go-ahead touchdown so you can figure out which of *your* kids to chew out for missing his block.

Referees

Don't be too swift to stop recording when the refs are doing their thing, either. For one thing, there's something dramatic about a referee signaling touchdown or incomplete pass, and it makes good highlight film footage. Second, in the 2003 season we had a spectacular come-from-behind victory over St. Helena in game two of the season. In the highlight tape, I used the footage of the penalty flags and the referees taking away our first two touchdowns to highlight the drama and intensify the feeling of dread. It made the comeback seem all that much more improbable.

Also, it helps the guy breaking down the film (that'd be you) to figure out why you went from a third and five, to a third and fifteen, to a first and ten.

Integrity

There's one more reason to keep the tape rolling while the referees are waving their arms about: it keeps them honest. Let's face it: while most officials are dedicated and hard working, there to do a good job and advance the game of football, there are some that are clueless, incompetent, or outright biased.

I can think of two examples that my own teams have faced. Both of the schools in question are in isolated communities, and the referees are all local boys. During the games it's not uncommon to see them address members of the home team by name and ask how their little brother is doing. Then, when the visiting team gets flagged for forty-five yards in penalties before they even snap the ball for the first play, it throws their bias into question. Having game film, and sometimes even casually mentioning to the referees that they are being taped every second, can work wonders towards keeping the game fair and balanced.

Penalty Hill

I'm also a bear on my own team for legitimate penalties. I watch the tape very carefully, and I make darn sure that anything called on my team actually happened. Then, I take the kids to "Penalty Hill".

Penalty Hill is a 50-degree, thirteen-yard-long slope next to our bleachers at Tomales High School. After every game, when I break down the game film, I tally up the entire penalty yardage we earned.

The next practice after the game, we hit the hill to work those penalties off. Each yard is worth one trip up and down the hill, so one holding call and one offsides is going to be fifteen hills.

I also add in any time we fumbled the ball, which is worth three hills, and if the other team recovers it, we run an additional two.

Another Quote From Jack Reed

Jack Reed is fond of saying, "What you tolerate, you encourage." I agree with him. I don't tolerate penalties or fumbles. I bear down very hard on them, and my teams generally respond by eliminating them. It really gets up my nose that there are millionaires playing this sport for a living that can't run ten consecutive plays without an offsides or a holding call, but I can keep my players from making the same infractions with just a little sweat.

By game three, I start getting mean. Each penalty yard will be worth two trips up the hill. I found that this became necessary because my teams got so good at avoiding penalties by week two that we were usually running only five or six hills. In order to keep conditioning them, I had to increase the punishment, which also worked to keep the penalties even *lower*. It became a vicious circle that has ended without a penalty in the last games of the season the last two years. I can't complain about that!

Penalties on Film

My players know that they aren't going to be punished for mistakes made by the referees. I have to clearly see the penalty on film before I'm going to make them run for it. This is one more reason why it's a good idea to get the referee's hand signals, because you tend to forget what was called when. If it's on film, though, you've got the reminder built in.

Down and Distance

It's not a bad idea to make the videographer focus on the sticks briefly to start each play. This gives you an idea what you were hoping to achieve when you called a certain play, and, especially on fourth down attempts, can heighten the drama. In that come-from-behind win over St. Helena, we converted on nine of nine fourth down attempts, including one fourth and eight on which we completed the only fade pass of the game after trying it five or six times. It made for a very dramatic highlight film.

If you haven't purchased the highlight CD from the 2003 Tomales Braves Junior Varsity season, you should consider doing so. (Shameless plug.)

Breaking it Down

Okay, you've got the taper, camera, tripod, and tape. You've filmed the game, beat your opponents 34-0, and it's now Sunday. Surely you don't need to break down the game film, right? I mean, you were perfect, weren't you? You can spend the day at the BBQ, right?

Wrong! I've never seen a flawless team in execution. Not even De La Salle High School, or Bellevue, the team that broke the 151-game, 13-year winning streak De La Salle had, was perfect in their execution. There were missed blocks, ball carrying issues, quarterback misreads, and a host of other things that are the hallmark of a football game.

No matter how perfect you think your game was; you need to make certain you carefully break down the film. I'm living proof of that. In 2002 I had just moved from the varsity staff to the junior varsity at Tomales, and I wasn't sure what my responsibilities were. At the varsity level, the head coach and the defensive coordinator were responsible for breaking down the game film.

For the JVs, no one else was doing it. Since it's not really in my nature to let a team I'm coaching fall apart through lack of effort on my part, I started watching the film.

We're Undefeated, We Must Be Perfect! ...Right?

Unfortunately, I didn't know what to look for. We won our first two games by a combined score of 66-12, and both of the touchdowns scored on us were gifts from the referees. I thought we were unstoppable.

Then we hit opponent number three. We couldn't move the ball, and we couldn't stop their offense. They just lined up and kicked our asses.

After that game I spent a lot of time watching game film over and over trying to figure out what the hell had gone wrong. I started to notice little things that had made a huge difference: footwork, angles to the ball, linebackers not taking on blocks properly, defensive linemen playing too high, offensive linemen blocking defensive tackles at the line of scrimmage instead of letting them through on the trap plays, etc.

Probably the worst thing I noticed was that our running backs had been breaking tackles in the backfield, a *lot* of tackles in the backfield. This is one sure sign that you're winning from talent, and not from execution. Your linemen are missing blocks, either from not using proper technique, or because they don't know who to block on a particular play.

If I'd been breaking down film properly before that disastrous third game, we might have had a better shot at beating our opponent. This led me to one of my favorite coaching sayings, "Either you guys beat our opponent, or I got out-coached."

Trial and Error

It took me forever to figure out what I was looking for. I had no clue what to watch and I had to literally trial-and-error my way through the films. That's where this book is going to help you. By the time you're done, you should know exactly what to watch for.

You must break down the film after every game. I'm going to take you step by step through breaking down offensive and defensive film, including giving you a checklist of things to look for.

Playlist

The first thing you need is a list of the plays you ran. On game day, we have two stat keepers that stand right next to the coaches. I'm usually all over the field, and on headset with the spotter in the booth. Our head coach, Bill Tucker, calls the offensive plays, our defensive coordinator, Bob Harr, calls the defensive fronts and coverages, and I usually call the linebacker stunts and the special teams.

The stat keepers need to be competent. It's a good idea to have them sit in on the conversation when you're talking with the cameraman. Give them an idea what terminology you use, so it's not totally unfamiliar to them on game day. One thing you cannot do is keep the stats yourself. I can guarantee you that you'll be distracted at the wrong time.

The main reason I want the stats kept on the field is to get an idea what's working and what's not during the game. You'll find that the video is more accurate, anyway, for recording your stats. What you'll need the most is the playlist. I print out several copies of the game form located at the end of this book. You'll use this again to break down the film.

On game day, when you call a play, make sure that the stat keepers hear the call. You might even consider putting them in the press box, and yes, put them on headset so they can hear the play call.

So, now it's Sunday, and you're sitting down to break down the film.

Get Ready

You'll need:

- Blank stats forms (at least four)

- The playlist from the game

- A couple of pencils (I tend to break mine when I'm watching botched plays, so get more than one.)

- The game tape

- A decent quality VCR (Spend as much as you need to get one without jitter when you pause. If it has frame-by-frame advance, that's an added bonus.)

- The remote control

- Something to drink, Mountain Dew™ for preference, because you're going to be here a while.

With every play, there are going to be five things you're going to look for:

(1) Did each player do what he was supposed to do?

(2) Did each player use correct technique in the execution of his responsibility?

(3) Were there any mitigating reasons why the player did not perform properly? (For example, did the umpire get in the linebacker's way so he couldn't make the tackle?)

(4) Where is your coaching weakest? (For example, are your players dropping passes? Fumbling?)

(5) Where is your coaching strongest? (Do your players stay low off the ball on offense and defense? Do your runners protect the ball? Are your defensive backs disciplined in their coverages?)

Watch it *All!*

This goes for your special teams as well. Coaches have a real tendency to focus only on their own team's offensive execution, and forget to look at the defense and the kicking game. You can't do that, however, and expect to be successful. I can promise you that the one aspect of your team you forget to study in depth will be the one that gives you problems later on in the season.

Kickoff

Starting with the opening kickoff, watch everything in slow motion. Typically, kickoff teams at the youth level are concerned with lanes. Each member of the kicking team runs straight down the field until they reach the level of the ball carrier, at which time they turn inward and swarm to tackle him. One player hangs back and stays directly upfield from the football.

Or, that's how it's *supposed* to look. Watch your kickoff coverage very closely. Since the field is 53.5 yards wide, you need to station one man every 5.35 yards in order to cover the entire field with ten men. They should stay in that relationship as they run down the field.

Coverage

Watch for gaps in the coverage. Even if almost everyone on the kickoff team does their job perfectly, and the ball carrier is tackled at the opposing twenty-yard line, odds are that the one mistake you don't catch, the wedge-breaker in the middle that follows his teammate downfield instead of covering his area, is going to open the door for an opponent's touchdown or long return later in the season.

Another thing to look for is the coverage men getting in front of the kicker. This is a penalty for illegal procedure, and will back you up five yards for a re-kick. Even if the officials don't call it, check your film, and work on it in practice, because the next crew might *not* miss the call.

Kickers

Keep an eye on your kicker as well. Good film can show you a lot of mistakes kickers make. I liken kicking a football to swinging a golf club. If you don't keep your head down and swing with a nice, smooth stroke, you're going to shank the ball.

The easiest thing to look for when you're trying to figure out head position is the helmet sticker on the back. Helmet reconditioners place a warning label on the back of the helmet every year when the helmet is certified for use. If you put a stripe down the center of your helmets, that can also be used, but for solid-colored helmets, the warning label is the best bet.

Make sure the kicker is placing the ball where *you* want it. I've never believed in kicking off deep down the field. This seems like common sense to me; why did the other coach put his two best athletes back there to return the kick again?

I have a specific angle I want the ball kicked, and a specific yard line I want the kicker to hit with it, adjusted for the exact kickoff return formation we're facing. If we don't hit that angle, or close to it, film should show the reason why.

I want every single player on the kickoff coverage within five yards of the football by the time the tape stops, with the sole exception of the safety. If your taper is stopping the tape two to five seconds after the whistle, then that should give your players ample time to get to that zone.

On the Return

When you're on kickoff return you need to have an even clearer picture in your mind of the responsibilities and techniques your team needs to execute. Kickoff coverage is mostly *reactive* in nature, just like defense, so it becomes a matter of finding out, *did that guy get to where he was supposed to be?* If not, *why* not?

Kickoff return, though, is *active* in nature. Not only do your players have to get to an assigned location, but they also need to attack a certain coverage player and execute a proper block.

Full Speed!

Regardless of the specific nature of the return you choose to run, it will bear many things in similarity to a football play. Most kickoff returns ask the front wall of return men to drop back towards their own goal line before turning and blocking. *They must do this at full speed!* I know of absolutely no kickoff return that requires the athletes to jog downfield, not one, yet this is one of the hardest places to get the kids to go all out.

I follow a rule when breaking down kickoff returns and coverages: either you sprint when we run it on game day, or you sprint when we run it in practice—five times for every time I see someone jogging. If you're not within the five-yard zone when the tape stops on kickoff, if the last frame doesn't show all ten players in that area, then we're going to run that kickoff five times in practice at a full sprint.

The same rule applies to kickoff return. You'll have to bear down on this, but it will make a huge difference in your kickoff coverages and returns.

Offensive Film

Once the teams line up to scrimmage, there are other things you have to pay attention to. I don't spend a lot of time worrying about the obvious errors. If a player drops a pass, everyone in the stadium is going to see it, so telling him, "You've got to catch that," isn't going to help anyone. It's better to try to and figure out *why* he dropped that pass. Is he getting enough passes thrown to him in practice? Did the quarterback throw it too hard? Did the free safety hit him so hard that his girlfriend had a coronary? Search for the little things.

What Did You Call?

The very first thing you have to do is ascertain what the play is, offensively, and defensively. It's not usually that difficult to figure out the offensive play, but defensively it can be a nightmare, especially if you don't track your defensive fronts, stunts, or coverages on game day.

Offensively, however, you should have that play chart that your stat keepers kept for you on game day. On your clean, pristine copy of the form, write down the name of the play. I strongly recommend that you use pencil, because there are times when you'll have changed the play at the last second and the stat keepers will miss the call. Hopefully this won't be very often.

Watch the play at normal speed the first time. Make sure it's the right one you wrote down. Then rewind the tape to the point right before the line gets into their stances. This is where it is extremely helpful to have a high-quality VCR with a frame-by-frame advance.

It goes without saying that burning the video to DVD will make this a much smoother operation.

Now, question one: Did each player do what he was supposed to do?

What Were They *Supposed* to Do?

In order to answer that, you need to have, in your head, a very specific idea of what each player's assignment was on that play. For example, if you run an I-formation system and on this play your flanker is supposed to line up in the slot to the left, motion across the formation towards the right, and then stalk block the nearest linebacker, then you need to know that.

What *Did* They Do?

Now, suppose you check the film and that linebacker is the one that made the tackle. Well, Jack Reed pointed out on his web site that most coaches at the youth level tend to think that their player *tried* to make the block, but was beaten by superior technique or attitude. (I think this is where the old sideline screech of, "You gotta hit someone!" came from.)

In reality, that is rarely the case. Even at the high school level, a missed block almost always comes about because the player assigned to block that defender went somewhere else, or made little effort to actually obstruct the defender.

Only after you have ascertained the specific failure on a play can you then investigate why that failure occurred.

So, you need to think about the whys and wherefores when you're assigning responsibility for a blown play.

So, what was the player supposed to do on the play?

Question one revisited: *Did he do it?*

Addendum to question one: *Why the heck not?*

If the flanker missed his block, was it because you were asking an 80-pound freshman to block a 210-pound sophomore linebacker? Was it because the defender blitzed and wasn't where he was supposed to be? Was it because the flanker wasn't in the right spot? Did he turn and block inward when he was supposed to block the outside guy?

Who Before How

After you have determined that, yes, the flanker was where he was supposed to be, made an effort to block the right guy, and he had some form of blocking advantage that should have stacked the odds in his favor, such as a blocking angle or a teammate that was supposed to help double team, *then* you can start looking at technique problems.

Specific blocking techniques vary, and you'll have to match the technique to the type of block your player is trying to pull off, but don't fall into the standby of saying, "He just wanted it more." In my experience, *all* the players want to make their blocks and execute properly. The only variable is whether or not they were properly taught how to do it.

I am a huge believer in the concept of teaching *who* before you teach *how* to block. Proper blocking technique is important, but what's most important is eliminating confusion. Your films should clearly show it if one of your players is blocking the wrong guy.

In our case, lets say that our flanker was in the right spot, and we know he's physically capable of making that block, but he put his head on the wrong side of the defender, allowing the linebacker to shuck the block and scrape into the hole, making the tackle after a three yard gain.

The Stats Form

On your stats sheet, fill in the rest of the information about the play, including the yardage gained, in case the stat keepers made a mistake. In the comments section, write down who fouled up and what they did wrong.

	Formation	Play	Ball Carrier	Result (+/-)	Comments
1	I-right, Slot Left	Laser 24 Ice	37	+3	#81, head in the hole

Now, I can already hear your question: what if more than one person screws up? There isn't a whole lot of room on that form. What if, for example, our center was supposed to block the playside defensive tackle, but stepped with the wrong foot and missed the block?

No problem. Use as many lines as you need. I do it like this:

	Formation	Play	Ball Carrier	Result (+/-)	Comments
1	I-right, Slot Left	Laser 24 Ice	37	+3	#81, head in the hole
2	• • • • • • • • • •	• • • • • • • • • •	• • • • • • • • •	• • • • • • • •	#53, near foot!

As you're probably thinking right now, this takes about six minutes less than *forever*. I'm always pleasantly surprised at the end of football season, when I see my wife again and realize how pretty she is. During the season, however, I'm usually too busy staring into computer or television monitors to look at her as much as I'd like to.

You're going to have to watch each play of the game at least—at *least*—eleven times in slow motion, once for each player on the field. A seven to fifteen second play is going to take you about three to five minutes to break down properly.

Good plays

Don't get cocky and fast forward past the great plays, either. Just because your tailback went 65 yards for a touchdown doesn't mean everything was hunky-dory. This was the crucial error I made in 2002, when I jumped to the conclusion that our 2-0 record meant that we were doing everything right.

Watch for times when the running back breaks tackles in the backfield, or is touched before he makes it to your goal yardage. Every play I have has a specific 'yards per attempt' average that I want to hit with it. If the ball carrier is touched by a defender, or has to dance around one, before he makes it to that goal, then we did something wrong.

Also watch for the quarterback dodging tacklers in the backfield on your passing plays. Just because he managed to throw the pass doesn't mean that he had the protection he was supposed to have. The ultimate goal for most drop back passing plays is five seconds of pass protection for the quarterback, and the ball should be gone within 2.5 seconds. Obviously roll out passes, screens, and play action are going to take longer.

Perfect Plays

I mentioned the hill we use to work off our penalty yardage and fumbles. There's another way to motivate the kids to execute properly, and I call it "Perfect Plays." If the execution on a play is flawless, everyone does it exactly as it's drawn in the playbook, with proper faking, effort, and discipline, then the only thing I write under comments is "PP." When I'm totaling up the penalty yardage, I take off one hill for each "PP" on the chart.

This is positive reinforcement. The kids need to know that they are capable of proper execution, and that the coaches will recognize it. They also need to know that it isn't going to be easy. You're going to have about five penalty yards for every perfect play, but the upside is worth it.

Faking

If you're running a misdirection offense like the Double Wing, Wing-T, Single Wing, or other system that needs effective sleight-of-hand, you need to make sure that your backs are executing their fakes properly. This takes some discipline, but it's one of the most effective ways to get the defense out of position.

I keep an eye on the fakes during the game, but film is where they're really going to be seen. My ultimate goal is for my fakers to be tackled by the defenders, since a defender tackling my tailback isn't there to stop the fullback from streaking past him on a 75-yard score.

I use the following chart to grade fakes:

Result of Fake	Grade
Faker Tackled	A (4.0)
Defender Pursued Faker	B (3.0)
Defender Froze	C (2.0)
Defender Paused	D (1.0)
No Fake	F (0.0)

On the grading form, this comment looks like this:

	Formation	Play	Ball Carrier	Result (+/-)	Comments
1	I-right, Slot Left	Laser 24 Ice	37	+3	#81, head in the hole
2	••••••••••	••••••••••	••••••••••	••••••	#53, near foot!
2	••••••••••	••••••••••	••••••••••	••••••	#41: B Fake

I average the fakes out for the entire game for each individual player, as well as for the entire team. Anything below a "B" is unacceptable. This goes for receivers running fake pass routes as well as the running backs pretending to carry the ball.

Some defenses are simply going to be more disciplined than others. You should be able to tell if your players were executing a proper fake that was ignored by a defender determined to cover his assignment, and a fake that just didn't fool anyone.

Playcalling

Keep an eye on yourself as well. You're going to call the game based on a number of factors. I can almost guarantee that when you see the films you're going to see some places where you're going to think a different play would have worked better. Make a note of these situations, mentally if not on paper, and when you encounter them again think about the new call.

Defensive Film

On defense, you've got a more difficult job to do. As I said before, recording the stunts, coverages, and all the other minutiae of the defense is virtually impossible to do at the youth level. It's prohibitively difficult at the high school level as well.

In a perfect world you'd have an abundance of intelligent, dedicated staff members that are willing to record stats and keep everything up to date. Unfortunately, we live in a world that is far from perfect. Something usually has to give. Fortunately, paying attention to the tape should tell you everything you need to know about how your defense played. I can usually pick my stunts out of the film, and from the stunts I can deduce the coverages pretty easily.

Your biggest problem in breaking down defensive film is figuring out what the other coach called and whether or not his players did their jobs correctly.

What is the Offense Doing?

For example, suppose your opposition lines up in the wishbone and the fullback dives to the right of the line, taking the handoff as he goes. Your defensive tackles do a perfect job of shedding blocks and meet him in the hole so he bounces outside where the defensive end has abandoned his responsibility and come down hard towards the middle. The fullback loops outside him, helped by a sudden reach block by the tight end, and is finally tackled after an eight-yard gain by your outside linebacker and free safety together.

Now coach, what play was called by the other team? Was it supposed to be a bounce out? Did that tight end put his head on the wrong side of the defensive end, and that's why the fullback could get to the perimeter?

You have to make some adjustments based on what you're pretty sure the offense is running. Keep an eye on later portions of the film: does that fullback bounce out every time he starts that dive? Does the tight end try to reach block your defensive end all the time?

You should have a decent idea what the offense was supposed to be trying to run from the scouting report that you prepared before this game, so refer to that when you're working on your game film.

Defense and the Game Plan

In order to properly analyze defensive film, you have to have a clear idea in your head what your defense was supposed to do in order to stop the play to begin with. If you're not sure what the defense was supposed to do, then there's no way they could have known.

Defense is about discipline and assignments. In the above example, that defensive end coming to the inside is not a good thing. As an offensive coordinator, I look for things like that as much as possible. Any time a defender is abandoning his duty, they are opening the door for a play that attacks his responsibility.

So the converse is also true. When you're on defense, you want your players to be as disciplined as possible, and to play their assignments. Defenses are always created with one goal in mind: placing a defender in an intersection point with a ball carrier. Hopefully the defender will be able to tackle the ball carrier, and the defense will win the battle.

Some Things Never Change

So, you need to answer the same questions about your defensive film:

(1) Did each player do what he was supposed to do?

Did your defensive tackles make the stop on the diving fullback? Did the defensive end stay home to prevent the bounce out? Did the playside linebackers scrape to their assigned gaps? Did the backside linebackers stay home and cross key for the counter?

(2) Did each player use correct technique in the execution of his responsibility?

Did the tackles dip and rip, swim, or bull rush, or were they just physically bigger and stronger? Did the defensive end maintain outside leverage on the tight end or tackle? Did the linebackers keep their shoulders square to the line while scraping?

(3) Were there any mitigating reasons why the player did not perform properly?

Did your corner drop that interception because the ball was wet? Did the backup defensive tackle shoot the wrong gap and leave your linebacker on his own? (You can forgive the linebacker, but you need to train the tackle better.)

(4) Where is your coaching weakest?

Did you jump offsides on a long count? Did the players fail to recognize an unbalanced line? Was your tackling up to standard? Did the players flow to and secure their assignments?

(5) Where is your coaching strongest?

Did the defensive backs stay home and cover the pass even when the offense showed run? Did your defensive line beat the offensive line off the ball? Did they get stronger or weaker as the game went on?

Getting Cocky

Don't get so wrapped up in the great plays that you miss the little mistakes. Just because your outside linebacker crashed and made the tackle for a five yard loss doesn't mean that everyone else was doing their job. In fact, it doesn't mean that *he* was doing his job, either, if you didn't call that stunt. In 1999 in Kodiak I had to bench a defensive end after his fifth tackle in a row for loss. Despite his assignment, he kept coming down the line and attacking the dive back, leaving the door wide open for sweeps to his side.

Eventually I had to pull him off the field to prove that I meant business. Although his tackles were great, highlight film material, they weren't his assignment, and the cost could have outweighed the benefits if our opponents had realized his mistakes and chosen to attack the perimeter.

Time

You should have a pretty good idea by now what to look for in your film. Those same five questions can be applied to each aspect of the game, offense, defense, and special teams, and answering them for each play will go a long way towards showing you what you need to work on in practice, and where your own coaching errors lie.

As you've probably realized, this is not going to be a five second task. One of the goals of any football team is to stay on offense. As long as you have the football, the other team can't score. This is a *good* thing. As a result, successful teams at the high school level shoot for about fifty offensive plays as a goal. Junior varsity teams typically aim for forty, and youth teams may aim for thirty to thirty-five. Coaches running a no huddle or hurry up form of offense such as Jack Reed's "Warp Speed No-Huddle" will probably find that this might even double for them.

Youth games are typically about sixty to seventy plays long. You should figure that competently evaluating and analyzing each scrimmage play is going to take between two and three minutes, and each kicking play another one to two minutes. You can assume that you're going to be spending approximately two and a half hours breaking down the average youth football game.

Getting Help

You're going to have to do this *every* week. If you can break things up with an offensive, defensive, and special teams coordinator that can watch their areas, you can save some time, but as the head coach, the bulk of the film watching responsibility is going to devolve onto you. (Plus, you're going to need assistants that are firmly on board and committed to the way you do things. If they think your 4-4 split defense isn't going to work, then when they break down the defense they're going to stress everything that makes it look unsuccessful. More about that in chapter six.)

Even if effective coordinators are working below me, as the head coach, since the success of the team is ultimately up to me, I need to be the one breaking down the film, even if it's just with a quick glance-through to get an overall idea.

Playing in Someone Else's Sandbox

I caution you to be very careful when you're dealing with other members of the staff and their areas of responsibility, particularly if you happen to be a coordinator or an assistant coach. If you're supposed to be watching the offense, and you start pointing out things that the defense screwed up on, odds are the defensive coordinator is going to have a few choice words for you. Additionally, if you're there to coach the running backs, don't be badmouthing the offensive linemen about missed blocks. Remember that coaching staffs have to be as much of a team as the players on the field.

Now What?

So you've finished watching the film, and you now have three or four pages filled with notes on places you can improve your team. The next thing you need to do is sit down with them and go over it.

Showing film to kids is an exercise in discipline and futility. I'm not sure I'd even do it below the eleven-year-old level. The younger the age group, the fewer plays you can get through before their brains shut off.

My recommendation is that you build a combination highlights/lowlights tape. Following the timeline of the game, snag one to three plays in each quarter and put them on one tape to show to the players. Add three or so plays from each quarter for each year above the age of ten. By the time you get to fourteen to sixteen years old, you should be able to watch most, if not all, of the game film.

Practice Time

This is going to steal practice time from you. Every week you need to balance the good of seeing yourself on film and the building of understanding that comes with it, with the very real knowledge that while you're in the coaches' office watching tape, you're *not* on the field honing your blocking and tackling, learning new plays, or preparing for the upcoming opponent. You have to take a hard look at the film and say you yourself, "Self, if I take fifteen minutes from practice to show this to the kids, *what is that going to take practice time away from?*"

If you think your kids would be better served on the field, then by all means do so. Film study is for *you* and your assistants, to help you figure out where you're making mistakes and how you can coach your players better. The kids can live without it.

Doing it Right

Here's another tip, if you watch video with your players. I sit my players down in the coaches' office, and we watch the film together. I don't use names when I break down film, not at all. If Juan Ruiz misses a block, I simply tell the team, "#71 has to make this block. Step with the near foot to the defender's midline."

I have a rationale for this. You'll find that some kids rarely screw up, for whatever reason. They might understand the program a little better, or they might be such a great athlete that they don't have to worry about the physical game, and all their concentration can be devoted to the mental game.

Unfortunately, you're also going to have a few kids that seem to always make mistakes. It's bad when you're calling the same number over and over. It's worse when the poor kid is making the same *mistake* over and over.

What using the numbers is there to reinforce is the idea that this is a football team, and when one person messes up, it hurts *all* of us.

Discipline

Watching film is not easy for young players. They'll get bored very easily and start making comments, or they'll be so busy looking for the good hits and the highlights that they miss the things you're going to be trying to show them. This is why I recommend keeping the list of plays you show them to a very small number.

On the other hand, you also have to have their attention during those five to seven minutes that you're showing film. I enforce discipline by, well, by being myself. I inform the captains that any talking during the film sessions will result in extra conditioning—for the captains—and then I let them handle it.

I've had to make good on that threat only one time. I took the entire team back outside to the practice field, and they made a circle around the captains, who did up-downs until the time I'd allotted for the film session expired. After that, the captains did a fine job of enforcing discipline on their own. (Sixty-eight up-downs will do that to you.)

This was a high school team, so I don't recommend that you try that exact route with your eight-year-olds, although the best coach I know at that age level is also the strictest disciplinarian I've ever met. His teams have been undefeated in the regular season for five years and unscored on for three. He makes me look like Mother Theresa.

Lou Holtz once pointed out that discipline isn't something you do *to* someone; it's something you do *for* someone.

Getting the Video to the Field

Most youth coaches don't have a practice facility, video room, or coaches' office to hang out in and watch video. All the ones I know of are lucky to be able to get grass instead of asphalt to practice on. As a result, you've got to be creative when it comes to showing the video to the kids.

You can give them their own copy of the clips you need them to see and admonish them to watch it, but the odds are low that they will. Just like playbooks, which are pretty much a thing of the past for the players, you'll find the tapes or DVDs all over the parking lot. Plus, you're looking at around a buck per kid per week for media, unless you make them purchase a DVD-RW and turn it in every week. Burning thirty copies of the game film or copying the tape thirty times every week could take forever, though.

Portable Video

A better idea is to get your hands on either a portable DVD player with a screen large enough to be seen by your entire team, or try to find a cheap VCR/TV combination. (You can get them for less than two hundred dollars now, if you shop around.)

You can power this from your car if you purchase a DC/AC inverter. It takes the power supplied by the car's cigarette lighter, which is DC, and converts it to AC that can be used by any plug-in device. You can then plug in the viewer, sit the kids down, and watch the film.

Other Options

You could meet over at a parents' house after practice on Monday to watch game film. Another cool idea would be to have a weekly pizza party at the local pizza joint with a TV, and hook up a VCR or DVD player to their TV (or bring your own TV with you).

If you make the decision to show the video to your kids as part of their football preparation, then commit to it and keep coming up with new ideas until one of them works. Remember, anyone can come up with reasons why something *can't* be done, but that's just interfering with *getting* it done.

Think of it like this: your boss ordered you to show video to your players or you're going to be fired. Think you can figure out a way to get it done now that you've been properly motivated?

The coaches, no matter what, absolutely must see the video. It's imperative that each coordinator have a strong grasp of the mistakes that were made on his side of the ball. The only way to fix anything is to first figure out what's wrong. For that, you've got to have the film. Football, even at the youth level, is so complex and happens at such high speeds that only by slowing it down on video can you truly ascertain where the mistakes are being made.

Fixing Problems

It's one thing to see yourself on video, and it's another thing to rationalize that the pixels on the screen are you doing something wrong and be able to correct it.

To make that a little clearer, here's an example. Let's talk about outside linebackers. In most defenses, the outside linebacker is responsible for protecting the perimeter from sweeps, and for either dropping into pass coverage in the flats, or providing a hard rush to the passer on passes.

Assume for a second that you're looking at film of your last game, and your outside linebacker keeps making the same mistake. Instead of attacking the upfield shoulder and hip of the ball carrier on the sweep, he's running right at the ball carrier, who is able to beat him to the outside of the formation and cut upfield for large gains.

In your video session, go ahead and show the outside linebacker what he's doing wrong. I guarantee it, though, that he's going to make the same mistake when you get back on the field. Seeing the pixels on a screen is *intellectual*, and performing the actions is *visceral*. It's almost impossible, even for high school players, to make the rational distinction between something they saw on a video and what they need to do on the field, *especially* at game speeds.

Wasting Time the NFL Way

In preparations for the 2005 season, during which most of this book was written, it suddenly occurred to me that we spent more time during video sessions talking than teaching. Since football is a physical game, it doesn't make a lot of sense to make corrections while staring at a video screen. The more I thought about it, the more I realized that video, at least at the junior varsity level and down, isn't really the best way to fix problems with your team.

Video has its uses. At the varsity level, the video session is also a decompression time. Most varsity coaches show the video to their teams on Monday after a Friday game, which gives their players a chance to physically recover and heal from the bumps and bruises incurred during the game.

I think this is a good idea for that level. At the junior varsity level, however, I've come to strongly believe that the players should be on grass during that period. Instead of sitting in a classroom watching TV, get them out for some slow motion "bird dogging" of the plays. Work on conditioning or speed work.

The combination that I hit on was a blend of charts for the assistant coaches and correction drills.

It Don't Fit On a Clipboard!

Most of the people that have seen me coach are amazed at the amount of crap I carry on the field with me. I generally don't carry a clipboard, as was fashionable among coaches some ten years ago. Generally I carry a *notebook*, and the reason is the number of charts I carry around.

I've had my bell rung too many times to be able to adequately remember what goes where with who about half the time. Sometimes it makes me repeat myself. Even worse than that, sometimes I repeat myself.

In order to make sure that I'm putting my practice time emphasis where my players need it, and to make sure that the film is being properly broken down, I've developed the idea of the film chart. In chapters six and seven we're going to divide our team into six blocks, with one coach working with two blocks every day. Just to preview, these six blocks are: offensive backfield, receivers, and offensive linemen; and linebackers, defensive backs, and defensive linemen. While I'm breaking down film I use a simple chart that looks like this:

Player Improvements: Running Backs

	Name	Done Well	Needs Work
1	Bobby	Kickout blocks	Securing the ball
2	Billy	Reading blocks	Reach blocks (1st step)

The next practice day, it's a simple matter to hand that paper to the coach responsible for working with that section of the team, and let him take it from there. There's a blank copy of these charts in appendix three. You have my permission to make as many copies of them as you need.

I don't play the touchie-feelie game that some people play where every negative comment has to be preceded and followed by a positive one. Sometimes there are only going to be negative things to say, and sometimes there are only going to be positive things. As a coach, I try to balance these things as much as possible, but you can*not* lose sleep over the fact that Billy had three great comments and Bobby only got one. Being fair means giving out the rewards and praise that is earned, not making things up or stretching the truth out of some misguided notion of "fairness."

Applying the Wrench

While it works to use the charts if you don't have a staff you can count on to break down film, it's a better idea to have your coaching staff watch the video as a group and determine themselves the largest mistakes your players are making. In the case of that outside linebacker who keeps trailing the sweep instead of turning it inward, we have diagnosed a problem, and now we need to correct it. That's what drills are for. Drills are tools for repairing the execution problems your team is having.

If your left guard keeps blocking the wrong guy on your isolation play, then showing him the video isn't going to help him nearly as much as ten minutes or so of "bird dogging." Bird-dogging is a very effective drill that involves the offensive players. Line them up and call a play. At the snap, each player takes his first two steps. This should be enough to show you whether or not the player is moving to block the correct defender, putting his head on the correct side, and staying low enough in his stance to execute a proper block.

Some coaches call this a "fit and freeze" drill. We start the season doing about fifteen to twenty minutes of this drill every day, and then after the games begin I allocate at least five minutes out of *every practice* just for this drill. I feel it's that important, and it's also a nice return on investment: you can bird dog a play ten times in one minute if you hurry and coach on the run. Even the fastest possible pace I've ever maintained running plays fully from start to finish with the whole team was just five plays a minute.

If your problem is linebackers not attacking their gaps, run some drills like the "Eye opener." In this drill, you put seven bags or cones on the ground and create a number of gaps. Use a ball carrier, who holds a shield to protect himself, and a tackler on the other side of the gaps from him. The coach stands behind the defender and points to a specific gap.

The goal of the ball carrier is to get through the line and advance five yards. The goal of the tackler is to scrape to the hole with shoulders square and make a secure tackle in the hole. The ball carrier can juke, jive, shake, and bake as much as he wants.

Drills

I'm not going to list every possible thing that could go wrong on game day, or drills to fix them all. My point here is that the film becomes a diagnostic tool. Try to break your film down into the smallest common denominator, as in, "What single skill did we fail in the execution of that caused this play to not succeed?" Now you have a clue what you need to rep over and over again with your drills. There are some drills in Appendix one that will help you with most of the skills you need to teach, and for other problem areas, try looking for books like Tom Bass's *Play Football the NFL Way*. (ISBN: 0312059477) I was astonished to discover that, despite the name, there are no drills for trash talking, improving touchdown dance choreography, or tackling with the head down. I'm thinking of writing a letter to Coach Bass to suggest that he change the name to *Play Football the Way the NFL Should*.

Coaches email me all the time and ask what drills they should be running. I'll talk about specific drills in chapter eight, during the discussion of practice plans, and also in my books on offense, defense, and special teams. For the most part, though, I'm going to tell you right off the bat that drills are the absolute *last* thing you should be doing. Drills are there for a specific purpose. Use them to fix precise aspects of your execution that need work. Try to avoid doing drills just to be doing drills. You'll end up with kids that are great at one skill, but have no idea where or how to apply it.

You know, like the *average* youth football coach.

CHAPTER FIVE
Dealing With Parents

Introduction

I've been very fortunate to have had few problems with parents. Part of that I attribute to my no-nonsense approach to dealing with them, and part of it is simply that I'm lucky. I've had great kids on my teams, and one of the reasons they were so great is that their parents were good parents, concerned with their welfare and supportive without being restrictive.

I've had the occasional parent grab his kid and take him hunting during our season, or schedule a dentist's visit during practice time, but the majority of them have understood the importance of commitment. Part of the reason for this is my open communications with the parents.

It's important to remember that *you're* the coach. Football is not a democracy. While in the past I have asked the players for input on what play they think would work well in a given situation, I have never once asked a parent for advice on playcalling, playing time, practice methods, or any other aspect of coaching this sport.

You are the expert. Hopefully this book will whet your appetite and you will begin to study the game in more depth. By the time you're in your second season, you'll probably have read a dozen or more books on the subject, and even possibly purchased a videotape or three about coaching and attended a few clinics. You've put the time in to study the game, and you deserve the respect that entails.

There's one thing I almost always tell my rookie players when they are getting ready to start for the first time. It applies to you as well: *You wouldn't be out there if you weren't the best man for the job.* Don't ever let anyone tell you that you can't coach, or that you're not coaching properly. Just by the fact that you picked up this book, you're already making the transition from *average* to *exceptional*. Parents can either recognize that and respect it, or they can take their kids and go home.

~D.

Square One	The first place you need to start when it comes to dealing with parents is, paradoxically, with your staff. In the next chapter I'm going to talk about selecting and divvying up your staff members and what kinds of help you're going to need.

No matter who is on your staff, you need to hold a couple of meetings with them prior to the beginning of the season—at *least* two to three months before the first practices. They're going to need that much time to learn their responsibilities and study the materials you've given them so they can coach their assignments. Along with handing out your tasks to them, you're also going to need to talk to them about how to deal with parents.

Parents Are Off Limits

I have a rule on my teams. No one talks to parents about this team but the head coach. No coaching staff is perfect. I have enormous respect for Bill Tucker, the head junior varsity coach at Tomales High School, but he and I are different people, with different philosophies of offense and defense. It doesn't make me right, and it doesn't make him wrong, but there are plays I would chop out of our playbook, and things I would do differently. I know for a fact he feels the same way about some of my ideas. (Ask him about my squib kicks sometime.)

I keep my mouth shut, as much as I am ever able to do. I'll make suggestions during a game, but if he overrules me, then I sit quietly (or as quietly as I ever am during a game) and that's the end of it. It is very rare that things ever go beyond that.

In the past parents have approached me that were under the mistaken impression that Coach Tucker should have done this or that differently. It's the responsibility of an assistant coach to defuse that immediately. I have actually been pretty curt with those parents, because I don't have a lot of time for people that show up just to carp and criticize after a loss. (I think my exact words were, "Where were you when we were undefeated?") With parents that might have a legitimate complaint, I simply tell them, "You need to talk to Coach Tucker. I'll let him know that you want some time with him." That's the end of it as far as I'm concerned.

On any team that I am the head coach of, assistant coaches are not to discuss coaching decisions with the parents. They can talk about the games, how exciting, difficult, or fun they were, but the mechanics—who played and who sat, plays that were called, techniques that were used, etc, are none of the parents' business.

Meeting With Parents

You need to hold a meeting with the parents before the season begins. I recommend about two to three weeks before the first practices. I strongly encourage you to make this meeting mandatory and adults only.

By mandatory, I mean that their kid doesn't play or practice until one of his parents is sitting in front of you for thirty minutes. Make the playing dependent on the parents' attendance, and if the parent doesn't show up, well, why practice a kid that can't play?

This is important. The meeting is mandatory because you need to make sure everyone is on the same page. Frankly, if a parent doesn't want to be bothered coming to a meeting about a dangerous and complex sport they want their kid to play, then they probably aren't the sort of parent you want to have around.

**Hey Parent,
Start *Parenting!***

I don't have kids, but I can tell you that if I did, I wouldn't send them to *any* practice for *any* sport unless I'd spoken to the coach first. There are thousands of youth football coaches out there in the world, and I don't think very many of them have done even the most basic research necessary to teach the sport safely, much less successfully. Even at the high school level, in the year 2004, I've heard coaches yelling to players, "You've gotta put your head down and move the pile!" Parents need to *check* this stuff!

When you get the meeting scheduled, you need to have an outline of how you're going to present yourself and your staff to the parents. I try to walk a tightrope I call the "tough but fair" look. I want the parents to realize that I'm a disciplinarian, because this sport demands it. I enjoy having fun and goofing around, but that stops when we step onto the field to practice a collision sport. I want the parents to realize that they can come and talk to me about things that bother them, but that they also need to know from the start who is in charge, and it ain't them.

**What Shall We
Talk About?**

Here's a rough outline of things to discuss with the parents:

I. Welcome to the program

    a. Introduce yourself and your staff

    b. Talk a little about your background as a coach

    c. Discuss your systems briefly

II. Team rules

    a. Attendance policy

    b. Grades policy

    c. Equipment policy

    d. Minimum-play rules

    e. Rule enforcement/punishments

    f. When to speak with the coaching staff and who to speak to

III. Help you need throughout the season

    a. Assistant coach openings (if any)

    b. Team mom, transportation coordinator, etc.

IV. Team building activities

    a. Pizza parties, team meals, etc.

V. Awards

    a. Black Lion

b.   Hardest working lineman of the week

c.   Additional awards

VI.   Open forum and questions for the coaching staff from the parents.

I'll go through the entire outline in some depth to give you an idea what kind of information to pass to the parents. One thing that I hate to break to you is that you need to get used to a certain amount of public speaking. I read somewhere that the fear of speaking in front of a crowd is the number one phobia in America, higher even than fear of contracting cancer.

Public Speaking

You're going to have to get over it. For the next two months at least, you're going to be in front of a crowd—your players—for about seven to ten hours a week, and you'll be coaching in front of an even bigger crowd during games.

I remember performing on stage when I was in high school, and realizing during our 1990 production of *Hamlet* that I wasn't getting stage fright at all. It took me a while to figure out why: preparation. I approached my directorial debut with my characteristic anal-retentive attention to detail. All the actors were required to have their lines memorized before we ever got on stage to work on the stage directions for a scene, and we probably did each scene twenty or thirty times before the first performance.

Stage fright and fear of addressing a crowd comes about because you're not sure you've adequately prepared for the presentation. You're worried about blowing your lines and looking like a fool in front of all those people.

Scout Motto

If you follow my advice, you should *never* get stage fright, because you'll be too well prepared. It's a matter of deciding what you want to talk about, getting it down on paper with a decent outline (Wasn't there one of those about a page or so back?) and practicing it a couple of times.

You need to pretend that you're addressing the board of directors at your company during a stockholder's meeting. Be as prepared to face those parents as you would be if your job was on the line. I think you'll find that any butterflies in your stomach will vanish within the first ten seconds of your presentation, when you realize just how prepared you are.

You're going to be thrown a little bit from time to time by parents with some interesting questions. If the parents have read anything by me, they're probably going to ask how you teach tackling to the players. (And your answer had *better* be, "*Without* using full speed, head on drills.") Don't worry about it. Just answer as best you can. If you know your material properly you'll be okay.

Section I: Welcome to the Team

I usually start the discussion with an introduction. One of the most fundamental questions a parent should have is, "Can I trust this guy?" Your expertise and previous knowledge should carry itself.

Don't be worried if you don't have a lot of coaching experience. In 1999 I had one year of experience as an assistant football coach from seven years before. I also have one problem you probably won't have: I *look* like a kid.

I was very concerned about parents acting as if I was clueless because at age twenty-five I looked nineteen. I was even more concerned because I *was* clueless. I combated this by presenting an appearance as the best-prepared coach in the league. I carried my notebook, not a clipboard, on the field. My playbook looked like it had been professionally published.

The Question of Credibility

What you're searching for is *credibility*. You're seeking to answer the question of "Can I trust this guy?" with, "Yes!"

It's unfortunate, but the only way to get experience is to coach. I had to laugh at one knucklehead in an online message board a couple of years ago. I had been asked a question and recommended a book I thought would give better information than my response. Out of nowhere some yahoo dropped in with his comments.

> *I've seen you answer several questions in here, and all you ever do is tell people to read books. There's no substitute for experience, and you can't get experience any other way than being on the field!*

He was partly right. There isn't any substitute for experience. Unfortunately, following his advice would lead to screwing your first five or six teams out of success because you're not sure how to coach them properly. At least reading some books on coaching will help you benefit from the experience that other coaches have gained throughout the years. I honestly never really figured out what his problem was.

What you need to do is make that clear to the parents. There's nothing wrong with telling them, "This is my first year of coaching football." Believe me, they'll be able to tell on their own, and they're going to give you a certain amount of slack.

The best thing you can do is tell them, "Look, I'm new to this, but I'm being guided by experienced coaches that have been successful." Get your hands on the books I recommended in chapter one and some of the tapes from chapter two. Preface the answers to questions about your system with the statement, "My research suggests…" This lends an aura of credibility to your comments because it underscores the fact that you've been working on improving your knowledge while the parents were eating Cheetos™ and sitting on the couch watching *Survivor*.

I always talk a little bit about the impending season and how much I'm looking forward to beating the ass off our upcoming opponents. (Note: you might want to be slightly more tactful.) Be enthusiastic and fired up. You're coaching this team because it's going to be fun, right? Well, show the parents that. Enthusiasm is infectious. If there's a team that beat us especially bad the season before, I make sure the parents know we intend to pay them back with a hard fought drubbing this season.

My Title is "Coach," Not "Day Care Operator!"

Too many parents tend to think of coaches as babysitters, and that's not your responsibility. This is one of the things you need to make clear to the parents at the meeting. I take special care to make sure that the parents know my staff and I are to be referred to at all times by title. I am not "Wade," or "Derek." I am "Coach Wade." This is an important part of teaching the players proper respect.

The players are also required to answer yes/no questions with "Yes, coach," or "No, coach." There are no exceptions. Even from one staff member to the next we refer to each other by title.

I had one coach tell me a horror story about a couple of "parents" that approached him after he laid down this law at a meeting. Seems those "parents" allow their kids to call them by their first names and felt it was inappropriate for the coach to demand his title be respected.

His reaction was kinder than mine would have been. Running through the modern teenager is a broad streak of entitlement and disrespect for authority that was created, in large part, by that sort of leniency towards actions of contempt directed at senior persons. Teachers are losing control of their classrooms, police are losing control of the streets, and it has come about in many cases because parents were more concerned with being buddies than being parents. Youthful rebellion has turned into scorn towards anyone in authority. I will not have that on my practice field or on my team. If someone's son has a "Question Authority" bumper sticker on his helmet, he and I are probably going to have some words, and they won't be gentle ones. He will be *very* sweaty when he leaves practice.

I've earned my title, and just by reading this book, so have you. Whether or not you choose to make your title mandatory, you deserve it. If you ever come to my practice field, expect to be called "Coach" and treated with the utmost respect by my players.

Your Staff

You should introduce your staff next. For offensive, defensive, or special teams coordinators, you might want to talk about their experience and training, but for assistants it's probably better to just mention their names.

I don't actually use coordinator positions, really. I would if I were able to coach with someone I really knew well and trusted, but for the most part I haven't had the luxury of coaching with a staff as obsessive as I am. I have three assistant coaches that are there to teach technique to specific players. These coaches are typically divided into running backs and linebackers coach, offensive and defensive line coach, and ends and defensive backs coach. In the next chapter I'll discuss my reasons for this, but to reiterate, this gives me the freedom to be a wanderer and move from section to section. Because my assistants are the primary teachers, I can function more as quality control and manager. I can also spend more time on developing them as a staff by providing immediate feedback on their coaching.

This is extremely important. Everyone has a different way to do things, and while mine may not always be the best way, on my team it's the *only* way.

Your Program

I don't go overboard during this section. I can happily discuss football in general and my program in specific for hours on end. There's an optional period at the end of the meeting for any parents that want some more in depth information on your program. In this section, I just tell the parents that we run an offense and defense that have been very successful across the nation for years, and that we as a coaching staff are extremely familiar with it and well-versed in coaching it properly and safely. If they want to learn more, they're welcome to stay after the meeting ends and you'll go through some of the plays and talk about the individual responsibilities.

Section II: Team Rules

This is the most important thing you're going to talk about with the parents all season. I have a number of team rules that need to be brought up with the parents from the start.

Probably the number one thing that gets me assed during the season is a player missing practice. I've never had so many athletes that one or two of them deciding to go home and watch cartoons didn't have an enormously detrimental impact on my program.

What I'm about to say next is not going to go over well. If there's one thing about your program that is going to stick sideways in the craw of the average parent, it is you telling them how to live their lives outside of football, but that is precisely what you need to do.

Be. At. Practice.

There is no such thing as an excused practice on my football team. The players are expected to be at every practice, no matter what. If they are ill, I wish them a speedy recovery, but either they come to practice and stand to the side, or they miss one quarter of football in the next game.

PERIOD!

I tell the parents flat out, "If you have a dental exam scheduled during practice, reschedule it. If you have a doctor's exam scheduled, change it. If you have a family vacation planned, re-plan it."

There is usually a murmur through the crowd at this point, so I go on to tell them, "This coaching curriculum stresses four things: 1) sportsmanship and respect, 2) safe and sound football fundamentals, 3) commitment, and 4) victory through hard work."

One of the most important things that young people need to learn is commitment. In a world of video games with reset buttons, anyone can start over or quit something any time things don't go their way. What does it tell the players when their parents tell them over and over to finish what they start, and then they turn around and say, "We're taking our kid camping during the first week of your practice. Sorry about that."?

I don't tolerate it. If a player misses two practices in a single week, they sit out the next game. If a player has more than five absences, there will be a meeting with the parents to determine his fate, which will probably be removal from the team.

Know When to Break the Rules

There are some exceptions to this rule. There are kids out there that desperately need football. One coach told me a particularly saddening story about a young man on his team in Illinois whose parents were divorcing. The father loved football, and so did the player. Mom, however, wanted to get back at Dad; so on the days that she had custody of their son, she refused to take him to practice.

The young man wanted to play, tried to be there, and worked hard. In a situation like that, denying playing time is punishing the player for the parent's transgressions. I confess that I don't think much of Mom for playing that game with the welfare and happiness of her son, either.

The coach that brought me that sad tale was asking for advice because other parents on the team were starting to ask questions because his policy was nearly identical to mine, yet this young man was still seeing a great deal of playing time. Now, I don't discuss playing time or positions with the parents very often, but they have a right to know why the rules are apparently inconsistent. I think the coach handled things the right way by addressing the team when the player was not at practice and simply saying, "Billy needs our support. He's having some problems, and we're part of his family." To the parents, the coach explained a little more detail, still keeping confidentiality as much as possible. I was extremely impressed with his discretion, to be honest.

There are some other things I'll consider making exceptions for. Death in the family, for example, although I pray I'll never have to do that.

Your Commitment

If the parents grumble too loudly during the meeting, one of the things I've found that generally puts a cork in it is mentioning your own commitment to the team. Before the first practice I have generally put in about 150 hours or more of preparation and study time specifically for that season. I work full time, go to school full time, and I will still be at every single practice from 6pm to 8pm Monday through Friday and at the games every Saturday. I will also spend Sunday breaking down game film and doing stats as well as preparing the scouting report.

This goes over *really* well when you do not have your own children on your team, by the way.

The point here isn't to make myself out as some kind of wunder-coach, able to leap tall goalposts with a single bound, because I'm not. However, I work at least as much as the average dad does, and I can not only be on time for each practice and schedule my life around football season, but I can prepare an entire program and teach it to thirty players.

I want families to spend time together. I wish my family had been able to do more when I was a kid. Unfortunately, the biggest concept that young people have to get their heads around is that when you are part of a team, you *belong* to that team.

I promise you that if you do not have some form of absentee policy in place, and if you do not describe it to the parents and enforce it precisely as you describe, it will come back to haunt you.

Grades

After the parents swallow the attendance guidelines, the next concept, your grades policy, tends to go down a lot more smoothly. Most youth leagues have a grades requirement, and I make sure that the parents know and understand that we will enforce it on my team. Because I am the type of person I am, I demand that my players not just succeed, but excel. Typically my team's grade requirements are at least one half grade higher than the league's requirements. I have learned through experience that the higher you raise the bar, the more players will make the effort to jump to it.

Equipment

I recommend that you have an equipment turn-in day planned and scheduled before your season even begins. It makes things go a lot easier when you can be up front and tell the parents, "We turn in equipment on November 13th." That way, if something doesn't come back to your program on time, you can remind the parents that it was discussed at the meeting.

Minimum Play Rules

Parents pay a lot of money so their kids can play football. You will note that I don't refer to my team as a collection of "practicers." That word is not even in my spell checker.

Even in leagues that have no official minimum play rule, I have my own. I want to get each and every player on my team into each game for around six to ten plays. Football is about hard work leading to success and rewards, and one of those rewards is the ability to go onto the field and strut your stuff.

Building for the Future

A completely separate point is my personal selfishness. See, I plan to win *next* season, too, and the guys sitting on the bench this season are probably going to start for me next season. If I can get them ten extra plays per game in a six game season, that's sixty extra plays, or the equivalent of one full extra game of experience ahead of the benchwarmers on our opponents' teams, who generally sit there looking disgruntled while my third stringers are playing. That makes a *big* difference when you're talking about long-term success.

There are some caveats to the concept of a minimum play program, however. To start with, most leagues have an extremely shoddy tracking system. Typically, if the league bothers to track it at all, then each team selects two parents to make tick marks next to each player's name on a chart that is then submitted to the league. Now, what happens if the parent decides to get his own kid into the game more often? What about the parent that isn't paying attention to his responsibility because he's watching the game and forgets to mark down a whole bunch of substitutions?

For the meeting with the parents, I would simply let them know that you do have a minimum number of plays that you're going to get each player into the game for, and that you are committed to seeing that happen.

Enforcement

This is a good place to transition to the enforcement of the rules, because a minimum play rule isn't a rule for the parents or players; it's a rule for you. Since I just bent the parents' ears about commitment and integrity, I feel it's necessary to establish a standard. If I fail to ensure that each player receives his minimum plays in each game, I will personally write a letter of apology to the player. I feel it's the least I can do for a screw up of that magnitude. I've made a promise to my players, and I don't break my promises lightly.

Enforcement of the rules is a tricky issue. I hate it when players are late to practice. I can get there on time, so I don't see why parents make such an issue of getting their kids there. Would you be late to work?

I make the kids run one lap after practice for every minute they are late, by my watch. No exceptions, no excuses. The kids then go home and tell their parents that they are being punished because the parents didn't get them to practice on time. The parents will hopefully then put some effort into making good on *their* commitment to get the kids to practice on time.

Yes, Mom, We *Do* Need Your Son at Practice!

I have only ever had one parent get upset by this policy. She was a soccer-mom type that didn't understand why it was important to be at practice on time until she saw her first football game. Something about seeing players get knocked down suddenly convinced her that maybe her son should be at practice early enough to learn how to protect himself. I had no further problems with her son from that moment forward.

A funny story about this policy happened in 1999 in Kodiak, Alaska. At that time I sent players on laps as soon as they arrived, rather than keeping them after practice. (I changed because it usually takes two or three minutes to run a lap, and that's a lot of practice time to miss. Besides, if a parent is going to waste my time being late, then I think they can handle the waste of a few minutes of *their* time when their son gets out of practice late.) While the players were running I went back to the drill I was supervising, and looked up a few moments later to see both their moms jogging side by side around the practice field.

I yelled over to them to ask what they heck they were doing, and they hollered back, "It was our fault they were late!"

One of the last things I discuss with the parents in this section is when to speak to the coaches and who to speak to. In chapter seven you'll find out that practice time seconds are like jewels and you should no more waste them than you should chuck your wife's diamond earrings out the window. (Although your players probably won't make you spend the rest of your life sleeping on the couch.)

Practice is for practicing. I do not speak to the parents during practice times, and the pre- and post- practice meetings are considered a part of practice. I make it to the field in plenty of time for the parents to bring any concerns to me before the meeting begins, and I don't leave the field for at least thirty minutes after the post-practice meeting ends. Parents are welcome to discuss things with me then.

Note that I say, "Discuss with *me*." Any concerns the parents might have need to be brought to me, and not anyone else on the coaching staff.

Section III: Getting Help

I try to go into every season knowing in great detail who is going to be coaching for my program. My first preseason meeting is held some four months prior to the first practice.

In some cases, however, it might be necessary to fill a coaching position from the ranks of parents. I prefer moms to dads for a lot of reasons. Here's a short list:

- Moms typically don't know much about football, so they ask questions and teach the way you want things taught.
  - Dads typically played before, and try to get you to do things their way.

- Moms tend to be more protective of the players, so they concentrate on teaching safety and sportsmanship.
  - Dads usually like to kick ass.

- Moms smell good.
  - Dads don't.

Don't even get me started on body hair.

Seriously, though, while it'll probably be a dad that offers to help you out, don't automatically turn down a mom (or dad, or older brother or sister) because they have no football experience. Just make sure you read over the chapter on choosing your staff before you make a pick.

Help!

Where you need the most assistance is not really the coaching. You can do that yourself if you have to. It's tough, and it slows you down a bit because you have to work with the entire team at one time, but it's eminently possible.

Pushing Paper

You're going to need help with the *administration.* You'll need a team mom to help you organize things like pictures and team dinners. You'll need a transportation coordinator to help you get the players to each game. You'll need a videographer to tape your games and at least a few of your practices. You'll need at least one substitution coach to work your sidelines and follow your substitution schedule to make sure all your players get in the game. Although I usually assign that task to one of my three assistants, it's a better idea to have a parent do it. .

What you absolutely do *not* need is someone to tell you what you should run or how you should run it. This is the problem a lot of dads have, because a lot of dads are football fans. If you've followed my advice and were crazy enough to buy the rest of this series of books, then you're using a system that doesn't look anything at all like what you see on TV.

Plus, from reading this book, you're using a practice schedule that looks completely unlike anything used by any coach twenty years ago, which is when most dads played. As I mention in chapter eight, if you get any complaints about the practice plan, they'll be from the coaching staff, not from the players.

Section IV: Team Building

I like to do a lot of team building in my program. At Tomales High School, Coach Feliciano recently put together a new tradition of a weekly team dinner. Every week the night before the game is a shortened walkthrough practice and the entire team goes over to one player's house for a team dinner. After dinner the coaches and captains present their feelings about the season, the upcoming game, and some of the positive attributes we hope to instill in the players, such as integrity and sportsmanship.

I think this is a fine idea, but it's also a difficult one. Preparing a meal for thirty people is a huge task. An easier and still great idea is a pizza party. I like to have one about midway through the season at the local pie parlor. Just ask the parents to chip in about ten bucks per kid, and that should take care of things.

Thanks From Coach Wade

Special note: in 1999 the uncle of one of my defensive backs took the *entire* team, including the coaching staff, out for pizza at the halfway point. I still think that was one of the most generous things I've ever seen. If Mr. Garcia ever reads this, thank you so much for that wonderful night.

Some other fun ideas that I've had are "optional practices." I usually do this in the preseason on a Saturday, where the kids meet at our practice field and play two-hand touch with the coaches for a couple of hours. No one is required to come, and it has nothing to do with actual football practice, so we usually don't have any problems with practice time restrictions. You could also have a potluck picnic at a local park or something like that.

Probably my favorite idea I stole straight out of *Remember the Titans*. I love to take the players on runs of about two to three miles. Since there isn't any time laid aside for that during practice, it's the sort of voluntary thing that makes the team come together a little bit more on an extra Saturday. Plus, you need to run off the pizza from the weekly team parties.

Never Mandatory, Always Great

Team building is about forging a bond together. Overcoming the adversity of a tough practice or a long run can really make a team begin to pull in the right direction. While none of these things have ever been mandatory, I've noticed that the number of players attending on their own is directly proportional to the success of the season.

Section V: Awards

I don't like giving out individual awards very much. Football isn't an individual sport, it's a team sport, and the success of the team rests on their ability to support one another. I think individual awards tend to take away from that, and they are usually given based on luck rather than hard work.

For example, a man and a woman meet in college, fall in love, get married, and have a kid that grows up to stand 5'11" tall, weigh 185 pounds, and runs a 4.6 forty yard dash as a freshman in high school.

Another set of parents turns out a kid that graduates from high school at 5'4" tall, 108 pounds and that runs a forty in 4.6 months. (Thanks for *nothing*, Mom and Dad!)

Life Isn't Fair

Which one of those kids is going to win the most accolades as an athlete? Assuming they both work with equal intensity, some players just have gifts that others don't. Giving out an award for most touchdowns scored to a natural athlete is sort of a smack in the face to the backup that didn't have the same advantages that the starter was born with.

If I'm going to give out an individual award, it's going to be an award that helps bind the team together as one. In appendix five you'll find information on the most important award I've ever given out, the Black Lion. That's one of the only two awards I'll give out on my teams.

The other is the hardest working lineman award, which is a weekly award announced at every home game. In fact, the hardest working lineman of the week leads the team onto the field, and stands in the captain's circle during warm-ups for the game. In the past, the award winner's parents were even given a certificate just before the game for two free hotdogs and sodas from the concession stand. This way the player feels that he not only helped his team and earned an honor for himself, but he also earned something for his family as well.

Section VI: Open Forum

I really try to keep the preceding presentation information down to twenty minutes or less. It doesn't really take that long to pass the facts. Now you can open the floor for questions about your program.

Be prepared to defend some of your decisions. Some parents, typically the ones you're going to have the greatest amount of trouble with during the season, are going to try to get up your nose about the policies you've unveiled. I tend to catch a lot of flak for one line: "If you have a vacation scheduled for August, reschedule it." Some parents feel that their family vacation is more important than their son's football team. You might have to answer the question, "Where do you get off?"

Keep the Faith

Okey-dokey. I don't get to tell people how they can think, even when they're wrong. I *do* get to lay down the law about who plays on my football teams. Any player missing a single practice for any reason doesn't play for a quarter. There is no discussion about this. Any player missing more than two practices in a week will sit for the game, and any player missing five practices will not play football for me. There are no exceptions to this rule beyond death in the family or serious illness.

The Hard Choice

It sucks that a player might have to make the decision between a family vacation and playing football. Unfortunately, that's the way things work. A long time ago I had to make a decision between playing football for my high school or getting involved in the drama program. I made the wrong choice, and wish I could undo it. I can't though, and my senior year I watched from the Homecoming float instead of playing in the game. I'm thirty-one now, and I'll never be able to undo that choice.

For your players, their family should be the most important thing in their lives. Football should be well down the list. If a player ever asked me what they should do, I would tell them unequivocally that they should go on vacation with their family. Family comes first.

But if you're going to play football for me, you need to be at practice. Schedule your family trip to Cancun in July. August, September, October, and at least part of November belong to your teammates. This rule is the primary reason why the parents' meeting is adults only. (Well, that and the one incident with the dancing girls, but we don't talk about that very often.) Be prepared to defend it.

Chalk Time

Sooner or later the conversation is going to drift around to your offense and defense. Usually it's a dad that's going to pop the question, but I once had a mom that was very curious about my offense because I had casually tossed off that it's set national scoring records and been used from peewee to pros.

This is where your personal preparation is going to pay off. If you've been doing your homework on your system, and hopefully procured a little intelligence on your opponents as well, there won't be a question you can't answer. This is also a natural transition to the Xs and Os of your specific schemes, which should cover the last ten minutes or so of the meeting.

No Big Words!

Stay away from the jargon of football. For one thing, it sounds like a snow job. When a parent asks you how your basic blocking attack works, throwing out phrases like, "We're going to zone out on a six-tech and send the flex end to the second level," is not going to impress the parents with how much football you know, it's going to impress them with your inability to teach things coherently. If *they* can't understand it, as adults with a lifetime of experience and at least some basic knowledge of football, they're going to start wondering how their eight-year-old sons are going to understand it.

Here's another point about that. One of the best clinic speakers and coaches I've ever had the privilege of listening to didn't even know what a nine-technique defensive end was. When someone asked him a question about blocking that guy he stared blankly at the whiteboard for a few seconds before asking, "Where's that guy lined up again?"

Considering that his offense scored 880 points in 1991 and set a national scoring record while earning an average score of 67 offensive points per game for thirteen games, I think it's pretty obvious that his players knew how to *block* a nine-tech, even if he didn't know what the heck one was *called.*

Be Fired Up

Above all, keep your enthusiasm about your program. Most of the time when the parents ask you a question about your offense or defense, they aren't going to really understand very much about the answer. The *way* you answer it is going to be more meaningful than the actual words that come out of your mouth. Remember, whatever specific offense and defense you choose to run, and I hope it's the ones I've put together for my forthcoming books, you've put a lot of time into research and development, and the reason you picked those systems was that you felt strongly that they would give you the best possible chances to win.

Take that same emotion and channel it into responding to questions the parents have about your program. Be prepared for some animosity if you run anything other than a spread passing system with an I-formation running game. People tend to be a little afraid of things that they don't understand, and the average fan only understands the limited football they see on TV. Don't be hostile, just be honest.

Playing Politics

Speaking of being honest, I'm a little more blunt about the way I do things than I recommend for most coaches. For one thing, it's a part of what I laughingly refer to as my charm. Second, I have enough experience and knowledge now to be able to silence nay-sayers and critics right off the bat. When a fan tells me that my offense can't possibly work at whatever level I'm coaching because it's impossible to teach kids that young to pull and trap, and then tries to convince me that a spread passing game is a better idea, I have plenty of research, study, and contacts, as well as my personal, on-grass experience, to point to in order to get them to back off.

Like the Bomb Squad – Defuse *Gently*

Probably the best line I ever discovered for dealing with nay-sayer parents is, "I think you'll be pleasantly surprised." This cuts through a lot of arguing. As much as I hate playing politics, there's no real purpose to winning the battle of wits with a parent on a subject like this. If you crush them abjectly (and you will, because you know what you're talking about and they don't), you end up with someone that's going to be badmouthing you and undermining you throughout the season. When things go wrong, and occasionally they will, you're going to see them sitting in the bleachers leaning over to whisper in the ears of the other parents.

Suffer With a Smile

To avoid that, be positive. Just tell them, "Hey, trust me on this. I can teach it, and your sons can learn it. Believe in them and we'll be fine. You'll be surprised how well we do."

I believe in open communications with the parents. While I don't discuss playing time, positions, or depth chart locations with them, one thing I keep in the front of my mind is that they do have certain rights. They deserve to know that you care about their sons (or daughters). When one of my former players was in a bad car accident two days before the start of the 2003 season I told his mother point blank, "He's my son, too, for sixteen weeks or so. I just don't have to feed him, thank God."

The parents deserve to know that you're there to protect their sons from harm, that you're going to work hard to make them winners on and off the field, and that you're committed to making football a life-changing, wonderful experience for them. They deserve to know where they stand with you, and that you're going to be as fair as possible.

What the Parents *Have* to Know

They also *have* to know a few things. They have to know that you're not there for them to abuse. You're not a babysitter. You're a professional in your own right. They have to know the consequences of certain actions, whether committed by them or by their son. They have to know that, as far as you're concerned, discipline starts from within, and is enforced from without.

Parents should be invested in your program through their children. Believe it or not, the number one reason why good coaches quit is dealing with parents. Most coaches get into coaching to be around the kids and for love of the game. They aren't there for political games. I make it a firm policy to avoid the politics of running a youth football program by concentrating on the coaching and letting the politics take care of itself. I respect the parents, but I do not cater to them.

The result is that I've been rewarded with some great parents and some great players. Their hard work has made me extremely successful. Approaching them the right way can reap incredible dividends for your team as well.

CHAPTER SIX
Selecting and Preparing Your Staff

Introduction

A staff should be an extension of the head coach. Your staff can make or break your team, and selecting someone to be a part of it should never be a light process. One seemingly minor mistake can infect your team with a cancer that can destroy your season, undermine your morale, and interfere with your players' ability to enjoy football.

Worse, it can get your players hurt. The sole serious injury I've ever had on the practice field occurred when one of my assistants decided to run a tackling drill that I had banned. The drill involved head on tackling at full speed. I had specifically avoided this drill because I've always believed in giving my players hundred and hundreds of slow motion repetitions to hone their tackling skills and letting them tackle at full speed only in controlled environments.

The player was a rookie, who dropped his head just for an instant, and took the impact on the crown of his helmet. The result was a neck stinger that took him out of contact for a week and earned him a ride to the hospital in the back of an ambulance.

It also earned my assistant coach the ass chewing of his life. It was my first year as a head coach. Had I then the experience that I have now, I'd have fired him on the spot and kicked his happy rear off my practice field, probably physically. Getting my players hurt is a sin that I simply do not forgive. Getting them hurt because you chose to specifically ignore my detailed instructions is even worse.

A good staff, however, can take a lot of the pressure off you as the head coach. They can help you scout, break down film, prepare game plans, and hone your players to a sharp edge. They can be your eyes-in-the-sky and make your game day run much smoother by handling your substitutions for you and keeping an eye on clock management.

Selecting and training your staff is one of your most important responsibilities as a head coach. You want competent, confident individuals that are going to teach what you want them to teach and teach if well. In this chapter, I'll give you a few ideas what to look for, the good and the bad, and I'll hopefully help you organize your responsibilities among your teammates—the guys in the polo shirts.

~D.

It's Not the Size…

One of the high schools in my area has a truly amazing staff. I think, for a student body of 310 and 57 players split between a varsity and junior varsity program, they have some fourteen coaches, including a person listed in their media guides as the "spirit coach," whatever that is.

In the four years that I have coached at Tomales, we've beaten them three times. In 2004 we took our three man coaching staff and sixteen JV players to their house and faced off against their twenty-eight kids in a battle that we won 30-0. A larger coaching staff does not automatically mean that it's a *better* coaching staff. (Actually, I give credit for that win to our players, who came out with guns blazing, caused and recovered a fumble on the eighteen-yard line on the second play from scrimmage, and allowed just two first downs all day. We as coaches had very little to do with things that day.)

By contrast, some of the best-coached teams I've seen at any level had coaching staffs composed of two or three highly motivated and dedicated persons. The coaches had a clear division of responsibility and they were highly skilled in their specific areas. They also stayed out of each other's sand boxes.

In his outstanding book, *Coaching Football Successfully* (ISBN 087322518X), Bob Reade describes the ideal coaching staff size as comparable to what your opponents have. "If they have six coaches, you should strive to have six coaches."

Jack Reed, by contrast, feels the ideal coaching staff is an army of one: you. Several times in his books and on his web site he mentions that having just one coach can avoid much of the hassle created by conflicting ideologies and football knowledge.

…It's How You Use It!

I think the truth lies somewhere in the middle. I don't want a lot of coaches on the field with me, because we'd just tend to get under each other's skin. However, I also don't want to be doing everything myself, and it really impairs your efficiency to work alone. At any given moment you'd generally have ten to twenty players standing around waiting to get into a drill or scrimmage, and that's not a good idea. I prefer to keep my players moving every second, but that means that someone has to be watching and coaching them every second as well.

In a perfect world I would have three assistants, one clock management coach who runs a timer at practice, and a pair of team moms to help me keep everything organized. I'd also have a dedicated scout who would go obtain film on my opponents. In a perfect world I'd also be six feet tall, and my helicopter would have a stealth mode on it. Too bad things are never perfect.

I've said several times that I don't believe in having offensive, defensive, or special teams coordinator positions on my staff. As an experienced head coach, I have a certain way that I want things to be run. Like the Phantom of the Opera, I want Mssrs. Firme and Andre to keep themselves out of my art.

Qualifications

There's a specific reason for this. I don't like to blow my own horn, but I have put a *lot* of time and effort into studying the game of football. I've read numerous books, watched countless videos, and spent what feels like years breaking down our game films. I don't think it makes any sort of sense to hand a critical portion of my football team over to another person whose two largest qualifications are that he's watched football on TV for twenty years and happens to be the father of the quarterback.

I want that guy to help me coach, but I'm not going to let him run the entire show. If you think about it, it's not really fair to him, either. Throwing a dad-coach into the fire against experienced coaches is asking for a bad situation. It's usually the inexperienced parent-coaches that are on the sidelines yelling, "You've got to hit someone!" and, "You tackle like a *girl!*" This comes about because of frustration; they can see that the magical, successful plays they drew in their heads are failing on the field, but they can't see why because they just don't have the know-how yet.

If there's one thing that Coach Feliciano at Tomales High School ever taught me, it's that the head coach is responsible for the development of his staff. Just like a younger player, I want to take my inexperienced coaches and give them a chance to learn their positions and be successful. Throwing them to the wolves right away is not fair to them *or* to the team we're going to screw while they fumble around learning their jobs properly.

In 1999 I got stuck with the head coaching position two days before the season began. Ten years of doubts and fears boiled up in an instant, and I spent much of that season terrified that I was going to screw something up. Not only was I afraid that we were going to lose, which is a pretty minor thing, but I was also afraid that my inexperience was going to result in a serious injury to one of my players. We went undefeated, but I know in my heart that my team was not well coached because I didn't know what I was doing. I don't want my assistant coaches to ever have to go through the sleepless nights and stress that I went through that season.

Organizing the Team

Therefore, it's my responsibility to be the coordinators, and the assistant coaches become my position coaches. Logically, if we break up a football team into its traditional components, your players are usually arranged into six groups: running backs, receivers, offensive linemen, linebackers, defensive backs, and defensive linemen. Quarterbacks generally practice with the running backs to work on the timing of the offensive plays, but they might be assigned here and there to work on the passing game with the receivers.

Since we rarely, if ever, practice offensive and defensive skills at the same time, we really have three groups in two sections:

Offense	Defense
Running Backs	Linebackers
Receivers	Defensive Backs
Linemen	Linemen

By no coincidence, these are the same positions we're going to need coaches for. One assistant coach will be assigned to coach running backs and linebackers, a second will be assigned to coach receivers and their defensive counterparts, the defensive backs, and the last assistant will be working with the big boys on both sides of the line.

Where, you might ask, does the head coach fit into this? It doesn't appear that there's any place left over for him.

This is by design. The head coach should be the master of the program, with a coherent plan in his head for how he needs and wants each specific position to be coached. It's his job to rotate from group to group every day, to make sure that his players are competently and confidently coached, and that his assistants are following the program.

Crop Rotation

By using this "crop rotation" idea, it makes it much easier for the head coach to oversee the minor details of his program. He can make sure that inexperienced coaches are coaching inexperienced players in the correct techniques. Since each day the head man works with someone new, this gives the assistants a chance to coach on their own without getting into too much trouble. They're never further than two days from being able to ask the head coach for advice and guidance.

I think crop rotation is a good metaphor. (Duh. I wrote it.) What you're doing by using this coaching method is sowing the seeds of a very successful coaching team in the future. By giving your assistants time to coach on their own, but still keeping your hand in the pot, you're able to consistently monitor their progress.

Selecting Who to Work With

Typically, I start each week working with the offensive linemen and the linebackers, both of whom are the foundations of their sides of the ball. You'll find in my practice plan that, for all its detail, I really didn't put much in there for the head coach. That's intentional. You're going to have to look at your own team as the season progresses and decide who needs your help the most. If you give up five touchdown passes because of missed coverage assignments, you should probably consider working a little more personally with your defensive backs.

On the other hand, if your receivers are dropping the ball too often (about once per game is all I can tolerate without throwing one of my famous fits), then you might want to work with the receivers a little more. It might even be necessary to work with the same group two days in a row. The head coach has to have that kind of flexibility in his schedule, so I leave it completely up to you.

There's an art to coaching your coaches, and I admit that I'm not stellar at it. No one likes to be told that they're wrong, and it's unfortunate, but you're going to have to do that fairly often, at least at first.

My problem is that I'm too blunt. Maybe it's the military training, maybe it's my anal-retentiveness getting in the way of proper communications, but sometimes I have had to almost physically stop myself from stepping in when a coach is teaching something incorrectly and calling them out in front of the players.

Honesty- It Really *Is* the Best Policy

The better way to handle it is to quietly correct the coach and let him fix the error with the players. If you keep total honesty with your staff and players, it usually isn't a problem. Far too many times in my career I've had to go back and "uncoach" something that I taught incorrectly. Because I always go out of my way to be honest with my players, they tend to be very forgiving when I make a mistake and immediately own up to it.

If your staff members approach the players with the same sort of honesty, they should find that same respect and courtesy extended to them.

Game Day

During the games, each coach should have a clear and specific responsibility assigned to them. Generally, one of my three coaches is in the booth, giving me real time information on our opponents via the headset, one of the staff is on the sidelines coordinating substitutions and helping me manage the clock, and the third will be out scouting. How you organize these specific tasks is up to you, and should take into account the skills and abilities of your staff.

Now that we've divided up the specific responsibilities, including your job as the head coach, it's time to go looking for a staff. Finding talent to put pads on is hard enough. Coming up with the guys to coach them can be even harder.

Dads

I really try as hard as I can to avoid drawing from the ranks of dads. Dads are usually football fans. They played twenty years ago, and they love the Lions, or the Bears, or the Bills, or the Seahawks (Go 'Hawks!). They follow a particular college (Go Huskies!), and, no matter how much they may try to deny it, they see their sons in their hearts as the next Brett Favre or Walter Payton.

The problem is, all that TV football gets in the way of reality. Not only can there be a problem with dad-coaches and nepotism, when they put their players in prime positions even though they are completely unsuitable for the spot, but the video-game football in the NFL and Div-IA College also breeds a certain amount of false knowledge.

Youth football is more than the I-formation and a spread passing attack. In fact, without a great deal of expertise and careful coaching, as well as a crapload of talent, those specific systems are not going to be successful at the youth level. Catching a thrown football when there is a linebacker steaming down to crush your helmet while your head is still in it requires a certain amount of skill and talent that many youth players haven't developed yet.

One of the worst displays of video game coaching I have ever seen occurred in 2004. Before my season started I spent two weeks helping to install the Double Wing offense with a local youth program. (Great kids!) I called the plays at their first scrimmage, and our first game was against a team that obviously had a parent-coach with no experience. They lined up in an I-formation to run between the tackles, the split-back formation to run outside, and passed from a shotgun.

By their sixth snap I was yelling the play to the defense as soon as they lined up, and I was never wrong. I even called the reverse out to the defense even though I hadn't seen them run it yet.

They had incredible talent on that team. We hit their running backs in the backfield on almost every play, but three times they broke loose for long gains. The result was that we lost the scrimmage, two touchdowns to three. During the handshake he told our head coach that it was his first year coaching. I'm sure that coach was very excited to have won his first 'game' and he probably did very well throughout the rest of the season.

What Happens Next?

Unfortunately, in the 2005 season, he probably didn't do nearly as well, when all that talent had moved on.

Don't get me wrong. I'm no super coach. In fact, just six years ago, I *was* that coach. His playbook wasn't a whole lot different from the one I used in 1999 with my Kodiak Lions.

My point here is that just being a fan and watching football on TV doesn't prepare you for actual coaching responsibility. If I'd been in charge of that league, that dad would have never been allowed (or forced) to be a head coach with no experience. He'd have been required to serve at least one year under a competent head coach.

The Bill of Rights

If you're going to open your coaching staff to the ranks of dads, make damn sure that you establish the guidelines right off the bat. I'm not really a rules guy. For all my anal-retentiveness, having a specific set of rules for the staff isn't my style. Thomas Jefferson never wanted to write the Bill of Rights because he was afraid it would be used as a maximum instead of a minimum. I feel somewhat the same way when it comes to my staff. About the only rule I pass out to them is, "Don't undercut the head coach."

If you think about it, this covers a *lot*. Don't undercut the head coach to *who* is not mentioned. This means you don't badmouth the boss to the kids or their parents or the league or even your wife. *How* also isn't mentioned. This means you don't tell the players, "Well, we're blocking this play like this, but it's not what I would do." It means you don't tell the parents, "I wouldn't have called that play in that situation."

I mentioned before that I never speak to the parents about the team in anything other than a positive way when I'm an assistant coach, and I refer everything else back to the head coach. I demand that my assistants follow the same policy.

Dads are going to have to realize that, unless they study the sport as much as you do, they really aren't in a position to pass judgment on anything you choose to do. Take a look at the way President Bush has been criticized for some of his presidential decisions. If you think about it, very few of the people carping about him have ever had a CIA briefing, and even fewer have graduated from Yale, so how do they know he's ever made a wrong choice?

Supporting the Head Man

Coaching football is the same way. I feel a certain amount of justification for my vehement complaining about Mike Holmgren and the way he has (mis)handled my beloved Seattle Seahawks. I see no reason why I shouldn't complain, vocally, viscerally, and with *volume* about the way Mike Tice refused to muzzle Randy Moss. As I write this chapter, Moss was recently fined a whopping $10,000 for his disgraceful mooning of the fans at Lambeau Stadium during a 31-17 Minnesota Vikings playoff victory over the Packers on January 9th, 2005. Moss can feel *very* lucky that he doesn't play for me. Somewhere his high school coach is crying himself to sleep every night.

I have every right to say these things, because I am a football coach and fan. If, however, I was ever accidentally lobotomized in a horrible proctology accident and decided to coach in the NFL for Coach Holmgren or Coach Tice, it would become my responsibility to *keep my mouth shut!*

Supporting the Team

Dads need to be informed that the same rules of conduct apply to them. Once they step on that practice field with a whistle and a polo shirt, they represent the team. Not just the team with the fancy logo and the oddly shaped ball, they also represent the team of *coaches*, and of that team, *you* are the quarterback. They don't have to agree with everything you do, and kissing your ass isn't going to be helpful to your team, but they need to know that anything negative should be brought up behind closed doors.

There's another significant problem with some dads: out of date information. This isn't a crime or a sin unless they try to use it on the field, but let's think a little bit. The average father of a ten-year-old boy is about thirty years old. He was last in high school twelve years ago, and the last time he played football was closer to *thirteen* years ago, because football is the first sport played in the school year.

I'm thirty-(mumble) years old. I can tell you that, just fifteen years ago, my football coaches were withholding water to 'toughen' us. I watched when a player on my team was sent to the sidelines with a concussion and *sent back into the game four plays later!* A dad-coach who went through the same playing experiences I did, without the benefit of years of research and study, can be a real danger to your players' health if he attempts to take those techniques to your practice field.

None of this is an issue if the dads you pick to help you will acknowledge your substantial knowledge of the game. Everything is just peachy if they'll smile and follow your lead.

Asking for Directions

The problem is that sports seem to be a challenge to the manhood of most men. We won't even ask for directions when we're lost, why would we ask for directions when we're coaching a sport we think we know everything about because we played it a decade and a half ago? It's unfortunately very natural for the average dad to get his ego wrapped up in coaching football, and be resistive to doing things other ways.

A dad that watches what passes for football in the NFL is probably going to tell you that you're out of your mind when you show up with my Double Wing playbook and tell everyone that you plan on pulling the back side of the offensive line through the point of attack. He's not going to listen when you tell him that kids as young as five and six have successfully run this offense. He's going to fight tooth and nail because "kids at this age can't pull or trap block" and "you need to know the limitations of the players!"

Then he's going to try to talk you into spreading out with four wide receivers in a shotgun set and throwing the ball twice in every set of downs, because apparently your players have a better chance of successful pass blocking and running precise routes than of pulling off double teams and angle blocks.

No, I don't understand his logic either.

Don't Despair!

I've told you the bad. Here's the good: this guy *can* become a great coach, and he's not necessarily *wrong*. I know a guy that coaches semi-pro and eight-year-olds, using the *same offense!* His system, developed by one of my mentors and friends, Ted Seay, is a spread passing game called the "Wild Bunch." (You can find out more information at http://forums.delphiforums.com/TedSeay/start.)

The difference is that the coach I'm talking about has worked many long hours to learn how to teach the passing game to the younger kids. He understands pass protection schemes and knows how to get his linemen to execute them. He comprehends the way defenses try to stop the pass, and designs his offense to take advantage of that. He did *not* just watch a few NFL games and put his offense together from that, or pick it out of Madden '05™.

I've told you all these horror stories because you need to be informed. Most new coaches are so thankful to get the help that they jump on the first raised hand in the parents' meeting when they ask for coaching volunteers. These guys are desperate for someone to take the load off of them.

The Consequences of the Wrong Staff

Unfortunately, the natural result is that they end up with a staff that wants to do things their own way. They end up with a staff that fights them, undercuts them to the parents, or doesn't teach critical skills properly. Because most rookie coaches also don't establish a 'crop rotation' coaching plan, either, some kids on the team may *never* be coached by the head coach, or may go the entire season learning the wrong techniques for playing their positions.

For some reason, this tends to happen to the offensive line more than anything else. Actually, I know the reason; it's because no one, including myself, ever dreams about being an offensive lineman. I never think about my playing days in junior high, when I was a guard. I think about playing in high school, where I was a free safety and corner, even though I think I was a better guard than defensive back.

Just for fun, try to find an NFL jersey with a number like "66" or "61." I've been looking for close to ten years and I still can't find one. Any jersey with a number 50-59, 70-79, or 90-99 is probably a linebacker, defensive tackle, or defensive end.

Football is *Not* Just the Offense!

When someone gets into coaching for the first time, they generally think about scoring touchdowns. They want to work with the running backs or receivers and quarterbacks, and the poor grunts in the trenches get stuck with the lowest ranking coach in the pecking order. Heck, many of these coaches don't work on special teams or defense *either*, ignoring both of those until the week before the first game or scrimmage.

What I want you to do is remember that you're actually building two teams at the same time. You need a coaching staff that is going to be on the same page, and that will, in turn, result in a group of players that are being correctly taught. That's going to translate into much more game day success than anything else you could do.

The Best Man for the Job— *Whoa! Man!*

Dads can be a good source of aid to you, but before I'd even look at them, I'd ask whether or not there are any moms that are interested in coaching.

You might laugh about this, but I'm dead serious. Most of the problems I've cited above that dads have can't be attributed to moms. Very few thirty-year-old women actually played football in high school, so they don't have dim memories of coaches shrieking at them to get in the way of proper instruction. Moms generally *know* that they're ignorant about coaching football, and they know that there's no shame in it. They have no problems with asking questions when something doesn't seem right.

For all the grief that men give women about not being logical, and God knows my wife has heard it *all* from me, when it comes to football and women, logic seems to hold immediate sway. When I've talked with parents about my offense, for example, the dads always think they have a better way, but the moms almost always nod when I describe why we angle block and double team instead of taking on our opponents' defensive linemen with a bunch of one-on-one blocks across the playside. And no, they're not nodding because they don't understand and are in "auto-bob" mode. The ladies just seem to *get* it faster than their husbands do, probably because they don't have twenty years of foggy memories getting in the way of their comprehension.

You Know, You *Can* Yell At Them!

The one issue you might have with moms is assertiveness. Moms tend to be a little more tentative with certain things. Punishment is one of them. Something about seeing the little buggers sweating seems to throw them off their stride. I witnessed one lady trying to organize a group of baseball players once that were about eight-years-old. After listening to her whisper, "Eyes on me, please," for the eighth time, I finally wandered over and barked, "Eyes on your coach, *now!*" Suddenly twenty-six eyes were locked on their coach while I stood at parade rest behind her and scowled in my best E-5 manner. I was actually only at the field to scout out a practice area for my football team while our field was being reseeded, so she was a little startled, but I think she appreciated the help.

The type of mother that is willing to help you is also typically an excellent parent, and part of parenting is disciplining, so this is definitely not an insurmountable problem.

Another good thing about moms is that they generally follow through on their commitments because they have something to prove. Most women know and understand that there are very few members of their gender involved in coaching in general and coaching football in specific. The mom you're looking for is the one that's going to see this as a challenge. She's going to want to hit the field as the most knowledgeable, energetic, and enthusiastic coach next to, well, next to *you*.

Preparing the Staff

Once you get the staff put together, you're going to need to divide their responsibilities. As I mentioned before, you need one coach for each of three primary aspects of the team: offensive and defensive line, offensive backfield and linebackers, and defensive backs and receivers/ends. This is a logical division of the team; if your players play both ways like most youth players, you'll probably find that your receivers play defensive back, your linebackers will most likely also play tailback, and the offensive linemen are typically the defensive linemen. By using your three coaches in this manner you're keeping continuity within the coaching staff for the players; the same guy is going to be working with the same athletes throughout the year. This goes a long ways towards assisting those players in getting comfortable with their coach.

Don't be overly attached to this, though. The running backs coach doesn't *have* to work with the linebackers if he's a better defensive line coach. Use your coaching talent where you need it most.

The next thing you have to do is put together a training program for your coaches. Much of the material you're going to hand them is going to be specific to your system, but some things are general. In the next chapter I'm going to give you a pretty universal (although by no means comprehensive) list of skills that every player that will ever play a game needs to know. By starting there, you should be able to put together a training plan for your coaches.

One thing I really recommend is that you get copies of this book into your assistants' hands. In fact, you should probably buy each coach two or three copies in case they lose the first one. You know, just to be safe.

On the serious side, if you're going to use the programs in this book and the rest of the series with your team, asking the coaches helping you to read through the material is pure common sense. This way you can literally be on the same page as your assistants.

It goes without saying that, as the head coach, you need to be comfortable with the information you choose to use on the field. If you're going to follow my advice and hand a copy of Lou Tepper's, *Complete Linebacking* (ISBN: 0-88011-797-4) to your linebacker coach and expect him to read it then *you* had better at least be familiar with it as well.

The Way Things Ought to Be

In a perfect world your assistant coaches would be the experts and you would simply be a manager. In a perfect world, you would decide on a blocking scheme for a particular play, and they would be able to instinctively teach the skills and come up with the drills for teaching the players everything else they need to know. In a perfect world you'd be able to concern yourself with the *strategy* of each play, while your assistant coaches concern themselves with the *tactics*.

I hate to be the bearer of bad news, but this world is far from perfect. One need look no further than the fact that Carrot Top made a movie to confirm that. In the reality that we all have to live in, no magic fairy is going to sprinkle her pixie dust in your offensive line coach's ear and make him a super coach overnight. *You're* going to have to be the expert, because no one else is going to be.

The informational roles are going to be reversed, at least for a while; until your staff gets comfortable working with you and you can get them fully trained in their responsibilities.

Staff Meetings

If you're like me, and I know I am, then one of the most frightening phrases in the English language is, "Staff Meeting," second only to the expression, "We'll have to cut it off." Regardless, you have to have at least two staff meetings, and each of your assistants is going to have to be there for both of them.

There are two ways to organize the meetings. If the purpose is to introduce a new staff to one another (and to you), while you discuss their responsibilities, then I would strongly recommend that you organize your meeting parameters along disciplinary lines. Have one meeting about your offense at least two months

before the start of practice. A second meeting should be defensive and special teams in nature and take place about four weeks before you get the players on grass. I usually have meetings at four months out, two months out, and one month out from the start of the season.

Meeting Plans

The meeting plans are a little vague because I don't know the specific systems you're going to run. These outlines should give you a basic idea of the information you need to cover. I'm operating under the assumption that you have already interviewed and selected these assistant coaches from the pool of candidates that beat down your door once you started advertising. I'm also assuming that the first time many of these coaches have met each other is when they sat down at your dining room table ten minutes ago to start this meeting, so there are probably going to be adjustments you'll have to make to get these plans to fit your particular needs.

One thing I highly recommend is that you swear, on a Bible or in blood if necessary, that the meetings will be one hour each in maximum. If you follow these plans and don't let yourself get sidetracked, you'll be within that time frame, and your coaches are going to be a lot more interested in coming to them. A coach that's willing to commit 250 hours to coaching a team can really bend his neck on the idea of sitting in a room for three hours on an evening, chatting about football instead of spending time with his family because no one followed the meeting plan. I have yet to attend a board meeting that I felt didn't waste about forty percent of the time we sat there. Don't let that happen with your meetings!

Your First Staff Meeting

Your first meeting is about your offense.

I.   Welcome to the program

      a.   Introduce yourself and give your background as a coach

      b.   Introduce your staff to one another by assignment

      c.   Discuss your systems briefly

II.   Team rules – Staff

      a.   Commitment

      b.   Scouting requirements

      c.   Handling parents

      d.   Summary: *Don't undercut the head coach!*

III.   Team rules - Players

      a.   Attendance policy

      b.   Grades policy

      c.   Equipment policy

d. Minimum-play rules

e. Rule enforcement/punishments

IV. Offensive Football

a. Brief history of your offense and why you selected it

b. Offensive philosophy

c. Offensive series (see Chapter seven)

d. Play breakdown

V. Open forum and questions

Section I: Welcome to the Staff

To start with, it's a good idea to introduce the staff to one another. Every year that I've coached football we've had turnover in some form, so whether you're bringing a group of coaches together for the first time or expanding a staff that has worked together for years, there's probably at least one or two new people that need to be welcomed onto the crew and introduced to the rest of the team.

I usually take about five minutes for this. I start with a brief background of my coaching experience, not to blow my own horn, but as a subtle reminder to the assistants that I'm in charge, and I actually do know what I'm doing. As with the parents, honesty is the best policy. If you have no coaching experience because this is your first year, don't try to hide it, and do *not* waste your staff's time talking about what levels you played at. Just tell them the truth: you don't have much experience, but you've been studying the sport for a while, and have selected a good program based on your reading and research.

This is a good place to naturally transition into a brief discussion of your offense. My description is usually pretty swift: "The offense we're going to run is the Double Wing. I've selected this system because it offers maximum power at the point of attack coupled with a highly deceptive misdirection game, and a precision passing attack. Above all, I've selected it because it's set national scoring records and been used successfully at levels from peewee to pro."

Section II: Don't Undercut the Head Coach!

I went and told you in the first part of this chapter that I don't give my assistants a huge number of rules to follow, and then I gave you a laundry list of things to tell them in this section. I'm not making an error here. The number one thing you need from your assistant coaches is *commitment*. They need to be at every practice, and they need to be at every game. You also need to make them aware that part of their commitment to the overall success of the team might mean *missing* a game because they have to scout somewhere else. Remind them that your collective responsibility is to train your players to the best of their ability, and to adequately prepare your players to face their opponents you need to have a quality scouting report. Someone on your staff is going to have to go get that report.

The wrap-up here has got to include the restrictions I alluded to in chapter five: only *you* speak to the parents about negative things. Ultimately, the staff must swear to adhere to the rule: *"Don't undercut the head coach!"*

**Section III:
Team Discipline**

It's a good idea to talk about your team rules with the staff as well. While you're going to be the one that enforces most of the rules, the staff should know two main things as well: 1) They represent you, and therefore you support them 100% when they are enforcing the rules that you have laid down for the team to follow, and 2) What forms of discipline you will allow them to use to enforce the rules.

Some coaches are terribly fond of the punishment lap. I'm not. I find it much more effective to keep players after practice for a few minutes of extra conditioning. For one thing, when Mom and Dad have to wait for Billy to do his extra conditioning, it generally makes them grouchy. Then they ask Billy why he's late from practice, and they get the response, "I was screwing around and Coach had to make sure it doesn't happen again."

Now Mom and Dad are involved in your disciplinary process, i.e. they're going to chew Billy's ass right off for making *them* late. (Be warned! Occasionally you're going to run into the parents that are convinced that their little darling *couldn't* have done anything wrong, or that you shouldn't be affecting *them* with your punishment.)

I also don't like using punishment laps because the players tend to jog rather than run. It's much more effective to hand out twenty up-downs, and it usually takes less time as well.

Pushups, barked orders, up-downs, sprints, etc. are all a part of the necessary discipline in football. They've been around for decades and they will be around for centuries. They are fine and acceptable ways to discipline your players, get their attention, and keep them focused.

**Hazing is Not
Allowed**

Taunting, harassment, hazing, and verbal or physical abuse are absolutely *not* to be tolerated in any form. I'm a very physical football coach. I demonstrate drills to my players, and when we have few bodies to work with I will even perform some drills *with* them. I do not, however, tackle them to the ground, blindside them, or otherwise physically abuse them. It should also be noted that I coach at the higher levels of youth football: JV high school, and my players are generally larger and faster than I am. I can get away with a lot by nature of the fact that my head barely tops the shoulder pads of my athletes.

What you have to make clear to the staff is the difference between allowed physical punishment and abuse. Yelling, "Get your head in the game!" is allowed, and might even be required by circumstances. Yelling, "You're a loser!" or, "You tackle like a girl!" or most of the things shouted by your football coaches in 1982 is neither allowed nor acceptable.

**Section IV: The
Good Stuff**

Moving on from the rules, it's time now to talk about the offense. In the next chapter I'm going to show you exactly how to divide your system into components to maximize your practice time. Part of the beauty of this is that you can take the same organizational chart to this meeting and use it as a stepping-stone to teach the basic offense to the staff.

Without being redundant, the basic division is by series. My Double Wing offense, for example, is divided into three series based on the primary play in each series. These are: the toss, the sweep, and the wedge. The offense is further divided within each series into core plays, counters, and big plays and passes.

It should take you no more than twenty minutes to get through everything in sections I-IV of this meeting plan. If you stick to the plan and keep on track, you should find that you've got plenty of time to go through your offense.

Drawing Plays

You'll need to draw up the plays against the most common fronts you're going to face this season, have faced in the past, or, if you have no idea what you're going to be looking at, against both an even and an odd front. Typically, I draw my plays against the 5-3 and the 4-4 split, which gives us a look at pretty much everything we're likely to face throughout the season.

Right now you already have an advantage. Most of the coaches you're going to be facing this season probably don't even have defenses drawn up at all when they chalk their plays. Your coaches, and the players they'll be teaching, are already better prepared than most of their counterparts.

It's probably going to take you about thirty minutes to get through the entire offense, figuring about ten minutes per series and keeping your series down to three or fewer, depending on the specific level you coach. I leave out the sideboarded plays, which I'll review with the staff right before we install them. Since we might not even use them, there's no real point in wasting the staff meeting time with them until we know for sure.

Can I just slip in one more comment about the size of your offense? If you can't *chalk* the whole thing to your staff in thirty minutes, how on earth are you going to teach it to your players in a couple of weeks of two hour practices? Start trimming, with an axe if you have to, until you can get through it all in half an hour.

If you have video of your offense, now is a great time for your staff to see it in action. Remember, the 2003 Tomales Braves JV Football Highlights are only $15, so if you decide to run the Double Wing you'll have a great example right there!

Section V: Open Forum and Questions

You'll note that our one-hour timeline has left us ten additional minutes after the chalk talk. This time is set aside for the open forum. Your coaches are bound to have some questions or ideas, and hopefully you'll start giving each other ideas. That's what this time is for.

One thing that should be absolutely clear to your staff long before you get to this point is that the open forum is a place to ask questions and bring up legitimate concerns about the offense *only*. It's not a place to trash talk your decisions. If you have decided to run the Veer with a team of ten-year-olds, and you've read this book, then you have already undertaken the massive effort of research necessary to understand how to coach that offense. You know that it is intricate and requires careful coaching. You know that there are hundreds of minute details that you have to pay attention to.

There is nothing that your staff can say on the subject that you have not already heard from me, or from your research on the subject. A brand new assistant coach with a shiny whistle is probably not going to have enough information at his command to be able to adequately state whether or not the system will be effective at your level.

Real Problems

Occasionally you're going to run into the coach with a few legitimate concerns. Going back to our example of the Veer, for example, it takes some careful coaching from the backfield coach to teach a quarterback and fullback to mesh properly in the less than a second they have to read the defense. I can fully understand why a rookie assistant coach who is looking at the Veer for the first time would be a little nervous about his ability to teach it to his quarterbacks properly. Frankly, as his head coach, I'd be a little concerned if he *didn't* have a question or two about it.

How you handle these concerns and questions is up to you. In our example, I would take great pains to make sure that my assistant knew that I was making myself responsible for teaching him how to coach his position properly, but that I was holding *him* responsible for getting with me and going over the information until he felt comfortable with it. You can't chase these folks around and make them learn from you; they have to take a certain amount of initiative, but ultimately, you still have to provide the knowledge to them.

Staff Meeting Number Two

Your second staff meeting needs to cover even more ground than the first one. You've already gone over the offense, which is typically more time intensive than the defensive and special teams material, and you've made whatever introductions are necessary. Now it's time to cover the parts of a football team that almost always get left out.

The second staff meeting will cover your defensive and special teams systems.

I. Meeting opener

    a. Introduce your staff to one another by assignment

    b. Discuss your system briefly

II. Defensive football

    a. Brief history of your defense and why you selected it

    b. Defensive philosophy

    c. Defensive responsibilities by position

    d. Chalk of defensive positions and basic alignments

    e. Chalk of adjustments to the basic defense for motion and unusual alignments

    f. Play breakdown against sample offensive plays

III. Special teams program

    a. Brief history of your special teams program and why you selected it

    b. Philosophy of special teams

    c. Rules pertaining specifically to special teams

    d. Chalk of special teams (Kickoff, KOR, Punt, PR, Field Goal. FG Block)

IV.   Open forum and questions

Section I:
Meeting Opener

You'll note that this meeting plan is significantly shorter than the last one. This doesn't necessarily mean that the meeting itself will be. You've got a *lot* of material to cover.

Since you already know each other, a quick refresher is probably all you need to get things going. I generally take a moment to remind everyone of their defensive coaching assignments during this first five minutes or so, but everyone should be fairly comfortable with their responsibilities by now.

Section II:
Defensive
Football

No matter the defense you've decided on, it has a history and a philosophy behind it. Systems like the 5-3 were developed to take advantage of the abilities of big, strong defensive linemen to dominate the battle up front and brutalize offensive lines. Schemes like the 4-4 split and the 3-3 stack were designed to allow smaller, faster players to use their speed and confuse blocking assignments of the larger, stronger offensive linemen. Systems like the "46" were invented to put tremendous pressure on the quarterback and interfere with the passing game while still clogging the running lanes.

Whichever defensive system you've selected to give your players the best possible chance to be successful, there's a reason you've picked it, and it probably has something to do with the philosophy behind it. From the philosophy of the system naturally come the concepts of specific position assignments and play. Whether your defensive linemen are to be trained to attack upfield through a gap or neutralize an offensive player and read the backfield will determine much of the specific coaching your team will receive.

Basic
Alignments and
Responsibilities

After you've discussed the background of the system, it comes as no surprise that the next step is a specific chalk of the basic alignments and responsibilities for each player. This is one of the most important things you can do with your defensive staff. Regardless what specific defensive system you choose to run, your basic alignment and responsibilities will be the foundation for each stunt, blitz, and coverage that you teach to your players. The coaching staff absolutely *has* to have a solid grasp of it.

What if...?

This actually includes the basic adjustments for some unusual alignments. If your opponent comes out in the Pro-I, with a tight end and flanker on the same side, and the split end on the other with an I-formation backfield, it's great that most defensive coaches have drawn their defenses up against that specific offensive formation. Unfortunately, what if the opponent lines up in a Wing-T "900" formation with a wingback and tight end on one side, and a halfback and split end on the other? What if the offense comes out in the 1940s single wing? What if they come out with an empty backfield and five wide receivers? What if they start out in a Pro-I and shift to a split back, or motion from a two wide outs on each side to a trips right look?

While you don't necessarily need to show each of these unusual formations to your staff at this exact moment, you need to convince them that the defense you've selected has an answer to any questions posed by the offense. Since we're operating under the assumption that your staff members don't have the experience or study time that you have, we can assume that they aren't going to be totally convinced that your system is the right one for the team. By describing situations that *they* haven't even thought of, you're subtly explaining to them that you've covered all the angles.

Action!

The last thing that I like to do is draw up a couple of basic offensive plays against the defense and show how the system you've selected is designed to put a tackler on an intercept course with the ball carrier. After I chalk out a couple of plays against the defense, I like to put on a short highlight video of the system in action, just like we did with the offense before.

Section III: Special Teams

After we get through the defensive section, which is probably going to take most of our time (I usually plan for about thirty-five minutes of defensive conversation.) the next step is to talk about the special teams program you intend to use. This should be a vastly simpler discussion, because there are only a few plays to discuss.

One thing I'm certain to stress to the staff is the importance of special teams. The kicking game is one of the most neglected and undercoached aspects of the game. I've heard dozens of coaches give lip service to how important they are, but come practice time, they always seem to be shunted to the side and ignored in favor of the offense.

It's *always* the offense for some reason. Actually, we both know the reason. It goes back to football coaches dreaming about touchdowns.

I'm an odd duckling. I spend a lot more time dreaming about blocked punts and kickoff returns that cross my opponents' thirty than I do about the touchdowns. I think one thing that has made me successful as a coach is that I dream about the things that get us into position to score. The touchdowns generally take care of themselves after that.

I am pretty firm with my assistant coaches that special teams is *not* an afterthought on my football team. We will put just as much, if not *more* emphasis into coaching the kicking game properly as we put into our offense and defense, and we start by doing the research necessary to make it happen on the field.

Right. A Special Teams Program... uh... Where Can I Find One?

Other than my forthcoming book on coaching youth special teams (Volume II of the *Impact!* series), I don't know of any specific special teams *programs* available. Each special teams coordinator or coach generally seems to select what he likes and discard what he dislikes from a variety of sources.

George Allen's Guide to Special Teams (ISBN: 0880113707) is a decent source of material for general special teams. Dick Arbuckle's *Special Teams: the Winning Edge* (ISBN: 1585183113) also contains some great information. The main problems with these two books are the intricate schemes they recommend. Because kicking plays occur so infrequently each play has a lot more significance on game day, and each play gets far fewer repetitions in practice than your standard offensive play.

For example, my basic off-tackle play, 24 Toss, might get practiced 350 or more times before we call it on game day. Even as anal-retentive as I am, however, it is highly unlikely that we'll be able to run our basic kickoff return more than seventy times before we're doing it to start that same game.

This means that the convoluted kicking plays described in most of the books on special teams are extremely hard to install and run successfully at the youth level. This is one of the reasons why I've spent the last five years collecting notes and gathering information to develop an integrated system of simple kicking plays and returns that are easy to teach and difficult to counter.

Unfortunately, until my next book comes out, you've got your work cut out for you when it comes to developing a program. Jack Reed's books contain some highly useful special teams information, and I recommend them very highly. See chapter two for my review of his book.

The Piecemeal Approach

There's nothing wrong with selecting your special teams the way coaches at the higher levels of football have been doing for decades. Find a set of special teams that you like by asking around. Talk to coaches online and at local schools and ask them for assistance with your special teams. Look for a set of simple returns and kicking plays that you think are going to be successful for you, and that you think you can teach properly. Make sure you understand them as well as you do your offense or defense, and chalk them out for your staff at the meeting.

Punt Returns and Fakes

I don't know why, but for some reason coaches always love to see punt fakes and punt returns drawn up. For that reason, if you choose to install a punt return, I recommend closing with it or with your most spectacular punt fake. Give your staff a high note to end on.

The Rules Pertaining to Special Teams

There are some specific rules for special teams that most fans and many coaches are not aware of. For example, not too many coaches, even at the high school level, are aware that you can fair catch *any* kick, not just a punt. This includes field goal attempts that haven't crossed the goal line, and of course, *onside* kick attempts that haven't touched the ground. I have actually taught my players on occasion to call for a fair catch even if the ball has touched the ground, on the theory that the coverage unit will slow down out of reflex. A good knowledge of the rules can give you a lot of ways to win games.

Section IV: Open Forum and Questions

As you did with the offensive meeting, it's a good idea to end with a brief question and answer session. Because most inexperienced coaches put more thought into offense, you're likely to encounter less resistance and confusion from your coaches at this meeting, but you should still be prepared to answer a few questions and explain a few things more fully.

Additional Meetings

These two meetings are the bare minimum. You might find it necessary to have several additional meetings, as well as individual training time with each of your assistants. I leave it up to you and your staff to decide how often you should get together and what you need to cover. The ultimate goal is to have your staff competent and confident to teach your systems *before* the first practice starts.

You might want to consider getting together with your staff one more time to discuss the practice plans, but much of that can be covered in the pre-practice meetings after the season begins.

Having a confident, competent staff is ultimately the responsibility of the head coach. By carefully selecting your help with the same attention to detail that you would put into hiring a staff member for your office, and putting in the effort to train them in your system before the season begins, you'll find your organization meshing like a well-oiled machine.

On the game field, your players will be better taught, more comfortable, and more successful—and isn't that really what this is all about?

CHAPTER SEVEN
PRACTICE PREPARATION

Introduction

Successful coaching of any sport is about preparation. Some sports—soccer comes to mind—are so simple in execution that it's possible to coach them with a hat, whistle, and a vague idea of the skills needed. Football is *not* that kind of sport.

In the next chapter I'm going to take you through an entire football preseason, practice by practice, in five-minute segments. Each skill necessary to playing safe and effective football will be taught, practiced, and honed to perfection.

Before we can do that, however, we need to figure out what those skills are. That's why this chapter is here. Unless you use my exact system, you're probably going to have to alter some things here and there to the practice plan in the next chapter, although I've tried to keep it pretty general. By thinking your way through your program from start to finish, using the guidelines in this chapter, you'll be able to make the adjustments you need to be able to fit everything into your practice plans.

In all the years I have interacted with other football coaches, I've heard them complain about a lot of things: referees, parents, facilities, the taste of green Gatorade™, but I have never once heard a football coach complain about having too much practice time.

Time is precious. Successful coaching in football means being efficient with your practice time, and that means starting *now*, long before the season begins, to think about the path you want to take.

My teams tend to be successful because I do not fall into the traps laid for the unsuspecting youth coach. I don't concentrate my efforts on my offense and ignore my defense and special teams. I practice all of them approximately equally, and I plan my practices to carefully teach each necessary skill and perfect it long before the players ever step on the game field. I don't give ten water breaks of five minutes each. I don't let myself or my coaches talk all practice. In fact, we almost never talk at all above a whisper, except for the chalk talk to end practice.

I am no better coach than you are. I'm just more anal-retentive.

Don't worry; you'll get there in time.

~D.

Teaching

As an electronics instructor for the United States Coast Guard, I've learned something extremely important to the football coach. Professional teachers already know this, and my first dim clue was watching my mother, a special education teacher in Washington State, working hundreds of hours over the summer to prepare her classroom and lessons.

This simple concept is: for every planned hour of instruction you need to spend at least *three hours* in preparation.

I'm not kidding. You think teachers don't deserve three months a year off? Trust me; the good ones are working their fingers to the bone. For sixteen years my mother took no more than four days of vacation a year, and never worked less than sixty hours a week. She worked harder over her "vacation" time than most people work during their regular job.

When you're preparing to coach a football team, this means that you're going to have to worry about a series of skills that need to be taught, and you need to consider not only *how* you're going to teach them, but *when*. You have to plan your practices down to the wire.

Boredom

Players are like dogs. I've said this for years. I've never met a dog that wanted to make its owners mad. I have three dogs right now, and they all have their own little personality quirks and annoying traits. Actually, the fat one does things on a daily basis that light off the boiler on my temper.

But, that's not his fault as much as it's mine. He's a Rottweiler/Australian shepherd mix. Those are both highly intelligent breeds of working dogs that aren't accustomed to sitting at home all day waiting for mom and dad to come home. He tends to get into trouble because he gets *bored*. In thinking about the times when I've gotten frustrated or angry on the practice field (It *does* happen. Even the most phlegmatic coach will start getting irritated when his players run the wrong play five times in a row, and undemonstrative is one thing I'm not.), most of the times when the players have set me off it has been my own fault. I spent too much time on one drill, or too much time flapping my jaws, and the players started getting bored.

The younger your age group, the more this is going to happen. You have to keep moving through the drills at a rapid pace, and don't give the players *time* to get bored.

Certain things are not going to change, no matter how boring they might be. Tackling and blocking, for example, will be done for a ten-minute period each to start every single practice, no exceptions. The trick is to do one of two things: 1) Use new drills as often as possible that can still move at a quick pace and teach the same skills, or 2) Keep the players moving so fast that they have no time to get bored.

When possible, do both.

The problem with number one is that every drill you use has to be taught to the players first. If you're going to spend ten minutes tackling, you can't waste three of those precious minutes teaching a new drill every day. The problem with number two is that familiarity breeds contempt. You have to keep an eye on the technique and make sure that it's still precise on the thirtieth day running the same drill.

Get a Timer

In 2004 I attended a coaching clinic at the University of California-Berkeley campus. The clinic started with a Cal practice, and I was one of hundreds of high school coaches watching open-mouthed at the way the Cal coaching staff ran things.

They practiced in the stadium where they play their games, and a huge countdown clock that was divided in half dominated one of the upper decks. The right hand side held a five-minute countdown timer. The left held a segment counter.

Segments

The entire two and a half hour practice was divided into twenty-four five-minute segments. As each segment counted down, the five-minute timer would reset, and the segment counter would go up by one. Thus, you could write out a practice plan like this:

Segments 17-18: Receivers- Stalk blocking, Backs- Pass blocking, Line- Trap Blocking.

Segments 19-21: Receivers- Hands drills, Backs- Ball carrying, Line- Pass blocking.

When the clock ticks down at the end of each segment, a horn that's built into the timer sounds, and the players immediately sprint to the next series of drills. The coaching staff can tell at a glance what segment they're on, and with a written practice schedule, can get hundreds of skills practiced in a single practice.

Got Any Extra Cash?

Now, you're probably not going to be able to afford the $1900 segment timer that Cal used. There are cheaper routes to go. I like the Cal timer because everyone can see it, no matter where you are on the field, and once you set it up and get it going, you just leave it alone. Unfortunately, I have yet to coach anywhere that a two thousand dollar stopwatch would be a practical addition to the coaching equipment.

One of the best investments I ever made in my football team was the purchase of a tiny plastic cooking timer. You can use the one on your watch if you prefer (I have a watch I purchased just for coaching.), but you need something that can count down. My watch is perfect, because it's a Timex Iron Man™ that doesn't need to have the time entered over and over again. I set it to five minutes, and after that it resets at the touch of one button, rather than setting hours, minutes, and seconds all over again every time you want to start a new segment.

When I bought the watch it was about fifteen bucks, but unfortunately the new ones are closer to fifty. That's heading towards the limits of my price range for a watch I'm going to beat hell out of demonstrating drills every day. (On the other hand, my $300 Skagen™ doesn't even come on the practice field!)

The five-dollar practice timer I bought in 1999 worked like a charm. It had a hole in one end for a shoestring, and I threaded my whistle cord through it. Not only was it really easy to use for timing practices, but it was also loud enough that I could set it for 2.5 seconds when timing my quarterbacks in their passing reads. If they heard the beeping, they knew they'd been sacked. I bought the timer at Wal-Mart, and until 2003 when it got broken it worked fine. I'm a lot more physical in practice than most coaches (I give out sodas to players that can knock me down with legal blocks.) so you're much more likely to keep from breaking your timer than I am.

Using the Staff

Later on in this series of books I'm going to talk about clock management a little bit, and one of the things you should really have is a coach or parent that is dedicated to clock management on game day. They should be very familiar with the rules for timing football games, and during your practices I would give them the timer and an air horn. Every five minutes of practice they should sound the horn (or yell, depends on how loud they are) and sound off with the segment number. (Radio Shack sells a mini-bullhorn for about thirty bucks. They come with a built in air horn.)

Practice Time

The typical youth football coach gets a two-week preseason with five practices per week. Then he'll get one week to prepare for the first scrimmage, and a final week to prepare for the first game. After that, he'll normally get three practice days a week until the end of the season. High school coaches typically get a similar preseason, but can practice four to five days a week with Friday night or Saturday afternoon games.

You're *not* going to have enough practice time. If you think you're going to have all kinds of time to talk and screw around, you need to get that thought out of your head right now. You can't waste a second of practice. I get absolutely furious with parents that come and "need" to talk to me during practice. I make it clear during the preseason parents' meeting that the only times to speak with the coaching staff are after practice or before practice, and the pre- and post-practice meetings are considered part of practice.

I'm There For *All* the Players, Not Just *Yours!*

There are a lot of ways to waste practice time, and the most annoying is the parent that won't shut up. I'm coming across as extremely caustic, and unwilling to even listen to the parents. That's not really the case. I have to make it clear, though, from the beginning that I am *not* there for the parents, and I'm not there for *your* player. I'm there for the players, the players *only*, and *all* the players. I have a commitment to *every one* of them, and that means that I need to practice for at least 119 minutes out of a 120-minute practice.

Pulling me aside to yammer for five minutes about the highlight tape, or ask me why I didn't start your son in the second half, or what time the game is this weekend, is interfering with my ability to give the other players my time and instruction. Plus, what if every set of 24 parents decided they wanted to talk to me for five minutes?

That's right, I just spent the *entire* practice talking. Your players didn't get ten seconds of instruction out of me. Keep that in mind, Billy's Mom, when you "just need a sec" to tell me something or ask a question.

This goes for the rest of the coaching staff as well. I tell my assistants, "Look, you volunteered for the position, and you made a commitment to be here. I need a solid 120-minute effort out of you for every practice. If you can't give me that, then tell me now and get off my practice field."

Harsh? Possibly, but unfortunately also a very real indicator of modern times. Too many people today think it's cool to make promises and not follow through on them. I don't have time for that, and neither do you. You have a team to coach.

You're going to have to be able to count on your assistants, because when you make your practice schedules you're going to be relying on them to supervise certain drills. I can, and have, coached a football team almost entirely on my own. It can be done, but it severely limits the number of additional skills and drills you can work on at any one time.

The Uselessness of Drills

Speaking of drills, in addition to parents, there are other, more surreptitious ways to waste your practice time. Drills are one of the traditional and prime time-wasters in all of football.

First off, what the heck *is* a drill? For the youth football coach that barely remembers playing in high school, or has never played at all, drills are something of a mystery. At least one email a week that hits my in-box has the question, "What drills should I run?" in it.

What is a Drill?

A drill is one series of movements, typically called a "rep" or "repetition" through an action designed to refine a specific skill. Drills have their uses because you can isolate particular problem areas that your players have and correct them with multiple reps of the correct procedure. Tackling, for example, is an ability that is hard to master at first, since it combines fear of collision with the desire not to hurt others and a general lack of coordination. It's also a dangerous skill when improperly performed.

Your players will need a number of repetitions of proper tackling form before they can become proficient at tackling safely. The best and safest way to obtain these repetitions is to run a number of different tackling drills that simulate game day conditions and situations that your players are going to need to react to.

There really isn't a specific target number of reps that you need to get to before a player becomes proficient at tackling. My goal is simply, "as many as possible." I'll show you later on how to get close to three hundred tackling reps in three weeks of practice using just ten minutes a day.

The problems with drills lie in three specific areas:

• Drills that are unnecessary to the system you run.

• Drills that take too much time to get through or are too complex.

• Drills that are dangerous.

We'll go through each of these specific problems in more detail. I want you to keep in mind, though, that the object here is not to avoid drills entirely, it's to avoid wasting time, and to eliminate as many potential dangers to the players as possible. By thinking your way through the criteria, you can avoid the huge time wasters and focus your efforts where they're needed.

Coach, Why Are You Doing This?

• Drills that are unnecessary to the system you run.

I know a coach, a very successful one, who runs a pitchout drill every other day in practice. He hasn't installed the play that needs that pitchout since 1998, but he still faithfully runs the drill for five minutes out of every day.

He's a thousand times the coach I am, but I can't figure him out. Over the course of a twelve-week season, he wastes about four hours of practice time with a drill he doesn't need. What if he put those five minutes every other night into teaching his backs to fake better, or put it into bad-ball drills to improve their catching?

Before you put a drill into your practice plan you've got to make sure that it serves a specific purpose for your team. Think your way through the skills necessary for your offense, defense, and special teams, and then do the research to find effective drills for teaching those skills. If you use the systems in my books, you'll find the drills are included in the program.

Coach, What Are You *Doing*?

- Drills that take too much time to get through or are too complex.

This one drives me nuts. I've watched a coach set up a drill for five minutes that involved six players at once, and took over half an hour for each player to rotate through each position. How is two reps an hour going to help your team?

What about breaking that drill into a series of smaller drills, concentrating on each individual portion of the skills involved. For example, while the "West Point" drill—that features three offensive linemen, two defensive linemen, a running back, and a linebacker, is a great drill for teaching the defensive line to fight through blocks, the offensive line to *make* blocks, and the linebackers to read flow—the complexity of the drill interferes with it. By the time the players get into the drill area, get set up in their stances, and are completely ready to go, you end up with one rep every two to three minutes unless you are really hustling.

Instead, you could simplify the drill by using Vince Lombardi's "Nutcracker" drill. Pull out one of the defensive and one of the offensive linemen, and run the drill with fewer players. Or, you could avoid the drill entirely and instead use drills that only concentrate on one or two skills for one group instead of three or four skills for each player.

Coach, Are You *Crazy*?

- Drills that are dangerous.

This scares the hell out of me. Unfortunately, it's all too common out there, since youth football has no nationwide official certification or training requirements. Most leagues do a background check to make sure you're not an axe murderer or a child molester, but they make no effort to ascertain whether or not you know what drills can get a child injured or even killed.

For example, remember those head-on tackling drills you used to do in junior high? I remember the dried brown grass of the practice field at Sumner Junior High, and lining up ten yards or more from my partner. At the whistle, we'd sprint towards one another at full speed and he'd try to run over me while I tried to tackle him. Then, I'd get the ball and he'd knock me down.

Invariably, one of us got hurt. It might have been a mild injury, it might have been more serious, but it was asking for trouble either way. (I sometimes wonder if the separated shoulder I ended up with my freshman year had been weakened thanks to a huge number of hard contact drills the week before.)

There are ways to make some drills safer. I do a number of head on tackling drills in my practices, but I start the players about three to four yards apart. There's no way they can get to full speed or even close to it in that shortened distance.

Here's the trick, though: the players *think* they are getting to full speed. This means that they build some confidence in themselves and their tackling ability. Then, on game day, they don't tense up or slow down, and they protect themselves with their kinetic energy. It's some of the greatest sleight-of-hand in football!

The Necessity of Drills

Sometimes drills are necessary. You can teach proper blocking technique much more safely and effectively by using a quick blocking drill than you can by lining the players up to run plays over and over. (Although if you only have time to do one of the two, run the plays.)

Think of it like this: At my best, full speed pace, I can run five plays a minute with my entire team. With backs alone I can run about eight plays a minute. That's about twenty-five blocking reps for the offensive line in a five-minute period.

During a blocking drill, however, I can get fifteen punches (first step off the line into a bag or sled), and about eight to ten five step drive blocking repetitions per minute, which is about 75 reps on the punch, or fifty drive blocking reps in the same five minute period. Essentially, that's doubling the return in the same amount of time.

Putting in Drills

The trick is to make sure that the drill is important, effective, and quick to run. There are three criteria for a drill before I'll install it.

- How important is the skill we're trying to hone?

Tackling and blocking are necessary for every player on the team. We're going to practice those every single day, and with every player. We're going to shoot for close to three hundred tackling reps, not counting any that come in scrimmages or non-tackling specific drills.

Blocking is a little more problematical, but we're going to shoot for close to five hundred punches and about two hundred drives. I have always believed that tackling and blocking are the cornerstone of everything you're trying to do on a football field. I admonish the players constantly, "If you can't tackle, then you can't play defense." And, "If you can't block, then you can't play offense."

What I *don't* tell them is that if they can't block or tackle, it's *my* fault, not theirs!

- How quickly can we get through the drill? (How many reps in one minute per player?)

This is going to vary as widely as the drills themselves. I work hard to shoot for a minimum of three reps per minute for each drill we run. Sometimes we're going to get more than that (such as punches), and sometimes we'll get less (such as deep zone pass coverages that take time for the receivers to get downfield).

- How long does it take to set up/break down the equipment for the drill?

If it takes more than a couple of minutes to set things up for the drill, then you need to scrap the drill, or figure out a quicker way to get things going.

A lot of coaches use water breaks as a sort of "time out" in which they set up the drills. Since I don't use water breaks, I've learned to move very quickly while setting up the drills. Think ahead, and use your resources. Sometimes I'll have the last few players in a line that are already done with their reps run and set up the next drill while I work with the remaining few.

Use the Staff— They're Out There Anyway!

Or, if you're lucky enough to have a decent sized staff to help you out, have one of the coaches be in charge of setting up the drills for everyone. The perfect coach for this is the clock management coach, since he's also carrying the timer and practice plan already. He can be thinking several segments ahead, and getting the field ready as he goes. Obviously you need to have enough equipment for him to set up one drill while you're finishing another one.

Probably the best example of this I have ever seen was when I went through the motorcycle safety course at Northern California Motorcycle Training. Dave Sullivan and his crew did a fantastic job of setting up the rider course. One rider coach would explain the drill while the other one went through and set up the cones. By the time the first coach was done describing the drill, the second was on a bike and ready to give an example. It was seamless. (NCMT can be reached at (707) 888-6268. I highly encourage everyone to take their course even if you don't necessarily have a motorcycle. The things you'll learn about driving vision and vehicle control might save your life behind the wheel, as well as astride a bike.)

Guidelines For Drills

Here are some guidelines to help you sort out your drills.

- The skill must be necessary for every person in the group

For example, I'm not going to do many cutback drills with my offensive linemen, because they won't be carrying the football and looking for a cutback lane. Likewise, my running backs don't need to spend a lot of time on pulling and trapping. Running these drills as a team is a waste of time.

- We must be able to get at least one player through one full repetition every thirty seconds of the drill, minimum.

This is very important. I've seen a lot of time wasted on football fields by coaches that were running some very good drills. Unfortunately, no matter how great a drill is, if the players can't get through it in a timely fashion and get a number of reps sufficient to improve their skills, then the drill isn't helping to improve your team, it's actually making it *worse*.

The West Point drill I described above is one of the examples of a great drill gone bad. I know of no other drill that's as effective for teaching contact, tackling, blocking, and physical running. Unfortunately, it's not easy to use because it takes so long to get the players through it.

- We must be able to set up and break down the drill in less than one minute.

You can have the best drill in the world, get your players a huge number of reps at it, and still waste an inordinate amount of time setting it up. This is one reason why I do tackling and blocking right out of the gate to start practice. It takes about five minutes or so to set up the various stations. I prefer to set it up before practice starts, when that time isn't slated for other things. I'm typically at my practice field about thirty minutes before the practice actually begins, and the pre-practice meeting only lasts for ten minutes or less. I use the rest of that time to set up the pads for tackling practice.

I Feel the Need…

I hope I'm making a strong point here for speed. There are a lot of reasons to move very quickly through your practices, and only the least of them involve the incredible number of skills you have to teach, sharpen, and eventually perfect.

One of the best things you can get out of a high-speed practice is the conditioning of your players. Players hate running wind sprints. I hated running them as a player, and since I made the 2002 decision to start running the conditioning with my players, nothing has happened to change my opinion about them in the slightest.

Sprints are time-consuming, boring, and exhausting. They're also only effective for cardiovascular increases, and they do nothing to strengthen the muscles you're going to need in football.

They can also build some bad habits in running form if you don't pay attention. Players tend to want to pop up before they start moving forward, so their momentum goes *up* instead of into their opponent. You can spend hours and hours drilling that out of them with punches and other quickstep line drills, only to turn around and run fifteen minutes of sprints in which they get right back into the bad habits, and reinforce them.

You can make your players sweat by simply running your plays at high speed, over and over again. If you hit five reps a minute, you're going to be getting the players in shape, and, best of all, they'll be using the exact muscles that they need to condition for game day.

High School Conditioning

There are a lot of high school programs around the country that have completely abandoned the wind sprint as an in-season exercise. Conditioning is performed in the weight room, generally starting before pre-season practice even begins and carrying through until the season ends, and the entire on-field time is spent running plays and drills necessary for the systems.

I still run some wind sprints as conditioning, but it is extremely rare. They have some hidden values. If you keep your eyes open, you can really find out who your leaders are on your team during a series of wind sprints. The leaders are the ones encouraging the others to push themselves harder, reminding the others about the snap counts, and other things to make the team better. I also use those to reinforce the snap count and to make my centers and quarterbacks practice snapping when they're tired.

Where I prefer to do things differently from other coaches is the types of wind sprints I do. I prefer conditioning exercises that have some basis in football. For example, I run a pursuit drill during defensive practice. This drill is designed to teach proper pursuit angles and get every defensive player in on every tackle.

It also involves running all the way across the bloody field chasing plays that go away from your position. The players tend to be very sweaty by the time we're done with the drill.

Then there's kickoff and punt coverage. I require all coverage drills to be performed at full speed, so the players end up doing five to ten forty yard sprints every time we practice special teams.

Again, the high speed that these drills are performed at gives us more reps in less time, and improves the team in a number if ways. Not only are we getting more skilful, but we're also getting into better and better shape as we go.

Any time you can get two goals out of one drill you're coming out ahead.

The number one conditioning method I use, however, is the simple requirement that the players do five pushups and five sit-ups every time we start a new period. More about that later on.

Water Breaks and Proper Hydration

I don't give the traditional water breaks. When you get to the next chapter you'll discover that there is no time set aside for the players to stand around and chitchat while holding bottles of Gatorade™. There's a specific reason for this. In my opinion, one of the biggest time wasters in football is the water break.

I've found a more effective and more efficient method to keep my players hydrated. Players are required to have a one-liter or larger water bottle with them at every practice, and at all times when a player is not actively engaged in a drill they need to have their water bottle in their hand. During the drills or instructional time when they are not performing, they need to be drinking in small sips.

Glutting water the way you and I did after practice twenty years ago is not efficient for the body. It can lead to upset stomachs and queasiness, as well as cramps. Severe cases can lead to hyponatremia, or "water intoxication," a potentially lethal dilution of salts in the body. In the case of carbohydrate-rich drinks like Gatorade™ and other sports drinks, the rush of carbs to the digestive system can pull blood from the muscles to aid in digestion if drunk in quantities that are too large.

It is far more efficient for the body to take in fluids in smaller quantities, but more frequently. To accomplish the goal of keeping our players hydrated in this manner, the most effective means is to have them sipping every second.

Cool water is best, by the way. Extremely cold water shocks the system and is harder to keep down.

Skills by Player

The following is a fairly comprehensive list of skills that your players are going to need to have. I'm sure that there are some things I've left out.

I've stolen some of this from Jack Reed's books, so I give him most of the credit for listing these out. I've made a few modifications, though.

Everyone Must be Taught

Every player on your team needs to know:

- **Tackling :**
    - Form
    - Front
    - Side
    - From Behind
    - Open Field

- Gang Tackling
- Sideline Tackling
- **Blocking:**
  - Drive Block
  - Left
  - Right
  - Double Team
  - Stalk (open field)
  - Reach blocks
- **Miscellaneous:**
  - Carrying the football
  - Stripping the football from the ball carrier
  - Catching the football
  - Substituting on and off the field
  - Safely recover fumbles
  - "Scoop and score"
  - Communications ("Pass," "Ball," "Run" at proper times)
  - Huddling on offense and defense
- **Rules:**
  - Your specific rules (Using coaches' titles, helmets on and mouthpieces in at all times, etc.)
  - Unsportsmanlike Conduct
  - Basic game play
  - Four down system
  - Scoring points
  - Penalties

As you can see, that's a lot of stuff that each person on the team needs to know. Then we can talk about the specific positions and what you need to teach them.

For the Quarterback

Your quarterback needs to know:

- Stance
- Snap Count
- How to take the snap
- What to do if the snap, handoff, or pitch is fumbled
- How to hand off

- How to pitch the ball

- How to drop back

- How to throw the football

- On the run to either side

- While stationary

- How to sprint out

- How/when/why to take a sack

- How/when/why to throw an incomplete and uninterceptable pass

- Throwing a pass

- Finding the open receiver

- Hitting the receiver's target

- Leading the receiver

- Passing in spite of the distraction of a pass rush

- How/why to take a safety

- Stiff arm

- Hurry up offense

- Slowdown offense

If you'll note, everything the quarterback needs to know is in addition to everything the entire team needs to know. Are you starting to get stressed out yet, Coach?

The Center

Your center/long snapper needs to know:

- Stance

- How to snap the ball

- Snap count

- When to get set

- Long snapping

Okay, if you're not pulling your hair out now, you should be. This is why I tend to get ever so slightly aggravated with those coaches that wander into the Delphi Football Coaching forums two days before their seasons begin and ask for, "a couple of plays."

The Offensive Linemen

Your whole offensive line needs to know:

- Stance

- Where to line up

- Split discipline

- Blocking assignments for each play

- Blocking techniques for each play
- Blocking calls for each defensive alignment
- Pulling
- Down blocking
- Double-Team blocking
- Wedge blocking
- Cut blocking
- Pass blocking
- How to break holds
- Rules pertaining to blocking
- Where you can hit the opponent
- What you can hit the opponent with
- Free blocking zone
- False start
- Illegal procedure
- Illegal use of hands
- Illegal blocking
- Illegal personal contact

I hope you're reading this several months before the season begins, because there's plenty more to go.

Receivers

Your receivers need to know:

- Stance
- How to catch the ball
- Look-in and tuck away
- What to do if the passer holds the ball an extended period of time
- Where to line up
- Blocking assignments for each play
- Pass routes and patterns for each play
- Release techniques against bump and run coverage
- Keeping one foot in bounds on passes to the sidelines
- Reading the coverage and finding seams in the zones
- Escaping man coverage
- Concentration on catch despite distractions
- Catching the ball at its highest point on jump passes

- Fighting for the ball

- Switching the ball to the hand farthest from the tackler

- Getting upfield immediately after the catch

- Stiff arm

- Reacting to and catching tipped passes

Did you find that bottle of Tums™ you were looking for? I'll wait until you're back.

Running Backs

Your running backs need to know:

- Stance

- Alignment

- Receiving handoffs

- Receiving pitches

- Blocking assignments for each play

- Blocking techniques for each play

- Path of the ball carrier for each play

- Faking technique for each play

- How to respond to a broken play

- Avoiding tip-offs

- Switching the ball to the hand farthest from the tackler

- Throwing option passes

- Stiff arm

- Catching technique

- Look-in and tuck

- Reacting to and catching tipped passes

Okay, now that we've covered the very basic skills necessary to play offensive football, it's time to move on to the other side of the ball. We're only half done, and you're probably already thinking that coaching soccer would be easier.

It would be. That's why soccer coaches do it. On the defensive side of the ball, there's more we have to do.

Defensive Skills

Your whole defense needs to know:

- Stance

- Alignment

- Pass rush technique

- Wide play pursuit angles
- Pass pursuit
- Move on movement (of the ball, not the man)

The Defensive Line

The defensive linemen need to know:

- Roughing the passer
- Breaking holds
- Charge (Bull rush)
- Rip technique
- Swim technique

Additionally, defensive ends need a few more skills:

- Stance
- Trailing sweeps that go the other way
- Pass rush
- Contain technique
- Pass pursuit
- Taking on lead blockers

The Defensive Backfield

Playing linebacker or defensive back requires an additional skill set.

- Stance
- Where to line up against each offensive formation
- How to respond to motion
- Job description for each type of offensive play
- Man pass coverage
- Zone pass coverage
- How to bat the ball down
- Catch technique
- Look-in and tuck
- Breaking on the pass

- Backpedal

- Bump and run

- Reacting to and catching tipped passes

That wasn't so bad, was it? I mean; it was much simpler than the offensive side of things. The reason for that is that defense is *reactive*, and if we load the players down with too many things to think about, they'll end up trying to problem-solve in the middle of the play. Defensive play needs to be instinct.

Special Teams Play

Oh, wait. We're not done. I've saved the best for last. Special teams is one third of the game, and it's a pretty darn important third. In 2003 the average change of yardage on an NFL punt was 31.4 yards. That's a long ways down the field.

Blocked punts led to immediate scores in 42 cases, and led to a score on the ensuing drive another thirteen times. Regardless of the level, special teams have an enormous impact on the effectiveness of a football team.

Punter

Your punter is going to need to know:

- Stance

- How to catch snaps

- How to drop ball

- How to kick ball

- What to do if the snap is bad

- Where to aim the kick

- How to play safety during the return

Punt Team

- The rest of your punt team needs to know:

- How to block for a punt/when to release

- Securing the field

- Swarming to the football

- Who has outside contain

- What to do on a "fire" call

Punt Returner

Your punt returner needs to know:

- How to catch punts

- How to fair catch

- Where to line up

- How to execute return plays

- How to react to a "Peter" call

- What to do with punts inside the ten yard line

Punt Block/Return Team

Your punt block/return team needs to know:

- Alignment against the punt formation
- How to rush the punter
- Running into/Roughing the kicker
- Who has outside contain
- What to do against a fake punt run or pass
- How to execute return plays
- What to do with a blocked punt
- What to do if the punt crosses the line of scrimmage
- How to react to a "Peter" call (a call to get away from a punt that hits the ground)

Field Goal Unit

Your holder and placekicker need to know:

- How to catch the snap
- Where to place the ball and at what angle
- How to approach the ball
- How to kick the ball

The rest of the field goal unit needs to know:

- How to block for a field goal/when to release
- Securing the field on a short kick
- Swarming to the football if it doesn't go in the end zone
- What to do on a fire call

Field Goal Block

The field goal blocking unit needs to know:

- Alignment against field goal formation
- How to rush the kicker
- Running into/Roughing the kicker
- Who has outside contain
- What to do against a fake kick run or pass
- What to do with a blocked kick
- What to do if the kick crosses the line of scrimmage

- How to react to a "Peter" call

Kicker

Your kicker is going to need to know:

- Stance
- Approach
- How to kick ball
  - How to kick a squib kick
  - How to kick a deep kick
  - How to kick an onside kick
- Where to aim the kick
- How to play safety during the return

Kickoff Team

- The rest of your kickoff team needs to know:
- When to release
- Securing the field
- Swarming to the football
- Who has outside contain
- What to do on a squib, deep, or onside kick
- What to do if the ball doesn't go ten yards
- When the ball is live

Kickoff Return Team

Your kickoff return team needs to know:

- Alignment across the field
- Who to block
- How to execute return plays

Now here's the good news, folks: you can delete a few of these skills if you don't need them. For example, I don't spend a lot of time teaching zone pass coverage at the lower youth levels. I feel that man-to-man is a better, more effective coverage scheme, and that zone is cumbersome to teach. It's usually only my safeties that are required to learn and play in a zone below the age of thirteen.

Rubber and Road

The next chapter is going to put the schedule together for you. I'm going to take you through every day for the first twenty days of practice. Of course, I'm assuming that you have a league that allows you a three-week preseason before the first game.

You'll probably still have to modify the practice plans to fit your exact system. Bear in mind, also, that these schedules are assuming that you plan to use the offense and defense described in my other books. If you decide to switch to a run and shoot system then you're going to have to adjust the schedule on your own. Also, no schedule is perfect. Even as anal-retentive as I am, I still have to adjust things on the fly.

Practice Everything

The typical high school practice week is divided into offensive and defensive days. I've never really understood this concept. Studies have shown that the best way to memorize and learn something is to work at it for a short period of time every day, rather than for a long period of time every couple of days.

Breaking your week into offensive and defensive practices also has some other problems associated with it. Say, for example, if your starting middle linebacker has an orthodontist appointment on Tuesday, the day you're going to show the upcoming opponent's plays to your defense. In this scenario, one of the players you most need to teach a thorough understanding of the opponent's system to just missed a crucial practice.

On the other hand, if you practice everything, every day, then you don't need to worry about that. So Billy missed Tuesday's practice; who cares? He was here on Monday and Wednesday. (Actually, I care, and Billy won't be playing in the first quarter of the game.)

Special Teams

The other thing that happens when you break off into days for each side of the ball is that special teams tend to get ignored. I notice that there never seems to be a day set aside just for special teams in these types of schedules. Offense has a day, defense has a day, and special teams are typically given a twenty-minute period somewhere on each of those days.

I don't like that, and not just because I've been a special teams coordinator for the past four years. You can steal a lot of games from opponents that are better than you on offense and defense if you properly coach your kicking game, and the only way to do that is to give them the time they need. This means something pretty close to equal time for special teams.

Blocking and Tackling

The two most important skills your players need to have on the field are blocking and tackling. These need to be practiced every single day in some fashion. I even recommend teaching the basic, slow motion form movements before you put pads on.

Typically, if a high school or youth team divides things up and practices offense on Monday, then that's the only day they tend to practice blocking. Ditto for tackling.

Let me put that another way for you. The two most important, basic, and fundamental skills in all of football are practiced only fifty percent of the time.

Later on in chapter eight I'm going to show you a drill progression I use that will give your players nearly 300 reps at form tackles in your two-week preseason alone. I'm also going to show you drills that will get hundreds of blocking reps in as well. The strength behind these drills isn't just the number of reps; it's the fact that the skills are practiced every single day. It really helps to get the skills into muscle memory.

Becoming Perfect

Here's an example out of my past. I trained in Isshitu-Ryu Issin-Ryu Karate for close to seven years. Before I qualified for my black belt, I literally executed the common techniques more than eighteen thousand times. We started every single training session with 50 straight punches, 50 reverse punches, 50 side foot stomp kicks, 50 roundhouse kicks, 50 back spin heel kicks, and 50 front kicks.

Think about that for a moment. In seven years, I probably went to 370 sessions, or just over one session per week on average. 50 times 370 is 18,500.

That's not scary. What's scary is the knowledge that my head trainer, an-Shidoshi Yotishoto Uechimi, had been training every day for *forty years*.

If he kicks you, you stay kicked. Trust me on this.

My point here isn't to talk about what kind of a badass I am in a bar fight. It's to make certain you understand the concept of perfectibility. Blocking and tackling are the two most essential skills in football. They are the foundation upon which every play you run and defensive stunt you call needs to rest. You need to be as perfect as possible when it comes to these two skills.

Safety

There's another reason, as well. Blocking and tackling are also the two most dangerous skills in football, since they involve a collision with another player, and sometimes with the ground. The more reps you get in practice, in a controlled environment where the drill determines the speed of execution, the more likely you're going to be able to keep yourself safe on game day.

As a coach, you need to be able to spot incorrect technique and correct it before it becomes a habit. Slow motion and half speed repetitions become vital, not just to your players as they learn and perfect the skills, but also to you as you troubleshoot them. Especially in the case of inexperienced coaches, who are just beginning to train their eyes to spot errors of technique, slow motion movements are critical for gaining experience without getting a player hurt.

According to the National Youth Sports Coaching Association, more than 80% of football injuries occur during practice. This makes some sense, because you'll practice about four times as long as you'll play a game. Of these injuries, more than *ninety percent* occur during tackling practice and scrimmages.

Slowing your players down and giving them many, many reps of blocking and tackling, then, seem to me to be the most common-sense approach to safety. I've been very lucky to have had only a very few injuries on my teams, and only one significant practice injury. A large part of that I credit to Jack Reed and Hugh Wyatt, whose books and tapes on coaching were my first introduction to coaching football, and as a result I kept my players safe through following their advice.

Your Coaching Staff

You're going to need some help from your staff to use this schedule efficiently. My recommendation is that you locate four assistants using the guidelines and information I passed to you in Chapter six. One of those assistants isn't really going to be a coach, he or she will instead be the timekeeper, making sure that you are always on task and where you need to be at all times.

The other three are going to be extensions of you. The practice plan is going to be put together so that you can literally Xerox™ it (you have my permission, by the way), hand it to your assistants, and say, "Do this."

Stopping the "I Can'ts"

Now, they need to do *exactly* that. If you don't follow the guidelines in chapter six, or the people you have helping you aren't what they seem at first glance, then you're going to have some issues. One of those issues is going to be a case of the "I can't's." This happens when your assistant comes to you and says, "I can't coach at this speed/teach this/run this."

Now, they probably won't say, "I can't," it'll probably come out as, "The players can't." I'm here to tell you that yes, they darn well *can*. It's simply a matter of never allowing them a way out. Like the ancient commander that burned his boats on the shore of the distant land and then told his troops, "Now advance, because you cannot retreat," you must never give the players or the staff even a moment to think that they cannot execute the grand vision you have developed called your football program. Once you allow an "I can't" into your practice, you've opened the door for a whole lot more of them.

Of your four assistants, none of them need to have any knowledge of football as long as you're using this book and the remaining ones in the series to put together your program. Everything they'll need to use is within their covers.

Who Are the Assistants?

As I said in chapter six, I break my assistants' responsibilities up into three groups of players. One coach is my running backs' and linebackers' coach, a second is the receivers and defensive backs coach, and the third is the offensive and defensive line coach. My fourth assistant, or an available parent, is the time manager. It's his job to stand in the middle of the practice field every night with a stopwatch and a bullhorn. Every five minutes he announces the segment number, and the players will move to a new set of drills or training.

Where's the Head Coach?

You'll note that I've left no place for myself. That is by design. Coaches like Jack Reed and Hugh Wyatt, two of my mentors, will tell you over and over about the dangers of assistants that don't know anything about your system or don't believe in it. They'll tell you stories about coaches that have been backdoored by assistants that tried to teach specific skills incorrectly because they didn't like the way the head coach wanted it taught, or simply wasted practice time badmouthing the system or the head coach.

Heck, I gave you warnings about those same sorts of assistants in chapter six. I even told you my personal horror story. Jack Reed, in fact, mentions on his website that the absolute best size of a youth football coaching staff is one. That way you don't need to argue with anyone about anything.

Me, I disagree. I've discovered that the best way to make sure an assistant is coaching what and how you want them to coach is simply be right next to them as often as possible. Obviously this is somewhat impractical if you want to be efficient, and efficiency is what we're after. There's no way to truly be efficient with one coach; he can only run one drill at a time. So use the crop rotation idea to keep tabs on your staff.

Coach *Everyone!*

There are other reasons to leave the head coach free as well. I got an email in late 2001 from a parent that was extremely distressed. Her son had been playing football on a program with 45 players, and the head coach refused to work with anyone but the starters. A third rate coach took everyone else and ran them through some half-hearted drills for the entire practice, and then on game day those players held the bench down. Most of them didn't even know the plays.

I used to be that player. I'm disgusted with that type of coach, and I admonish you not to be him. Those players are going to look up to you, respect you, and trust you. Coaching them all is your job.

This is the main reason I leave the head coach free, and, while the rest of the reasons are good ones, they don't even come close in importance to this one. You don't have a specific group of players to coach because you're going to work with a different group every single day. I typically start my week working with the offensive line and the linebackers, the following practice I work with the running backs and defensive backs, and then the third practice I work with the defensive line and the receivers.

Coaching the Coach

When I say, "work with," I mean I coach the coach as much as the players. This takes a special skill and tact. It's important not to undermine your coaching staff in the eyes of your players, but you need to make sure that the little things are being taught correctly. A well-intentioned coach that teaches something seemingly minor incorrectly can do as much damage as an intentional saboteur. Take reach blocks, for example. To reach block effectively, you need to step with the foot closest to the defender *first*, and place it as far past the defender's midline as possible. Imagine the havoc that could be wrought by a coach that teaches the wrong foot, or fails to teach it at all!

"Coordinator"

You'll note that I don't have an offensive, defensive or special teams coordinator. I wear all three hats simultaneously. I recommend that you do the same, at least for the first season that you're using this program. In the next year, when you're with a staff that you know and trust, you can consider pulling back a little from one side of the ball or the other and allowing someone else to take over as the coordinator.

Good luck. Hopefully you're less anal-retentive than I am.

Getting Started

Okay, you now have three coaches carrying whistles, and one more carting around a bullhorn. You've selected an offense and defense, and you're ready to hit the field, right?

Sorry, there's still more work to do. The next thing you need to do is determine which of your offensive plays fall into what categories, and what parts of your defense are base. You also need to organize your special teams into a logical and consistent series for instruction.

Organizing the Defense

On the defensive side, this is relatively minor. Every defense has a base, which I think of as a "default" setting. For example, the default setting for the Ram linebacker in my 4-4 is to read and scrape to the B-Gap on run and drop to hook-to-curl support on pass. Unless he's stunting or covering for the outside linebacker stunt next to him, that's what he does every play.

No problem. Just drawing your defense up against a typical offensive set should give you a pretty good idea what you need to get into the player's heads right off the bat.

Don't Forget Special Teams!

Many coaches tend to ignore special teams. I really don't recommend that at all. It's one third of the game, and, to put it another way: you can win a lot of games from coaches that don't put any effort into special teams by coaching your kicking game properly. Imagine what can happen if your opponent throws his punting unit together in one practice while you make a concerted effort to teach an effective punt-blocking scheme to your players.

Take it from me, there's nothing more disheartening to a coach than hearing that double thump on a punt, and there's nothing more exciting than hearing it when you're on punt return.

Organizing Special Teams

I break my special teams down into two major sections: offensive and defensive. Offensive special teams are the kicking plays in which we are turning over the football. Defensive special teams are those in which we are returning the football like kickoff return and punt return.

Some of these are going to require more work than others. Coverage is generally easier to put together than returns because it's usually just a matter of teaching the players to stay in their lanes and sprint downfield before closing to the ball carrier. (Understand that I'm talking about ease of basic installation, not game day execution, which is a lot more complex than that.)

Once the basic special teams are organized, it's not that difficult to spend ten minutes a day installing the foundation that you'll build on later in the season. You can put the special teams details off for a little while, because you typically won't be using them until your first game. While you can't ignore them, you can get a lot of basic work done in a limited amount of time.

Organizing Your Offense

Offense is a little more problematical. I don't remember who said this, but the relevant quote is, "Offense is about execution, but defense is about reaction." The only way you can get the execution you need is to rep your plays over and over, and that takes practice time.

You're going to find that the first week or so of my practice schedule is going to revolve around the offensive execution. In fact, while this isn't one hundred percent accurate, I think you could average it out and say that the first week is about sixty percent offense, thirty percent defense, and ten percent special teams.

I think it's extremely important to keep your defense and special teams as simple as possible. Much of those two aspects of the game is going to be reaction to whatever the other side is doing. The more complex you make something, the more your players are going to be thinking instead of reacting.

Your Players Have to Learn *Both* Sides of the Ball

Remember also that most youth coaches don't have the luxury of a platoon system in which each player plays only on offense or defense. In other words, that means that each one of your players is going to have to learn both sides of the ball and a special teams assignment as well. Anything you can do to simplify something for them is going to make things easier all the way around.

The Double Wing offensive system I describe to you in my book on offense is "series based." This means that the plays are all designed to look as similar as possible for the first second or two after the snap. You need to determine the following three things about every play:

- How often will I call this play?
- Why will I call this play?
- How crucial is the success of this play?

You're thinking about these things because you need to know how much of your offense is wrapped up in this one play. For an example, this book is going to use my Double Wing offensive system.

In my version of the Double Wing, everything revolves around one play: the toss. In his book on the offense, Jerry Vallotton calls it "the hub of the wheel." It's *that* important. Double Wing coaches sometimes call that one play thirty times in a game. Everything we do in the entire offense is based on that one play.

Obviously that play is the first one we install, and the one we work on the most to perfect. Knowing the first play is part of the battle, but it's not all of it, not by a long shot.

Dividing the Offense

You really need to divide your plays by series. My Double Wing, for example, is divided into three specific series: 1) Toss Series, 2) Buck Sweep Series, and 3) Wedge Series. A team that runs the Pro-I might have the Isolation, Counter Trey, and Pitch Sweep series.

Once you have made this division, the next thing to do is further subdivide the series into the following areas:

Core – These are the main plays. You'll call these most of the time, and use them to set up the counters.

Counters – These are the home runs. When you need a longer gain than usual, you'll bank on the defensive overpursuit and desperation to stop your main core plays. Counters typically have a much greater average yards gained than the core, if for no other reason than because they take advantage of the defense "selling out" to stop the main plays. Mathematically, you should call about six or seven core plays for every counter.

Passes – You need to be able to throw the ball. While I'd love to live in a world where passing is completely unnecessary, the reality is that the defense is going to stop you cold on occasion on the ground. If they put ten defenders "in the box," you had better be able to throw over the top. (You will, don't worry.)

Big Play – These are the plays you need to call when you're behind or otherwise need huge chunks of yardage in a hurry. You can think of them as trick plays, but I don't like that term. Trick plays are usually plays that you call once a season and I think that's a waste of practice time. Big plays, however, are plays you have complete confidence in because you've practiced them almost as much as the core plays. They're also plays that tend to lose their effectiveness if you show them to the defense too many times in one game. (Five or six is about the limit.) In that five or six attempts, though, you might get thirty yards per attempt and two touchdowns.

Sideboard – These plays are ones that you'd like to have, more arrows in the quiver, but they aren't essential to the success of your offense. Maybe it's a pass play designed to get the ball to a hard working tight end that usually blocks on your passing plays, or it's a counter that's just a little different than the main one you already run—useful against certain defenses, but not crucial to the rest of the system.

Almost There

Once you've made this subdivision, you're almost ready to start putting the practice schedule together. Some coaches make a practice schedule the night before the practice in question, but I really don't like that at all. You have to think of your practices like a teacher would. If you're teaching a math class to a bunch of third graders, you can't leave anything out. What happens if you walk into class one day to teach division and then realize that you've forgotten to teach subtraction? You're going to end up with a lot of confused students. Most teachers will have a grand schedule of their course curriculum from start to finish, and they'll adjust it every day as the class goes. So if one section needs a little more time or the students pick up something really easily they can modify as they go.

Coaching football is the same way. You need to have a logical order that starts with the extreme basics and moves to the advanced portions of your program. The basic foundation of stance and movement is eventually going to be the underpinning of attacking the ball, blocking, and tackling, and those are in turn going to be the groundwork for every play and defensive stunt you run. Later, you may find that you don't need so much time on basic footwork because the players are doing really well. Fine, use that time for other things, like working on ball stripping drills or something else that always seems to be left behind in the hurried practice scheduling world.

Think Your Way Carefully Through the Season

What I'm driving at is that you need to put some thought into this. Too many coaches make it up as they go along, and then they go into the first game with their players ignorant of some crucial skill or bit of knowledge. Probably the worst I've seen was a high school coach that had neglected to tell his players that a punt becomes live if the receiving team touches it and doesn't recover it. We recovered *three* punts against them because of that little slip—in *one game*.

It will help you significantly if you can estimate how many players you're going to have on the team. There's some math involved in figuring out how long it takes to get each player through a drill rep. The schedule in the next chapter is written with an eye to a team with thirty players on it. You might have to change things here and there to make it fit your team.

CHAPTER EIGHT
PRACTICE PLAN

Introduction

In 1999 I was, for all intents and purposes, a complete rookie to coaching football. The last time I'd carried a whistle on grass was in 1992, when I was fresh out of high school. (Fortunately, at that time I knew everything.) I'd only coached for one season, and never really understood much more than the basic skills of the positions I'd played.

I joined the Lions' Club Lions staff in June of 1999, and met with the head coach, who named me his defensive coordinator. Thanks to some research I'd done on the web, I'd ordered a copy of Jack Reed's book on coaching defense. I was prepared and ready to go to work.

Practices were to start on August 3rd. On the evening of July 31st I received a phone call from David Jones, the KFL administrator. My head coach had quit and since I was the only one on the staff with prior football coaching experience, he wanted to know if I would consider taking the team as the head coach.

While I was trying to say, "No, I don't think I would do a very good job." I somehow slipped and said, "Okay, if there's no one else."

I was fortunate in that I'd had some experience with the Jack Reed coaching philosophy before this came about. My defensive practices were well structured (Xeroxed from Jack's book, if you must know.), and I had a pretty good idea what I needed to do and what I needed to avoid. Or at least I thought I did.

I was therefore surprised, when a player's dad brought his new camcorder to our practice and then gave me the tape, to see that many of the things I was desperately trying to avoid, like players screwing around, coaches running drills just to run drills, and colossal time wasting, were happening on *my* practice field.

We were lucky. We won our first game 32-13. By the time we faced our toughest opponents, the laser-precise ACS Environmental Chiefs, we were getting the most out of our three practices a week. The basic principles of Jack Reed's philosophy took root, and the result was a 14-13 win that we eked out on discipline and training that manifested itself in an interception return for a touchdown thanks to one drill—a drill I hadn't had time to run the previous week because I'd wasted too much time.

~D.

Starting Out

I am assuming several things in this practice schedule. Number one, I'm operating under the assumption that you have never met your players before. Either you had a quick draft, or you might be a school coach that doesn't get to pick his talent. If that's not the case, and you already know where every player on your team is going to be playing, then skip right to day three and start installing things. This is a great situation for you, because it means that you get an extra two days to rep your plays, and you might even be able to get into your sideboard before the first game (personally, I still wouldn't, but it's your call.)

Keeping Track

Take a 3x5 index card and turn it sideways. Write the name of each player you have coming to the first practice across the top of one card. Here is where you're going to make some notes about that player during the first two days, and those notes are going to be a big part of where the player plays. Down the side of the card write:

20

10

Jingle-Jangle

Agility 4

Strength 4

Agility Ladder

Strength Ladder

On the back write: Notes

These are the seven drills you're going to do over the next two days that are going to give you a rough idea how quick, agile and strong your players are to start out. In the notes section, you're going to write some things about how they responded to instruction, whether they can punt, pass, kick, or catch the ball extraordinarily well, and additional notes and feelings you might have about their play. Much of this is going to come from the "Deer Hunter" game and the two-hand-touch games you're going to be playing on days one and two.

Plan Ahead For New Players

It's a good idea to make up a couple of extra cards without names on them for new players that show up on the first day, or even later, unannounced. Remember the scout motto?

You'll note that day one's practice does *not* start with spending thirty minutes fixing equipment issues or otherwise wasting time. For one thing, you probably won't be in pads the first day, anyway, and for another, I require every player to check their equipment prior to the first practice, and to be at practice thirty minutes early if there is any problem with it. I also said earlier that I don't talk to parents during practice, so once the bullhorn sounds, we need to be moving at full speed.

This description matches to the practice plan in appendix two. It's probably easiest if you buy a second copy of this book so you don't have to keep flipping back and forth between them.

Day One, Segments 1-2: Coaches' Introduction

The very first thing you need to do is gather the team together and address them as a single group to introduce the coaches. I do this before we do anything else, because the players need to know who those guys yelling at them are. I usually take this opportunity to talk up the coaches. I tell the players that each one is an expert at coaching their position, and they are lucky to have them, so pay attention and learn everything you can from them. I say this even if the coach is so brand-new that he's reading my book behind me while I'm talking.

You have to build confidence in your team that the coaches know what they're doing. The players are going to have to trust these coaches, sometimes over their own parents. (Ever have a parent try to teach one of your players how to tackle "properly?" I have, and it almost got the player badly hurt before I put a stop to it.)

The first two segments of the practice are a brief "Welcome to the team" speech and an introduction of the coaching staff. I've scheduled ten minutes for this, but it usually takes less than five. I mean, how long can you really talk about yourself?

One of the other things I pass at this speech is the expectation of effort from the players and the rules for moving around on the practice field. Since I don't do traditional wind sprints-style conditioning in my practices, I instead condition the players with tricks. One of those is a rule that whenever the players switch to a new station, they will sprint there and do five pushups, five sit-ups, and then break down to a good hit position or three-point-stance. It's during this speech that we're going to teach these stances as well, and it will be the task of every coach running a drill to check and see to it that every player's stance is checked and corrected every time they start a drill period. (Note: The sole exception to this rule is the internal blocking and tackling stations of the foundation period. We're trying to maximize our reps in two segments, so we don't even have time to waste ten seconds on pushups and sit-ups during that period.) Later on in the season we'll start incorporating other exercises into this conditioning program, from jumping jacks to up-downs, and other traditional calisthenics, but to start out, pushups and sit-ups are all we need.

Day One Segments 3-4: Speed Training

From the welcome speech we move right to our speed work, which is performed on a twenty-yard long field. The players start by doing five pushups and five sit-ups as soon as they get to the drill area, which I usually set right next to wherever we were talking. Then we fan out and check their hit positions before putting them on a line for speed drills.

The first day we're only going to do five exercises: <u>Drill A</u>: Butt kickers, <u>Drill B</u>: High Knees, <u>Drill C</u>: Frog Hops <u>Drill D</u>: Forward Leap, and <u>Drill E</u>: Form Running. It is crucial that you start in right off the bat and teach proper sprinting form, and then stick to it for the rest of the season. Most players simply don't know how to run, and you have to teach them carefully.

Speed work is very, *very* important. Many coaches complain about not getting decent talent, by which they usually mean speed. It was also "common knowledge" until just a few years ago that you couldn't coach speed. The reality is that you can coach it very well if you just put your mind to it.

Muscle Tissue

Human muscle tissue is composed of two main types of muscle fiber. Each contractile unit of muscle possesses different characteristics and capacities. In general, type I fibers are referred to as "slow-twitch" fibers. Think of these as the long-haul fibers of the muscle tissue. They exert less force, but for a longer duration. They are smaller and suited for the utilization of aerobic energy because of the large amounts of mitochondria, endurance enzymes, capillaries, and triglyceride stores they possess. Marathon runners tend to possess highly efficient type I fibers.

Type II fibers are fast twitch, and may be thought of as the "bursting" fibers. They are larger and superior for anaerobic use because they have more glycolytic enzymes and phosphate stores. Power lifters trained to explode in one rapid series of movements would have efficient type II fibers.

"Possession" of fibers is not really an accurate term; we all possess both types of fibers. It is impossible to convert one type of fiber to another, but exercise of a certain type can improve the efficiency of one type of fiber.

Muscle Fiber in Football

In football, you need to condition and train both types of fibers. You need type I muscle fiber for the endurance necessary to play four quarters of football at full speed, and you need to have type II fibers to be able to burst from the line and deliver the first blow, hitting your opponent before he can hit you.

Speed work is designed to improve the efficiency of type II fibers, as well as work on form running, which will make your players faster because they won't be wasting kinetic energy flailing their arms or carrying them as dead weight.

Like everything else we do, these five basic exercises will be done every day for the rest of the season. Although we will add new drills here and there periodically to keep the boredom at bay, we'll always start with these, and we'll always expect perfect form.

I think it works best to line up the coaches and have them break the team into fourths to watch during the speed training. In a thirty-player team, each coach is only looking at about seven to eight players, which makes it manageable. They absolutely *must* be anal-retentive about correcting every tiny detail that is incorrect.

I've noticed that the players tend to ignore instruction that takes place during a rep. If you're doing high knees and you yell, "Johnny! Use your arms!" Johnny will usually pretend that he didn't hear you until the rep is over. It's for this reason that we established the rule, "Do it right, or do it again." If one player fails to use proper technique while doing any speed work drill, the *entire team* does another rep. Turn them around at twenty yards and make them do the same exercise back to the starting line, instead of a new one.

Do not accept excuses, and do not accept anything other than perfection on this. This is also your dynamic stretching period, which is more efficient and safer than traditional static stretching, so make sure the players are doing it right.

Day One, Segments 5-8: Form Tackling and Blocking

As soon as you finish the speed work, it's time to start working on the most important fundamentals in football: tackling and blocking.

While you were doing speed work your timing coach should have been setting up the bags for your blocking drills. When you have completed the speed work, the players should sprint, not jog, to the stations. Divide the team in half while they are doing their five pushups and sit-ups. (Remember those? The players won't, so remind them. I usually remind them by doubling it, so this group of exercises is going to be *ten* pushups and *ten* sit-ups.) Try to keep players of approximately the same size, weight, and talent level together.

As soon as the players are finished, they need to break off into their two groups, and there should be about fifteen players per group. Two coaches should go with each group.

There is only one tackling drill we're going to do today, and it's the most important one you'll do all season. In the drills section it is tackling <u>Drill A</u>: Slow Motion Tackling. You can and should do this drill whether you are in pads or not. With zero impact, all you're doing is teaching and reinforcing form.

Call and Answer Back

You need to make sure that the players know all five points to a proper tackle. The best way to do this is the "call and answer back" method. You call out the name of a tackling point and the players respond by calling back the key to that point.

Here's an example, taken directly from this drill explanation in appendix one:

Steps for a proper tackle:

Coach yells, "Break it down."

Players yell, "Eyes on the belt!"

Coach yells, "Hit."

Players yell, "Numbers to numbers!"

Coach yells, "Wrap."

Players yell, "Grab cloth behind the neck!"

Coach yells, "Lift."

Players yell, "Take the hips with you!"

Coach yells, "Drive!"

Players yell, "Short, choppy steps!"

Pause briefly between steps and have the coaches correct any mistakes in tackling form. After the first few reps, to keep things interesting, when the tacklers reach the fifth step, "Drive," I usually allow the ball carrier/tackling dummy to attempt to escape. This reinforces the desire to grab cloth and hold on. If a ball carrier escapes from the tackle, the tackler does five pushups. If a ball carrier *fails* to escape, then he will do five pushups.

You Don't Need to Hit to Learn How!

If you're going to do one drill to absolute excess every season, make it this one.

The other group of players is going to be working on blocking form. They'll be doing two specific drills, <u>Drill A</u>: Punch and Goes, and <u>Drill B</u>: Drive Blocking Form. Of these, the most important is the first. While we need to finish blocks with good form and consistent driving of the feet, we can accomplish most of our offensive goals by simply beating a defender off the line and getting into him before he can react. Establishing the "first punch" mentality is highly important to offensive success.

The hardest thing to watch for is the proper three-point stance during the reset phase of <u>Drill A</u>. Both coaches working with this group are going to have to be extremely watchful and pause the drill if necessary to correct stances. Above all, make certain that each player keeps his head up.

Finishing the Blocks

After the first segment ends, this group is going to move to practicing drive blocking with <u>Drill B</u>. This is where the players are going to work on finishing the blocks. Make sure that the whistle isn't blown until the defenders are driven back at least five yards. You have to ingrain into the players' heads that this is the minimum accepted effort on every play. If you find that one player doesn't put forth the effort necessary after repeated admonishments, have him stand there while you give ten pushups to the rest of the group. They should call out, "One! Thank you [Billy!]" "Two! Thank you [Billy!]" on every rep. You should never have that problem again after that, and it took seconds to fix. (No, it is *not* mean. You've already told him to do it right at least twice.)

As soon as segment six ends, have the players sprint and rotate to the other group of coaches. They should do their five pushups and five sit-ups, and then you'll do the same drills again. What you've done is simply broken the group into manageable sections to correct form, You'll find that this also uses a lot less equipment as well, so you don't need thirty blocking shields, because you'll only have a few players using them at any one time. Most of the drill periods are broken up like this.

Day One, Segments 9-12: Assessing Agility with the Deer Hunter

As I mentioned above, the main thing you need to do right off the bat is assess your talent. One of the ways you can do this quickly and efficiently is by playing a couple of quick games. You've got four coaches, so I would break up into two groups of fifteen players for this next series of segments.

I actually break things up before the practice even starts. Remember those cards I told you to make out before practice? Divide them into two groups of fifteen and give them to the coaches that will be running the two Deer Hunter games.

I am deeply indebted to Kevin Thurman, formerly of Madison High School and currently on staff at Lewis and Clark College in Oregon for introducing me to the Deer Hunter at the 2004 Double Wing Coaches Symposium in Dallas.

The Deer Hunter is a conditioning game. It moves very quickly so you don't have to use up a lot of practice time and the players have a lot of fun with it, so they'll run their asses off without even realizing how much they're sweating.

You'll be running two Deer Hunter games simultaneously. Mark off two forty-yard by forty-yard boxes using cones. Get three or four Nerf™ footballs per box, and give them to a few of the players. These players are the 'Hunters'. Everyone else is 'Deer'.

The Rules for Deer Hunter

The rules are:

Hunters have to chase down the deer and hit them with a Nerf™ ball. They can throw it; tag them with it; whatever they want.

Everyone must stay within the box.

Once a deer gets hit, he's out and must sit down right where he is.

Coach walks around with a "Silver Bullet": a real football and any deer that gets the Silver Bullet tossed to him can get back up and continue the game.

Last four deer standing win and become hunters for the next round.

You can even add a couple of twists: the deer switch with the hunters if they manage to catch a hunter's ball when he throws it at him, or yell out that for the next two minutes the hunter can't throw the ball, he has to physically tag the deer like in baseball.

While you're watching this game, take some careful notes on what's going on. Keep an eye on who moves well, and who doesn't. Make a note of anyone that catches a hunter's ball. Keep an eye on how well the deer dodge the hunters when they're being chased.

This game should give you some very useful information when it comes time to start working on the depth charts tomorrow evening.

Day One, Segments 13-16, Agility Assessment Drills

After you finish playing Deer Hunter, have each coach take half of each group. This should give you four smaller groups of about seven to eight players each. Each coach is going to have one specific drill he's going to time. Don't forget to have the players do their pushups and sit-ups!

These drills, and the spreadsheet described in the descriptions of them, are the result of hard work by Jack Gregory of Dallas, Texas. The spreadsheet is available for download from his web site at:

www.gregorydoublewing.com

Let me take a moment here to thank him for putting everything together into an easily understandable spreadsheet that can be used to rate your players for the draft or the depth chart.

The four drills you're going to time are the twenty-yard dash (to measure speed), the ten-yard dash (to measure quickness), an agility drill called the "Jingle Jangle" or pro agility drill, and the four-corner agility drill. You should be able to get two times for each player in one five-minute segment before rotating to the next drill station. The players need to do their pushups and sit-ups at every station. Make sure that you write down each player's time on his card. Believe it or not, I've had a coach forget to do this.

Day One, Segments 17-20: Two Hand Touch

As soon as the final segment ends, have each player sprint to where the head coach is, and do five more pushups and sit-ups. The head coach should collect the cards and shuffle them into six piles of five cards. Each pile is going to be a football team for a game of two-hand-touch.

I feel that the best way to determine whether or not someone can play football is to simply let them play football and watch them carefully. Like the Deer Hunter game, you're going to learn a lot about who can run pass routes, who can throw the ball, who can catch, and who can move their feet. This is information that is going to be invaluable when you're sitting at home trying to figure out who is going to be your starting fullback. If you've got three guys that all time out the same, but you can remember one of them catching everything that was thrown anywhere near him in five-on-five, it doesn't take a genius to figure out who should be the first string fullback. It also helps to show you some errors you might have to correct in your early practices.

I give them forty by thirty-yard fields and two completions for a first down, simple rules, and you can use one coach as a referee for each game while you take notes, moving from field to field. The only other thing I require is that there has to be a center, long-snapping the ball to the quarterback, and no person can center more than two plays in a row. This will give you a good idea what players have a talent for snapping the football in a quick, sure movement without much arc. That's going to come in handy in a couple of days when you start working on your punt formation.

Intangibles

Keep track of as many of the intangible things as you can. I never worry as much about who is scoring touchdowns or catching passes during these two-hand-touch periods. I'm more concerned with the players that are able to organize things. Who's drawing up the plays? Who are the other players listening to? Those are going to be the players that you'll look to when you need a captain or a leader on the field.

You've got twenty minutes, four segments, to run this set of games, so if you want you can do ten-minute games and rotate opponents. With tomorrow's session, you could even make it possible for every team to play every other team and find out who the champions are. I think it might be a little more effective to randomly shuffle the cards again the next day, though. You might find that one player caught a bunch of passes on day one because his best friend was the quarterback, and only threw the ball to him.

Day One, Segments 21-22: Punting and Kicking Contest

After the final segment, it's time to get back to serious football. You're still trying to fill in a few gaps in your team, and no gap is more important than the specialists. It's extremely important to find out who can punt and kick the ball. These are two different skills, and you may find that one player is better at kicking and another at punting. Just because one guy has a strong punting leg doesn't necessarily mean that he's a good placekicker.

As soon as the players finish their pushups and sit-ups, break the team into four groups and send each group to one corner of a box that extends from sideline to sideline and from the fifty-yard line to the goal line. Put one coach and a football with each group, and give a kicking tee to two of the groups. Give each coach the cards for the players in his group and tell him to write down their punting and kicking distances.

Finding a Kicker

Each group will kick the ball to the group directly across from them and then rotate clockwise to the next group. The object here is to see who can punt and kick the ball the farthest. Although you're not going to be kicking deep very often if you follow my special teams program, having a stronger leg can make a lot of difference to your field goal attempts and your squib kicking. You're also *definitely* going to need a decent punter.

In John Madden's book, *One Knee Equals Two Feet* he talks about the New York Giants in the early 1980s. They didn't have a great offense or defense, but they needed to find an edge. They found it in their special teams. The great punter they traded for and a good special teams coordinator allowed them to kick the ball deep and pin their opponents in their own territory. This gave their defense an advantage, and provided them more field to work with.

On the other side of the ball, the good placekicker they signed helped them score points even when they couldn't get the ball into the end zone. This kept them competitive until they could get their offense and defense up to snuff.

Don't Be Stupid

I'm not advocating that you become an NFL team and starting kicking field goals like they're going out of style. Remember that we're talking about *youth* football here, and kicking field goals is not easy even at the high school level. (My kickers at Tomales have kicked three in four years.) However, once again this is an arrow in the quiver for you to score points with, and it's best to sharpen its point as much as possible.

This drill will give you a chance to watch for a couple more skills as well. Tell the players that you want the ball caught in the air and watch to see who does it. For some reason players always seem to be nervous about a kicked football. I think it has something to do with the spin. It freaks them out. Once they get a few reps, I think you'll find that they'll catch it as easily as they catch a spiral.

Tomorrow you're going to take the top five kickers and punters and have a kick-off to see who is going to be the starters, so today you just want to give each player a couple of reps. Try to get three or more kicks from each player.

You've got two segments to get through this, and it should only take a few seconds per rep, so keep the players moving and don't worry about the time. This is one of the few places where you can go a little over the allotted time if you need to. Coming up, you've got a chalk talk period of ten minutes, one of the longest of the season, so you can take an extra one or two minutes if you need to.

Day One, Segments 23-24: Chalk Talk – Basic Football Information, Being Part of the Team

As soon as everyone has gotten two to three kicks, have the players sprint to the head coach and do five more pushups and sit-ups. I think you'll find that the kids have done somewhere between 50 and 65 pushups and sit-ups by the end of the practice, which is about where you want them. They've also been doing them in the same manner in which they'll use the muscles on game day: rapid bursts of effort followed by resting periods. They should be getting pretty good at their hit position stances by now, since they're getting constant input on them every time they move to a new drill.

This is an area that inexperienced coaches usually have problems with. Football stances are not intuitive at all, and it's the foundation of everything in the sport. Typically, players get little to no instruction on their stances, and as a result they have no explosion or power. This translates to ass-kickings on the field, both in practice against their teammates that caught on a little faster, and on game day, when their problems still haven't been corrected.

Instead of letting those poor stances get worse and worse, you're going to give constant instruction to your players, correcting the tiny details until every time they take a stance it's perfect. Just that one little detail can make your team a whole lot better.

If you don't use this program for a single practice after this for the rest of the season, you're still way ahead of the average youth coach, who teaches the hit position once, and then almost never revisits it. You've also begun a daily conditioning program that will make the kids stronger and faster, and you haven't wasted a second of practice time to do so.

Now You're a Teacher

The kids are going to have a chance to rest while you teach for a moment. I was a second year player before I ever figured out the four-down system. My coaches assumed that we knew what was going on and never bothered to explain anything. I only knew how much a touchdown was worth because I saw so many of them scored against my teams.

For the chalk talk you're going to need something to write on, like a large portable whiteboard. Have the kids take a knee around you while you talk about the basic rules of football. There are three main things you want to cover:

1. The offense must move the ball ten yards in four attempts, which are called "downs." If they do so, they get another four tries to go ten more yards, and so on. The defense tries to stop this.

2. The objective is to cross the goal line with the football and score a touchdown, which is worth six points. You can also kick a field goal which is worth three points, and that's what those goalposts are for.

3. There are several different positions on each side of the ball. Offensively, there is a center, two guards, two tackles, and two ends all on the line, and a quarterback, fullback, and two halfbacks in the backfield. Defensively, there are tackles, ends, linebackers, corners, and safeties.

K.I.S.S.

Obviously you want to keep things simple for this first chalk talk. There's no need to go into detail about defensive guards or unbalanced offensive lines. Just give the players a basic understanding of football. If you speak quickly enough, you should have a couple minutes left for questions before the team yell. Then, let the players go home and get some sleep, because tomorrow they come back to do it all again.

If you followed the practice plan as closely as possible, I think you'll find that the kids had a lot of fun, worked their butts off, and learned quite a bit. In fact, tomorrow, you're going to be pretty surprised how much they retain about football and the skills that you taught today. You've put down the foundation.

The Cards

There's one more thing that you need to go over with your players before moving on to the team yell. I have a number of business cards printed out for the players. They're cheap to produce and *very* important.

On the cards, I print my name and cell phone number as well as the names and at least one phone number for the rest of the coaching staff. There's also one blank line. When I give them to the players I tell them, "There may be a time this season, or next season, or whenever, where you're in harm's way. Before you do something that could get you hurt or killed, find a phone and call one of us."

The blank line is for the players to write down the name and phone number of one other member of the football team, a player they don't know yet, but someone they can call if they need help and they don't feel it should go to an adult yet. Sometimes I've seen this simple phone number exchange turn into a great friendship.

Team Yell

The very last thing we do is our team yell. This is actually where we "script" our pre-game stuff. As soon as we're done with our chalk talk, we put the players into a large circle, fingertip to fingertip with the captains in the middle. One of the captains calls, "[Mascot] Jacks! Ready, *begin!*"

Mascot jacks are somewhat of a time-honored tradition in football. My first experience with them was as a wrestler at Sumner Junior High in 1985. It's a standard four-count jumping jack, but instead of counting a number the players yell out a letter.

Thus, if your team is the *Tigers*, your captain would yell, "Tiger Jacks! Ready *begin!* One-two-three-*TEE!* One-two-three-*EYE!* One-two-three-*GEE!*" etc. The end goes "One-two-three-*ESS!* We!-Are!-The!-*Tigers!*" Then the captain yells "Ready- *Hit!*" and the entire team breaks down to a good hit position.

This is about all the scripting I do for my pre-game warm-ups. Some coaches go crazy with elaborate rituals. In my opinion, it's a waste of practice time to worry about that stuff when you should be running plays. I've lost a lot of warm-ups, but my players have won a lot of games, so I think I'll leave things as they are.

Post Practice Meeting

As soon as practice is over, you need to get with your staff and talk about the practice. Right now you should be completely preoccupied with the depth charts. Sift through your player cards and jot down some notes and impressions. When you get home and start pounding numbers into the computer, it'll help considerably if you already have a rough idea where to play each kid. You should have your depth chart about 75% completed by the time practice starts tomorrow.

I try to keep post-practice meetings to ten minutes or less. I can happily talk football for hours, but most assistants want to get home and eat some dinner. Plus, as soon as this meeting is over you're probably going to need to talk to the occasional parent that was forced by your policy of no parental conversations during practice to wait until after the meeting ended.

One thing you need to do is talk to your staff and make sure that everyone is on track for the next day's practice. Tomorrow should be a little bit easier, because the players are going to have a better idea what's going on, but it's still going to take high speed coaching to get everything done, and tomorrow you're going to work on a lot more specific skills and drills.

Day Two, Pre-Practice Meeting

Before practice begins on the second day, talk to your staff about the decisions you made at home the night before. You should have gone home and punched all of the times you recorded into the spreadsheets you downloaded from Jack Gregory's web site. This should have given you some numerical justification for some of the decisions you made. What you were really looking for during the first practice were backfield players. Today you're going to run drills and work on some things to determine who your offensive linemen are. The most important of these is the Sumo drill you'll be doing midway through practice. You've got another two-hand-touch period scheduled, and some makeup time for getting times for kids that missed practice or didn't have time to get recorded yesterday.

Day Two, Segments 1-2: Speed Training

Right off the bat the players need to crank out their pushups and sit-ups. Then it's time for speed work.

Start off with the same speed drills that you used on day one. We're still trying to build young muscles, so we're not going to add anything new yet. You have two segments to warm up and do speed drills, so I would do two sets of each exercise. Do the first set at twenty yards, half speed to stretch, and the second set at higher speed. Once again, follow the rule of do it right or do it again. Spend some time focusing on the players' three-point stances as well, and try to break bad habits of stance and body positioning *before* they get ingrained.

The half speed set is very important, since some of the players will be sore from the exertion of the day before. Working the muscles at half speed allows them a chance to burn lactic acid—the source of that soreness—out of their muscle tissues. (Note: Any soreness that lasts longer than a week or doesn't seem to get better might be a torn muscle or sprain, and the player should see a doctor.)

Day Two, Segments 3-6: Tackling and Blocking

We're still not in pads, so we're going to stick to the same blocking and tackling drills that we did yesterday. Once again, make sure that the players sprint to the blocking and tackling stations, and start each drill with five pushups and five sit-ups before coming to a good hit position. This is the day that the players will start making mistakes on hit position, so make sure that the coaches are correcting tiny details.

It's very important to be detail-oriented at this stage. Too many coaches start out with a desire to work on all the little details and then start to let things slide as the season goes on because they get caught up in "bigger" things. You need to keep perspective on two things:

• Big things are made of little things.

And,

• Part of the reason you're working on this schedule and planning things ahead is to focus on all the tiny little details so they get taken care of.

So don't let up. You've established a set standard, now you need to hold to it.

New Players

Today we're also going to work on form tackling and blocking again. New players tend to arrive during the first couple of days, so there's a good chance that you'll need to teach the steps over again. No problem, we've factored that in. Things should still go more swiftly than the day before, so you'll get quite a few more reps. You should be able to take any newcomers to your team and get them integrated without any significant issues.

Day Two, Segments 7-8: Demonstration Period

This is a very important period that you need to put some attention into. If you look further down the schedule you'll see that there is a one-segment period for missing or new players to get timed on the agility drills you did yesterday. If you have very few new players, that should become your fluff time and you should seriously think about expanding this series of instruction and putting in some drills to practice these skills.

You have four main skills that you need to demonstrate and give the players a rep or two at. They are handoffs, carrying the football securely, catching the football, and scooping and scoring with the football. Break the team up into four groups and have one coach take each group for a two-minute period. You have to move very quickly, but you need to demonstrate the proper way to take a handoff, carry the football securely, catch the ball, and scoop up a fumble on the run. At this point in the season it's not really necessary to give the players a large number of reps at this. You'll get plenty of time to practice these skills later on.

One thing I've found that can be very effective is to have one or two coaches that check three-point stances instead of hit position after the calisthenics. By tomorrow you'll be installing plays, so it's always a good idea to start making sure the players are performing the foundations properly.

Day Two, Segments 9-11: SUMO!

It's now time for the one drill your players are likely to enjoy the most, Sumo, otherwise known as blocking <u>Drill D</u>. You'll need three Sumo circles with each of your assistant coaches watching one match at a time. You should have about five groups of two opponents. The quickest way to get through a Sumo drill is to have the two smallest players go out and compete, with the winner staying in the circle and the next largest player coming in to challenge him. Each individual match should last for thirty seconds or less. You should take careful notes on who wins the Sumo matches for each circle.

When each circle has determined a clear winner (there will probably be time for one or two rematches), it is time to declare the Sumo champion. Take the top two Sumo wrestlers from each circle to the center circle and have them compete against each other. Again, this will move fastest if you have the players compete by weight and work their way from the lightest to the heaviest.

Most likely, your best five Sumo wrestlers should be the starting offensive linemen. You'll probably find that they might be your best athletes as well, so you might have to use one or more of them in the backfield. Bear in mind that you need to have the best possible offensive line, no matter what offense you use.

Day Two, Segments 12-14: Strength Drills

While you were running Sumo, your timing coach should have been setting up for the assessment drills. There are only three drills to get through today, strength four corner 5x5, agility 5x10x5 ladder, and strength 5x10x5 ladder. While your assistant coaches run those, you can be getting agility times for any players that missed yesterday's practice, or you can be finalizing your depth chart. By the time you get to segment 21 today, you need to have the depth chart nearly completed.

Again, the players need to sprint to their coach, do their exercises, and then demonstrate a good hit position or three-point stance. The coaches need to check these every time. Don't let your assistants get in the habit of just glancing over the players and not fixing the stances.

Each player should get at least two reps at each of the remaining assessment drills. Make sure these times get recorded on their cards.

Day Two, Segment 15-19: Makeup Assessments, Two-Hand-Touch

As soon as you complete the strength drills, use the next segment to get missing times for any players that weren't at yesterday's practice, or simply want a shot at improving one or two of their scores. When you have finished with this, it's time for another series of five on five two-hand-touch games. While your assistant coaches run these games, you need to sit down and put together the final depth chart based on the information you've gathered.

You should have everything you need to put together your basic depth chart. Understand that this is a living document. There is no law that says the names you write on the depth chart need to stay in those positions for the rest of the season. In fact, they might not last through the evening.

Don't Get Married to These Positions!

You still have some numbers to crunch based on the strength scores, and it could be that one of the players that missed the first day will turn out to be your best ball carrier. You won't know until a little further into the season when everyone starts to get more and more proficient in their skills.

You're also going to find out that raw strength might have had a lot to do with why Johnny won the Sumo challenges, but by next week, Billy's technique will be so good that he'll be able to knock Johnny out of his starting position. This depth chart is mostly going to be used for the next day or so, and you should be revising it every night.

Make sure that the players understand that the depth chart changes, too. Not everyone can be a starter, but nothing demoralizes a young player like thinking his lot as a third-stringer has been cast in stone.

Day Two, Segment 20: Punting/Kicking Finals

When the two-hand-touch games are completed, it's now time for the final punting and kicking contest. Take your top five punters and kickers and put them all on the goal line. Stagger the rest of the team from the fifty-yard line to the thirty and have them spread out to field the kicks. Each kicker gets two attempts to kick the ball. The player that catches the ball needs to stop where he catches it (like a fair catch). This will give the coaches time to write the distance down. Any player not catching a ball he should have caught does ten pushups.

You've got one segment to get this done, so you have to move at a pretty good clip. You should end up with two good punters and two good kickers by the time you're finished with this.

Day Two, Segment 21-23: Basic Offensive and Defensive Alignments

It's show time! Everything you've done so far has led up to this moment. It's now time to put the players into the basic offensive and defensive formations.

If you broke down your offense the way I recommended, you have probably realized that your core plays revolve around one basic formation. For example, the Wing-T coaches in the crowd will probably use the 100 and 900 formations. A Double Wing coach will use the two tight end "Tight" formation. An I-formation coach would probably use the Pro-I with one tight end and one split end.

Regardless what specific formation you selected, this is where you're going to actually line the players up in it. You've got five minutes, so make the most of it, and make sure that each player on your team knows right where he's going to be playing (for now). After the players are lined up properly, walk them through one or two reps of your first core play to each side. This is an instructional technique called "front loading." By showing the material to the students today, you're going to drastically reduce the amount of time it takes to teach the basics tomorrow.

Honestly, in five minutes I can front-load both 24 and 45 Toss from the Toss Series, and the backfield action of the Wedge and Buck Sweep Series. Teaching wedge blocking is a little more problematical, but the basic blocking of the buck sweep is easy to get through.

It is most effective to line the players up as a team in two groups: first and second string, based on the temporary depth charts you've created. Any third stringers you have should be scattered evenly between both groups. Have the players walk through each play a couple of times and then you should be out of time.

At the end of segment 22 it's time to switch gears to defense. Line the players up in your base defensive formation and explain their primary responsibilities. This doesn't have to be anything too excessive at first, but you might think about using pads to represent offensive linemen and walking through a couple of common plays like dives and isolations from the I-formation. Show the players their assignments against each of these basic plays and get them thinking about reading their keys properly.

Day Two, Segment 24: Chalk Talk-Sportsmanship

Thanks to the NFL and NBA, we youth coaches now need to put extra effort into our practices to make sure that our athletes don't emulate the criminals in the pro ranks. During day two's chalk talk you need to discuss a few of the more annoying professional tendencies and make sure that the players understand they are not tolerated on your football team. Pay particular attention to the touchdown celebration and the sack dance, two contemptible practices that pro football is rife with now.

On my teams there is only one allowed form of celebration after a touchdown. In fact, it's required. I demand that all running backs and receivers thank the offensive line after they score a touchdown. This is something we're going to practice whenever we can, and it's not optional.

The Sack Dance

After a sack or other great defensive play it's natural to be excited and happy, but high fives and hugs are the only tolerated celebration. Make sure the players understand that there is to be no trash talking to their opponents. They are gentlemen, and they are expected to act like it at all times.

I would also take some time to demonstrate what to do if an opponent picks a fight with them on the field. Let's be honest, if you are running this program, you're going to be far better prepared than almost all of your opponents. It's been my experience that the more poorly coached a team is, the more likely they are to throw tantrums on the field when the score starts getting out of hand. (Sadly, a few well-coached teams seem to do this as well when they're winning.) Coach your kids to be respectful, and to walk away from the poor sport that wants to pick a fight with them or talk trash. I even role-play this with one of my assistants. I either pick a fight with them, or vice versa, and the designated "good guy" has to walk away. It's very effective.

Day Two, Post-Practice Meeting

As soon as you finish the chalk talk, run through the team yell again. After the practice ends, you should meet with the rest of your staff and talk about the depth chart. One nice thing about organizing your program the way I've recommended is that you don't have to fight another coach for talent. Some head coaches, typically ones that are offensive coordinators, don't like to have their starting quarterbacks or running backs used on defense. Unfortunately, I have never had that kind of talent to burn, so I'll use my best players wherever I can put their skills and abilities.

That might mean that my starting quarterback is also a corner or free safety. It might mean that my running backs are also linebackers. Oh well. Even the NFL is starting to use more and more of their better athletes on both sides of the ball.

Planning for Day Three

What you need to do with your staff at this meeting is, first, make sure that no one noticed any glaring problems with the way you've put the depth chart together, and second, make absolutely sure that there are no questions about responsibilities or assignments for tomorrow, because tomorrow is the day you are going to install your first play, and it's going to be installed piecemeal first before you run it as a team.

Day Three, Segments 1-6: Foundation Period

This means that your offensive line coach is going to take the line and install the plays, while the running backs coach takes the backfield and works with them and the receivers coach works with his guys. Then, these three disparate sections of the team will meet and run the plays, and believe it or not, it will actually work.

One of the reasons *why* it's going to work is that *you're* going to work with the offensive linemen. Typically, at the youth level, the head coach wants to work primarily with the running backs, and the offensive line is relegated to the most junior and incompetent member of the staff. I don't say this to be offensive. I say this because it's true. Fortunately, you're not the typical youth coach, and your players are going to be coached by the best man for the job, the one that has done hour upon hour of research and preparation: *you*, at least for this first day with the offense.

Day three should be your first day in full pads as a team. Today you're going to do your first actual hitting drills. The players, and their coaches, should be excited and fired up to play football.

Don't let that get taken too far. Safety is still the number one thing that should be on your mind. You'll start practice with another warm-up period of speed drills, and today you're going to add one new drill: double frog hops. The object is to continually build explosive type II muscle tissue and make your players faster. Try to get two reps of twenty yards per exercise if you can, one slow, one faster. You might have to do one or two of the exercises only once to fit everything in.

After the speed drills, you'll move directly into the tackling and blocking period. Make sure your players are doing their pushups and sit-ups.

Today is the first day that you'll be doing the four station tackling circuit. It won't be the last. This series of drills in a natural progression from simple to advanced is going to make your players better tacklers than you ever thought possible.

Remedial Tackling

I mentioned before that the timing coach isn't really a coach. This is the one part of practice where things are going to be different. The timing coach is also going to be the remedial tackling coach. His job is going to be to take the kids that tackled incorrectly and make them do five slow-motion tackles correctly, emphasizing the correct tackling form, before sending them back to their group.

Start out by breaking your team into four groups. Each coach will take one group to their station. For the next two and a half minutes each player must move at full speed into and out of the tackling drill at that station, getting the highest number of repetitions possible. Each tackling station is specifically designed to teach and refine a particular type of tackle, and it's a good idea to alter these every day or so.

The Importance of Slow Motion Repetitions

For the rest of the week, at least one station will always be tackling <u>Drill A</u>. The players are going to need those slow motion repetitions to perfect their tackling form. I also think it's a good idea to periodically revisit this drill throughout the season, perhaps during every Monday practice, to keep the skills honed and make sure the players don't develop any bad habits.

For today, the four drills are <u>A</u>, <u>B</u>, <u>C</u>, and <u>D</u>. These are the four most essential drills in the tackling progression. In fact, if you were to run nothing but those four drills every day until the season ended, you would probably finish the season with the best tackling in your league.

These drills are, 1) Slow motion form tackling, 2) Head-on tackling to the pads, 3) "Eye opener" pursuit and tackling drill, and 4) "Box" drill angle tackling.

Whenever a player fails to tackle using the five correct tackling steps, send him to the remedial tackling coach. This isn't a punishment; it's simply a reinforcement of the proper tackling form. After a few trips to the remedial tackling coach, the players will concentrate harder during the drills, and they will learn to tackle properly.

The remedial tackling coach is also the person timing the drills. Every two minutes they should sound the alarm and rotate the players, who have thirty seconds to get to the next drill station and get into position. This is the only drill period in which the players do *not* do pushups and sit-ups after each rotation. You'll need the time to work on the skills.

Blocking Period

Nothing changes during the blocking period. You've already thrown a number of different types of tackles at the players. Now let them relax slightly with something they already know how to do properly.

Day Three, Segments 7-12: Individual Offensive Installation

It's time for your first offensive play. You should have broken your coaching assignments up into offensive line, backs, and receivers, and your backs and receiver coaches should be well prepared for today.

When you divided your offense into core, counter, pass, and big play, you should have determined the most important plays in each series you run. These are the plays you're going to install right now. On game day, you'll be calling these about sixty percent of the time, if not more.

Coaching the Backfield

The offensive backfield coach should put out three cones in a line with a slight offset in the middle. The end cones should be as far apart as your end man on the line of scrimmage is, excepting any split ends. The middle cone is your center. Place a marker of some form, like a flat disk cone, a rag, or a scrimmage vest, at the point of attack where the hole is supposed to be. It needs to be low and easily visible, because the ball carrier is going to run right over the top of it.

Take a look at this diagram to make that clearer.

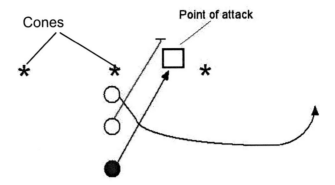

Then, line up the players behind their positions, treating the cones as if they were offensive players. The object is to teach the plays, focusing attention on fakes, ball handling, and running angles.

Jerry Vallotton's outstanding book, *The Toss; A New Offensive Attack for High Scoring Football* calls this drill the "timing" drill, and that's exactly what you're trying to accomplish. Work on the timing of each individual play without the offensive line getting in the way of the backfield movements.

Coaching the Offensive Line

The offensive line coach, assisted by the head coach, has a much more difficult task. I still use cones as much as possible. For this first day, you need to teach defensive front recognition to your center or guards, depending on who is going to make your blocking calls. My blocking calls are usually made by the centers on our Toss Series, and by the tight ends on the buck sweep series. (Both are taught to make dummy calls to keep the defenses from keying on the specific plays and sequences. There'll be more on that in Volume IV of this series.)

Take a bunch of cones and lay out three defensive lines with them. For the first day, I would lay out an odd front, with one cone over the center and one cone on the inside shoulder of each tackle. Then make a second line of cones in an even front with two cones to represent the defensive tackles on the guards and two more to represent defensive ends on the outside shade of the tackles or on the tight ends.

Finally, a third set of cones should be used to show the "covered" or T-N-T look of the eagled front.

Walk, Not *Talk!*

I take my starting offensive line and go through the blocking calls as rapidly as possible. Resist the urge to keep yammering and get the players into their positions. They need reps, not lecturing. Usually, I start the line with the odd front and walk them though the play twice. Then they move forward to the even front and walk through the play again twice. Then they move to the covered front and walk through it again.

Then they move to the back of the line while we work with the second and third stringers, one group at a time moving through the fronts as quickly as possible.

You've got to make sure that whoever is assigned to make a blocking call makes that call every time. Don't worry about dealing with blitzing linebackers or defensive line stunts yet, just concentrate on blocking the right defensive player (represented by a cone) at the right angle.

In three segments, fifteen minutes, you should be able to get twenty or thirty walk-through and jog--through repetitions. By then you should be proficient at running the plays properly, and you can move on to the next core play from your second series. Run it the same way as the first play for two segments, and then finish up with your last core play from your third and final series.

Coaching Receivers

Receivers can be more problematical to coach. Most of the time any split end or flanker will be assigned to block a man in space, such as a stalk block on a cornerback or a cutoff block on a free safety. On certain rare occasions they might be asked to crack block on a linebacker, but that's not usually a core play, because cracks tend to lose their effectiveness the more you call them against a certain defense. The other task usually given to a receiver on a running play is a "clear out" route in which they fake a pass route downfield.

Tight ends are the easiest of the receivers to coach. Typically, since my Double Wing offense uses two tight ends, I'll simply take them with the offensive line. This works out perfectly, because it essentially puts *three* coaches focusing on the most important part of the offense: the line blocking.

If you run an offense that uses split ends and/or flankers, such as the Veer or the Wing-T, you won't be able to use their coach to help with the offensive line. In the I-formation, most of the time the receivers will be running something that looks like a pass route, even if it's to gain depth and blocking angles on the defensive secondary. By using one of the receiver "trees" you can assign the receiver responsibilities based on pass routes, and the receiver coach can work with them on that.

Your receiver coach needs to take at least one segment to run Receiver Drill A, "One Thousand Hands." Every receiver you have should have a minimum of twenty passes thrown to him every day. During *every* offensive period there should be at least one segment just for this, and if possible, two or more.

The receiver coach needs to spend some time concentrating on the mechanics of catching the football: catch with the hands, fingertips and thumbs touching on a high ball, pinkies crossed on a low ball. Bring the ball to your body immediately with the eyes on it, and cover up both points. Maintain four points of pressure on the ball at all times ("Eagle claw" over the point, forearm, other point tucked behind the bicep, pressure from the stomach.) Each player needs to practice these mechanics on each catch, and after the first three or four passes, if he fails to execute the procedure properly he needs to start doing pushups.

Do *not* give out pushups to players for dropping passes. This tends to make a problem with catching even worse because it makes the kids rattled. Correct what they did wrong and get them back in line.

Dividing Your Installation Period

Your installation time is divided up into segments just like any other period. You have six total segments for working separately and focusing on the individual assignments of the backs, line, and receiver corps. You can divide these segments any way you want, but I would strongly encourage you to pick one primary series to be your absolute most important, and that's where you should put the majority of your practice time.

Think About the Assignments

In my practice plan, I have three segments devoted solely to the toss plays, right and left (24 and 45 toss, respectively). Two more segments are set aside for the buck sweep series, and a single segment is committed for the wedge series. I did it this way because the backfield action for the wedge and buck sweep is virtually identical. The only change is that one uses motion and the other does not because the ball is snapped on the quarterback's first sound.

You're going to have to take a long look at the offensive system and series you're using and determine which is your core series, and what you need the most work on. It's important to remember that even though the backfield action might be the same, the line blocking may be different. In fact, for the line, the buck sweep series I use is actually comprised of four different plays (sweep, trap, sprint out, and pass), with three disparate blocking schemes (sweep, trap, and pass)!

Of course, to make up for this, every one of the wedge series plays uses the same line-blocking scheme. This is actually intentional. Not only does it limit the amount of stuff I need to shoehorn into the skulls of my players, but it also helps on the misdirection of the series. If I find a defense is keying my offensive line movements, then a few plays from the wedge series should break their keys handily.

I have specifically structured my practice plans to focus on one play out of each series every day until the entire series is installed. You need to do the same. Of course, if you're using my Double Wing, you can just use the plan in appendix two, where everything is already written for you. There is also a blank plan in that appendix that you can use to put your own program together. Feel free to make any necessary modifications or copies of these practice plans. They're there to help you.

Day Three, Segments 13-17: Team Offense

No football play can be successful unless the players are well trained to work together as a functioning whole. You need to bring everyone together to run your plays as a group in segment 13. I have discovered that the quickest method for doing this is to break up the first, second and third stringers into three groups. After they finish their pushups and sit-ups, each group should huddle about ten yards from their ball, with the starters in the middle and the backups about on either hash mark.

The head coach/offensive coordinator should call the play, and the starters should sprint to the line and run the play against air. If you have a few fourth stringers you can toss them in as defensive linemen in odd, even, or covered fronts to give the center someone to make their calls on, but give them shields to protect themselves and *make sure that they get their offensive reps!* They need to be swapped into the offense as often as possible.

Remember, you coach *everyone*, not just the starters.

Coaching on the Run

Here's the tricky part: your assistant coaches must coach at high speed and in a whisper while the starters return to their huddle. They also need to keep an eye on the next group, who will be running the same play seconds after the starters clear the line of scrimmage. In fact, the second stringers should be lining up on the line within three seconds of the first snap of the ball.

Air

You need to run this against air or a very few defensive players at first. It's going to be a couple more days before you can put in a complete defense. Right now you need to work on the basic timing of the plays. The sole exception is if one of your core plays is a trap play (which would be very unusual). In that case, there should be a coach with a stand-up tackling dummy that represents the victim of the trap block. Line him up in his normal position and alternate charging across the line and sitting in the hole to give your trapper practice at rooting him out.

This also gives the rest of the offensive line practice at not blocking the trap prey at the line. Not only is this a waste of a blocker, since someone is already designated to whup that guy's ass, but it also means that no one is blocking the linebackers. They will inevitably scrape to the gap and make the tackle if your playside linemen do not go second level and get in their faces.

You need to get five reps a minute. More if you can do it. Before you start making excuses, understand that I coached twenty-four players by myself in 1999. I was a brand new head coach with only one previous year of coaching experience, and that was lost in the mists of time. I was able to maintain a steady four snap per minute pace, and I'm sure that adequate help from my assistants would have gotten us to a five or even *six* repetition pace.

Yes, you *can*!

AAAARGH!!!

It's going to feel like you're herding cats. This day, more than any other, is going to be the day that the assistants come to you with the "I can'ts" after practice. *Remain calm.* They can, the players can, and *you* can.

Keep moving. Your goal today is just five to ten reps of each play for each string. You can do this. If things are moving too fast for you, then slow things down between groups.

Backups for the Backup's Backup

Don't forget about those fourth stringers, or, if you have a smaller team, those third stringers that don't fit onto your first or second team. They need some reps, too. Ultimately, you want to make your third-stringers as competent at running your offense as your starters are. They might be smaller, slower, or younger, but they need to know everything that your starters know. It's the only way that you can trust them to execute properly in a game, and you're going to have to get them in games *this* year if you want them to play next year.

Running off Players

By the way, before you start thinking how much easier it might be to run that player off so he's not "wasting" your practice time, let me tell you about Casey Karlow, our last-place fullback in 2003. As a freshman Casey was 110 pounds and slower than a tax refund. He had good hands, but we despaired of ever making the kid a football player.

However, in the off-season Casey committed to a solid workout program. He filled out, and also grew about four inches, hitting close to six foot. He worked with me every week for six weeks on speed training and shaved at least three tenths of a second off his 40-yard dash time.

In 2004 he was our leading receiver, strong side defensive end, right tight end, and team captain. In one game he intercepted two option pitches and took one of them back for a touchdown. In another he caught four passes, two for touchdowns. Now how stupid would we have been to run him off the team in 2003 because he was too small and too slow?

Your goal as a coach is to make your worst players as good as the league's best players. No, it's not easy. If it was easy we'd call it *soccer* and it would *suck*.

Organizing Team Time

You have twenty-five minutes, five segments, to rep each of the plays you installed during individual time. I usually install about four plays on the first day (a step up from my previous pace of one play per day only because I have improved my efficiency throughout my practices). This gives you five minutes per core play, with an extra five minutes to call them all at random.

In other words, I'll call nothing but 24 and 45 Toss for the first five minutes, running the same play over and over again to each side of the field, repping the backfield movements and the line assignments over and over against air.

As soon as segment 13 ends I'll shift gears and go to the next play on the list, 49 Jet Sweep. For five minutes we'll run that play over and over. Note that we did not install the companion play to the other side yet. There's a reason for this; we want to perfect the entire *series* in one direction before we swap things around, since the buck sweep series is more complex for the offensive line.

At the end of segment 14 we'll start with the 30 Wedge. The backfield action is identical to 49 Jet Sweep, with the exception of motion, so it's almost as if we're getting more reps at the sweep.

When segment 16 starts we have an option. 24 and 45 toss are the same play to either side, and we've only run each one for two and a half minutes. We can either run it for another five minutes, or we can start in with our randomized playcalling. Whatever you do, you need to keep track of the number of times you practice each play. This is tremendously significant, because it helps make game day decisions for you. I flatly refuse to call a play unless I've run it fifty times in practice—perfectly, and the only way to know when a play is ready is to count the reps. Ultimately, you're shooting for about 350 reps per play.

Keeping Count

This becomes extremely important later on in the season when you start putting in your sideboarded plays. You want to make sure that you continue to get a high number of reps with the core offense; don't let that suffer just to put in some fancy new play, and you also need to make sure that you rep the new play sufficiently to give you a reasonable chance to run it properly on game day.

Included with the practice and installation schedule is an Offensive Repetition Checklist. I strongly suggest that you use it, or something like it, to keep track of the number of times you run each play as a team. Don't count repetitions run by the individual sections of the team; only count the reps run as a team.

Don't Worry About Situation Football Yet

Don't stress out about situations right now. All you're going to be doing for the next few days is putting in your plays and repping them as closely to perfection as you can get. After you've gotten most of the base offense installed, then you can start worrying about teaching your players (and coaches) clock management, goal line, and panic techniques.

By the way, "panic" is a term for an offense that is backed up within its own five-yard line. This isn't a good place to be for several reasons, but one of the key ones is the way it compresses your punt formation. Punters normally stand fifteen yards back from the snapper at the high school level and higher. If you're on the one-yard line, the punter can be, at most, eleven yards from the snapper. To put it another way, it means you're four yards *closer* to the guys that want to block the kick. Not good.

Typically a panic offense uses straight ahead plays that aren't designed to get big yards, but will hopefully shove the defense back a couple of yards to give the punter a chance to kick the ball. Most coaches *hate* the thought of their punter kicking out of the end zone. (By the way, don't forget that, if you have a decent kicker and your opponent is punting out of his end zone, you can think about having your return man fair catch the ball. You're allowed a free kick from the spot of the catch, and if it goes through the uprights, it gives you three points. The difference between that and a field goal is that the field goal is a *scrimmage* kick, and can be blocked. A free kick cannot; the defenders must be ten yards from the ball!)

I'm pretty sure you won't have to spend much time or effort teaching your coaches how to panic. They'll do that on their own, probably with very little input from you. I encourage this. It keeps them out of my hair.

Day Three, Segments 18-21: Defensive Period

In the practice plan this period is divided into the installation period and the team period, and that's not entirely accurate. You basically have four segments to play around with your base defensive formations. If you are going to use my defense, I would strongly encourage you to avoid getting into the blitz package for a couple more days.

I have coached defenses on either end of the spectrum, from great to poor. I can tell you that the 1999 Kodiak Lions were so good that they should have been unscored on, and would have been if I hadn't made a couple of boneheaded coaching mistakes. I can also tell you that the 2004 Tomales Braves JV was confused and unsure of their assignments, and allowed 23.1 points per game, the most of any team I have ever coached. (By contrast, the 2003 JV Braves allowed 19.4 points per game and pitched four shutouts. Take away the 34 points scored by Middletown on us, and our average goes down to 14.3 per game.)

Limit the Confusion

Defense is about playing assignments and reacting to the offensive plays. Offensive plays are *designed* to confuse the defense. Defenders are already at a disadvantage, and anything you do to further confuse your players is only going to dig the hole deeper.

I strongly recommend that you use one base formation, or two that "interlock." You need to have some form of goal line set, and you need to have some form of standard defense. There's no law I know of that says you can't use your goal line defense as your standard front, either. It depends on what you're going to face. At the youth level the deep ball is a fairly insubstantial threat, so what purpose is gained by putting in a nickel defense? In fact, the goal line defense that I use with my 4-4 split is also the *only* defense I used in Kodiak. It worked very well.

Interlocking

When I'm talking about interlocking, I'm talking about choosing defensive fronts that fit together and don't require special skills or talent. For example, if you run a 4-4 as your base front, you're going to be concentrating your time with the defensive tackles on teaching them to shoot gaps and engage blockers from the side. (You had also better spend some time teaching them to counter trap blocks.) What you will probably *not* be teaching them is how to engage a blocker head on and shed the block to pressure the backfield.

In other words, you are *not* teaching them to play nose tackle. Now, if you shift to a 7-Diamond defensive front, which features a nose, in goal line situations, you're looking at either teaching an entirely new set of techniques, or getting the center of your defensive line blown back on every play. (I promise you that if I notice you've shifted from an even front to an odd or eagled look, I'll wedge you until you go back to the even front. Then I'll probably wedge some more because it's my favorite play.) A better match for the 7-D would be an odd or eagled front like a 5-3 or "46". A happier marriage to the 4-4 split is the 6-5 or the Gap-8, sometimes called the Gap-Air-Mirror or GAM.

The Wade 4-4: Like Most of My Stuff—Stolen From Other Coaches

The two defensive formations I use are the Gap-8 and the 4-4 Split, as popularized by Joe Roman and Pete Noble, and with my own stamp on things. You'll have to wait for my book on defense to get all the particulars on the system.

To summarize in one sentence what I just spent the last three pages telling you, this first few days you need to make sure that everyone understands their most basic assignments on an instinctive level. There can be *no* confusion in the players' minds about who covers what gap, or who covers what eligible receiver. (Here's a tip: there can't be any confusion in *your* head, either.)

Splitting Up

I would strongly recommend that you take the first two segments of the defensive period to split up into linebackers and line, and defensive backs. Defensive backs can go with their coach to work on coverages, and you, the line coach, and the linebacker coach need to work with the front two levels of the defense.

There are three main things you need to teach today:

1. Alignments

2. Gap responsibilities

3. Primary pass coverage responsibilities

If you are using any defense with linebackers, the pass coverages are going to change every time you send one of the linebackers on a blitz. Right now, you need to be concerned with the "default settings." If you slip and fall on the sidelines and the kids don't get a play in from you, what are they going to do?

Stopping the Isolation

The one play you absolutely must learn to stop is the Isolation, sometimes called the Lead, Blast, or Power. It is an I-formation play that can be found in other systems as well. Essentially, it is a base-blocked front with the fullback leading the way for the tailback. It can be run from a huge number of offensive formations, although the NFL and college teams seem to have collectively forgotten this and run it almost exclusively from the I-Formation.

By far this is the most common play in football. It's used in the Delaware Wing-T and called the thirty series. It's used from the two back Veer formation and called "Power," and, of course, it's used from the I-formation constantly and called a bloody boring play.

Stopping the isolation is actually not that difficult, on paper. It hinges on the linebackers attacking the line of scrimmage as soon as the fullback takes a step in their direction. They need to hit him at full speed and blow him back into the path of the tailback while the other linebackers stay alert for bounce-out to the playside, and cutback and counter to the back side.

The problem is, the desire to run into people at full speed is not a survival trait for the human species, and most kids are born without it. You need to condition your players to do it instinctively when the fullback takes a step towards them. Linebacker <u>Drill A</u>: Crunch Time is specifically designed to counter this play and the counters off of it, and you'll be running it nearly every single day. Tom Bass's *Play Football the NFL Way* (ISBN: 0312059477) also has some great drills for focusing on this type of play.

Trick Plays

There are a few more plays you need to condition the players to deal with, but those need to wait until you get everyone together as a group. Once you have the basic defense put together you need to walk through a reverse, a fake reverse, and a double reverse. You also need to give your players a chance to see a halfback pass. Someone, somewhere, is going to run one or more of those plays against you.

The beauty of it is that if you prepare your players properly for those plays, when your opponent calls them they're going to be thrown for horrendous losses. You want your players to focus on their assignments and be disciplined. This means breaking the "single-exchange mentality," as Jack Reed calls it. Typically, youth football players are so used to seeing one exchange, from quarterback to running back, that they completely forget that there are other people that can carry the ball. Once they see the handoff, safeties plant and come up, corners abandon their coverages, linebackers take pursuit angles... and they get burned when the tailback pulls up and throws a pass back to the quarterback down the opposite sideline.

My advice is to burn them in practice so many times that they are conditioned and ready for the plays when they see them in games. Two or three times a week I'll toss a trick play into my stack of cards. After about week one the defense usually snuffs it out and throws the scout team for a significant loss.

It's In the Cards

Speaking of cards, I have a stack of 5x7 index cards with plays on them from several years of coaching. To start each season, when you're not sure what sort of offensive systems you're going to be facing, you need to draw up some new cards, pretty much at random to show some plays to your players. I usually grab a few cards out of the stack and just shuffle them together for the first few scout team days.

There is one mistake that a lot of youth football coaches make. I remember very clearly being in junior high and running our own offense against our own defense. We would have been in great shape if anyone we faced ran a Wing-T and a 5-3, but when we faced Lakeridge and their Wishbone, we got cold-cocked. Likewise when Aylen hit us with the Pro-I.

The object of team time is to show your players what they are going to be facing in the game. You need to line up a scout team, comprised of your backups and extra bodies, such as parents and coaches, and run plays taken from your scouting reports against your defense. This is *vital*.

I have said it before, many, many times, that if you're not scouting, then you're not coaching. There are complete sections on scouting for each part of football in each of my books on offense, defense, and special teams. There's no excuse for not scouting your opponents. If you intend to work as hard at coaching as you ask the players to work for you at playing, then you need to be scouting.

Of course, you're in day three of the season right now. You haven't got any scouting reports yet, so what do you show your players?

Make Something Up!

Thanks to several years of coaching experience, I have a pretty extensive library of scout team cards to draw from. If you don't have that, then your other option is to sit down with a couple of books on coaching and draw a few plays on some cards yourself. It's not really that hard, but make sure that you put some blocking assignments on there for the scout offensive line. Make it as realistic as possible. It also helps to put a sample situation on the card as well. Tell the defense it is third and one before running a dive, or second and six before a sweep.

Here's the way I run my scout offense. I give all members of the scout offensive backfield a number from one to five. Then I hold up the card with the play that we're going to run on it and I point to each eligible receiver and give that receiver a number, one to five, plus the quarterback. Each player matches his number to the number I call out, and executes the assignment shown on the card. It takes about three seconds to call each play.

Mix in the Tricks

I mix in at least one or two completely random "trick" plays that sort of fit the offense, like a flanker reverse out of the I-formation if the offense we're facing is an I-formation system. If the offense we're facing runs a trick play, and I've got it on the scouting report, I'll usually put it in a couple of times.

Like anything else, start at a slow speed and walk, and then jog through the assignments. Typically, I'll only run three or four scout team plays on this first day after showing the trick plays. After you show each play a couple of times increase the speed to full.

Quick Whistle

Remember that your players have not been tackling very long. They need to get a lot more practice at tackling before they tackle someone to the ground under game-day conditions like a scrimmage, which is what you're doing. For this reason, it is vital that you use a quick whistle. I actually blow the whistle the instant *before* a potential tackler touches the ball carrier, at least for the first few days.

Believe it or not, this is going to make your players into *better* tacklers on game day. Most of tackling is the approach angle to the ball carrier, squaring up, and getting into a good breakdown position. What you are doing right now is emphasizing that portion of the tackle. Kids tend to think that it's all about the hit, so they leave their feet to deliver a smashing blow—and get dodged by a nimble runner.

In this form of scrimmage, though, the kids have to establish a good breakdown position on the tackler, almost without touching him. This is called a "thud" scrimmage, and I use it extensively.

Starvation

There's one more thing this type of practice does: it absolutely *starves* your kids for impact. My players tend to be the hardest hitters in their league because they almost never get to hit in practice. When they get to the game field, they tend to crush their opponents, especially the ones that hit every day and are still afraid of it because they get banged up all the time.

Getting Religion

In his excellent books on coaching youth football, Jack Reed talks about "getting religion," which is when a football player, typically a rookie or relative newcomer, suddenly realizes that hitting is fun. You can see the actual transition in them, when they start to deliver a blow while running with the ball instead of accepting the force from a tackler and when they speed up slightly before contact to give themselves more kinetic weight.

I disagree with Jack, but only slightly, on the execution of finding religion. Jack states in his books that players get religion from doing contact drills and discovering on their own that hitting doesn't hurt. In my opinion and experience, the players develop religion when they are completely confident in their ability to defend themselves on the field. Now, this might come from the execution of contact drills, but I think it's more likely to come from hundreds and hundreds of slow and one-half speed repetitions until the movements and mechanics of hitting are second nature. In fact, one of the most successful coaches I've ever met is a 5A high school coach in Washington State who has made fifteen straight playoff appearances and won seven state championships at last count. The *only* live contact he does at his practices is during spring training—ten days a year. The rest of the time his players thud. In the video clips he showed of his program, his players looked like Brahma bulls rampaging through a pet store.

This works at higher levels as well. John Gagliardi of St. John's College in Minnesota hasn't done a full speed hitting drill since he got into coaching in 1959. In 2004 he passed Eddie Robinson of Grambling University as the most successful college coach of all time, with 409 wins.

So, in my practices I really strive to give the kids just enough hitting time to get them a taste, just enough to show them how much fun it is to flatback an opponent. Everything else they're going to do is for working on form. With enough reps, the form will be perfect, and game day will be nothing more than a hitting drill, this one *finally* at full speed.

Day Three, Segments 22-23: Special Teams

Today is the first real day that you're going to put some effort into special teams. I always start with the kickoff, simply because it's the easiest kicking play for the kids to grasp. It really involves nothing more than lining up on the field and running in a straight line, at least for now.

One thing I recommend in my book on special teams is that you create a depth chart for each kicking unit just as you have for the offense and defense.

You're going to need your ten best tacklers on the kickoff, as well as the kicker you selected yesterday. At this point in the season it's a little premature to try to figure who those tacklers are, so I mostly go with the guys I've pegged for defense. There are going to be one or two kids you're going to just *know* need to be on the kickoff team, and there are also probably going to be one or two that you absolutely *don't* want on the team.

Like almost everything else we do, we line the backups up directly behind the starters in a second, and even third huddle. For right now, there are only two kickoffs to worry about calling: squib and mob kick.

Kickoffs

If you use my special teams program, and you understand why it was put together, you'll understand that kicking the ball deep down the field to the best two athletes on the opposing team in the open field, behind a screen of blockers, is sheer stupidity. Inexperienced coaches do that because they usually have misplaced confidence in their coverage team. Experienced coaches do that for the same reason.

I want two things:

1. The ball

2. To prevent a runback

Not too terribly complex.

Kickoff Procedure

We use a choirboy huddle with three of our hardest hitters in the front. Before we ever break a huddle the kicker raises his hand and obtains the ready to play whistle from the referee.

Usually after that he'll call, "Squib left" and then break the huddle. The rear line jogs out to their positions to the left, and the front line jogs out to the right. When each player is settled in his lane he will turn inwards towards the kicker and put both hands in the air to show that he is ready. One of the hitters will then call, "Ready-*Hit!*" On hit, each player will turn to face downfield and get into a three-point stance. The kicker will start his approach, and they will start down their lanes after he passes them.

In a nutshell, that's my basic kickoff. There's a specific reason for everything we do, but you'll need to buy the special teams book for that stuff.

The Mob Kick

The second kickoff that we use is the mob kick. This is our onside kick. I love to call it at random times because it really forces the kickoff return team to be paranoid. I like that.

Instead of breaking the huddle after the ready-to-play whistle, the kicker will call, "Mob kick at ##," where "##" is the number of the poor guy from the other team that we're going to obliterate.

When the kicker is ready he will turn and kick a slow dribbler that should stop exactly eleven yards from the tee and directly at the opposing player whose number he called in the huddle.

The three hitters have one job. They don't care about the ball, and in fact need to avoid it. I'll chew their butts off if they ever recover it. They are there to hit the guy at ground zero as hard as they can. They can get in front of the football (in fact, they *have* to), but they cannot touch it.

Everyone *else* needs to recover the ball after it goes ten yards. The kicker should hang back as a safety, just in case the return team does something fruity with it.

Remember, This is Day Three

The goal here is to get a couple of reps at the kickoff, not to perfect it, so jog through a couple of reps with each crew. Here's one tip: kick off from the fifty-yard line towards the goal line. Then, turn the players around and kick from the goal line towards the fifty. (Why waste time running all the way back to the initial starting position?) After the players do their pushups and sit-ups, set them up in three huddles, one behind the other, and then jog through a rep.

An alternate method of speeding this up is to put one kicking team at each end of the field and have them kick to each other. Whichever you choose, get through this at high speed.

Like everything else, try to get two to four reps per player at the kickoff. I usually put a coach back as a receiver, at least to start out, and the players are taught to stay in their lanes until they are even with the person who is returning, and then swarm inward. Now is also a good time to start working on the "ten hats" philosophy, which means you want every person on the kickoff team except the kicker in on every single tackle. I simply hand out pushups every time the players aren't within five yards of the ball carrier when the whistle blows. Five the first time, ten the second, fifteen the third, and so on is usually sufficient.

In ten minutes, you can actually make this look pretty good. You won't be ready to handle a return team yet, but you'll have the basic understanding of lane discipline in the players' heads. Heck, ten minutes is more time than most youth coaches spend on their kickoff teams all *season*.

Day Three, Segment 24: Chalk Talk-Leadership

Have the players do their pushups and sit-ups, and then gather them around on a knee. The subject today is leadership. I take today and speak to the players about what it means to be a leader and what it means to be a follower. I also talk about the role of the captain in football. Every week I assign captains for the game at the first practice of the week, and I make those captains write a 500-word essay on the responsibilities of leadership, due the day of the game.

This is a trick you can thank my brother-in-law for. He teaches Tae Kwon Do in Massachusetts, and for each grade level his students obtain they are required to write an essay on the responsibilities of that level. I liked the idea so much that I stole it unashamedly from him.

If a captain fails to give me his essay the day of the game, then he is not allowed to be a captain for that game. There are no excuses and no recriminations. He has simply demonstrated that he is not ready to be a leader of the football team yet. He is not blacklisted, and might even be selected as a captain the next week, if he proves himself in practice.

I don't grade the players in any way on their essays. Grammar, spelling, and punctuation are nice, but not absolutely necessary, as long as I can read the darn thing. The main thing I look for is the knowledge that the players are accepting personal responsibility as captains.

For the end of season banquet I'll take a few choice phrases from the essays and read them aloud, anonymously. The parents, especially, love it. I think it helps them see a side of their sons that they don't often see at home. Everyone wants to think that their kid is going to grow up to be a leader of men. I also find that the best parts of my coaching scrapbook come from these essays, especially when they've been written by players that spent a couple of years in my program.

After you're done talking about leadership, perform your team yell and send the players home. Tomorrow is another day.

Post Practice Meeting

Today's meeting should be a quick one. You've already got the depth chart mostly done, although it's probably going to change every day. What you need to be talking about today is any problems you encountered while installing the plays.

Did any of the players have significant problems catching on to what you were trying to do? Do any of the coaches need extra help from you as the head coach?

Tomorrow, you probably need to work with the running backs. It's the day you should be installing your main counter from your primary series, so you need to be on hand to stress the fakes you want your backs to execute. Counters also typically require very precise footwork and timing, so that's another reason you should probably be there to assist.

Snaps

This is also the first day that you need to have the quarterbacks and centers stay after practice for a few minutes. The most important part of any football play is the snap—the exchange between the center and the quarterback. If you can't get a snap off, you can't run a play.

Mud and Blud

You also need to plan ahead for foul weather. Coaches always seem to forget that the sunny, warm weather they practice in during August is going to be long gone by the playoffs. Do you really want to see your team sent home because of a fumbled snap? Practice it daily in August and September, and you won't have as many problems in October and November when you're playing in the mud.

I require fifty snaps without a fumble every night. There are no excuses, and I tend to get really snippy with parents that get in my face because I'm keeping their kids after practice. They usually don't have any problems with their son's selection as the quarterback or starting center, but when it comes time to put in the extra work that those positions entail they start getting antsy.

Ignore the parents that complain. Fifty snaps should take less than five minutes. Get them done. Tell the parents to go get a latte and shut up.

Oh, by the way, if you've selected a long snapper, which you should have by now, then they need to stay after practice and long snap. I require thirty perfect long snaps to a punter, and twenty perfect long snaps to a holder for field goals. Don't push this too hard, however. If a player's snaps are normally perfect, and he starts to get erratic, break it off early. Don't force him to practice through it, because you might end up causing him to reinforce a bad habit.

At this time in the season, though, the snaps are probably going to be a little crappy. Accept this as a fact of life and give them enough reps to get better at it. Use Mark Ingram's video, reviewed in chapter three, to coach your long snapper on the proper mechanics.

You may consider having the quarterbacks and centers face you while you're talking and do their snaps quietly during the chalk talk. I would only do this if league rules absolutely prohibited taking that extra five minutes for four players. It's something to consider, but try to get them after practice to minimize disruption. (I have personally never seen a practice field clear in less than thirty minutes at the youth level, even in a thunderstorm. Someone should always be hanging around, so there really isn't much room for the league, or the parents, to complain.)

Day Four, Segments 1-6: Foundation Period

Your fourth day of practice is going to start out like every other day so far. Your speed work will consist of the same exercises you did yesterday. You should already be seeing improvement in the players' ability to move with alacrity. Remember, if the player is hammering at the ground with their feet, they're wasting energy driving downward that could be used to move forward. Ideally, they shouldn't make a sound.

Don't forget to continue the pushups and sit-ups before starting every drill period.

The tackling and blocking drills are the same today as yesterday. By now you should really be seeing some improvement in the basic form of each technique. Believe it or not, your team is already better at blocking and tackling than some of the teams you're going to face, because you're working on the skills every day to perfect them.

Day Four, Segment 7: Offensive Drill Period

After you're done with the foundation drills, break up into your offensive groups. Today is a little different from yesterday, because you're going to work for one segment on some additional skills. The backs need to sharpen their handoff skills, so they'll be doing Quarterbacks and Running Backs Drill A: The Handoff Machine. Receivers should continue to run the hands drill they did yesterday, Drill A. Offensive linemen should work on Offensive Line Drill B: Double Teams. This is all skill work that needs to be done in addition to the foundation work you've already done today. Don't forget to have the players do their pushups and sit-ups.

You only have five minutes, so get as many reps as you can with each player and then move on.

Day Four, Segments 8-13: Offensive Period

You need to start out by reviewing the plays you ran the day before. You've got three segments set aside just for this, although, in all honesty you can probably get away with two. That's fine, and it will give you more time to work on installing the counters.

If you're following my advice then you're working with the offensive backfield today. You need to stress proper faking. I require all faking backs to execute their fakes for ten vertical yards, minimum. That means heading towards the opposing goal line or being tackled in the attempt.

Crack down on backs that slow down after a couple of steps, or stop to look back at the ball carrier. I tend to hand out up-downs and pushups fairly liberally during this day.

You also need to put some pressure on the handoffs. Any time the ball hits the ground I tend to explode. You absolutely can*not* let the kids think it is okay to fumble the ball.

Counters are usually very similar to the play they emulate, so your reps here should be of very high quality. In fact, if you're running a series-based offense like the Wing-T or Double Wing, in a lot of cases you can practice three or more plays at one time because the backfield movements are identical for the first few steps after the snap.

Day Four, Segment 14-17: Team Offense

After you install the plays and get some repetitions as individual groups, following the same methods you used yesterday, then put the kids together as a team and run the plays, starting with a review of the plays you installed yesterday.

Today is the day you need to start adding a defense to the mix. Give blocking shields to six or seven players that are not on the starting offense and arrange them to represent one half of a defense on the side you're running to. Walk through the blocks for each of your plays in slow motion several times, gradually speeding things up until you're running each of the plays at full speed. As you did yesterday, coach on the run and get as many reps as you can.

The slow motion walk through of a football play is called "bird dogging." I use it extensively, even later in the season. It's a great tool for confirming who blocks who and at what angle on a particular offensive play. When I want to bird dog a play, I call it in the huddle like this: "24 Toss, bird dog." This tells the players to take only their first two steps at the snap and then freeze.

This takes a lot of time, but it fortunately doesn't need as many reps. You should have already gotten most of the timing down in your individual periods, so some bird dogging here isn't going to hurt you.

Shoot for another seven to twelve reps of your core plays, and eight to twelve reps of your counters during this period, and don't forget to rotate in the bag holders so they can get some practice at the plays as well.

Day Four, Segment 18: Defensive Drill Period

Next you're going to move into a defensive drill period. The drill you need to work on the most right now is Defensive <u>Drill A</u>: Pursuit Drill. This is extremely important for teaching your defensive players to swarm to the ball. Try to get at least five reps, and make sure that all of your players get into the drill for at least one rep.

Day Four, Segment 19: Defensive Install

As soon as the defensive drill period ends, move into the defensive installation period. Typically, this period is where we install our first blitzes. I don't recommend sending defensive backs on blitzes, since they are typically smaller and weaker players not as physically impressive as linebackers. For this reason, the defensive backs should be working on Defensive Backs <u>Drill B</u>: "W" Drill while the linebackers and linemen work on the blitz package. Footwork is extremely important to the defensive back, and breaking on the ball is highly significant. Make sure you teach your defenders to call "Pass!" "Ball!" and "Bingo!" to let the entire defense know the type of play, when the ball is in the air, and when you've intercepted it, respectively.

When it comes to installing the blitzes, I almost always start my blitz installation from the outside in. In my 4-4 Split each linebacker is responsible for knowing about two blitzes and each defensive lineman is responsible for knowing about the same number of stunts. Effectively, this means that we have thirty-two stunts we can call by mixing and matching the calls, but each individual player is only required to remember and execute a very few. If a lineman or linebacker is not involved in a stunt, he simply executes his base assignment.

However you break your defensive installation time up, you have one segment to install the new blitz before the defensive backs join you for team defense.

Day Four, Segments 20-21: Team Defense

Like yesterday's period, today should be a period of scout team offense showing plays you're likely to face in the first few games or the scrimmage. Today is the day that I'll usually put in a wrinkle or two as well, with some traps and misdirection. I may also align the scout team in a non-standard offensive formation like the single wing or the short punt and walk through one or two reps of the main plays from those systems, just to keep the players sprinkled with some new stuff. Don't forget the trick plays, and make sure the players are still doing their pushups and sit-ups.

Day Four, Segments 22-23: Special Teams

Today you're going to put together the most important play in football: the punt. The only reason we didn't put it in first is because it's easier to teach coverage if you start with the players already spread out like they are for the kickoff we did yesterday. Now that they understand the concept we can move on to the idea of spreading out to their coverage lanes.

I run two punts; a tight punt and a spread punt; and two fakes, an option run and a pass. Today we're not going to worry about the fakes; we're just going to walk through the responsibilities of the basic punting unit.

In short form, the responsibilities of a punting unit are to block the rush, then cover the kick. It's got to be in that order, and neither of those is more important than the other. Your blockers must step and protect the inside gap, especially the wingbacks on the outside edge of the formation. They need to keep their hips to the inside while "making themselves big" to the outside and steering any outside rushers deeper and preventing the inside rush.

Your personal protector absolutely can *not* step backwards at any time during a punt.

You should have enough time to jog through three or four reps of both tight punt and spread punt with all of your players before this period ends.

Day Four, Segment 24: Chalk Talk

Today's chalk talk is one of the most important ones you'll have all season. In Appendix Two there is detailed information about the only real individual award I give out, the Black Lion Award. To give you the basics here, the award was started in 2000 by football coach Hugh Wyatt in memory of Don Holleder, a 1956 graduate of West Point and former Army Football player. In 1954 Cadet Holleder was an all-American end on the 7-2 Army team. Unfortunately, the Cadets lost most of their offensive starters through graduation, and prior to the 1955 season their coach, legendary Colonel Earl "Red" Blaik approached Holleder and asked if he would be willing to make the switch from all-star honors to quarterback. Coach Blaik and Holleder both knew quite well that Cadet Holleder would not be a great, or even a good, quarterback, but Colonel Blaik felt he would be an efficient leader.

Cadet Holleder thought about the switch all night before deciding to give it a shot and stepping in at quarterback for the good of the team. While his stats were not impressive, they included a win over the dominating Navy team that knocked the Midshipmen from first place.

Major Holleder was killed on October 17th, 1967 during the Battle of Ong Thanh. When members of his company were wounded and pinned down by sniper fire, Major Holleder sprinted from the fire zone to find a medic and attempted to lead that medic back to the wounded. He was gut shot by the sniper and died within minutes.

This is a Football Award, not a Military Honor.

The Black Lion Award is not a military or even militaristic award. It is given in honor of the one player that best exemplifies the courage and commitment of Don Holleder. If you have a third string player that continually pushes the players above him to get better, or takes on the responsibility of running the scout team defense for you, or otherwise displays exemplary leadership and personal sacrifice, they are a candidate for the Black Lion Award.

While I encourage anyone and everyone to give out the Black Lion, I also discourage giving it rampantly. It pains me to admit this, but there have been teams I have coached where I truly felt that no one was worthy to receive the award. I beg you; please do not treat this in "trophies for everybody" fashion. Give it only to players that earn it.

Post Practice Meeting

As soon as the chalk talk ends, do your team yell, and then get your snappers together with the quarterbacks and punters and get their fifty snaps while you hold your post practice coaches' meeting. Once again, find out if there are any issues with the basic plays you've installed or players that are having troubles. If things are going according to plan, you should actually have a pretty good-looking offense, and your defense should already know their most basic assignments.

Tomorrow you work with the receivers, and start working on your passing game. Hard to believe you started all this just four days ago, isn't it?

Day Five, Segments 1-6: Foundation Period

You've established a routine now. Today you'll add one new speed drill, Drill F: Leaping run and change to double frog hops. Make sure the players are still doing their pushups and sit-ups, and by now you should be getting preposterous numbers of repetitions at both your blocking and tackling drills. You should start seeing some of the more inexperienced players starting to show tangible results in their blocking and tackling form.

By the way, it's usually about this point when coaches tend to get lax on things like running form during the speed drills and warm-ups period. If anything, you need to bear down harder on the players at this point. You have established a standard, and the players have been with you long enough to know what is expected of them. *Never* accept anything less than their best. Remember, tolerance is just another word for encouragement, and you never want to encourage anything less than perfection.

Day Five, Segment 7: Offensive Drill Period

Here we are again with another period exactly like yesterday's. Start out with the pushups and sit-ups after the players have broken into their groups. By now your receivers are probably getting sick of Drill A, so I would work in variations one and two of the drill. Plus, this gives you a chance to make sure they know the pass routes. You'll probably want to demonstrate the arm over and dip and rip techniques for clearing the line to them before they run these drill variations. Your backfield is going to do the same drill they did yesterday, but the offensive line needs to get working on pass blocking with Offensive Line Drill C: Pass Blocking.

Day Five, Segment 8-13: Offensive Install Period

Today you have four segments for review and only two segments to install anything new. You shouldn't need much time at all for the installations, actually, because the new plays should come off the same backfield movements. All you really need to do now is work on the fakes, add in the pass routes and pass protection scheme, and start throwing the football around the practice field.

When you get to the installation period, have the receivers work with the backfield players and put in the passing plays.

Thanks to passing guru Ted Seay for a little trick he gave me for practicing passing plays that really cuts down the practice time. I almost never give my quarterback more than two reads. So, take your two quarterbacks and have the backup stand behind the offensive formation, approximately where he would be standing to throw the ball if he were running the play, only a little deeper. The starter runs the play, executing any fakes that need to be performed, and then throws the ball to the primary receiver in the pattern. Behind him, the backup quarterback checks the primary read, then throws to the *secondary* read in the pattern. Now swap in your backup to take the snaps. He'll execute the fakes and then throw the primary read, while behind him the starter checks off the primary and throws to the secondary.

Basically, you're doubling the reps for the quarterbacks, and practicing the immediate coverage recognition necessary to keep him from forcing the ball to a covered receiver.

Put in a Defense

Speaking of coverage, after about three reps I would take some extra players and have them align in a cover three look. This is the most common youth pass coverage because most youth teams put eight players up tight to the line to stop the run. This leaves three deep for coverage. Put some scrimmage vests on those defenders, and give the quarterbacks a chance to look at the defense. This is really important.

It also helps to teach your receivers to read man or zone. For years I thought this was a complex process, but it's really not. Have the receiver run with his eyes open. I even have a pre-snap read that receivers and quarterbacks are assigned to do on every play to determine cover one or cover two in the defensive secondary. (They count safeties. It ain't that hard! Even I can do it!)

Eyes Up!

Once the receiver gets into the pattern he needs to make sure he doesn't try to run across the field on a zone or he'll get killed. The tip is to simply look and see if someone in a different colored jersey is in front of him. If the answer is yes, it's a zone defense, and he should be coached to break off his route and settle down between the zone defenders. If there isn't anyone from the other team in front of him, it means that the coverage is *behind* him, and the defense is probably blitzing. He needs to get to his designated spot as fast as possible, especially if he is a Q, or hot route receiver.

This sounds incredibly complex, but I know of teams of eight-year-olds running this sort of passing game without a problem. Your players can do this; you just have to coach them.

Day Five, Segments 14-16: Team Offense

Have the players do their pushups and sit-ups, and then start your team offense by reviewing everything that you've already installed. Then work in the new stuff. As you did yesterday, start putting a few players out there to act as a defense.

It is extremely important that you practice against a defensive secondary when you throw the ball. When you're getting the timing of the routes down you can run against air, but you have to do most of your practice work in the manner you're going to play it, and you're going to find very few football teams that don't put defensive backs in the game.

What tends to happen if you don't practice with a secondary is that the quarterback gets used to throwing to a single receiver without checking coverage. He'll glance and throw whether the receiver is covered or not. Heck, he'll usually glance and throw whether the receiver is *standing* or not. Quarterbacks also have a nasty habit of always throwing to the deepest man in the pattern, whether he's covered or not.

Practice Against a Defense!

Let's put some thought into this. Everyone that has ever coached football on the defensive side of things has told their defensive backs and linebackers to stay as deep as necessary to cover the deepest man in their zone. So, where are the most likely coverage mistakes going to be against a well-coached and disciplined team? Will they be in the deep defensive backfield, with players that have the sole job of covering the deep ball, or will it be the linebackers who are concerned about stopping the run as well?

I'll give you a hint: it's probably not the deep man. The exception to this is if you can force the defensive back to make a mistake, such as getting him to bite on play action. Once again, though, you're basing your success on your opposite numbers coaching their players incorrectly. I don't like those odds.

You have three segments to work on your passing game. Make the most of them by keeping a quick rotation; don't wait for your receivers to get back to the line of scrimmage to run the next rep, just put their backups in and snap the ball again. Also, use the same quarterback technique that I described earlier: have your backup stand at the location he'll be throwing the ball from and throw to the number two read while the starter throws to number one. Then rotate him in and reverse the assignments.

You should be able to get 15-25 reps of the passes you installed, if you keep to a quick enough pace, plus some reps at the running game. As always, keep moving, and remember to mark each successful rep off on the checklist.

Day Five, Segments 17: Defensive Drill Period

The drills you're going to be doing are all quick-repetition basic drills that hone specific skills necessary for the defensive players. Defensive backs are going to work on the first part of bump and run pass coverage with Defensive Backs <u>Drill A</u>: Punch and Go. Defensive linemen need to concentrate on getting off the ball as soon as the center lifts it from the ground. They'll work on that with Defensive Lineman <u>Drill A</u>: Get offs. Linebackers need to work on defeating isolation blocks and staying home to watch for counters, for that they'll use Linebacker <u>Drill A</u>: Crunch Time.

You've only got five minutes for this period, so you're not going to be able to do more than explain the drills, demonstrate them, and get a few quick reps. That's fine. Remember, we build a foundation of constant daily practice. Next week you'll be able to simply run the drills with little explanation, and gradually you'll start to get more and more proficient at them.

Day Five, Segments 18-19: Defensive Install Period

It's time after this to get into some more of the blitzing. While the linemen and linebackers are working on that, have the defensive backs work on <u>Drill C</u>: Man-To-Man Coverage. Whenever you blitz you'll probably be using man-to-man, so you need to make sure the players are well coached at that, before you start playing around with any zone coverage you might have in the playbook.

Day Five, Segments 20-21: Defensive Team

Once again put together a scout team and run some opposing plays at the defense as soon as the players finish their pushups and sit-ups. This is typically the day that I'll start calling scout team plays based on down and distance. You need to reinforce to the players that football games are composed of situations, and the most common situation is simply the down and distance.

Usually I assign a linebacker to call the defensive front and any stunts or blitzes, and the free safety is assigned to call the down and distance and the coverage. This needs to happen on every play, and you can install it earlier if you like and the players are keeping up.

You want to try to keep to a three play per minute pace throughout your scout team period, so you should be able to get in thirty plays in two segments. Make sure that you rotate your backups into the practice as often as possible; they need the reps, too.

Day 5, Segments 22-23: Special Teams

Today is the first time you're going to walk through a return, so be prepared for a few false starts and missteps. Fortunately, kickoff returns are generally a little easier to install than punt returns, because you don't have to worry about teaching methods of scraping through punt protection or kick blocking techniques.

I run one kickoff return. Some coaches have all kinds of returns; reverses, starbursts, traps, wedges, etc. The reality, though, is that most youth players can't kick far enough to set up most of the more complicated returns, and some of the ones that can, *won't* because their coaches will be competent and will teach them to squib the kick rather than do you the enormous favor of setting up your return for you.

Second, there are more important things for you to be worrying about. If you have comparable talent to your opponents and a halfway decent blocking scheme, any of your running backs can break a long return. *Covering* a kickoff, on the other hand, takes a lot more work and effort. Put your emphasis there, and go easy with a simple return.

When teaching kickoff returns the quickest thing I've discovered to do is to take the starters on the return team and put them into my kickoff return formation. They walk through the return against air once, maybe twice. Then the backups take up positions as a kickoff team and jog down the field. This gives the return team a person to block.

Freeze!

I teach a hit, stick, and freeze method to troubleshoot my kickoff return blocking. The fastest and easiest way to check your blocking is to have the players blocking and being blocked stop moving as soon as they make contact with one another. The blocker should be at the correct angle, proper location on the field, and making contact in the right blocking surface. Anyone touching an opponent from behind or below the waist earns the return team fifteen pushups. I call this "sticky" blocking.

You need to run at least five reps of this at a jog for both your starters and your backups. You should note by now that I treat special teams no differently than my offense or defense, and I keep a depth chart for *everything*. If Billy gets hurt on game day, I don't want to be searching the sidelines for someone that can throw a moving block on the kickoff return; I want to know immediately that Johnny can do it.

Two segments, ten minutes, should be plenty of time to get five reps a piece at the kickoff return, and then it's time to move on to today's Chalk Talk.

Day Five, Segment 24: Chalk Talk-Grades

Gather the players and have them crank out their pushups and sit-ups. Today's chalk talk is about the importance of grades. I don't screw around with grades. Typically schools require a 1.7 grade point average in order to participate in extracurricular activities. That's a high D+/low C-. Frankly, I don't think that is acceptable.

In my world, football players are the leaders. My goal is for everyone in the school to look to the football players and say to themselves, "I want to be like *them*."

This means that the football players have to be the type of persons that put in the extra time. They work hard for grades, they help out underclassmen, and they aid their teachers. I don't tolerate the idea that a student-athlete is an athlete first and a student second. About the only thing that makes me angrier than that is hearing that my players are thugs in school.

I require complete honestly from my players. If a player fails a test, or is having problems getting their homework in on time, I want to hear it from them, not from their parents or their teachers. If it's a matter of not understanding the material, I'll do whatever I can to help out. Sometimes this means that I stay after practice to help them out with their homework, or come in early before hand. I'll also talk to the teacher about getting some form of extra instruction for the player.

Extra-Credit

I said extra *instruction*, not extra-credit. Extra-credit is what kids ask for when they haven't met the requirements for a course and, suddenly, it's grades time and they're failing. I don't want that. What I want is something that will help the player get the material down well enough to pull his grades up on his own.

If the player is just being lazy, then there's going to be a different form of remedial instruction. At Tomales High School, it's called "Penalty Hill" because it is the hill on which we work off our game-day penalties. One yard of penalties in a game is worth one trip up and down the 14-yard, 65-degree slope.

I tend to get really ornery when players don't listen to me; poor grades are fifteen minutes after practice every day on the hill until the teachers give me a grade report showing one full grade of improvement.

Raising The Bar

It has been my experience, in everything that I have ever done with young people, that the lower you drop the bar, the less effort they put into reaching it. The higher you hoist the bar, the higher they'll jump to get to it. For this reason, my absolute minimum grade requirement is a 2.3, or C+. I feel this is an attainable goal for the players to reach for.

During today's chalk talk, I discuss with the players the importance of grades and personal responsibility. I also point out that grades have a definite reflection in playing time and starting positions. If I have two players of approximately equal talent and skill, and one is getting a 3.7 GPA and the other a 2.5, I'm more likely to start the one with the higher GPA.

Exactly how you monitor and use the grades is up to you and to your organization. The most significant point I can make about them is simply this: our job as coaches is to make young people better than they start out and to push them to their full potential. Every player has the ability to reach a 4.0 if they work hard enough. It's simply a matter of deciding which is more important: play time or study time.

Day Five, Post-Practice Meeting

Don't forget to have the quarterbacks, centers, and long snappers stay with you to get their fifty snaps. You should be in the habit now of getting your coaches together and going over what needs more work and where your team sits at the moment. You've got one week in the bag, and you should now be comfortable with the practice organization and installation procedure.

That's good, because you're going to follow almost the exact same schedule every day for the next week as well. By this time next week you should have the entire offense and defense in place, be completely comfortable with your special teams operation, and be looking forward to the scrimmage or jamboree where you're going to unveil your highly trained and physically fit players.

The Week in Review

In the past week you've installed about seven offensive plays and probably three to five defensive stunts, coverages, and formations. You've put together three different special teams, and begun a speed training series that will drastically improve your program on both sides of the ball. You've also started a conditioning program that is going to make your players lean and mean; still playing hard in the fourth quarter of the first game when their opponents are going to be gasping for breath because they were conditioned with traditional, inefficient methods instead of using a football-oriented program.

If you stop reading this book right now, you should still be better prepared than almost all of your opponents—except the ones that read the whole thing.

One thing that I've noticed is how much the players love this schedule. With no time to stand around they're never bored, and so they don't screw off, which means that the coaches aren't screaming in frustration at them all the time. When I think back to every poor practice I've ever had, on both sides of the whistle, it's been because the players were uninterested and goofing around instead of concentrating on the task at hand, and the coaches got more and more exasperated until they burst into a screeching frenzy.

Nobody wants to be a part of that, on either side.

Over the Weekend

Take the weekend and think about your depth chart and any changes you might need to make to your system. The first practice day is going to be a review day, and then after that you're going to be back to installing new plays.

By now you should also have a pretty good idea what plays you're going to be depending on throughout the season. By this I mean that you've got enough of the playbook installed to see how your offense matches up to the players, and you can start thinking about things like getting the football to certain players in certain situations. If it's fourth and one, for example, I want to know which of the four backs in my backfield have the surest short yardage ability. If my 4-Wing has a nasty habit of dropping like a prom dress any time a defender comes near him, I don't think I want him carrying the football in such a crucial situation.

On the other hand, if my fullback is strong like ox, but also moves like ox, smells like ox, and thinks like ox, then putting the ball in his hands during a fourth and thirteen situation might be a poor choice, unless his ox-like stench can make the linebackers miss when their eyes start to water.

The Games in My Head

I actually play games out in my head. I try to think my way through varying game day situations and, using the playbook we have installed at any given moment, how would I call the plays to get out of that situation and get the first down.

Try to be realistic about this. It's normal to fantasize about the linebackers being completely suckered on the sweep action and totally missing the trap to the other side of the field, but it doesn't help you plan for the worst-case scenario.

Day Six, Segments 1-6: Fundamentals Period

Today's foundation period is much like day five's. Start out with the pushups and sit-ups, and your speed work should be exactly the same. You'll change the drills slightly tomorrow. The main difference in this period is that instead of doing <u>Tackling Drill B</u>: Head on Tackling, the shift is towards more angled tackling with <u>Drill E</u>: Angled Pad Drill. Likewise, we need to make a shift from pushing the defender away when we're blocking, to running through him and knocking him flat. For this, <u>Blocking Drill C</u>: "Splatter" is the preferred choice.

Day Six, Segment 7: Offensive Drill Period

As soon as you finish the blocking and tackling period, break the players up into their offensive groups and send them with their coaches. The head coach should be working with the offensive linemen today. I almost always start out the week with the big boys.

For my offense, which features a lot of pulling that requires the offensive linemen to get through the hole and block downfield, I put a lot of emphasis into offensive line <u>Drill A</u>: "Search and Destroy." You may choose a different drill, but the object here is to reinforce specific skills that your offensive linemen need to play the position. If you're a passing coach, try working some time at <u>Drill C</u>: Pass Blocking instead.

For the receivers, run <u>Receivers Drill A</u>. Remember, the goal is to get to 500 passes by the first game, so get those players out there on the pass routes and throw until your arm comes off.

I also make sure to spend some more time with the running backs and quarterbacks on their <u>Offensive Backfield Drill A</u>.

Day Six, Segment 8-13: Offensive Installation Period

This description is kind of a misnomer. Although it's labeled an installation period, you're really going to be working on reviewing the plays you installed last week. I recommend putting in only one new play on this day, and in my system it's a passing play, which means that the running backs and offensive line don't have much new to learn.

You have four full segments to review the entire offense up to this point, and two segments to install the new play. In the past I've actually never needed more than one segment to install the new play, and I've been able to put five segments into review. You should be able to get between twelve and thirteen reps of each play you have installed before you break up for team time.

Day Six, Segments 14-16: Offensive Team Period

Although today is a review day, it's time to start working live against a full defense. Place a full defense on the field if you can, in defensive fronts common to your league. You need to have each position coach individually responsible for making sure that his players swap in and out, and you need to run plays like madmen. You need to hit four plays a minute, *minimum*. Ideally you'll be somewhere around five plays a minute.

After the first segment, this is the day I typically begin to introduce situation football to the players. There are a number of different situations that will crop up on game day, and the better prepared your players are for them, the more likely you are to overcome them.

Situation Football

A few of these situations are:

1) No score, ball at midfield

2) No score, ball inside opponent's twenty

3) No score, ball inside your twenty

4) No score, ball inside opponent's ten

5) No score, ball inside your ten

6) Your team ahead by more than a touchdown, early in the game

7) Your team behind by more than a touchdown, early in the game

8) Your team ahead by more than a touchdown, late in the game

9) Your team behind by more than a touchdown, late in the game

10) Your team ahead by less than a touchdown, early in the game

11) Your team behind by less than a touchdown, late in the game

The significant things to remember are the time remaining in the game, the ball position on the field, and the score. There's a certain logic that you need to follow almost all of the time when you're in games. For example, any time you are behind in the game you should be trying to get the lead as soon as possible, since statistically the team in the lead at any given time has an 86% average chance of winning the game. (This increases the later you get in the game.) Special thanks to Jack Reed for his outstanding book on clock management in which he analyzed over 600 games.

Breaking the Rules

Now, what if you're facing a ridiculously superior opponent? We've all had a few of those. You have two main choices once you start to fall behind; you can start to pass more, which may help you catch up in a hurry, and is the logical thing to do, or you can try to run the clock by keeping the football on the ground as much as possible, thereby keeping your opponent's offense off the field and shortening the game and the accompanying ass-kicking.

Regardless how you decide to execute a specific game-day plan, you need to touch on some of the situations. In 2003 my Tomales Braves faced a physically superior team in the St. Helena Saints that put us down 19-0 by halftime. Fortunately, though, we had been practicing situation football all week long, and the players were able to flawlessly execute our "burn" offense to come from behind and score the winning touchdown with 0:23 on the clock. That 20-19 comeback victory is by far the most thrilling I've ever been involved with.

The Most Important Situations

Of all the situations we practice, there are four main ones I concentrate on teaching the players:

1) Goal line offense

2) Panic offense

3) Hurry Up

4) Slowdown

Everything else listed above is really extra gravy. Ahead by a touchdown or more is a "slowdown" situation, and behind by the same amounts is a "hurry up." Inside the tens is either a panic or goal line situation, depending on which side of the field we're on. If the players have a general idea of *what* you want them to do, and a vague idea of *why*, then they don't really need the exact details to be able to execute. You can tell your running backs to stay in bounds in a slowdown situation "to keep the clock moving," and let it go at that. Now it's up to you to determine precisely when that slowdown is needed.

Hidden Benefits of High Speed Practice

Here's where the real beauty of this practice system comes into play. Since you practice everything at full speed, your kids should already be used to sprinting to the line and getting the play off as fast as possible. Without even knowing it, you've been teaching a hurry-up this entire time!

To slow down your offense, all you really need to do is call your plays slower. I start a timer on the sideline when the referee blows the ready-to-play whistle that tells me we have twenty-five seconds to get the play off before we get called for delay of game. I'll let ten or fifteen seconds run off the clock before I signal in the play or send in a runner, and by the time the players get to the line and snap the ball, we're usually down to three to five seconds.

You can really work some precision into it by yelling a countdown from the sideline. I've done that several times when we've needed to kill clock late in the game. Simply start the timer at the ready to play whistle and count down vocally from twenty-five, telling your quarterback to start their cadence with four seconds left. Typically, this results in the ball being snapped on two or one.

I usually don't worry too much about this unless we're in a very close game against a team with an offense capable of scoring quickly on us.

On the Practice Field

Today I won't get too hot and heavy into the situations. Remember, this is a review day. I just move the ball to a yard line and say, "goal line offense." Then we'll work on a few of the tricks of playing on the goal line, such as getting an extra push to get into the end zone, and heading for the pylons on sweeps. We'll also make sure the players know that once we're inside the five, this is going to be "four down" territory. We *will* score. We *must* score.

After one segment of goal line offense we'll switch and start in with panic offense. Remember that the goal of a panic offense is to get enough room to punt without getting it blocked. This is where I'll also go over the mechanics of taking an intentional safety. If we're having a hard time dealing with punt blocking pressure, there are times when it makes good sense to take a knee in the end zone and kick the ball away from the twenty rather than give up a cheap touchdown.

Day Six, Segment 17: Defensive Drill Period

As soon as you're done with the team offensive period, break up your players into their defensive responsibilities and have them do their pushups and sit-ups.

Today you'll spend some time working footwork for the defensive backs with Drill A: The "W" drill. Linebackers should continue to work on Drill A. Defensive linemen should work on Drill B: Defeating trap blocks. Trapping is a key factor in successful misdirection plays, so it's vital that you give them a goodly number of reps at defeating the trap block and taking on the blocker. It also helps to teach the defensive linemen to "get in the hip" of a puller and follow him to the ball carrier.

Day Six, Segment 18-19: Defensive Installation

Bring the linebackers and linemen together when the drill period ends. The defensive backs should work with their coach on Drill C. By now you should see the players making some adjustments on their own to determine whether they are going to bump their assigned man or give him a cushion in coverage. I generally leave it up to the individual player to make the call. If they have the speed to cover the man downfield they can risk a bump a lot more often than if they're on the slow side. You should find that most of your players are pretty honest with themselves and with you about this.

My first season at Tomales I called the pass coverages from the sideline, and I would call the bump as part of the man-to-man assignment. Unfortunately, my addiction to the bump and run philosophy put us in some poor situations when we were out-talented on the perimeter. Fortunately, I had some smart kids that season, and we talked about it in practice. I decided after that conversation to let the players make the call, and our pass coverage improved dramatically.

This should be one of the last days that you actually need to install your defensive stunts. Today is primarily a review day, but I'll throw in a minor wrinkle, usually something that doesn't change assignments for more than two players. You should be nearing the end of your list of stunts, so after tomorrow, it's nothing but blitz package review and scout team offense time.

If your defense is more complex than most you can still work in a few more stunts, but you really shouldn't need the time. In five practice days your stunt package should be almost perfect.

Day Six, Segments 20-21: Team Defense

After your players get together for team defensive time and have done their pushups and sit-ups, it's time for some more work with the scout team. Throughout the preseason I hit a few offensive systems fairly hard, because they are either systems that are difficult to stop, or because they are common systems that we're likely to see a lot of, or both.

Today, for example, I put together as complete an I-formation offense as I can, with a passing scheme and ground attack that takes into account as much of my scout team personnel as possible. For example, if I have a good running back that doesn't play defense, I know I can use him on the scout team in the tailback position, which is where an opposing coach would probably put him. This gives my defense a good look at the entire offensive scheme.

You have two segments to run the scout team offense against your defense. In that period of time you should be able to get between twenty and forty plays run against your defense, depending on how long it takes you in the huddle. You're probably looking at closer to twenty, since this is your first time, but you should always be trying to move faster, while still getting quality repetitions.

The first segment I usually use as a basic scout team period, but I try to divide the second segment into goal line and pressure defenses. Pressure, by the way, is the good side of a panic situation, when you're trying to keep your opponents bottled up inside their five-yard line. You're not going to get a lot of time in at this, but it gives the kids an idea of what they're trying to do. You'll get more time at this later on in the season.

Day Six, Segments 22-23: Punt Return

Today's special team is the punt return. I practice two basic forms of punt defense: a block and a return that is structurally very similar to my kickoff return. In fact, my block unit is my goal line defense, so I'm not really teaching that much that is new.

There are two main things you need to teach your block team. The first is to stay off the kicker, and the second is how to block a kick properly. You need to practice these things, and you cannot expect your kids to execute them properly without reps.

Teaching the Block Technique

Place a towel or scrimmage vest on the ground about two yards in front of where the kicker is going to be standing, and on the same side as the kicker's dominant foot. Take a Nerf™ football and stand as the kicker. Then tell your blocking team to charge you, one by one, starting from the leftmost player to the rightmost.

Each player needs to approach at an angle that crosses the marker in front of you, without touching you. As they approach they should shoot their hands out with their thumbs together and moving from low to high. This should result in taking the football "right off your foot." Kick the ball into their hands and yell, "Scoop and score!" They should roll to their feet, sprint to the ball, and either fall on it or scoop it for a runback.

Although this sounds like an individual drill, if you're running the special teams program I use, you're actually practicing the entire block team in individual parts. It should take you less than one segment to get each player on your starting and secondary block teams at least one rep.

The Return

The return is a little more problematical. As I said above, my punt return is very similar to my kickoff return. For both of them the goal is to create a tunnel down the middle of the field for the return man to travel.

You need to realize that the long, high kicks of the NFL, or even high school football, scene are probably not going to happen on your game fields. I put a lot of effort into designing a great wall return that worked wonders at the JV level—the only time my punt returner fielded the ball. Every other time it was punted to us, the opposing kicker was either so excited, or specifically coached, that he kicked the ball out of bounds or so far away from the returner that there was little, if any, return.

AAARGH!

I still advocate using a return. Blocking punts is a difficult task, largely because the punters are usually the more talented players on the opposing team. When pressured, they're more likely to tuck the ball down and take off, and sometimes they'll break a play for a first down or a touchdown. Believe me, there is nothing that makes me want to bite through my hat faster than watching a punter slip contain and get a first down on a 4th and 11.

On the other hand, these players also usually kick the ball away when we don't put them under pressure. Since our ultimate goal is to get possession of the ball, wherever it lands on the field, sometimes playing the return game is a smart thing to do.

The Punt Return Walk Through

Similar to the kickoff return, I line a scout punt team up and walk through a common punt formation. It's extremely important that you coach your players to watch for fake punts, and each player needs to have a specific defensive assignment as well as a returning assignment.

I don't put a lot of effort into teaching fake punt defense on this day, however. Remember, we used one complete segment teaching the punt block. All I want to do today is teach the basic return assignments. As with kickoff return, I place cones on the field in the locations my return team is supposed to drop back to after they see the kick is away, and then we jog through the return once or twice per group with me kicking the ball. (I kick about as well as a youth punter.)

Use the same hit, stick, and freeze method that you used with the kickoff return to make sure that your players are covering their blocking assignments properly. Remember also that open field blocking is not a matter of laying a big hit on someone; it's about control and getting in the way of the coverage man.

Day Six, Segment 24: Chalk Talk-Nutrition

Today's chalk talk deals with a subject that is largely beyond the scope of this book: nutrition. Youth football players need to keep themselves properly fueled and hydrated in order to play at their peak level.

I strongly recommend that you limit the amount of straight Gatorade™ that your players consume. Although the commercials would have you believe otherwise, water has nearly as many electrolytes as Gatorade, and is actually more effective at re-hydrating the body. The complex carbohydrates in the sugar of most sport drinks require water to break down in the tissues. Most college and pro teams offer Gatorade on their sidelines, but dilute it with water to a half and half mixture. It goes without saying that soda has no place on a football sideline. I used to drink Mountain Dew™ like it was going out of style, but the only thing I ever drink on a sideline is water.

The most ideal nutritional balance for a football player is not the huge steak and protein mixture you might think. In fact, protein should only be about twenty percent of the total dietary intake. Carbohydrates in both simple and complex forms should be about seventy percent, and fats should be ten percent. Eliminate supplements, and tell your players to get their nutrition from foods, not multivitamin pills.

I'm not going to offer any further advice about nutrition because I am not a nutritionist or a doctor. I encourage you to do some further research on your own before putting the final touches on this chalk talk.

Sources of Information

I highly recommend two great books on nutrition to help you out. In fact, these books are so good that my 2004 American Military University class in Nutrition used them. They are *Nutrition for Serious Athletes* by Dan Benardot, Ph. D, RD. (ISBN: 0-88011-833-4) and *Training Nutrition* by Edmund R. Burke, Ph. D. and Jacqueline R. Berning, Ph. D., RD. (ISBN: 1-884125-22-0).

Day Six, Post-Practice Meeting

As usual, have the players taking snaps while you hold your post practice meeting. Since today was mostly a review day there shouldn't be many surprises. Make whatever notes you need to adjust your depth chart, and get ready to do this all again tomorrow.

Tomorrow you're going to get hot and heavy into installing new plays. If you're using my offensive system you're looking at the left handed versions of some of the plays your players are already familiar with, and this is going to present you with a choice to make.

Some coaches flop their offensive line when they want to run a left-handed version of a play. Typically this is at the lower levels of youth football, and it cuts down on training time considerably.

I've never liked that idea very much. Personally, I prefer to teach right and left-handed versions of most of my offense. I don't like tipping the defense off that we're running to the other side by moving my linemen, and I don't like hinting to the linemen we moved away from the point of attack that they are somehow not good enough to run the play to their side.

Hugh Wyatt, producer of the *Dynamics of the Double Wing* series of videotapes advocates having the players teach their opposite numbers the responsibilities. I think this is a pretty good idea. My offense is put together specifically to keep assignments as simple as possible, so I've never needed to use that tactic, but it's a good one.

Day Seven, Segments 1-6: Foundation Period

Bring the players together and get them doing their pushups and sit-ups. Today you're going to add a new exercise to the speed drills. You've been doing double frog hops for a few days now, and it's time to work in triple hops.

When you finish the speed training, break the players into their groups for tackling and blocking, and use the same drills that you used yesterday. You'll probably note that we don't add very many new drills to this period. Every new drill you add has to be taught, and you only have two minutes to rep each drill before the players rotate.

Day Seven, Segment 7: Offensive Drill Period

Are you starting to notice a rhythm to the practice plans? After the foundation period is completed, break the players up into their offensive position groups and get them working on their drill period. Receivers should be running <u>Drill A</u>, in as many variations your receiver coach wants to run. Backs should run their <u>Drill A</u>, and be honing their handoff and reception skills, and linemen should be focusing on driving their opponents off the ball with their <u>Drill B</u>. The head coach should be working with the running backs today.

I'm going to put in a little flexibility here. If you're repping the plays as much as you ought to be, and if you've been running the Backfield <u>Drill A</u> as much as I've recommended, your players are probably getting very, very good at handoffs. If you were able to get through your offensive period yesterday without fumbling, then I would take your backfield over with the receivers and run drills with them for today's period. You have to work in some time for the running backs to work on catching the ball. Since they are probably your top athletes you need to find ways to get the football into their hands, preferably in the open field. One of the better ways to do that is by throwing it to them.

Oh stop it. I never said passing wasn't effective, I said it wasn't *easy* and takes work.

Quarterbacks

Part of that work is the drill that the quarterbacks are going to be doing while the running backs work with the receivers. This drill is not in the drills section of this book because it only applies to your system if you use a roll/sprint out passing game. If you run some form of waggle or rollout, then you should focus some practice time on this drill from week to week.

Put your quarterbacks about fifteen yards apart and have them run down the field from goal line to goal line at a pace that is slightly less than a sprint, slightly more than a jog. Typically, I pace just behind them to keep them at about the right speed.

They should have a football, and they need to throw it back and forth between them while remaining fifteen yards from one another. This teaches them to throw on the run. When they reach the far goal line, have them turn around in place and run back, throwing from the opposite shoulder.

Don't overcoach throwing on the run. I usually keep my mouth shut during this period, other than to tell them to speed up or slow down. They need to train the myriad reflexes they'll use to deliver a well-thrown football while running away from the pass rush. Later on in the season we can increase the speed to something a little closer to a sprint, but remember to keep this reasonable—it's 200 yards, after all.

Day Seven, Segments 8-13: Offensive Installation Period

After the drill period ends, break the players back off into their groups and have them do their pushups and sit-ups. Today you're back to installing plays. Fortunately, if you've put your offense together and organized it properly, there probably aren't any completely new plays to install. Your players already have a working knowledge of today's stuff, because they learned the right-handed versions last week.

Today you have three segments for review, and three segments for installation of new plays. I've never really needed more than ten minutes to install these new plays, so you should have ample time to review your entire offense and get the new stuff in before the installation period ends.

Day Seven, Segments 14-16: Team Offense

At the end of the installation period, bring the players together for team offense and have them do their pushups and sit-ups. Make sure that you and your assistants are still checking their stances. By now I usually randomly call whether I want them to pop up to a three-point stance or a hit position.

As usual, you need to concentrate on speed. Make sure that you're still marking off the team reps of each play as you go. I can't stress enough how important this is. I refuse to call a play on game day until it has been repped at least fifty times in practice. The only way to know when a play is ready is to track it. Be anal-retentive. Trust me, it's necessary.

Think about this as well: you should be able to wrap up everything else in your offensive installation over the next two days. Day ten should be nothing more than a review day in which you work on fine-tuning every little detail of the offense until your players can run it in their sleep. From then until your first game, it's nothing more than tweaking things here and there to refine them.

Day Seven, Segment 17: Defensive Drill Period

We'll have the players sprint to their respective position coaches and do their pushups and sit-ups before we start our drill period. For today, the drills are, defensive backs: Drill B, linebackers: Drill A, and defensive linemen, Drill C: Pass Rushing. The only new drill is for the defensive line. You have one segment for drills, but you're going to pick up some extra time for the defensive linemen during the next period.

Day Seven, Segment 18-19: Defensive Installation Period

By this day I typically have the entire stunt package installed, and the players have been drilled incessantly on their responsibilities in the basic fronts. It's now time to start working on one of the more complex parts of defensive football: zone pass coverage.

You won't need the defensive linemen for this period, so I would have them stay with their coach and continue to run Drill C for the first segment and then switch to Drill B for Segment 19.

Why Run Zone Coverages?

I am not a big fan of zone coverage at the youth level, but it does have its uses from time to time, especially when you avoid standard landmark zones and give your opponents a slightly different look. A typical landmark cover three, in the words of Rex Ryan, son of the late Buddy Ryan (creator of the 46-defense that won the 1985 Chicago Bears a Superbowl), is "useful only against the deep ball." Since that's the *least* likely threat at the youth level, thanks to the relative weakness of the quarterback's arm, I tend to avoid cover three most of the time.

The number one reason you need some form of zone coverage, in my opinion, is to combat the triple option, especially a veer-style attack that uses the outside receivers to run off your defensive backs. Whatever you do is going to be wrong: if the defensive back stays in coverage the opposing coach calls a run or option keep and the ball goes downfield. If the defensive back comes up to play the run, the coach calls a pass to the receiver left alone downfield.

Some form of basic zone is usually necessary to face these defenses. I don't like it, but it's one of the facts of life.

You have two segments today to get your players used to dealing with the new form of pass coverage. Like almost everything we do, this is just a basic walkthrough to get them familiar with their responsibilities, so don't go berserk.

Day Seven, Segments 20-21: Team Defense

Bring the players together as a team and have them do their exercises. Today we need to work on another common offense you're probably going to face: the Wing-T.

The Wing-T has a long a varied history. It's the one offensive system out there that rivals the I-formation in flexibility and common usage. In fact, I would venture to guess that if you, dear reader, played football, you probably played in either an I-formation or Wing-T offense when you were a player.

You're probably going to run into this system at some point. Do some research into the system and create a short playlist of common plays from the basic 100 and 900 formations. Almost all youth-level Wing-T teams run some form of the 20 series and the 30 series, which are, respectively, the buck sweep and the power. You may also find Wing-T teams out there that run an option-based system as well.

Once again, divide this period into a basic period and a pressure/goal line period with one segment for each. This helps focus your kids on situation football.

Day Seven, Segments 22-23: Special Teams Period

After the defensive period ends, gather the players together and have them do their pushups and sit-ups. Today's special teams walk-through is the field goal.

I always start by kicking from the three-yard line, where point-after-touchdown tries are attempted. There are two schools of thought about the extra point. Some leagues offer one point for a run, and two points for a pass or a kick. Others offer two points for a run or pass and one for a kick. You have to take that into account when making a decision about how you're going to try for the point after.

At Tomales, we have a tradition of always going for two points. There are some drawbacks to that, though. Kicking PATs is a good way to practice your field goal unit in a live fire condition. It helps your kicker stay calm if he's kicked fifteen or twenty extra point attempts in previous games before lining up to try the game winning field goal with eight seconds left in the game against your biggest rivals. Also, going for two points when you're up by a lot is kind of tasteless.

On the other side of that coin, though, is the knowledge that, in an offensive battle, being able to hold your opponents to seven points while you get eight can be the difference in the game. You also need to develop a confidence in your players that they can score at will, and the best way to do that is to get *more* points after you've already scored a touchdown.

Weighing the Odds

I tend to take all these factors into account and call my PAT attempts based on each of them. If my kicker is decent and we can get the blocking against this team, we'll probably go for the kick. If we can get into the end zone with ease on a run or pass, we'll go for that.

Regardless, though, if you don't practice it, you can't call it. Some coaches may find that they would rather put their practice time and effort into working on their running attack or honing their passing game, since those plays are multi-use and can be used anywhere on the field. That's up to you. If you decide not to put in a field goal unit, then I would strongly recommend that you use all the special teams time earmarked for field goal to work on your punt team instead.

Like everything else we do, we practice field goals at high speed. I send my two punt/kickoff return men to positions behind the goal posts, where they need to catch every kick in the air. I also require them to fair catch every other kick. They have to spread out a bit to be able to cover the ball. I require them to catch every ball that they touch.

Everyone else is either on the kicking team or the blocking team. Field goal is one of those special teams plays that must be practiced live, and you have to make sure that the players know that the ball is treated like a punt once it crosses the line of scrimmage.

Without getting too in-depth, the important thing about the offensive line and wingbacks is that they block inside gap first, and then make themselves big to the outside by bumping any defenders at the shoulder to knock them off their path.

Practicing the Field Goal

The holder needs to catch the ball in his hands and place it as close to center on the tee as is possible. At the younger levels, and with straight ahead kickers, you might find it easier for your kicker to get necessary height on the ball by having the holder tilt it slightly towards the kicker.

I usually have six footballs at practice. We put all six of them on the three-yard line in front of the snapper. We'll do six PAT attempts and then back up five yards and move to the hash mark where we'll kick three more. Then we'll move to the other hash mark and back another five yards for another three kicks. In ten minutes you can generally get twenty to thirty kick attempts. I recommend that you try to end on a successful one if you can. Sometimes, if I have an extra moment (there's a rare occurrence!) I'll move the spot closer to the goal line if we are missing kicks to give my kicker a better chance to end on a successful kick.

Canard!

One important safety tip for you: face the kicker at all times. In 2002 I was working with the Tomales varsity team for the playoffs and placed myself downfield from the kick about twelve yards so the returners could throw the balls to me. I had just caught a ball and turned to toss it to the snapper when the latest kick attempt missed my head by about eighteen inches. Had I been normal-sized, it would have taken my head off. Now, I stand twelve yards downfield and outside the hash marks, so if a kicker hits me, he's going to be doing a *lot* of up-downs.

Day Seven, Segment 24: Chalk Talk-Supplements and Steroids

Today's chalk talk is a short one. I usually bring up the subject of weight lifting with my players on this day, and part of that is a discussion of supplements and steroids.

I have been lifting weights since I was about thirteen years old as a wrestler at Sumner Junior High in Washington State. In that time, I've taken only a protein supplement.

In 2004 I took a look at my diet during a Training and Conditioning class at the American Military University. It occurred to me that my diet already had more protein in it than I could assimilate in a 24-hour period. The protein supplement I had been taking was nothing more than an extra 140 calories that my system had to burn off instead of attacking the fat storage I wanted to get rid of.

I'm going to direct you towards a book here that has nothing to do with football. The title is *Don't Get Duped*, by Doctor Larry Forness. (ISBN: 1573929220) You'd be surprised at the amount of money Americans waste on fitness supplements that they don't need.

Steroids are not necessarily bad things. Under the supervision of a doctor, for example, steroids are commonly used to treat breathing problems, allergies, and muscle damage from surgery or injury. The main problem with steroids, like with most drugs, is in how and why they're used.

I'm not going to stand on a soapbox here and tell you what you should tell your players about steroid and supplement use. I will tell you that you should pass to them this phrase, "Be informed."

Day Seven, Post-Practice Meeting

You should be in the habit now of getting your snappers extra practice during this meeting and by now they should be able to do so with a minimum of supervision. If your quarterbacks are the leaders they should be, then you probably won't have much to do at all, other than reminding them that they need to slow their cadence down and not fall into a rote repetition of your snap count.

Tonight's meeting should focus on the fact that you should have roughly three plays left to install in your offense. You and your staff should be thinking about how your players are doing so far. Is anyone lagging behind? Is anyone really causing problems?

Also, how are the *plays* doing? Are there any plays that stand out as ones the players can run extraordinarily well? Are there any plays that the players keep screwing up? What's been going wrong? What about your defense? Were there any significant problems with the concepts of the zone coverage you installed today? Are your linebackers stunting through their gaps properly and securing before pursuit? After today, your defensive practice should be little more than a few skills drills and practice reps against common offenses until you begin to use the scouting reports to practice specifically against your opponents' systems.

Like the Hitchhiker's Guide Says: "Don't Panic!"

In two days you'll install the final offensive play of your base offense, and from then until the first game you'll do nothing but rep them over and over, while perhaps adding a formation or two as a wrinkle to keep defenses honest. Don't worry too much about problems with some of the plays. Remember that, if your preseason is typical, you'll have another ten practice days to do nothing but hone the offense. That's as much practice time as you took to install it, just to practice and refine. Even some pretty significant problems can be worked out with ten days of practice time.

Day Eight, Segments 1-6: Foundation Period

Here we are again starting out another practice with the foundation period. Make sure that the players are doing their pushups and sit-ups. Continue with the same exercises you've been doing the last two days on your speed work, and in your tackling circuit. For the blocking circuit, go back to Blocking <u>Drill B</u> for one of the drills, to reinforce that proper blocking involves driving the defender back out of the hole with correct footwork.

Younger players tend to forget the necessity to keep the feet moving, and overusing <u>Drill C</u> can cause them to concentrate more on the big hit than on continuing to maintain a push against an opponent. I try to bounce back and forth between <u>C</u> and <u>B</u> to work on both aspects of proper blocking form.

Day Eight, Segment 7: Offensive Drill Period

We've done this before. Have the players do their pushups and sit-ups and then get them together in their position groups. During today's offensive drill period you need to take stock once again of the performance of your running backs and quarterbacks. If you had any problems at all with fumbling yesterday, then do <u>Drill A</u>. If, however, they're doing okay, then you can instead spend the time as you did yesterday, giving the running backs a chance to work on their hands and the quarterbacks a chance to practice throwing on the run.

The offensive line should work on <u>Drill C</u> to hone their pass blocking technique. You've probably noticed by now that there are three main drills for each position, and that we practice them over and over again, changing things up just enough to hold off the ennui, but not wasting a bunch of time teaching and re-teaching drills that are designed to do the same things. If you have favorite drills or drills that are more specific to your offense that you would like to work into this period, by all means do so.

Day Eight, Segments 8-13: Offensive Installation Period

After the drills, you need to get one or two more plays installed. Of the four segments scheduled for this period, you should need only one to install your new plays. The remaining fifteen minutes is there to get speed reps for review of the rest of your offense.

Once again, this all comes down to good organization. If your offensive system is properly put together, you should find that all of your remaining plays are somewhat familiar to your players, because they have seen their mirror images. At this point it's a matter of turning your players vague conceptualizing into a reality.

Day Eight, Segments 14-16: Team Offense

Have the players do their pushups and sit-ups when you get together for team work. At this point, you'll probably notice that it's getting a little more difficult to get all your plays repped. Even at a high pace, running the plays during the team period can be frustrating.

Usually it's at this point in the season that I get tempted to rob Peter to pay Paul. I'll start asking myself if we *really* need all that defensive time if the defense has been installed already. Is it *really* crucial that we get the field goal block unit installed today? Couldn't we put that off until later on and rep the plays some more?

Stand fast. You have time before the first game. Remember that this entire schedule is designed to be a gradual progression. You have one more installation day, and then it's nothing but reps, reps, and more reps until game day. If you take away from your special teams now, you're going to have to put it back later on, when you're frantically trying to hone your offense for game day.

As per usual, I typically run at least one segment of goal line offense and one segment of panic offense. It's important to remember this and put a little effort into it each day.

Day Eight, Segment 17: Defensive Drill Period

After you finish the offensive team period, break the players up into their defensive positions and have them do their pushups and sit-ups. Yesterday you taught the team basic zone defense fundamentals, so today you should have the defensive backs run <u>Drill D</u>: Zone Coverage. Linebackers should be getting extremely familiar with their drill, <u>Drill A</u>, and the defensive linemen should run <u>Drill A</u> to get some more time in perfecting their explosion off the ball. By today the defensive linemen should definitely be running <u>Variation 1</u> of the drill.

Day Eight, Segments 18-19: Defensive Installation Period

Depending on the complexity of your defensive system, you may be able to use today's installation period as a seven-on-seven pass defense period. If this is the case, have your defensive linemen do drills B and C from their section for one segment each while you work with the defensive backs and linebackers.

Seven-on-seven is an excellent way to hone pass coverage skills. In short form, it's a game of football pitting the linebackers and defensive secondary against the quarterback, center, running backs, and receivers. I use blocking shields to represent the rest of the offensive line, and I use this period as a chance to cheat on my center/quarterback snaps by putting a center in to snap the ball to my quarterback. Using cards to show the scout team offense the plays your opponents will use, you can focus specifically on your pass coverages.

Each card should be marked with the down and distance in which the opposing team typically uses the play. This gets your defensive players thinking about game situations, and learning how much they can flex to keep any completions underneath them.

Seven-on-seven is also a great time to work on teaching your quarterback to read pass coverages and find the open spots in zone coverage. I think much of the reason why my 2003 Tomales quarterback, Joey Moreda, became such a great passer was the near-daily work he did with the varsity as a sophomore. His scout team and seven-on-seven training really helped him learn "pocket poise" and skill in delivering the ball.

Day Eight, Segments 20-21: Defensive Team Period

After the seven-on-seven period ends, have the players come together as a team and do their pushups and sit-ups. Today's scout team is an offense you should be fairly familiar with if you're running my program: the Double Wing.

The history of the Double Wing as an offensive formation goes back to the early days of football and Pop Warner's system. The modern, flexible version of the offense was originally developed by Don Markham in the early seventies, and perfected throughout the eighties and nineties. Coaches such as Hugh Wyatt and Jerry Vallotton have honed the system, and developed a very effective power running game that is supplemented by misdirection and precision passing.

You can't face the Double Wing expecting it to be like other offenses. While I certainly don't have the secret to stopping the system, I can tell you right now that Double Wing coaches are a special breed of cat. We like to hit people in the mouth. We love power. After power, the only thing we love more is a misdirection play that fools the cameraman, the referees, half the spectators, the entire defense, our own sideline, and at least two thirds of our staff.

Double Wing coaches think in terms of four downs, everywhere on the field, and we generally throw the football only when we've decided to score. The only way to really stop a Double Wing team is to hope they stop themselves with an ill-timed fumble, interception, or penalty. Most of the time, because Double Wingers tend to think in terms of three yards per play, you need to put them into a fourth and five or more before they really think seriously about punting the football. Again, I'd divide this period into a mini section of pressure and goal line situations so that the players can work on learning game situations.

Day Eight, Segments 22-23: Special Teams Period

Today's special team is a team you've already installed without realizing it. I use the exact same block for punt that I use for field goal. Essentially, I line up in my Gap-8 defense that I use for goal line situations, and we hit every gap in an attempt to split the line and put pressure in the backfield.

I strongly recommend that you put more effort into teaching proper blocking form than anything else. Offensive line blocking at the youth level is so poor, and kickers are generally so erratic, that you shouldn't have a problem getting the penetration that you need to block the kick.

On the other hand, you need to make certain that your blocking unit doesn't touch the kicker or the holder unless they get a hand on the football. I teach the field goal block the same way I teach the punt block; with a bunch of Nerf™ footballs. The only thing that's different is that I have one of the players take a knee as a holder and make a fake catch and placement before I kick the ball.

Again, shoot for speed, trying to get everyone on the block team through at least two blocks from the correct angles before you end the period.

Day Eight, Segment 24: Chalk Talk-Drugs and Alcohol

After the special teams period is over, gather the players and have them do their final pushups and sit-ups for the day. After you check their stances, have them take a knee for today's chalk talk: drugs and alcohol.

By the way, it really bugs me that coaches even have to bring this up at all.

Drugs are prevalent in society. While the evidence, if you speak to some people, is inconclusive that certain drugs are "gateway" drugs that lead to more and harder drug use, the bottom line is that drugs are an insidious form of self-destruction. Typically, drug users exhibit signs of low self-esteem and lack of ambition. Since the whole purpose to youth football is to increase the players' self-confidence and teach them character, integrity, and devotion to a goal, drugs are anathema to everything we're trying to do.

Ecstasy

There are three main drugs I try to make my players aware of. These are "ecstasy," alcohol, and marijuana. These are the cheapest, most easily accessible drugs for young people. Because of their near legitimacy, these drugs are also slowly gaining popularity as "recreational" drugs. For the last decade, for example, there has been a widely held belief that ecstasy holds no dangers. It has become popular over the last decade as a "club drug" that is often used at raves and underground parties as well as on the streets.

Using ecstasy brings about a heightened sense of feeling, pleasure and euphoria, but it affects the user in a number of different ways and can cause depression, confusion, paranoia and anxiety. These effects can take place while a person is using the drug or even weeks after use.

Many people have negative physical reactions to ecstasy. These may include an increase in heart rate, muscle and jaw tension, nausea, fatigue and excessive sweating. Habitual users of ecstasy or people who have adverse affects to the drug can also be in danger of long term brain damage to the part of the brain responsible for critical thinking and memory. People who use ecstasy are at high risk for permanent brain damage. Long-term effects can also include liver damage and a tendency towards problems such as Parkinson's disease and paralysis later in life.

Alcohol

Alcohol is also an insidious drug. My own bloodline has a history of alcoholism, and it claimed my stepfather as well. Alcoholics generally don't even really understand the effect their drinking has on them, and even their families see alcoholic behaviors as somehow "normal." For example, it was perfectly normal for my stepfather to need to go out to the car and take a nap during the high school production of *The Hobbit* in which I played Gollum.

Alcohol causes inevitable destruction of the liver as well as a physical and emotional addiction. It impairs judgment, and in at least one study has been called the most significant date rape drug ever produced.

Marijuana

Marijuana is the most commonly used illicit drug available in the United States. In the short term, its effects can include problems with memory and learning; distorted perception; difficulty in thinking and problem solving; loss of coordination; and increased heart rate. In fact, some studies have shown that the user's risk of heart attack more than *quadruples* in the first ninety minutes after smoking marijuana.

Because marijuana users hold the smoke in their lungs longer than tobacco smokers, they place themselves at a higher risk of absorbing carcinogens present in the smoke. Marijuana smoke has been proven to have between 50% and 70% more carcinogenic hydrocarbons than tobacco smoke. (http://www.nida.nih.gov/Infofax/marijuana.html)

Marijuana has also been proven to have severely deleterious effects on learning by affecting blood flow to certain sections of the brain.

None of these drugs are safe. Some of them are tolerated to a greater or lesser degree in our society. The bottom line, however, is that the only way to avoid the ill effects associated with the drugs, is to avoid using the drugs. Keep your players safe by educating them.

At the end of the chalk talk, have the players do their team yell and end practice.

Day Eight, Post-Practice Meeting

While your long snappers, centers, and quarterbacks get their snaps in, have another quick meeting. Tomorrow you will install your very last play, so you should get a quick baseline idea of where everyone is sitting in their comprehension and execution.

Your installed plays should be starting to look pretty sharp by now, and if you followed my advice on selecting a fully interlocking and series-based offense, you should already have most of the groundwork done for the play you're going to install tomorrow. Day ten is going to be nothing but review, but tomorrow is going to be pretty light on the installs because you've only got the one new play. This means that tomorrow is essentially an extra review day as well.

Day Nine, Segments 1-6: Foundation Period

By now everything we're doing should be a routine, and the players should be getting faster, stronger, and more proficient every day. Start with the pushups and sit-ups, and the speed work, using the same drills we've been using for the past three days. Tomorrow you'll tweak one of the speed drills to "load" it for next week's practice.

For the tackling and blocking period, I recommend that you stick with tackling drills <u>A</u>, <u>B</u>, <u>C</u>, and <u>D</u>, and for the blocking I recommend that you go back to drills <u>A</u> and <u>B</u>. Footwork and finishing is still the most important part of the blocking instruction.

Day Nine, Segment 7: Offensive Drill Period

After you have the players do their pushups and sit-ups, today I recommend that you work a little on protecting the football. Instead of handoffs, which you should have down fairly well by now, I advise you to place your focus on maintaining a secure grip on the football after you receive it. Running backs <u>Drill B</u>: The Gauntlet is a great drill for working on those skills. Offensive linemen should focus their time on <u>Drill D</u>: Down Blocking.

Receivers, of course, should run <u>Drill A</u> again. By now you should really be noticing a positive impact on their receiving skills from catching ten to fifteen passes every day. Imagine how good they're going to be in a couple more weeks when you get them into a game.

Day Nine, Segments 8-13: Offensive Installation Period

Maybe this should be titled "Offensive installation, *period*." After today, the only plays you'll be adding are ones to expand your offense and keep your players from getting bored.

As usual, you have six segments to work individually before you work on team offense against a defense. You should devote five of those segments to reviewing the previously installed offense before you add your final play.

In my system, every individual element of the last play has already been learned. The line already knows their responsibility, the backs are already well versed in their assignments, and the receivers are trained to perform their jobs. The only thing remaining is to put everything together. Installing the final play has never taken me more than fifty seconds, so you should have ample time to get everything reviewed.

That's it. You're *done* with the offensive installation! Can you believe that your entire program is in? Two weeks ago your players didn't even know how to take proper stances, and now you have a complete offense, defense, and special teams program installed. After this, it's just working on perfection.

Day Nine, Segments 14-16: Team Offense

Part of that perfection is getting the players together as a group as much as possible. Have the players do their pushups and sit-ups and then get them going against a scout defense. By now running the plays at high speed should be second nature to you and to your players, but let me stress again that you have only three segments—fifteen minutes—to run twenty offensive plays at least five times a piece. You're probably not going to be able to get each play as many reps as you'd like, but don't worry about it. Because you're tracking the reps on your handy checklist, you can tell which plays you need more work on for tomorrow, and you can plan your review periods accordingly.

Day Nine, Segment 17: Defensive Drill Period

For today's defensive drill period we need to give the defensive backs some more practice at playing zone defense. Zone is tough because the backs are looking into the offensive backfield and watching the fakes as they occur. It takes a lot of discipline to stay in a zone when you've seen ten or twelve running plays in a row, and here comes a thirteenth play that looks just like the last ones.

For this reason, the backs need some more work at <u>Drill D</u>. Linebackers should keep on running <u>Drill A</u>, and the defensive line should put some more time in on <u>Drill B</u> to work on defeating trap blocks.

Day Nine, Segment 18-19: Defensive Installation Period

You're probably wondering why this section is still labeled "Installation" if we finished installing the entire defense three days ago. The reason is that not everyone who reads this book is going to run my defensive system and be able to get everything installed in the first six days like I do. For those folks, we're keeping the labeling the same, but for you and I we'll change things around a bit.

If you need to work on defensive installation, go ahead and do it. Otherwise, take segment 18 and work on seven-on-seven while the defensive line does <u>Drill C</u> to work on pass rushing.

By the way, you might have noticed that we're not working on <u>Drill A</u> with the defensive linemen very much any more. The main reason for this is the incorporation of the elements of get offs into each other defensive line drills we do. There's no reason to practice defensive explosion by itself unless you need to concentrate on that because you've noticed your line being beaten off the ball by the offense consistently.

If you don't need it for installation, use segment 19 as the start of your team defensive period, and work on getting more reps against the scout offense. It can only help in the long run to get more reps.

Day Nine, Segment 20-21: Defensive Team Period

Today you need to show your defense another common offensive system that is commonly used at the youth level. This offense is the split back formation sometimes called a "pro" formation. Some coaches call it the "Veer" formation, because the Houston Veer developed by Bill Yeoman used this formation much of the time.

There's a horribly accurate key that drives me ballistic when I've encountered it on the game field. There are coaches out there whose offenses are so poorly put together that they line up in an I-formation to run between the guards, and in a split back formation to run outside, whether it is off tackle or around end. I've encountered it on several occasions, and it drives me nuts to be able to nail my opponent's tendencies that easily. That's just poor coaching.

The Effectiveness of the Split Backs

For coaches that are well-prepared, the split back is a much more versatile formation than it first seems. For one thing, as I mentioned above, the Veer is commonly run from this sort of formation, and the simplicity of the triple option attack from this set makes it ideal for the youth coach willing to put in the time to coach it properly. Second, the most feared play in youth football, especially at the younger levels, is the sweep. With two backs stationed wide behind the guards (or even wider on occasion) the formation is perfectly suited for the pitch sweep to the team's best athlete. Some similar principles to the Delaware Wing-T can also be applied to the running game, such as the power and buck sweep series. The Packer Sweep was run from this formation most of the time.

Lastly, the formation is perfect for the passing game, since it places both backs in prime position to pick up the edge rushers and assist in the pass protection or run short routes while the quarterback stands in the pocket.

On the other side of that coin, defending this basic system is no more complex than defending an I-formation team. By using the backs to block on the edge, the offense sacrifices much of the play action game, so your defensive backs and linebackers can commit to their receivers or zones without much worry once they read pass.

In all, the split backs formation gives the offense a number of advantages when competently coached, and puts them at a number of disadvantages if the coaches are *not* competent. If your opponents know what they're doing, they can be very effective from this set. Again, the more reps you give the defense at facing this style of offense, the better they'll be able to defend it on game day.

Day Nine, Segments 22-23: Special Teams Period- Kickoff and Kickoff Return

Today you're going to work on two special teams for the first time this season. You have one segment to devote to each, and if you move at full speed you shouldn't have any problems. Both of the special teams you're going to be practicing have been installed before, so this should be easy for you.

In segment 22, work on your kickoff, concentrating on getting both your first and second team kickoff coverage units onto the practice field for at least two reps apiece. It should take you less than thirty seconds per rep, so you should have plenty of time. In segment 23, run your kickoff return, trying to keep to the same pace.

It goes without saying that you should practice this live if you have enough players. In fact, you'll probably find that your starting kickoff and return teams are composed of the same players, which means you should be able to run your second team kickoff return against your starting kickoff team, then swap and run the starters on the return while the backups kick off to them.

For now, since you have approximately two more weeks before game day, I would concentrate on maintaining the "sticky" block I talked about during the installation. Right now we need to reinforce the blocking and concentrate on correct angles and approaches. While we should go full speed, for at least the first few reps I'd tell the kicking team to stop the moment a return team player makes contact with them. This allows you to see the blocking and make sure that it's set up properly.

Day Nine, Segment 24: Chalk Talk

Today's chalk talk is about heroes. After the players do their pushups and sit-ups, I have them take a knee so I can talk to them a little bit about the people we call hero. In today's society, we have a problem with title inflation. It's virtually impossible to watch a professional sports game of any stripe and not hear some athlete referred to as a hero.

Frankly, that burns my ass. Heroes run into burning buildings. Heroes lay in muddy or sandy foxholes in far off countries to defend our freedom to sit at home in comparative luxury and coach a sport.

Heroes risk their lives for the safety or security of other people. Professional athletes do not.

I make a consistent effort not to use the word hero to describe any athlete, and certainly not the individuals in the ranks of professional sports. In a time when steroid scandals rock baseball, brawls tarnish basketball, and celebratory antics disfigure the face of football, it's important that kids understand whom they should and should not look up to.

Who is *Your* Hero, Coach?

I talk to my players about my heroes. Probably the most important hero I've ever had to look up to was my grandfather. He served two tours in Viet Nam and was wounded on each tour, once so severely that the lead from the shrapnel could not be removed from his back. I remember it used to bleed through his skin and discolor his shirts. Jumpmaster qualified, he finished his last two training jumps in 1988—two years *after* a heart attack destroyed all but 28% of his heart. He had a goal, and he went after it.

My grandfather grew up dirt-poor in Wisconsin, and joined the Army to take care of his family, ending his career as the first official CW05 in Army history. Unfortunately, he was on life support at the time, dead of a massive heart attack during surgery. I was fifteen when he died.

Barry Bonds thinks he's a hero because he's hit a few baseballs over a fence. Randy Moss would love for you to think of him as a hero because he's caught a few thrown passes. Shaquil O'Neal wants you to buy into the heroism he's displayed by dunking a few basketballs.

None of them have gone to war to defend your freedoms. None of them have run into a burning building to save a child. None of them have worked twenty-hour days to put themselves through college while taking care of a baby.

I hope you keep that in mind when you're coaching the next generation of potential heroes.

Day Nine, Post-Practice Meeting

After the chalk talk is over, have your snappers get their reps while you talk with your coaching staff about tomorrow's practice. From this point on, almost everything we're going to do is going to be a review of things we've already done. We may add a new play here and there, or try a slightly different blocking scheme, or adjust our defensive stunts, but for the most part, the entire framework is in place.

I would bet that if you got a call from the league tonight and they told you they were going to move the first game to this weekend, you'd be better prepared than your opponents. While not perfect, you'd probably still do very well.

Right now, you need to find out where your weakest points are. What plays are giving you the biggest problems? What kinds of problems are they? Timing problems are easy to fix with more reps of that play. Blocking problems are a little more difficult. If the players are having problems remembering their blocking assignments on certain plays, you might have to simplify things, or put more time in bird dog drills.

This meeting is going to determine the next few days of practice emphasis, so you should make some pretty careful notes.

Day Ten, Segments 1-6: Foundation Period

After the players do their first pushups and sit-ups, you're going to make one small but crucial change to the speed training for today. To continue our growth of type II, "fast twitch" muscle fibers, we're going to also add in reverse frog hops.

This exercise is excruciating, so I strongly recommend that you don't go down and back with it. Twenty yards of reverse hops, on top of everything else, should be sufficient.

Make sure that you and your staff members are all paying close attention to the players' form during these exercises. We're entering a part of the season when coaches tend to start sloughing off on the tiny details because they're starting to get nervous about the "big picture." This is highly important, so make sure you put the effort into it.

Your blocking and tackling drills aren't going to change. Next week we'll get into some new drills as we prepare for the scrimmage. For right now, let the players become proficient in the drills they already know.

Day Ten, Segment 7: Offensive Drill Period

Today you should either have your running backs work with the receivers on catching the ball, or you should have them run the gauntlet again, using yesterday's Drill B. Receivers should keep running Drill A, and don't worry, next week they'll have a new drill. Offensive linemen should work on Drill A and focus on getting downfield and into their blocks.

Day Ten, Segments 8-16: Offensive Installation Period/Team Offense

You have a brief install period just in case you have a play or two that you had to put off installing for some reason. You should have everything in, though, and this section is here for you to get some quick individual review before coming together as a team for six segments.

For the most part, this is the way you'll run your offensive practices from now on. There'll be a brief drills period, followed by some individual review time and installation time for any new plays you want to run, and then most of the period will be taken up with team offense against a live scout defense. After you finish your individual review, bring the players together for team work. Have them do their pushups and sit-ups, and then run your plays against a defense.

I tend to put most of the time in today's period into bird-dogging the offense. It's vital that you make sure all blocking assignments and running paths are instinctive. For the next week of practice you're going to be trying to get as many reps as possible, and it's crucial that your players are practicing the right thing. Trust me on this; you do *not* want to spend your time trying to undo something that you practiced incorrectly.

Day Ten, Segment 17-19: Defensive Drill/Installation Period

Break the players up into their defensive groups and have them do their pushups and sit-ups. Then have the defensive backs do Drill C, the linebackers do Drill A, and the defensive linemen do Drill C.

Just like yesterday, if you're finished with your defensive installation, use segment 18 for seven-on-seven with the defensive backs and linebackers while the linemen work on Drill C to hone their pass rush. Take segment 19 straight into the defensive team period and start working on getting your defensive reps.

Day Ten, Segment 20-21: Defensive Team Period

Today's scout team offense is a system from the birth of football that has been given new life, especially at the youth levels, thanks to books by Jack Reed and Doctor John Aldrich and the dedication of a small group of devoted coaches: the Single Wing.

In the early 1900s Glenn "Pop" Warner developed an offensive system that began with power, and slowly evolved into a misdirection attack. Using a shotgun snap, this offensive system used the quarterback as a blocking back, and fired the ball from the center directly to the running back who could carry it on a running play, hand off or pitch on a misdirection play, or pass on a passing play.

The modern Single Wing is as flexible as the Wing-T, as powerful as the Double Wing, and as effective as any other offense out there. Although some ignorant coaches may claim its effective day is over, the fact remains that there are still many teams around the country that are running this system with great results. (In fact, next to the Double Wing and the Veer, the Single Wing is my next choice for offense.)

With almost a century of experimentation and adaptation, the Single Wing system has hundreds of permutations and series. It can be fairly difficult to create a simple version of the system for your scout team. My recommendation is to get your hands on a copy of Jack Reed's book, *Coaching Youth Football, 3rd ed.* (ISBN: 0-939224-45-3). Coach Reed's offense is very simply laid out, and contains the basic framework of a Single Wing offense that can be used as a scout team version until you scout any opponents you might have that run the system and can prepare for their specific plays. (Most true Single Wing devotees, however, feel that Jack Reed's offense is too simple for any but the lowest levels of youth football.)

Day Ten, Segment 22-23: Special Teams

After you finish the scout team period, gather the team for special teams. Have the players do their pushups and sit-ups, and then it's time to go through your punt and punt return again. This is also the same day that we install the punt fakes. It really doesn't take that long, and you only need a couple of jog-throughs before you get to the real meat and potatoes of the period.

If possible, follow the same procedure you used yesterday; have the starting punt team kick to the second string return team before trading sides. If that's not possible, you're going to have to pick up the pace a bit.

Don't forget about your fake punt. I don't call a fake very often. Usually if it's close enough to go for it, there's a play in the playbook that will probably work better. On the other hand, it can be a game breaker, and can force the defense into covering something that they're not used to seeing.

I usually shoot for three or four reps of the basic punt, and one to two reps of the fake before we swap and work on the return/block. I don't practice the block nearly as much as the return, because the return takes more careful timing, and the block is our standard goal line defense, just like on field goal, so we're already getting plenty of practice at that. Typically, I run the punt return a few times and then have the players align in the punt block and rush, one at a time, to block a kick off my foot, just like we did on Day six. This should only take a few seconds to get everyone at least one rep.

By the way, I still recommend that you have your coverage team freeze as soon as a member of the return team touches them. This really makes it easy to see if everyone is blocking the right person.

Day 10, Segment 24: Chalk Talk- 'Atta-Boys

After you finish the special teams period, have the players sprint to you and do their pushups and sit-ups. Today's chalk talk isn't about anything earth shattering, but it's still important.

I like to take the final day of the installation period to tell the players how proud I am of them. Sometimes this gets left out, and it really shouldn't. By now, kids that have never been on a football field before have learned the basic fundamentals of football. They're faster. They're getting stronger. They can run an entire offense and defense, recognize some common offensive systems and the most common plays run from them, execute two returns, two blocks and two kicking units on special teams. They know how important teamwork and leadership is. They know to focus on their grades. They know how dangerous drugs can be, and what a waste of time and money nutritional supplements usually are.

They've come a long, *long* way from where they started the season. By now, if things are going at all well, you should have a team gathered around you, instead of the group of individuals you had ten days ago.

The players need to know that you appreciate their hard work and effort. Next week is going to be a countdown to the first live-fire test of your system, the intensity of practice is going to be much greater, and the players should know that *you* know that they can handle it.

The Best Man...

This is also the best time to talk about substitutions. Young people aren't stupid, and they know who the best athletes are. It's perfectly normal, especially as you move up in levels, for the backups or even the inexperienced starters to be nervous to a greater or lesser degree. While a part of them can't wait to get in the game, another part is terrified that they'll drop the pass or miss the block and let down their teammates.

I always try to take this chalk talk and make sure the team knows that we, as coaches, pick a player for a position and situation because we feel he's the best man for the job. If we put Billy in at running back on 4th and three, it's because we feel he's got the best chance to get us the three yards we need for the first down.

A big part of teamwork is learning to trust your teammates. This chalk talk is hopefully going to help instill that trust in your players. Obviously, it's going to take more than your say-so, but talking about it briefly can't hurt.

Day Ten, Post-Practice Meeting

As usual, have anyone that snaps or receives a snap stay after practice during the coaches meeting. Today's meeting is going to be one of the most important of the preseason. When you come back on Monday to start your third week, you're no longer going to be teaching general football theory. You'll need to be focused on the specific things your opponents are going to do against you. You'll have to put together a scouting report, and you'll have to plan how you're going to teach your players to execute against the systems your opponents use.

Scouting for a scrimmage is difficult. I generally don't worry very much about it, because my systems are designed with specific rules on offense and defense that simplify things immeasurably for the players. Since the scrimmage isn't technically a part of the season, I'm more concerned with how we apply those rules than I am with how many times we score or are scored on.

Obviously I want to do well. I believe very strongly in scouting our opponents. Since we can't scout in the preseason, we'll have to come up with something else. If you can, get your hands on game tapes from last season. I wouldn't put too much effort into breaking them down, because there could have been a lot of changes to your opponents' programs. What you're looking for is simply a rough idea on what systems you're likely to face.

The best place to get this information is from your game tape of last year's scrimmage, which will typically have the same teams you're going to face this season. It will also give you an idea of how well prepared your opponents are going to be. Some teams are great starting out the gate, and some are still putting things together in the third week of the regular season.

Sorry About This... Please Bend Over

Today you're also going to have to screw over one member of your coaching staff. Next week you're going to have a scrimmage, and the odds are that your first opponents are also going to be scrimmaging somewhere. One of your coaches absolutely *must* be at that scrimmage. If your league allows you to scout with a video camera he needs to tape the game and bring it back for you. If not, then you need to teach him how to scout properly and send him to get intelligence on your first opponent.

Unfortunately, what this means is that one of your coaches is not going to be at *your* scrimmage. It sucks, especially for the coaches with sons on your team, but scouting is imperative. I recommend that you establish a rotation so that no one is stuck with all the scouting duties. As the head coach, you *have* to be at your team's games, and so do the individuals responsible for calling offensive plays and defensive schemes. Everyone else is superfluous. You can have a parent track substitutions and keep stats for you, but you typically cannot ask a parent to scout for you.

Honestly, I try to settle this issue long before the season begins, during my staff meetings over the summer. This coaches' meeting is more of a reminder than anything else. It's still an important topic, however, and if at this point you have not found someone to scout, then you need to do something we in the military call "select and direct."

It's got to be done. This is where the fun of coaching runs headlong into the responsibility to do it right.

Scrimmage Week

Most youth football programs are given a preseason in which they can practice five days a week for two hours a day. This preseason period typically lasts for two weeks, which is what we've planned for. These leagues usually then give an additional week of at least four practices, with a scrimmage on Friday or Saturday.

This next section of the practice plan is going to be devoted to preparing specifically for the game-like conditions of the scrimmage. I'm going to plan out five complete practices for you, but you might have to compress your timelines if you're given fewer days.

Day Eleven, Segments 1-6: Foundation Period

Some things are never going to change, and the foundation period is one of them. We have added all the speed-training exercises we need to add, and from now on we're going to be much more concerned with technique than we have been up to now. Gather your players and have them do their pushups and sit-ups before you do your speed work. Your coaches need to scrutinize every detail of each exercise of the speed training.

When the speed work is done, have the players split up into their groups for tackling and blocking. Today is the first time you will not be doing the slow motion tackling Drill A. By now your players should be highly proficient at tackling correctly in drill circumstances, and it's time to increase the game-like conditions in preparation for the scrimmage.

For that reason, I recommend Drill H: Lane Tackling. This is an advanced tackling drill that hones open field instincts. For today, I recommend that you dispense with the shield and have the tacklers break down to a good hit position at the proper tackling angle to the ball carrier. *Do not* allow contact in this drill without the pad. If this drill goes well, tomorrow we'll try adding the shield and allowing the tacklers to make contact and drive the ball carrier as long as they do not tackle to the ground.

Day Eleven, Segment 7: Offensive Drill Period

Have the players break up into their offensive groups and go with their coaches. Since this is the first day of the week, you should be working with the offensive linemen. As soon as they do their pushups and sit-ups, have the running backs work on Drill B. The offensive line should work on their pass blocking with Drill C, and the receivers will finally get a new drill, Drill B: Concentration.

Anyone that has seen footage of the 2004 Seattle Seahawks on offense will understand the frustration of seeing receivers drop passes. This typically happens because the receiver loses concentration on the football for whatever reason. He might be unused to making an adjustment to a badly thrown football, or he might be nervous about his first pass, or he might be thinking about the linebacker bearing down on him. No matter the reason, he's got to maintain concentration on the football and tuck it away securely.

He should already be very familiar with the mechanics of making a proper catch while running a pass route, and if your arm is as bad as mine is, he's had plenty of opportunity to catch poorly thrown footballs. Now we need to focus on securing the football in traffic.

Day Eleven, Segment 8-14: Offensive Period

After the drill period ends, move to running the plays with each individual group. You have three segments for this, so work on honing each player's assignments. Focus on proper stance and footwork, and on blocking the right man from the right angle.

For the backs, the biggest problem I have at this time of the season is the freelancing. You might need to crack down and make some noise if your running backs insist on bouncing outside on the off tackle, or dancing around instead of hitting the hole square. This might even have to go as far as demoting a running back that has been consistently ignoring your attempts to steer him in the right direction (i.e. shouting). They need to make an effort to focus on taking no more than one jab step and then hitting the hole as square to the line of scrimmage as possible.

Because my offense is based around the power running game, receivers might be getting a little bored. The new drill should help with that, but you really have to crack down on them to focus on the little things. Receivers like Jerry Rice and Steve Largent didn't become great only because they caught passes, but because they weren't afraid to block for their teammates. Most of the time your longest runs from scrimmage are going to come about because a receiver threw a block downfield. This is a fact no matter the offense you happen to be running.

Team Offense

At the end of segment 10, bring the players together for team offense and have them do their pushups and sit-ups. You now have four segments, twenty minutes, to focus on running the plays as a team. You really need to focus your time on running against the scout versions of the likely defenses you're going to be facing. If nothing else, work on facing an even front (4-4, 6-2), an odd front (5-3, 3-5), and a covered front (7-Diamond) interchangeably.

The final segment of the offensive period should be devoted to goal line offense. Where before we ran goal line and panic on the same day for about a half segment each, today we're going to focus solely on the goal line. Bear in mind that if you choose to go for a two-point conversion and your league requires that you run a play for the attempt, then you need to be able to get three yards with one play. You have to practice that at least once per week.

Day Eleven, Segments 15-21: Defensive Period

After the goal line offense, bring the players together as a defensive group and have them do their calisthenics. After they finish that, do defensive <u>Drill A</u>: Pursuit Angles. You need to do this drill at least once per week from now on. Some coaches even do this drill every day. Whether or not you start doing that is going to be determined by your team's ability to play in the scrimmage this weekend. If the players are taking correct pursuit angles and trapping the ball against the sideline properly without leaving cutback lanes then you can keep running this drill only once per week.

On the other hand, if they're trailing the ball carrier or attacking the near shoulder instead of the upfield shoulder and hip, you're going to have to up the number of reps you get at this drill.

When you've finished with the drill, break the players up into their defensive groups and send them with their coaches. After they do their calisthenics, have the defensive backs do <u>Drill A</u>. The defensive linemen have a new drill today to work on a skill they'll need to learn: <u>Drill D</u>: Splitting Double Teams. The linebackers also finally get a new drill today: <u>Drill B</u>: Attacking Sweeps. The sweep is the most feared play in youth football, and up until now we really haven't given it a great deal of thought, choosing instead to focus on the off-tackle. Don't worry, because Team Defense <u>Drill A</u> has been preparing your players for stopping the sweep, and your linebackers won't need a whole lot of work to get proficient at their new drill.

Blitz Period

At the end of segment 16, have the linebackers and defensive linemen work together on gap control during the blitz period. It's always a good idea to grab your scout team cards and put a few of the backup linemen and linebackers on the offensive side of the ball as a skeleton. When I do this, I generally do what's called a "half-line." If I have four backups to use, I'll put one at guard, one at tackle, one at fullback, and one at tailback. Then you can run your opponent's plays towards the side of the line with the real players, and use dummies or shields to represent the other side of the line.

This works very well for teaching the back side of the defense to stay home and slow play for counter/cutback. The first few times you run plays you're going to see them leaping towards the side of the offense with the live bodies, and if you jump on them right then, you'll be able to correct that before it becomes a bad habit that can open the door for some long gains.

Seven-on-Seven Period

While the linebackers and linemen are working on that, have the defensive backs run <u>Drill D</u> with their coach to work on their zone coverage techniques. At the end of the blitz period, break off the defensive linemen with their coach and have everyone do pushups and sit-ups before the linebackers and defensive backs get together to run a seven-on-seven period.

Use your scouting information from the scrimmage tapes or whatever intelligence you have, or you can simply grab some passing plays out of the offenses you taught in the preseason. While the linebackers and defensive backs are engaged in seven-on-seven, the defensive linemen should be focusing on <u>Drill C</u>, using those same offensive plays.

Team Defense

For segments 19 and 20, bring the players back together and have them do their pushups and sit-ups before you run scout team offense for them. Again, either use the information you have available on your scrimmage opponents' likely programs, or simply use a random selection of plays from the cards you made up last week. Make sure that you're still using the occasional trick play such as the reverse, fake reverse, and double reverse, and the halfback pass. Your players need to be comfortable defending those plays from a variety of offensive sets and defensive stunts.

Keeping Track

Another thing I recommend when it comes to teaching your defense to stop scout team plays is to make a plus or minus sign on the back of the card each time you run it in practice. If the defense stops the play for a minimal gain or a loss, mark the card with a plus. If the play works for more than three to five yards at a time against your team, then mark a minus. Gradually you'll begin to develop a sense of what plays your team has trouble with, and you can work them into your scout team effort more often.

In segment 21 shift to a goal line period and do the same thing. At this point, remember the logical play calls for an offense that is within the ten-yard line and trying to score in four downs. By this I mean that most of your opponents' tendencies are going to be for dive and off tackle plays, with the occasional sweep or pass. You will most likely find very few youth coaches that will empty their backfield and throw a pass in that situation, although the NFL influence seems to be insidiously seeping down to the high school level, and I suppose it's only a matter of time.

For now, though, concentrate your efforts on stopping dives, off tackles, the occasional sweep, and the rare pass. Remember that unless your opponent watches too much TV or has an incredible field goal unit, odds are you're going to have to play defense for four downs instead of three.

Day Eleven, Segments 22-23: Special Teams Period

After you finish the goal line defense period, it's time to shift gears to special teams. You've probably noticed that we're still not really putting a lot of emphasis on this third part of the game yet. The reason for this is that very few scrimmages have any form of special teams period. The closest I've seen was a field goal competition at the high school level. Right now, we need to understand the importance of special teams without taking away from our offense or defense to prepare a part of the team that we're still not going to be using until next week.

I can also promise you this: most youth football coaches don't even think about special teams until the week of their first game. You've been practicing yours since week one. You already have an advantage over the guys that are going to randomly throw things together.

Segment 22 is for the kickoff team. Try to get between three and five reps of the kickoff against a live kickoff return team. If possible, I'd have my return team do some goofy things like starbursts and reverses, just to give the coverage unit a look at them. To do this, you might have to take a few coaches and put them back there as returners. Try not to use the elderly ones, though.

Segment 23 is for the kickoff return team. Again, try to get between three and five reps of the return, and it's a good idea to spring some surprise onside kicks and squibs on the returners. At this point in the season, now that we've managed to teach the basics properly, it's time to start preparing our team for the tricky stuff they might see.

Day Eleven, Segment 24: Chalk Talk-Goal Cards

Today's chalk talk is going to become a staple of our practice. I stole this unashamedly from Coach Feliciano, my mentor and head coach at Tomales High School. In turn, I think he stole it from De La Salle High School. Wherever it came from, it's a great idea.

The first practice of every week is going to be devoted to goals. Each player is going to be issued a 3X5 index card to take home. On this card they need to write their name and what their goals for the scrimmage are. These goals can be as team or as individual as they like. We do this on the first practice of the week so that the players can work towards their goals every day.

I think you'll find that this will bring your team together a little bit more than would otherwise have happened. When the offensive linemen write things down like, "Each back in the backfield to get 150 yards and one touchdown," you'll know that your players are starting to think less about themselves and more about playing and winning as a team.

The cards need to come back at the next practice. Any player forgetting their card owes me 500 yards of wind sprints, no excuses or exceptions. Goal setting is an important part of what we teach as coaches, and I put a lot of stress on making the players accept some responsibility for remembering these cards.

During tomorrow's chalk talk we'll flip through the cards and read a few of the goals aloud anonymously.

Not Just for Kids Any More

By the way, these goal cards aren't just for the players. As a coach, I, too, have goals for each game. I've been told that there are such things as unwinnable games, but I've never seen one. Maybe if my JV players were facing off against the 2004 San Francisco 49ers the game might be unwinnable for us, but considering the record of the "professionals" that played for the 2004 49ers, possibly not.

My goal cards don't change often. Here's my standard goal card for a game:

1) No more than ten points allowed.

2) Hold opponent to fewer than 150 yards of total offense.

3) Allow zero completed passes.

4) No more than three missed tackles.

5) Score once or more on defense.

6) Block or cause at least one poor scrimmage kick.

7) Return at least one punt or kickoff for touchdown.

8) Never let the opponent outside the thirty-five on a kickoff return.

9) Score thirty points on offense.

10) Gain 300 yards rushing, 120 yards passing.

11) Complete 80% passing. Average seven yards per rushing attempt.

Extra Goals

I figure if we can do all these things, we will win the game. I have other goals, too, that sometimes get added. Sometimes these are more important.

1) Get Jimmy his first touchdown.

2) Let Bobby play the entire fourth quarter.

3) Throw a pass to Billy.

Sometimes the game is already won or lost, but there's a player that's worked extremely hard in practice and deserves a little extra time on the field. I feel that, as a coach, it's my responsibility to give every player a chance to excel on the field, so part of my goals is getting the players into the game to have that chance.

Day Eleven, Post-Practice Meeting

Get your snappers and snap-takers together for another fifty snaps while you have your post-practice meeting. Today's meeting should be focused on the upcoming scrimmage. There's an art to getting each team emotionally ready to play football. I can't tell you when to really start firing up the players, because it's going to change from season to season and even week to week. Ideally, you want the players to reach their emotional peak about ten seconds before the opening kickoff.

Mostly, my goal for this meeting is to remind the coaching staff to put the pressure on ourselves throughout the week. For at least a few players, this is going to be their first-ever football contact outside of practice. The more you can look like a duck on a pond: calm and self-assured, the more the players are going to focus themselves and also remain calm.

Take Acting Lessons If You Have To

It's normal for the players to be nervous. Heck, I usually can't eat either the night before or the day of the first game, and it doesn't get appreciably better as we get into the season. Unfortunately, fear is infective. If you allow the players to think that you're in doubt about the outcome of the game, then they're going to start having doubts as well.

Another thing to go over at the meeting is anything picked up from film study or other intelligence about last season's scrimmage. Who is traditionally the toughest opponents and why? Who are typically the league doormats and why? This is information you can use to focus your efforts on scrimmage day.

Speaking of film, make sure you have a videographer prepared and ready to go by today. Don't be running around at the last second on scrimmage morning trying to find someone willing to climb on top of the press booth to tape for you, and do *not* assign that to your assistant coaches. On game day or scrimmage day they'll have far more important responsibilities to worry about!

You also want to make sure that you have at least one person ready and willing to keep stats for you during the scrimmage. This is going to be highly important when we're breaking down the film, since the planned script you're going to put together in a few days is nothing more than a rough draft.

Day Twelve, Segments 1-6: Foundation Period

Before you do anything else, gather the goal cards from the players. Throughout practice, take a second or two to glance over the cards and make a mental note of some of the best goals to talk about at the end of the practice.

Some of the things I look for are goals like: "Gain 200 yards rushing," from an offensive lineman and, "Get an 'A' on my fakes," from a running back. These are the sorts of things that show that the players are starting to think as a team, and that they are placing the success of the team above their own personal goals.

There's nothing wrong with a running back picking, "Score three touchdowns and get 250 yards rushing." That's his job, just like the offensive line's job is to block for him.

Have the players do their calisthenics before starting their speed work. Make sure the coaches are keeping a careful eye on stance, start and form during the speed training exercises. It's normal to slowly stop noticing the details and things that seem minor because your mind fills in the blanks when you look at the same things over and over every day. This is why sentries on military installations change the guard every two hours or more. It keeps them alert, and prevents their mind from filling the blank spaces for them.

Unfortunately, this speed work is trying to overcome a lifetime of poor running habits with a couple of weeks of exercises. It can be done, but every drill you run in which the players don't use proper form is simply retraining them with the bad habits we were trying to eradicate.

There are no changes to the tackling and blocking periods, except that today you can give the ball carrier a shield during tackling Drill H and allow the tacklers to make contact with him. Do *not* let the tacklers drive him to the ground. They need to wrap up with proper form and drive their legs through the ball carrier, but you should keep a quick whistle to keep the players from going to the ground. Continue to use tackling drills C, D, and E in any variations, and also blocking drills A and B, also in any variations.

Day Twelve, Segment 7: Offensive Drill Period

After you're done with the foundation period, break the players up into their groups for the offensive drill period. During this segment we need to work on continuing to hone specific skills and techniques. We're trying to work slightly different skills every day, as you've probably noticed if you've gotten this far into the chapter. Today's drills are Drill B for the running backs to work on keeping hold of the ball, Drill A for the receivers, who still need to concentrate on running precise routes, and Drill D for the offensive linemen to work on their down blocking.

Day Twelve, Segments 8-14: Offensive Period

There are no significant changes from yesterday to today as far as the offensive period goes. Continue trying to maximize your reps and focusing on the little details of each offensive play. Make sure that you're paying proper attention to footwork and blocking angles.

To start segment 11, gather the players for team offense and have them crank out their pushups and sit-ups. Then, following the same format you used yesterday, rep your plays at high speed against even, odd, and covered fronts.

I recommend that you pull out your handy-dandy little repetition checklist and keep an eye on the plays you have repped. Obviously you need to rep your core and core counter plays every single day, but you're going to find that you had to go a little light on a few of the additional plays yesterday. That's fine, today you can make up for that, and go a little light somewhere else.

For example, if you run a Pro-I as your base offensive set, and you run the standard plays from it, then you need to practice the isolation and the trap every single day, since those are your core play and your counter. After that, perhaps you ran the wingback counter fifteen times yesterday, and only practiced the draw five times. No problem, today you practice the draw fifteen times, and rep the wingback counter three or four.

Keeping It Interesting

I think you'll find that this method of repetition also keeps the players more interested and focused, because things are always changing slightly, just enough to keep them on their toes. That's a good thing, because it means that they are going to be retaining more of the information you're passing to them than their counterparts on the opposing teams that are trained using the traditional, less efficient methods of instruction.

Balance your practice time so you can get everything the maximum number of reps. Once again, I think the value of the anal-retentive philosophy shows through. Most coaches don't keep track of the number of times they call each play in practice, so they end up repping certain plays to death, and a few of the plays they might really need just don't get enough practice time.

Aren't you glad you bought this book?

Panic!

Yesterday we practiced the goal line offense for five minutes. Today, turn the team around and put their backs to the wall. For five minutes today you need to practice the panic offense. Concentrate on high percentage plays that will drive the opposing team back from the ball and give you room to punt. It's probably not a good idea to call draws, sweeps, screens, and passes out of your own end zone. The risk of a sack, fumble, or tackle for loss is too great.

You won't need to practice this often. About once a week is generally enough. I like to do it now and then as a change of pace, but mostly this is a situation that you, as the coach, need to be thinking about.

Day Twelve, Segment 15, Defensive Drill Period

When you've finished putting the panic offense through their paces, it's time to move on to defense. Start out by breaking the team into their defensive groups and getting their calisthenics out of the way. Then have the defensive backs work on Drill B to hone their footwork and break off the ball, the linebackers work on Drill A some more, and the defensive linemen work on Drill B. By now the linemen's reaction to a pulling offensive lineman across from them should be almost instinctive.

Day Twelve, Segments 16-21: Defensive Period

As we did yesterday, group the linebackers and defensive linemen together to work on blitzes and pass rushing. The defensive backs will spend segment 16 working on Drill D to continue improving their zone pass coverage. Segment 17 they'll work on Drill C to sharpen their man-to-man coverage skills.

This gives you ten minutes to run scout team plays at the linebackers and defensive linemen. Remember: high reps and coach on the run. Since you're only working with roughly eight live players and a few backups, make sure everyone gets as much time as possible to learn their assignments.

Pass Rushing Angles

At the end of segment 17 have the defensive backs join you, and send the defensive linemen off with their coach. While the defensive backs and linebackers run seven-on-seven to perfect their pass coverage, the defensive linemen should work with their coach on Drill C. It's vital, no matter what defense you run, that your defensive linemen maintain proper pass rushing angles to the quarterback. Much of the time at the youth level the quarterback is one of the most athletic members of the offense, and the defensive tackles are slower and less agile. If the defensive linemen take incorrect angles to the offensive backfield while pass rushing, they open the door for the quarterback to break to the outside and head downfield. This is *not* a good thing.

After segment 18 ends, bring the defense together and have them do their calisthenics before you run scout team plays. You have two segments to work on showing an assortment of scout team plays to the entire defense. Remember to throw in some trick plays. Your team needs to see a reverse, double reverse, fake reverse, and halfback pass about once per week. I also make sure to show my defense a flea-flicker and the hook and lateral about once every two weeks or so, unless I know that a team we're about to play runs them, in which case I'll call it at least once every day during that week's practice. Don't forget to keep a tally of pluses and minuses on each card to get an idea of how well your team is doing against those plays.

Goal Line

In segment 21 it's time to work on goal line defense again. You'll notice that we aren't putting much time into practicing a pressure defense. The reason for that is that *you* need to have a plan for a pressure situation, but the players don't really need to be as honed on that situation. About once every two weeks I'll review the situation with them, but mostly I just keep in my head that we need to be concerned about dives, off tackles, and the one-step passing game.

Protecting your own goal line, however, is vastly more important, and something you should work on as often as possible.

Day Twelve, Segment 22-23: Special Teams Period

Once you're done with the goal line period it's time to work on special teams. Today's two teams are punt and punt return/block. It's perfect if you have enough players to practice the starters against the backups, but if you don't, you should still take as many of the non-punt-team players as possible and move them to the punt return side to put some pressure on the punter. By the way, if your punt returner is on the punt team, he should get one or two reps, and then spend the rest of his time on the other side of the ball catching the punts. He'll need the practice.

We run the punt and every member of the punt team pursues to the ball. Then we set our huddle there and punt back to the original starting position rather than wasting time jogging back. You'll be surprised how much time this saves. You should also have the return team show some trick returns, such as a reverse wall and a throwback. Again, use coaches if you need to so the coverage team can see these trick returns in action.

Don't forget to practice your punt fakes as well. Try to get one to two reps in before the segment ends and you have to move to practicing the block. Again, try to give each player at least two reps to practice the correct approach angle and blocking technique on the block, and then practice your return. Like we did yesterday with the kickoff return, try to surprise the return team with something unusual, like a fake punt pass or direct snap run.

Day Twelve, Segment 24: Chalk Talk- Review Goal Cards

When you gather the players, have them do their calisthenics. Long before now they should be doing them on their own, but I'm leaving these reminders in here just in case. When they're done and you and your staff have checked their stances, have them take a knee to talk about the goal cards.

I always pick one or two cards out with especially meaningful things. I really like to talk about backups who put things like, "I want to cheer my team to a win." I've had players do that before. Obviously, I want to get all the players into the game, but they're usually pretty realistic about how much playing time they're likely to get if they happen to be the fourth string running back.

I also read a couple of my goals out to the players. Anything that directly involves one player, such as trying to get Billy into the game, I usually leave out. There have been a couple of times, though, when I have actively told the team, "Our goal this week is to get Bobby into the end zone. We need to make it happen." Sometimes, particularly later in the season when the team has grown together, a goal like this might help motivate the team to work harder.

Day Twelve Post-Practice Meeting

Pretty much the rest of this week's meetings are going to be brief chats about the way practice is going. What and who needs more work? Which sections of the team should the head coach work with the next day? There really shouldn't be anything earth shattering uncovered during the rest of the week. Don't forget to have any player that forgot his goal card do his 500 yards of wind sprints. I let the player choose: 10 fifties or 5 hundreds.

Make sure your snappers get their fifty snaps and you're out of there, with three days to go before the baptism of fire.

Day Thirteen, Segments 1-6: Foundation Period

By now you should see the players doing their pushups and sit-ups and jumping into lines for their speed work without any supervision at all. Today, I wouldn't change any of the drills for the tackling period from what you did yesterday, but it's time to go back to Drill C for the blocking period. Keep working on the first step with the punch and goes in blocking Drill A.

Day Thirteen, Segment 7: Offensive Drill Period

After the foundation period ends, have the players break up into their offensive groups and do their exercises. Today the running backs should work with the receivers on Receiver Drill A again. While they are doing that, have the offensive linemen work on Drill A. Downfield blocking after a pull isn't an easy thing for most linemen to do, so you should work that in at least once per week.

Day Thirteen, Segments 8-14: Offensive Period

Peel off the running backs from the receivers and start repping your offensive plays by group as per usual. Again, concentrate on footwork and timing.

At this time in the season you can start playing some tricks if you want. Try having the running backs that are not actively repping plays run Running Backs Drill A behind you, while you go through the plays with another group. Every two minutes, rotate the players. The goal is to keep the players from getting bored and horsing around, while still making sure to get the reps we need.

You can do the same thing with the offensive linemen. Have the backups work on Drills A, B, C, or D while you work with the starters, and then rotate every couple of minutes. You can sneak in a lot of extra reps at those drills that way.

The problem is that this takes an extra coach. Someone has to observe the drills while you're watching the plays. You can really only double time on days when you as the head coach are working alongside the position coach with that group.

After the group period is over at the end of segment 10, bring the team together to work against the scout defenses. Start with their pushups and sit-ups, and then go through your plays rapidly against even, odd, and covered fronts. Make sure you're still keeping track of the team reps, and remember: fifty isn't a goal; it's a *minimum*. You should be getting enough reps by now that the plays are starting to move very smoothly, and the players are very comfortable facing any defensive front, so be ready to start making them *un*comfortable again by having the scout defense blitz, change pass coverages, and take unusual alignments. In running my Double Wing offense, I've seen some bizarre desperation defenses that were completely unsound. Make sure the players have a working reference framework for dealing with anything they see.

You should be pretty close to fifty reps per play by now on almost the entire offense, so remember to tell the players how well they're doing. I can almost promise you that there will be teams in your league that will finish the season with certain plays in their playbook that haven't hit fifty reps yet, and your team has managed to do it in a couple of weeks.

Segment 14 is for the goal line offense. Make sure the players get their reps at things like attacking the pylon and knowing where the back of the end zone is on pass routes. You've got one segment to work on this.

Day Thirteen, Segment 15: Defensive Drill Period

After you've done your goal line work, split up the team for defense and have them do their calisthenics. Then the defensive backs should work on man-to-man coverage with <u>Drill C</u>, the linebackers should focus on stopping sweeps again with <u>Drill B</u>, and the defensive linemen should work on splitting double teams some more with <u>Drill D</u>.

Day Thirteen, Segments 16-21: Defensive Period

When you've finished with the drill period, bring the linebackers and defensive linemen together for the blitz/pass rush period. Today you should put your concentration on any plays that gave your defense troubles over the past couple of days. Remember to try to keep the situations as realistic as possible when you're running scout team offense; run misdirection plays on second and long and passes on third and long. While the linebackers and defensive linemen work on recognizing and reacting to offensive plays, the defensive backs should be continuing to work on <u>Drill D</u> and honing their zone pass coverage skills. For segment 17, have the defensive backs shift gears to <u>Drill C</u> and concentrate on their man-to-man skills, including bump-and-run coverage.

At the beginning of segment 18 bring the defensive backs together with the linebackers for seven-on-seven, and send the defensive linemen with their coach to work on <u>Drill C</u> and hone their pass rushing skills.

Segments 19-20 is the team period, so bring everyone together and have them do their calisthenics before you run scout team plays at them, just like yesterday. As you did during the blitz period, focus your attention on plays that you had problems with yesterday. If there's a misdirection play that confused your linebackers, or a play action play that caught your defensive backs out of position, make sure you see those plays at least three times a piece.

Segment 21 is for the goal line defense again. You can't really get enough practice at this vital part of defensive football. It takes a certain amount of pride to prevent an offense from scoring when you're playing inside your own five-yard line. Really, the only way to create that pride is to give the players as many chances as possible to succeed in practice. That will carry over to the game field, and you'll find that in crucial situations you'll be able to count on them.

Day Thirteen, Segment 22-23: Special Teams Period

When you have finished the goal line period, move on to special teams. Today you need to work on field goal and field goal blocks. Remember, use six footballs and kick all six from the PAT attempt line, then back up five yards and move to one hash mark or the other. Kick three and then move back five and to the other hash mark, following that pattern until you get back to about the twenty-five yard line. You should also run your field goal fake at least once or twice.

If possible, station your kickoff returners back behind the goal posts and make them catch the kicks in the air. Every little bit of practice helps.

When you switch over to field goal block, run it just like you did the punt block yesterday, giving each player a chance to block a kick from the proper angle and using the proper technique. You should be able to get through a couple of reps per player before the end of the period.

Day Thirteen Segment 24: Chalk Talk- Scrimmage Preview

Today's chalk talk is about the upcoming scrimmage. There are always minor details at this time of the season that need to be covered. Who is riding with whom to the field? What uniforms need to be worn?

One thing I strongly suggest you pass is a rule about equipment. On my teams, if you don't bring your own equipment, then you don't play. Forget your cleats? Warm the bench. Forget your hip pads? Warm the bench.

Some coaches are tempted to rape a backup's equipment in order to outfit a starter that forgot something. I completely disagree with that. Put the backup on the field in the starter's place. The backup, by virtue of his responsibility, has demonstrated the ability to be a starter. The starter, by virtue of his *irresponsibility*, has demonstrated that he is not ready to be a starter.

To avoid this entire problem, I lay down the law at least two practices before the scrimmage. Every player will have his own equipment, in its entirety, prior to the scrimmage. Our final practice of the week will be a complete walk through of our offense, defense, and special teams in full game-day uniforms including pads and helmets. That should make it nice and easy for the players to make sure everything fits and is ready to go.

Day Thirteen, Post-Practice Meeting

While your snappers work on practice snaps, you should direct this meeting to cover similar topics to the ones you talked about with your team during the chalk talk. Unless you're very lucky, odds are that you haven't worked with your staff before, so this scrimmage might be the first time your coaching staff has worked a sideline together. You'll need to have a clear-cut plan in place for sideline operations, and its best to think that through before hand.

If your league allows communications from the booth to the sidelines I highly recommend the creation of a booth kit that contains a pair of ten power binoculars, at least two (preferably four) multi-channel two-way radios (walkie-talkies), spare batteries, and headsets for the radios. One coach, preferably the one that is assigned to the booth, should be responsible for the maintenance and pre-game checks of this equipment.

The booth kit is important. Without a good set of eyes in the sky, it's almost impossible to accurately read a defense and attack its weak spots or, worse yet, figure out why the opposing offense keeps tearing your defense apart.

Unfortunately, some leagues do not allow any form of communications from the booth to the field; so make certain you check with the league prior to donning a headset on scrimmage morn. (Tip: Turn off your cell phone as well. I know one coach whose wife called him during a game. The referees flagged him for illegal communications. He never did explain to me why his wife was calling him in the middle of a football game. He also never clarified why he *answered* the phone during a game.)

Day Fourteen, Segments 1-6: Foundation Period

Your players should continue to get themselves into lanes for speed work, as well as perform their exercises pretty much on their own. Continue with drills H, C, D, and E for tackling, but move back to Drills A and B for blocking. Again, concentrate on proper form, but don't be afraid to move at high speed into and out of the drills. You should really be seeing some sharp tackles, and some excellent blocking by this point.

Day Fourteen, Segment 7: Offensive Drill Period

After the foundation period ends, move into the offensive drill period. The backs are again with their coach to run Drill B, and the receivers can start work on their new drill, Drill C: Basketball Drill. The offensive line should get some more reps at pass blocking with Drill C. Remember that the players should still be doing calisthenics as soon as they move to their coaches, but feel free to have some fun with things if you're tired of pushups and sit-ups. At this point in the season, using up-downs, mountain climbers, and other conditioning exercises works just as well. I'm sure the players will appreciate it.

Day Fourteen, Segments 8-14: Offensive Period

Now it's time to get reps on your offensive plays. You should be in groups as usual, to make it easier to spot problems in execution. To be perfectly honest, however, there should be very, very few problems with the execution of your plays at this point, and you're probably going to be tempted to start working on the sideboard.

Resist this temptation. After you smash your way through the opposing defenses at the scrimmage in three more days, then you can start thinking about it—of course first you're going to have to troubleshoot and fix any problems that come up during the scrimmage. Probably best to worry about the sideboard after the first game.

When segment ten is over, bring your groups together and run plays against defensive fronts. Remember to move at high speed, and get your backups into the rotation as often as possible. Your last segment of team offense is for panic offense. Remember to panic.

Day Fourteen, Segment 15: Defensive Drill Period

When you've finished the panic offensive period, split up the team for defense and have them do their exercises. Today I strongly recommend doing team defense Drill A. Wide play pursuit is going to be a big part of playing successful defense in the scrimmage, and getting your kids ready is going to be important.

Day Fourteen, Segments 16-21: Defensive Period

After you've worked the wide play pursuit drill, split into your sections and have the players do their exercises. The linebackers should be doing all the variations of Drill A by this time. Defensive backs can move on to Drill D to hone their zone coverage skills, and the defensive line can work on perfecting their ability to counter trap blocks with Drill B.

Following the individual time, bring the linebackers and defensive line together for a blitz and pass rush period. As you've been doing, run your scout team plays against the skeleton defense without the defensive backs. During this period the secondary should be working on <u>Drill C</u>. Remember, most blitzes require man-to-man coverage, so a skilled defensive backfield is a must. You only have one segment for this today, because we robbed this period for the team <u>Drill A</u> in segment fifteen.

At the end of the blitz period, segment seventeen, send the defensive linemen off with their coach to work on <u>Drill C</u> after they do their exercises. During that time run some scout team passing plays against your defensive backs and linebackers in seven-on-seven. You have one segment for this before you move into scout team defense against multiple offensive systems and plays.

Like we've done all week, the very last segment of the defensive period is for goal line stands. By now you should really have to work to trick your team and allow your scout team to score. Make a huge deal out of it if your defense can go the entire segment without allowing a touchdown.

Day Fourteen, Segment 22-23: Special Teams Period

Today's special teams are the kickoff and punt. You have two segments to get as many reps as possible. As usual, set up a return team with your second string players and kick to them, but don't forget that those second stringers need to get some reps at their positions too. It's a good idea to make sure that you're running some tricky returns, too.

Continue to focus on lane discipline, making sure that the players don't follow their own color downfield.

Day Fourteen Segment 24: Chalk Talk-Scrimmage Preview Again

Your chalk talk today should revolve around the upcoming scrimmage. Compliment the heck out of your players, and remind them that they've worked very, very hard to be where they are right now. At this point, there will be few teams that are as well-prepared as your team is, and you should be very proud of them. Tell them that.

Don't forget to remind them of their responsibilities as well. Every player needs to plan ahead and bring the following items to the scrimmage:

- Water bottle (the same one they have at practice every day)
- Cleats
- Pads (Shoulder, thigh and knee in the pants, hip and tail pads in the girdle, any additional pads such as elbow or "flak jackets")
- Socks
- Helmet
- Mouthpiece (attached to the helmet)
- A snack of some form (granola bars or something high in carbohydrates and low in fat)
- Transportation to and from the scrimmage
- Any additional items you require

Lines of Communication

The easiest way to make sure that this happens is to create a parents letter with a removable section. In the parents letter put all the information that you have about the scrimmage, such as where, when, what to bring, etc, and send it home tonight. The parents are to read the letter, sign the form, and give it to their kids to bring back tomorrow.

Of course, any player that forgets his signed form or doesn't get it signed gets some remedial conditioning after practice tomorrow. If the form doesn't come back to you by the day of the scrimmage, the player doesn't play.

Tomorrow's practice is going to be in full game regalia, so the players should have few excuses for not having their equipment with them on scrimmage morning.

After your team yell, dismiss the team, and get together with your assistant coaches while your snappers work on their snaps. By now there should be no fumbles, and the players should be conditioned to get snapping on their own without needing much prompting from you or your staff.

Day Fourteen, Post-Practice Meeting

You've already covered most of the material pertaining to the scrimmage in yesterday's meeting, and the chalk talks from yesterday and today, so there shouldn't be much more to worry about at the meeting. You should already have someone assigned to scout your first week's opponent, and return with a competent scouting report. You should also have things organized for your sideline, with someone handling substitutions and spotting from the booth if that's available.

You need to have a list similar to the players' of things your coaches need to have with them. This is going to be slightly more esoteric, and a lot more important.

Stuff to Bring

In addition to the booth kit I described earlier, you need to also have:

- Ear pads for helmets of varying sizes, at least four pair.
- A helmet maintenance kit containing screws, clips, and chinstraps. (Don't forget a screwdriver and a pair of needle nose pliers!)
- A shoulder pad repair kit containing straps, clips, shoelaces, and other repair items.
- Several extra mouthpieces.
- At least two pairs of socks. (Yes, I've had players forget those before.)
- A medical kit with athletic tape, prewrap, break-and-shake ice packs, tape scissors or knife, band aids, latex or equivalent gloves and other assorted medical supplies.
- A fluid system. By this I mean that you can get a giant thermos and fill it with Gatorade™ like the pros, or you can by bottles of water, but you need to have something on your sideline as a hydration system in addition to the players' own water bottles. (Plus, your throat is going to be dry from all the yelling of encouragement.)
- An extra jersey or three in case one is damaged beyond repair and has to be replaced.
- At least one complete set of extra knee, thigh and hip pads in case they get damaged or lost (it happens on the field all the time).

- Medical insurance/release forms for each player. Many emergency medical services won't provide treatment without parental authorization, and these forms give you permission to approve that if the parent isn't available.

- Footballs. It's sort of tough to play the game without them.

Start putting this stuff together now if you haven't already. You don't want to be running around like mad on scrimmage morning worrying about all of this crap when you should be concentrating on honing your team's excitement and getting them ready to whack heads.

One of the best ideas I've ever come up with was putting all the coaching equipment together in a wheeled toolbox. Home Depot™ sells them for about thirty to fifty bucks. They're made of plastic and are about waist-tall (on me). It basically looks like two or three toolboxes stacked on top of one another, with a handle and set of wheels to make it easy to move around. By dividing the "toolboxes" into sections, you can easily put together a helmet repair kit, pad repair kit, medical kit, and booth kit and even have room for administrative paperwork. They're well worth the money.

Think Ahead

Additionally, have a game plan of things you want to accomplish at the scrimmage. Some of them came from the goal cards we did on day eleven, obviously, but over the week of practices I'm sure there were several additional things you've discovered that you'd like to work on.

Scrimmages are the *only* contests that I script out, by the way. In my opinion, scripting plays in a game is completely asinine. It's an NFL trick that George Siefort popularized when he was the head coach of the San Francisco 49ers. Siefort, Bill Walsh, and Mike Holmgren worked as a staff to read the defense's reactions and set them up for certain plays based on the scouting report and talent matchups.

Why I Script Scrimmages

I script the scrimmage because my goal is to see my entire offense against a live defense that isn't composed of my junior players. In a game I might call one play fifteen times in a row if the defense isn't stopping it, but in the scrimmage my limit is about two or three, because the object isn't to drive the field and "win," it's to see how my players are executing their assignments.

The problem is that I'm human. Although I've been bitten by a number of spiders in my life, none of them have been radioactive, sadly, and the net result is that I tend to forget things (hence all the charts I carry around). To remind myself that we need to see each and every play in our offense several times, and preferably at least once for each player on the depth chart, I script out the scrimmages.

The quickest and easiest way to script out a scrimmage is in two columns. The first column is the "better case" scenario, in which each play is getting close to its minimum acceptable gain. (I'll talk more about the MAG in my book on offense. In short form, each play has a certain amount of yardage it needs to get every time I call it.) Obviously this is a "better" case scenario; because the *best* case is that you scored on the play.

The second column is for the "worse" case scenario. Note that it is "worse" and not "worst." There's a difference. The "worst" case is a fumble, interception, sack or other catastrophe.

Here's an example of my scripting chart, using my Double Wing offense:

	"Better" Case	**"Worse" Case**
1	24 Toss	--
2	30 Wedge	30 Wedge
3	49 Jet Sweep	49 Jet Sweep
4	34 Quick Trap	18 Waggle Pass
5	24 Toss	30 Draw
6	45 X-Toss	24 Toss Pass
7	24 Toss Pass	30 Wedge Keep

You'll note that I start out with the core offense and the base plays from each series, and then work through the secondary plays. The "worse" case side is the bigger plays designed to break for more yards. If we continued the "better" case side you'd eventually see those plays crop up, but they'd be further down the road after we've run the core a number of times.

I recommend that you start preparing this chart at least two days before the scrimmage. Each of your coaches should have a copy of it. Plan for about sixty offensive plays.

Now it's time for the dress rehearsal.

Day Fifteen, Segments 1-6: Foundation Period

Start today out by gathering all the returned forms from the parents. Handle the players that don't have their forms by assigning extra conditioning after practice, as usual.

Your players should be fired up for today's practice, since tomorrow they bang heads for the first time with another team, or set of teams. As a result, you might have some more disciplinary problems today than usual. Try to channel that energy without stifling it. You *want* the players pumped, but not disruptive. Keep things businesslike as much as you can.

As always, start the day with speed work and then move to the blocking and tackling of the foundation period. Continue with drills <u>H</u>, <u>C</u>, <u>D</u>, and <u>E</u> for tackling, but take advantage of that youthful exuberance and do <u>Drill C</u> for blocking. Let the players safely "splatter" themselves a bit.

The Virtues of Starvation

A trick I've used a couple of times is to starve the players for contact today. In all the tackling drills, only allow "thud" contact. Even on the blocking <u>Drill C</u>, don't let the players hit full speed. Move the blocker closer to the player with the pad if you have to, but don't let them hit today.

Tomorrow they'll be about ready to smash anything that moves. This trick is remarkably effective, especially at the twelve to sixteen-year-old range, where the players have developed a taste for hitting.

You also might want to consider reigning in your assistant coaches a little in the conditioning department. If you've been slowly creeping the number of pushups and sit-ups you've been doing when the players move from coach to coach, or you've been gradually adding in more challenging exercises, today is a good day to back off a little bit. No more than five of any exercise, and I'd really just stick with the pushups and sit-ups.

Day Fifteen, Segment 7: Offensive Drill Period

When the foundation period is completed it's time to move into the offensive drills. Break the players up into their component groups and have them do their calisthenics. Take a moment and look, really *look* at their stances when they pop up. Don't they look sharp now? It's hard to believe how far they've come in just three weeks.

Today's drills are going to be close to what you worked on yesterday. By the way, you might notice that we're spending an awful lot of time working on <u>Drill C</u> with the offensive line lately. There's a reason for that. You spend most of your time working on your run blocking, and your players get a lot of time to practice down blocks and double teams. Because you're focusing on that aspect of the game, your offensive linemen aren't getting a lot of practice reps on blocking for the pass.

To keep that from coming back to haunt you, I recommend that you use these drill periods to focus on that. Run as many variants of <u>Drill C</u> or any other pass blocking drills you might have at your disposal during these periods.

The backs should work on <u>Drill B</u> again, concentrating on holding onto the ball in traffic. Your receivers can do any of the drills, but I prefer to have them concentrate on <u>Drill A</u>. Tomorrow you're going to be chucking a few passes at them, and they're going to want to make some catches for Mom and Dad in the stands.

Day Fifteen, Segments 8-14: Offensive Period

After you're done with the drill period, keep the players in their groups and work on the plays, trying to get as many reps as possible in the three segments we have allotted. Today they should be a machine, lining up and running plays with a minimum of instruction from the coaches. Typically, by this point, we simply call a play, sit back, and watch them execute.

When segment ten ends, call the players in as a single group and run your plays against scout team fronts. Today's scout team work is a little different than normal, however. Today we need to move a little bit slower, about three repetitions per minute, and we need to make sure that we run every single play in our playbook at least once for each kid. This is the dress rehearsal for the scrimmage tomorrow, and there should be ample time to get through the offense if you hurry.

Today, in fact, I might even not do a goal line offense if I have so many players that I can't get all of them their reps in a timely manner during segments eleven to thirteen. Making sure that all of your players know their assignments like the back of their hands is very important. I'll leave that up to you. Most, if not all of them, should be ready, but there might be the occasional late bloomer or minimum-play-player that needs a little more coaching. It's a little late to find that out now, but if you need the time, use it.

Goal line offense and defense generally requires a lot of hitting, too, and we're trying to starve the kids for contact, so keeping that to a minimum isn't a bad idea. It also tends to keep the injuries down, as well as let kids recover from bumps and bruises, and that's always a good thing.

Day Fifteen, Segment 15: Defensive Drill Period

When you're done with the offensive period, switch gears and break the players up into their groups for individual skill work. Have the defensive backs concentrate on their footwork with Drill B while the linebackers focus on sweep defense with their Drill B. Give the defensive linemen some work on splitting double team blocks with Drill D.

The defensive linemen are pretty much the only players that are really going to get physical today, because they need the practice at defeating double teams. The double team block is one of the more effective used in youth football, and it's a favorite of many coaches, so the more work you can get for your players, the better, even the day before the scrimmage.

Day Fifteen, Segments 16-21: Defensive Period

When segment fifteen ends, get the defensive linemen and linebackers together for a blitz/pass rush period. Have them work against as many scout players as possible, but be certain to rotate the backups in frequently. It's hard to make sure that every player sees every possible scout team play often enough to recognize it, so the only real way to make it happen is to substitute liberally. Your defense depends on it. This is a jog-through period, and I say "jog through" because we're still trying to starve our players for contact. Give them a refresher of what the plays look like, but don't let them hit.

You'll probably need to slow things down a bit to and put your emphasis on any plays that have been giving you trouble. You've got two segments, so you should have enough time to really focus on the trouble spots.

While the defensive linemen and linebackers are working on this, your secondary should be with their coach working on pass coverages with Drills C and D.

At the end of segment seventeen, bring the defensive backs together with the linebackers and have the defensive linemen go off with their coach to work on Drill C. Work the defensive backfield on seven on seven, again focusing on those plays that have given you trouble over the last few days.

Scout Team

You'll follow that pattern into segments nineteen and twenty, which is a scout team period. Bring all members of the defense together and have them do their exercises. Then put together a scout offense and, again moving at a jog, go through as many plays as you can in the two segments allotted.

The goal line defense period is much like the goal line offense period was earlier. If you need to use it to get additional reps, do so. If you do run it, go for half speed as much as possible, and don't let the players tackle to the ground.

The object of this period is to get as many repetitions as possible against the plays that have been giving you trouble, especially for the players that need additional work. If one of your backup linebackers got cheated in the blitz period or the seven-on-seven time, then make sure he gets makeup reps here.

Day Fifteen, Segment 22-23: Special Teams Period

Despite today's focus on the scrimmage tomorrow, and the corresponding lack of kicking game most scrimmages entails, we don't want our special teams to suffer, so I recommend at least two walkthroughs each of the kickoff return and punt return. Continue to use "sticky" blocking and concentrate on the angles and approaches.

Day Fifteen Segment 24: Chalk Talk- Last Call for the Scrimmage!

Tomorrow is the big day. For the first time your players are going to be facing opposing teams, albeit ones that are probably not as well-prepared or focused as they are.

I like to center today's chalk talk around some of the goals that we talked about on days eleven and twelve, from the goal cards. It's just a brief reminder for the players that they have some things they set out to do this week, and they've worked hard to get to them.

Also, cover for the last time where the scrimmage is and when, where the team's going to meet and when, and make sure that the players understand in their little heads that no equipment equals no playing time, so make sure they take off every piece of padding they're wearing right now and put it into their football bag for tomorrow without forgetting anything.

Tomorrow is the big day.

Day Fifteen, Post-Practice Meeting

Today's meeting should be one of the shortest of the preseason. While your snappers grind out their snaps, go over any missing items from the previous day's list. Make sure that everything is set up and ready to go. You need to plan for the eventualities if something breaks, and try to think of other items that might need to be on the list that I didn't mention, such as replacement cleats and a cleat removal tool if your league allows removable cleats, assorted braces if you have players nursing sore joints, and things of that nature. Today is also the day you make your substitution list for the parent or coach that will be cycling players in and out of the game for you. In his books on coaching youth football Jack Reed elaborates on a very effective method for this, so I won't go into it here, but you need to have something on paper for keeping track of each player's plays.

Don't load yourself down incessantly, but make sure that you have everything you need. Halftime is a pretty poor time to be out searching for icepacks, take it from me.

Beyond that and a brief talk about players you want to see in action tomorrow and plays to focus on, keep things nice and short and get out of there early so you can get a good night's sleep. (Yeah, right. I've never once been able to sleep the night before the first scrimmage or the opening game. I don't know that I ever will.)

Scrimmage Day

I recommend that you get to the meeting site at least forty minutes before your team does and go through a mental checklist of everything you're going to need. Youth scrimmages usually start early in the morning because they have several levels of scrimmage games to get through in one day. If there are six teams at each level, each team plays three twenty-minute games (ten minutes offense and ten minutes defense is normal), and there are four levels, you're looking at six straight hours of games. That's a long time. Typically the fields for scrimmages are only fifty yards long, and at least two games are played at once, but it can still be a long, tiring day.

Get there early and find out where your team will be playing each game and when, and also what changing facilities are available. If the scrimmage is at a local high school the teams may cycle through the locker rooms, so find out when your changing time is.

Unfortunately for those riding the anal-retentive bus like I am, these events are *never* coordinated in advance. Just once I'd like to show up for one of these things with a mental map of precisely where I need to be and when.

I recommend that you keep your team together at all times, and keep them under adult supervision. Kids being kids, they're going to get bored and want to wander off. Try to keep that from happening. Good luck. Consider buying ten or twelve rolls of duct tape.

No Junk!

Above all, *keep them away from the snack bar!* I have yet to see anything even remotely healthful offered for sale at a youth athletics snack bar, an irony if I've ever seen one. The last thing you need is your players loading up on crap food right before your games begin. (Remember that nutrition chalk talk along about day six?) A Snickers™ doesn't really satisfy when it's on the way back up.

I usually like to take a moment, if possible, and watch my opponents if we aren't playing first. Take a couple of notes on threats to avoid, and what defenses they run. It's too late to make drastic changes, but sometimes even being able to simply tell your players, "Hey, they're running a covered front. We've seen this before," can really calm them down.

You need to be back with your team by at least forty-five minutes to your first game. You'll need about ten minutes to warm up, five minutes for offensive skills, five minutes for defensive skills and then about ten minutes each to jog through your offensive and defensive units before you start smacking heads. The extra five minutes is to make sure you get where you're supposed to be on time.

Warm ups

On game day or scrimmage day we don't really change much from our warm-ups. We start by breaking into our lines for speed work, and yes I have the players do five pushups and five sit-ups as part of the warm-ups. This is the only time we'll do the calisthenics today. Then we do our speed work the same way we open every practice, except for two things: we only go about half speed at best, and we only go about ten yards. We also only do exercises <u>A</u>, <u>B</u>, <u>C</u>, <u>D</u>, and <u>E</u>.

After the warm up period, we break up into our offensive groups and run through some very basic drills. Receivers' <u>Drill A</u> for the running backs and receivers, and blocking <u>Drill B</u> for the linemen. You can do it without bags as long as you keep things to around half speed so the linemen don't maul their "blocking dummies."

At the end of five minutes, bring everyone together and run your offensive plays against the scout team defense at about half speed. Use whatever notes you garnered from your intelligence gathering earlier. If you don't have anything new, move the defense around here and there to get a look at all three main fronts: even, odd, and covered.

You've only got ten minutes, so move quickly. When you're done, break up into defensive groups and run some basic drills like you did with the offense. Have everyone do their group's <u>Drill A</u>, and then move into a scout team period, using the cards that you've been using, and focusing your efforts on plays that have been giving you some trouble or plays that you noticed the opponents running in your intelligence gathering earlier. Run everything at about half speed.

The very last thing we do is the mascot jacks we've been doing as a team yell. Make them loud, and make them proud. I think it's one of my favorite things in football, to be in the center of a team doing those jacks on game day. Enjoy it.

By the time you're finished the referees should be ready for you.

The First "Game"

I have one significant rule for game day, and it applies to scrimmages, too: after we leave the field when warm-ups are completed, we take the field as a team, and we do it as a charge. I usually stand just off the field and stop all the players from going on. I spend a few moments pumping them up, and reminding them that they are the Braves/Lions/Junior Cardinals, and there's only ever going to be one team like this. Then the last thing I let out is, "Braves! *Take the field!*"

The players usually charge the field while letting out an earsplitting roar. For the next twenty minutes it belongs to them.

Getting the Most Out of Scrimmaging

Use the scrimmage. Following the script you put together, call your offense with an eye towards moving the ball well, but also on seeing each of the plays you run in action and building faith in the core. Remember that the script is only a guideline; so if you see a defense that's begging for something, feel free to hit them with it.

Remember that your core plays should be your "default settings." If you find yourself in a quandary, unsure about what to call, you should probably call one of them. I've found that not only does this make these plays more polished and effective, but the players begin to have faith and confidence in them as well. That's worth a mint on game day.

Make sure that your substitution coach, or the parent that is handling matters for you, is rotating the players in and out of the scrimmage. I strongly recommend that you do your best to get each player a minimum of eight plays in each contest, regardless of your league minimum play rule. If it's more, then obviously follow their requirements, but if it happens to be less than that, the extra experience these players will gain will make you successful next year, and that's a good thing.

The substitution coach is also the coach that I make responsible for keeping the sidelines clear. All players need to be at least two yards off the sidelines unless they are in immediate conversation with a coach. Some referees are really touchy about this, and may even flag your team for it. It's best to start out during the scrimmage working on this from the get-go.

The other coaches that are present are going to be your eyes. If you have a press booth, use it and the walkie-talkies. In *Volume IV: Offense* I'm going to detail a chart called the "Eyes on" chart that I use to make sure that my assistants are all helping me watch different parts of the defense when I call a certain play. This *vastly* improves the counter game, because I literally have eyes in the sky watching for certain defensive mistakes that we can capitalize on.

Post Scrimmage

I'd like to think that you're going to crush your confused and enfeebled opponents without much trouble, but let's be honest: that might not happen. There are too many variables. If you did extremely well, that's great, but don't get cocky.

Remember that there is a kicking game and a field position battle to fight out. Remember that scrimmages are nothing more than preseason practices against other teams.

This doesn't mean that you shouldn't congratulate your players all to heck. When my teams have a successful scrimmage, I trumpet it from the top of the tallest towers in the land. They've worked hard for the past three weeks, and they deserve to be praised.

Scrimmage as a Tool for Fixing Broken Things

There is the other side of the coin, unfortunately. One of the reasons I like scrimmages is that they give you a chance to locate problems in your system before you make it to game day. If the scrimmage doesn't go all that well for your team, still be positive. Tell them the truth: you saw a lot of really great things (You did, didn't you?) but you've got a lot of work to do before the game next weekend.

Send your players home on a high note. Remind them to drink plenty of water and get some rest before the next practice. Some of them will inevitably be banged up a little bit, so make sure that they know the proper treatment for bumps and bruises.

Where Do You Think *You're* Going?

When the players take off, you should have a ten-minute coaches' meeting, to briefly cover some of the things you saw in the scrimmage. Don't get too detailed. Everyone is going to be tired and emotionally drained from the scrimmage, so just hit the high points; who looks really good, who needs more work, how well things worked with the communications and sideline management.

Collect your tape from the videographer and head for home.

I usually like to watch the tape of a game or scrimmage on the night of the game. Sometimes this is physically impossible. In 2003 when we traveled to Merced, CA for a game it was a four and a half hour trip each way. I had no intention of watching the video at three thirty in the morning. I'm dedicated, but not *that* dedicated. Besides, the best VCR is in the bedroom, and the wife would have killed me.

If possible, though, I like to run through the tape at least once, making general notes while the game or scrimmage is still fresh in my mind. Tomorrow you can break down the film using the methods outlined in chapter four.

Goal Cards

One more thing I want to do tonight is grab the goal cards that the players filled out during the first practice of the week. I go over each card individually and, when a player meets a goal that took a lot of effort, I'll write a response to it. It's just a little "good job" for the player, but I think it's important to acknowledge them. If the player didn't quite make it to his goals, I try to write something to encourage him to work a little bit harder for them next week.

During that same 2003 season one of the parents drew me aside after practice and told me that her son had kept every one of those goal cards and put them into a scrapbook. That's one memory of coaching this sport that will always be with me. I think it answers all those questions people keep asking about why I do this.

Game Week

The week before your first game is like no other week in football. Even the playoffs don't have the same sense of anticipation mixed with apprehension.

There's the bowel-twisting terror that one of your players may be injured, and there's the glorious sense of freedom that comes from looking at a clean slate and wondering what wonderful pictures are going to fill it.

There are going to be some changes to our practice plan this week. For one thing, the kicking game is going to take on some added importance, since we're finally going to get to use the special teams. Additionally, we've got a list of mistakes and execution errors from the scrimmage that we need to correct; thanks to the careful film breakdown you did the day after the scrimmage. Make sure that you have the correction sheets for each of your assistants to work on with their players. Remember that the drills recommended in this description are only there as a generic reference. If your team needs a lot of work at pass defense, or your upcoming opponent runs an "air it out" style of offense, then by all means, structure your practice plans and drill periods for that.

Another thing we've got to do is get the kids fired up to play, but not let them peak at the wrong time. One of the most frustrating things that has ever happened to me is losing a game because we practiced like maniacs on Wednesday, and played like maids on Saturday. Getting your team's energy to crest at the right time is much more art than science. Each team is different, and each coach approaches them in a different manner.

Toning Down the First Practice

One more thing that you might have to worry about, especially later on the in the season, is that the players are getting banged up. At the high school level, nearly every school in America has a light half-pads or helmets-only practice on Monday following a Friday or Saturday game. At the youth level, however, you really can't afford to lose that contact time.

It can be a fine line to walk. Three to five twenty minute scrimmage games should not have banged up your players enough for you to really be concerned about it for the first practice of this week, but later in the season you might want to give that some thought.

Yet another thing to be concerned about is the practice schedule I've put together for you. I'm assuming that you had no highly significant problems with your team during the scrimmage. If that's not the case, feel free to modify things as much as you need to. If your linebackers didn't do a great job of playing sweeps, substitute Drill B in place of Drill A. If your defensive backs covered well in man-to-man situations, but not in zone, then put more emphasis into that. Remember that these practice plans are merely a guideline for you to use. They aren't sealed in stone.

Game Week – Practice One, Segments 1-6: Foundation Period

Some of your players might be sore from the scrimmage, so you can consider doing lighter speed work today. If you're going to do so, I recommend the same workout that you did on the day of the scrimmage, only at normal speed. I'll leave that up to you.

My concession to their potential soreness is to use tackling drills A, B, E, and the main variant of drill H. The object is to limit the amount of collision the players have to endure on this first day back to practice and to continue to reinforce proper body mechanics in the execution of form tackling.

As far as the general blocking goes, however, Drills A, and B are still the best of the lot for reinforcing proper explosion and effort.

Game Week – Practice One (Day 16), Segments 7-8: Offensive Drill Period

When you're finished with the foundation period, break the players into their groups and send them to their coaches. Have the players do their calisthenics and work them through some drills. You have two segments to work with.

The running backs should do <u>Drill B</u> for the first segment, and then move to work with the receivers on their <u>Drill A</u> for the second segment. The receivers should start with their <u>Drill B</u> for the first segment, and then start <u>Drill A</u> when they are joined by the running backs.

The linemen? Well, today they get to do something special. Today is the day that the backups get to challenge for a starting spot. You have two segments to use <u>Blocking Drill D: "Sumo"</u>. Any second stringer may challenge a starter for the right to start in his place in the upcoming game, and any third stringer may challenge the second stringer above him.

This period is one of the primary motivations for the offensive line. No other position on the field is able to challenge for the position in this manner. Want to be a starter? The spot is yours, *if you can take it from the incumbent!*

As the head coach, I strongly recommend that you work with the offensive linemen today and make certain that this drill is done fairly and in the most fun manner possible. Put the sumo circle out and gather the rest of the offensive linemen around it to cheer each other on.

Not Exactly Traditional, But Fun Anyway

The way I run this drill is to make it like a ceremony. I call the position, "Starter! Right tackle!" and the starting right tackle steps into the center of the circle. I then bellow, "Call for challenges!" I'll count to ten, and, if there are no challenges I'll yell out, "No challenges! Starter retire!"

Only the second stringer can challenge the starter, so the third stringer must first challenge the number two man on the depth chart before going after the top spot. Players can only challenge at their assigned positions. I don't want the number two left guard challenging the number one right tackle just because he thinks that guy is a pushover.

It's natural for some of the players that didn't win to be upset, so make sure that you keep things positive and remind them that there's a lot of season left to go.

Game Week – Practice One (Day 16), Segments 9-13: Offensive Period

When the drill period is over, run your plays as groups, concentrating on high speed, and thinking ahead to the scouting report for your upcoming opponent's defense. Try to get as many reps as possible and make certain that you concentrate on the core plays first. You only have two segments for this, so keep the players moving.

At the end of segment ten, bring the groups together for team work. Here is where it's absolutely vital to have a decent scouting report on your upcoming opponent. Again, you have two segments to get through as much of your offense as possible, concentrating largely on the core plays. Don't worry quite so much about the non-core material. Since you're keeping track of the number of reps you're getting, you can easily see which plays to focus on tomorrow.

You have two segments for scout team offense before you begin working on goal line defense. Again, use your scouting report and reiterate to your players the importance of coming away with six points any time you're inside the ten yard line.

Game Week – Practice One (Day 16), Segment 14: Defensive Drill Period

It's a good idea to start the week with defensive <u>Drill A</u> to work on wide play pursuit angles. Once again, though, if you had significant issues defensively during the scrimmage, feel free to modify this practice plan and consider some group or team drills to reinforce the areas you need to strengthen. Remember that I'm probably not going to spend a lot of time on your practice field, so the best these plans can be is guidelines for you.

Hey, do I have to do *everything?*

Game Week – Practice One (Day 16), Segments 15-20: Defensive Period

Following the drill period, break your team into their defensive groups and have the linebackers work with the defensive line on their blitz/pass rush period after they do their calisthenics. Use a skeleton offense to run your opponent's plays at your skeleton defense as many times as possible, and, like you were doing in preparation for the scrimmage, keep careful track of any plays that you have significant problems with.

Additionally, if any plays from the scrimmage gave you problems and your upcoming opponent has those same plays or similar ones in his repertoire, it goes without saying to make sure you put some emphasis into those as well.

Your defensive backs should be with their coach working on man-to-man and zone coverage with drills <u>C</u> and <u>D</u>. At the end of the blitz period, swap the defensive backs with the defensive linemen and run a seven-on-seven period, focusing on your upcoming opponent's passing offense. During this segment your defensive line should be focusing on pass rushing with <u>Drill C</u>.

At the end of segment seventeen use the scouting report to run your opponent's entire offense at your combined defense. You have two segments for this, and one segment for goal line defense. Try to focus your time on plays your opponent is probably going to think of as "core." Although a lot of youth football coaches fall into the "Madden" mistake of getting bored and calling plays somewhat at random, there are certain patterns that they tend to follow.

If you had the opportunity to break your opponent's tendencies down into a list of plays they tend to run on first, second, third, and fourth down, then use those situations with your teams as much as possible.

During the goal line period, remember to restrict your playcalling to plays that the opponent is likely to call in that situation. Again, a tendency-chart of some form is highly beneficial.

Game Week – Practice One (Day 16), Segments 21-23: Defensive Period

When you've completed the goal line period, switch gears to special teams. You have an additional segment today to focus on perfecting your kickoff and kickoff return. By now these plays should already look great, and it's simply a matter of getting more reps and making sure that everyone is comfortable with their assignments.

You can choose to run some special teams drills if you're happy with the way your kickoff and kickoff return look. Consider taking a segment and kicking dribblers to the front line of the kickoff return team while another coach throws or kicks high spirals and end-over-end balls to the returners themselves. Give a scout kickoff return team shields and have the wedge breakers practice turning into human torpedoes to break up the wedges. Take one of the three segments and work on specific drills to make the individual kickoff and kickoff return teams more successful.

Make sure that you get at least six perfect kickoffs and six perfect kickoff returns before you worry about drills, however. The plays themselves are far more important than drills. Generally I'll run my special teams plays first, and then if we make it through the required number of repetitions we'll add in some drills.

Play Football the NFL Way (ISBN: 0312059477) by Tom Bass is an excellent resource for drills that are special team-specific. Or you can look for Volume II of this series.

Game Week – Practice One (Day 16), Segment 24: Chalk Talk- Goal Cards and Captains

When the special teams period ends, gather the team and return to them the goal cards for the scrimmage with your written comments on them. Take a moment here to congratulate those players that pushed themselves to reach their goals, and challenge those that didn't quite get there.

After you return the goal cards for the scrimmage, hand out blank ones for the upcoming game. Dare the players to set new, higher goals and to work for the rest of the week on obtaining them.

You also need to assign captains for this week's game, and make sure they understand the essay requirements. Captains should be people that the team looks up to, and some coaches even have their players vote on the weekly captains. That's fine, but I prefer to have more input. Occasionally I'll move a player that some people might think is too shy or too inexperienced to a captain's position. I think it's important to give some chances to some of the players that don't always get them—and much of the time I get a pleasant surprise from that player.

Most of the time I draw my captains from the ranks of the offensive linemen, but not always. With seven to twelve offensive linemen and six to ten games in the regular season, it's easy to run out of captains if you confine yourself to just one part of the team. The captains are required to write a five hundred word essay that is due on the last practice before the game. The topic is, "Leadership and Being a Captain."

The last thing you should do is have any new members of the offensive line stand up and be recognized. Then do your team yell and break for the evening.

Game Week – Practice One (Day 16), Post- Practice Meeting

Tonight's meeting should be a relatively quick one. Like your players, your coaching staff has undergone a live-fire drill, and they should now be a highly effective unit. Other than the standard, "Who looks good? Who needs more work?" questions that we ask ourselves after every practice, there should be very little to cover. Generally this meeting is over even before the snappers finish their practice snaps.

Game Week – Practice Two (Day 17), Segments 1-6: Foundation Period

Start your practice by collecting the goal cards for the game. Handle anyone that forgets their goal cards with extra conditioning after practice. Then get the players together for the foundation period. Have them do their calisthenics, and then move them through the speed work. Today you're back to doing the exercises at normal speed.

For the tackling drills, use <u>C</u>, <u>D</u>, <u>E</u>, and <u>H</u>. The blocking drills stay the same as <u>A</u> and <u>B</u>. You can go back to normal hitting (if you haven't already) now that the players have had an extra day to recover.

Game Week – Practice Two (Day 17), Segments 7-13: Offensive Period

Your offensive period starts, as usual, with offensive drills. For today, have the backs work on their gauntlet (<u>Drill B</u>) unless you've been noticing fumble-itus lately, in which case have them do <u>Drill A</u>. The receivers are back to doing their <u>Drill A</u>, and the offensive linemen should be focusing on their <u>Drill D</u>.

When you've finished the individual drills you have two segments to put the groups through the plays before you get together as a team. Your scout team work is going to revolve around quality rather than quantity and facing the opposing defense, so make sure that you get as many repetitions as possible in the individual time to make up for a slightly slower pace as a team.

You have four segments for team offense when you're done with the individual period. Three of these segments should be devoted to the scouting report of the opposing defense, and the last segment should be specifically for goal line offense. Then it's time to switch gears and move into defense.

Game Week – Practice Two (Day 17), Segments 14-20: Defensive Period

Your defensive period starts with individual drills, so break the players into their defensive groups and have them perform their calisthenics. Make sure that you're checking stances carefully, even at this late date. Don't start to cut corners.

Defensively, the drills we're going to cover today are <u>Drill A</u> for the defensive backs to work on the first motions of the bump, <u>Drill A</u> for the linebackers to work on stopping the power running game, and <u>Drill D</u> for the defensive linemen to focus on splitting double teams.

After the drills period is completed, bring your defensive linemen and linebackers together for a blitz period while the defensive backs work on their coverages. During the next two segments the secondary should be working on coverage skills with drills <u>D</u>, and <u>C</u>. During the blitz period, use the scouting report and run the opponent's plays at your skeleton offense.

At the end of segment sixteen, swap the defensive backs with the defensive linemen and have the linemen work on <u>Drill C</u> to hone their pass rushing skills while your linebackers and backs concentrate on stopping the opponent's passing game in a seven-on-seven period.

When this period has ended, bring the defensive linemen back and work on scout team, running the opponent's plays at your defense. Like you did in the offensive scout team period, concentrate on getting high quality repetitions, especially of the plays your opponent is most likely to use against you. You have two segments for scout team defense and then one final segment for goal line work before moving into the special teams period.

Game Week – Practice Two (Day 17), Segments 21-23: Special Teams Period

Like yesterday's, today's special teams period is one segment longer than the previous two weeks has been. You have punt and punt return to get through today, and again, you need to get at least six repetitions of each before you consider running any drills you might have in mind.

If it's possible, have your punt returner always field the punts to get additional practice at catching the high, arcing punts. Remind your punter, however, that on game day he needs to kick the ball *away* from the other team's return men.

Game Week – Practice Two (Day 17), Segment 24: Chalk Talk – Read Goal Cards

During today's chalk talk, we're again going to read a few of the goal cards that the players have written. Like last week, keep the names out of it, and concentrate on the goals that have some significance for the team. Remind the players that their individual efforts are what makes the team great, and the harder they work on game day, the more everyone will succeed.

I think that you'll find the players are starting to realize this on their own.

Game Week – Practice Two (Day 17), Post-Practice Meeting

Today's meeting is another of the shorter ones without a very specific agenda. You'll probably discover that, at this point in the preseason, there isn't that much to cover in these meetings unless something goes catastrophically wrong somehow.

About the only thing you really *have* to cover is the necessity for someone to scout your next opponent. If you don't have an assigned scout to take care of this for you, then you're going to need to make sure that someone steps up to fill this role immediately, even if you have to select and direct an assistant to do this. Let me stress one more time how important that scouting report is to everything you're trying to accomplish when it comes to preparing your team.

Game Week – Practice Three (Day 18), Segments 1-6: Foundation Period

By today you should be able to cut the anticipation with a rubber knife. Your players should be excited, and you should make sure to remind them constantly how much they've accomplished in the last three short weeks. Make sure they know how well-prepared they are, and remind them of the success they had in the scrimmage last Saturday.

Today's foundation period is identical to yesterdays, except for the drills used during the blocking period. The tackling drills remain the same, but for blocking use drills <u>B</u> and <u>C</u>. Tomorrow we're going to start scaling back the amount of hitting that we allow, so we'll shift to some of the padded or non-contact variants of the drills we're using, but today we can butt heads and enjoy it.

Game Week – Practice Three (Day 18), Segments 7-13: Offensive Period

When the foundation period is over, break the kids up into their offensive groups and work on the drills. Today, I would recommend putting the running backs with receivers and work on receiver's <u>Drill A</u> to get them some more practice at catching passes. If you decide that your backs are doing fine at that, or the emphasis should be put in other areas, running backs <u>Drill B</u> is probably a good idea. The offensive line should work on their <u>Drill B</u> as well, to hone their ability to double team and drive defenders off the line.

After the drill period ends, work the kids in their groups for two segments, again trying to make up the number of reps you're going to lose in team time while you're here in the individual periods. Don't let the high speed interfere with your need to develop quality as well as quantity, but with fewer players in motion at any one time mistakes should be much easier to diagnose and correct while still maintaining a quicker pace.

When segment nine ends, bring the team together and have them do their calisthenics. Then, using your scouting report of the opponent's defense, run your plays against your backups at about three quarters to full speed. Make sure that you use a quick whistle, as always, to reduce the likelihood of an injury. You have three segments to work on basic offense before you move to goal line offense. Remember to emphasize the importance of always scoring from within the five-yard line. If you always attempt a two point conversion, or your league doesn't allow PAT kicks, this becomes even more important for you.

Game Week – Practice Three (Day 18), Segments 14-20: Defensive Period

Segments fourteen through twenty are for defense. Break the team into their defensive groups by position and send them with their coaches. Each group will do their <u>Drill B</u>, so the linebackers will be working on sweep defense, the defensive backs will work on footwork, and the defensive line will work on defeating trap blocks. After one segment of this, bring the linebackers and defensive linemen together with the scouting report. After the players do their calisthenics, run the scout team plays with your skeleton defense and practice your blitzing.

By now it should be second nature to you to focus your practice time on those plays that your players have problems with, but one more thing that I would recommend is that you also throw in a couple of those trick plays we talked about before. Try to pick ones that "fit" with your upcoming opponent's offense, or adjust plays you've seen to work. More important than defending the actual play is the necessity to keep your players on their toes and ready to defense anything.

While the defensive linemen and linebackers are working on the blitz period, the defensive backs should be working with their coaches on drills <u>C</u> and <u>D</u>. Remember to use all variations available of these drills to really reinforce good pass coverage.

At the end of segment sixteen, send the defensive linemen off with their coach to work on pass rushing while the defensive backfield comes together to work on seven-on-seven for one segment. If your opponent has any trick passing plays, such as the "hook and lateral" or the "flea flicker," now is a good time to work those into the practice.

After the seven-on-seven period ends, call the linemen back and put together a scout team. You have two segments to get through the scouting report, and one additional segment for goal line defense.

Reinforcing Situation Football

Since today is the last day we're going to be hitting all out for the week, I like to do some fun stuff during the goal line period. I'll give the defense a situation, such as "ahead by three with sixty seconds left in the game and the opponent knocking on the door from our five yard line." Then I'll run the offensive plays in a hurry-up offense style, moving as fast as possible and not giving anyone a chance to rest. The offense gets four tries to get into the end zone, and then we'll move them back to the five yard line and start over, with another sixty second period to defend the doorstep.

The players should be dripping with sweat by the end of this period, but they should also have a lot of fun. Remember to use a quick whistle to keep hard collisions with the ground to a minimum, but encourage a certain amount of hitting. Goal line defense is largely a matter of attitude, and the team that is prepared to hit the hardest in this situation is typically the one that wins the battle. The problem is conditioning your players to do this without getting them hurt.

Game Week – Practice Three (Day 18), Segments 21-23: Special Teams Period

When you're done with the goal line period, bring the players together to practice special teams. Today you need to work on field goal and field goal block. Again, if you can, try to get as many reps as you can in a short period of time. If you can cheat by running your second string block team against the starting PAT/Field Goal unit, then try that. Whatever you do, shoot for about twelve to fifteen repetitions from several hash marks and distances, always starting from the PAT line.

By the way, don't forget that you can have the ball spotted *anywhere* along the three yard line inside the hash marks after a touchdown. If there's a big mud puddle right on the PAT mark, it doesn't make a lot of sense to kick out of it, so you might want to practice the occasional PAT from the three-yard-line on a hash.

If you can, try to get through enough of your reps that you can devote some extra time to field goal blocking drills. Don't forget to practice your field goal fake, too.

Of course, if you're in a league that doesn't allow field goals, feel free to use the extra time where you need the most work. I would generally put the emphasis on defense or another special team, but if your offense needs it, then by all means use it.

Game Week – Practice Three (Day 18), Segment 24: Chalk Talk – Game One Preview

Last week, before the scrimmage, we talked with the team about some of the rules we were going to enforce. We need to do the same thing today, and focus it on the upcoming game. Everyone needs to have their full equipment, and the last practice of the week is going to be in full game regalia once again.

There's a bit more to it than that. I usually end up spending a little time quelling some nervousness. Remind your players that they are the most disciplined football-playing machine in the league. They're stronger, faster, and better trained than anyone else, and when they step on that field in three days, everyone in the stands is going to see it as well.

Reinforce to them how proud you are of everything they've accomplished, and tell them how much you're looking forward to seeing them play in the game for the first time. Make sure they understand that butterflies in the stomach are normal, and after the first play, when they smack someone, those bugs are going to disappear.

Above all, encourage them to keep their focus and their practice intensity up. Winning a championship means playing like champions, and playing like champions means *practicing* like champions. So far, they've been doing that just fine, but remind them to keep working hard.

Tomorrow we're going to have our last hitting practice of the week, then a walk through on the day after, and then we're going to hand out a shellacking to our opponents.

Game Week – Practice Three (Day 18), Post-Practice Meeting

Again, today's meeting should be a simple affair. As you head into the first game, you should already be well aware of any areas where your players need extra work. Gather input from your staff to help you provide focus for the remaining practices of the week. Like yesterday, your meeting will probably be over before your players finish their practice snaps.

Game Week – Practice Four (Day 19), Segments 1-6: Foundation Period

Today is the final day that we're going to have the accelerator pressed to the floor in practice. While we want to keep the intensity high tomorrow, and we also want to continue coaching at high speed, we need to make sure that the players are slowing the tempo enough to rest their bodies for the first game.

At the youth level, this is rarely a problem, but we're still going to scale a few things back slightly today. To begin with, during the foundation period speed drills, have the players concentrate on slowing their movements down and exaggerating the exercises. The extra practice at form will help them, anyway.

For fun, try running Tackling Drills I, H, G, and E to give the players a change of pace. Note that most of these drills are lower impact, but still reinforce proper tackling form. Consider using the non-contact variant of tackling Drill H to reinforce the breakdown and begin the "hitting starvation."

For blocking, use drills A and B again. Remember to keep the players focused on a good explosion during both drills, but don't let them drive their partners to the ground.

Game Week – Practice Four (Day 19), Segments 7-13: Offensive Period

Today's offensive period is very similar to yesterday's. Since we're moving towards less and less contact in practice prior to the first game, we need to limit the hammering the players are going to take in the drill period. For this reason, the offensive linemen are going to focus on Drill A, which puts the emphasis on pulling and attacking the defender rather than on collision. The receivers, of course, will do Drill A, and by now they should be ball catching machines.

The running backs have something of a conundrum to face. They should be completely comfortable in their handoffs, and the ball should be nice and secure when they're carrying it. I recommend that you either work them on either of these skills as needed, with securing the ball as the most important responsibility (Drill B) or put them with the receivers for work on pass receiving.

After the drill period ends, use the scouting report to run your plays in the groups against the opposing defense. You have two segments for this, then bring the players together as a team and have them do their calisthenics before you get into the scouting report again. Like yesterday, you have three segments for scout defense with one final segment for goal line offense.

Game Week – Practice Four (Day 19), Segments 14-20: Defensive Period

Switch gears to defense at the end of segment thirteen. Break the players up into their groups and have them do their exercises before working on their individual drills.

Linebackers can go back to their Drill A, or focus on any set of skills you feel they need additional work on. The defensive line should center their attention on splitting double teams again with Drill D, and the defensive backs should work on either man-to-man coverage with Drill C or on zone coverage with Drill D, whichever you feel they need the most work at performing successfully.

As usual, after the individual drill period ends, have the linebackers and defensive linemen come together for the blitz period after they do their calisthenics. The defensive backs have two segments to work on pass coverage while the linebackers and linemen concentrate on snuffing out the opponent's scouting report. At the end of segment sixteen, send the linemen to work with their coach on pass rushing with <u>Drill C</u> and bring the defensive backs over for the seven-on-seven period. Again, use passing plays taken from your opponent's offense.

For segments eighteen and nineteen, bring the defensive linemen back and work on the full scout team. Today is your last real scrimmage before the game, so work your players hard. Call out the down and distance to go before every play, and try to put as many real life game situations into the period as possible. Remember to use a quick whistle and "thud" tackle to prevent injury and keep the players hungry for contact. Segment twenty is for goal line defense.

Practicing goal line defense with thud tackling can be difficult. The main trick is to blow the whistle just before the tackler makes contact with the ball carrier. The ball carrier should fight, but not full strength, for additional yardage. Tacklers should focus on the wrap portion of the tackle.

Game Week – Practice Four (Day 19), Segments 21-23: Special Teams Period

Today's special teams period is slightly different than the others we've had leading up to the first game. In the previous three practices this week we had fifteen minutes to devote to two different special teams. Today, we only have one: the punt.

In *The Hidden Game of Football* (ISBN: 1894963237), Bob Carroll describes the punt as "the most important play in football." I believe this to be entirely accurate. At the youth level, especially, punting is a highly important and usually forgotten part of the field position game. A punt, even at the youth level, can move you thirty yards closer to your opponent's end zone in one play.

Most coaches at the youth levels don't bother with punting. I've seen teams vying for a national championship go for it on fourth and fifteen from their own twenty-five yard line before. In my opinion, this is a result of absolutely atrocious coaching and a lack of responsibility in the coaches.

Think of it like this: if *you* can punt, and your opponent cannot, in a game in which neither offense can move the ball, then every time you get the ball you're going to come away with a net gain in yardage. Eventually your opponent is going to be playing panic football, and your chances of coming away with a score and winning the game go up by about ten percent for every thirteen yards closer to the end zone you start your drives.

Your punt team should look very good. The snaps should be crisp and accurate, and the punter should be able to face a rush unfazed and get the ball away, making sure to kick it *away* from any return men on the defense.

Extra Practice For The Most Important Play In Football

Having said that, in two days your punter is going to be staring into the teeth of a defense that wants to rip off his helmet while his head is still in it, and that long snapper is going to have to focus on his snaps while a defensive tackle snorts halitosis in his face. Taking fifteen minutes and devoting it to your punt team *now* can make a big difference in your health on game day. If possible, put your punt returner back to get extra practice at catching the ball.

Game Week – Practice Four (Day 19), Segment 24: Chalk Talk – Game One Preview

Just as we did with the scrimmage, we're going to talk today about the upcoming game. Make certain that the players are well aware of where they need to be and what time they need to be there on Saturday. Like we did for the scrimmage, I strongly encourage you to put all pertinent information into a handout for the parents and send it home with the players this evening. Again, make the parents sign the form stating that they read the information, and have the players bring back the signed form or face your wrath.

Remember, tomorrow's practice is in full game-day regalia, so all the players need to be in uniform.

Game Week – Practice Four (Day 19), Post-Practice Meeting

There are two main topics for tonight's meeting. 1) What do we need to put extra time into tomorrow? And 2) Is all the equipment ready for the game? Everything that was listed as necessary for the scrimmage is also necessary for the game. Whoever is in charge of the equipment needs to have the kits checked out and ready to go by the end of practice tomorrow.

All snappers should get an extra ten snaps today to prepare themselves for the game.

I recommend that you go home tonight and put some time into scripting out your opponent's offense for use in tomorrow's scout team defensive period. You're going to have four segments for nothing but scout team, and the best way to get your defense ready is to run it like a game. Following as closely as possible the offensive tendencies of your opponent, write a script of game situations that start from the opening kickoff, and move through at least forty plays, which is two per minute.

Don't forget to script a scout team goal line offense from your opponent's plays as well. You'll have one segment for that.

Game Week – Practice Five (Day 20), Segments 1-6: Foundation Period

This is it. Your last practice before you butt heads with another team in a real, live game. Just a few short weeks ago you had a bunch of crazy young people running around doing their own things, and now you have a solid team that works together like a well-oiled machine.

Today's practice is mostly a walk-through. Think of it as a dress rehearsal for the game tomorrow. We're going to limit contact as much as possible, and keep our exercises to a minimum. No more than five calisthenics of any type when the players change drills, and speed drills should be done like we did on the first practice of this week: full speed, but with reduced distances. This is also the same warm up we're going to do at the game.

Start out by collecting the parents' forms you sent home with your players yesterday, and mete out punishment for after practice conditioning as needed. Don't forget to collect the captain's essays as well.

Limit contact in the tackling and blocking period as well. For tackling, I recommend the non-contact version of Drill H, and drills A, B, and E. It's okay to do blocking drills A and B.

**Game Week –
Practice Five
(Day 20),
Segments 7-13:
Offensive
Period**

After the foundation period ends, gather the team and break them off into their respective offensive groups. The backs should concentrate on <u>Drill A</u>. It's always a good idea to reinforce proper ball handling right before a game. Receivers should practice <u>Drill A</u> some more, and the linemen should focus on pass blocking with <u>Drill C</u>.

This period is to get some last minute practice. By now, since they've been practicing it every day, your players should be very skilled at these core proficiencies. You'll note that there is no individual time today. When you're done with drills, bring the team together immediately to walk through the scouting report.

Actually, "walk through" is something of a misnomer. The players should move at a jogging pace and you should run every play in your offense at least three or four times for every player. Segment thirteen is a goal line period, but you might want to add segment twelve as well to make sure that every member of your team is as ready as possible.

One good idea, if you can pull it off, is to have your substitution coach standing on the sideline keeping track of which players need to sub in and out of the game. Whether or not you can do this is going to depend on how many players you have available. It can be difficult to constantly shuttle players back and forth from the scout defense to the offense while still maintaining a decent pace. Try it out and see what happens.

**Game Week –
Practice Five
(Day 20),
Segments 14-
19: Defensive
Period**

When segment thirteen ends, change your focus to defense. As you did for the offensive period, there won't be any individual drill time. In fact, the only drill you're going to focus on today is <u>Team Drill A</u>. Extra practice at wide play pursuit is a good idea before you get into the game.

When you've finished the one segment period devoted to this drill, put the scout team offense together and jog through your opponent's plays using the script you prepared last night. Make sure that you give your players the down and distance and game situation as a part of the pre-play information. You have four segments for this, so you should be able to run at least forty plays.

Again, concentrate on quality and on getting every member of your team on the field. The fluid game situation of defensive football makes it impossible to give every player a certain number of reps against every possible offensive play from every possible formation, but you still need to make sure that the mechanics of playing their position and pursuing the ball are being executed properly.

As per normal, your final segment of the defensive period is for scout team. Follow the script you put together last night, and concentrate on making sure that the players are putting themselves into position to make the tackles.

**Game Week –
Practice Five
(Day 20),
Segments 20-
23: Special
Teams Period**

Today's special teams period is vastly different from the previous ones. You have one extra segment for special teams, and you're going to need it, because today you need to walk through each special team, including fakes, at least three times with each member of your team.

Make sure that each player knows which special teams he plays on, and what his responsibilities are. Use the "sticky" blocking method I described earlier to make sure that your players are blocking the right men on the return teams, and move as quickly as you can without sacrificing quality.

For the punt and kickoff, if possible, put your returners back to field the balls, and make sure that you surprise your kickoff return team with a couple of onside kick attempts to keep them on their toes. If you can practice two teams at once: punt return versus punt team, kickoff return against the kickoff team, it will make this period go much more smoothly for you.

I like to end the practice with field goals. We'll kick four or five of them, and then tell the kicker that we're down by two points with just one second left in the game. It's up to him. Sometimes I'll move him a little closer, but most of the time I'll simply let him sink or swim on his own.

One thing that you might have noticed is that I told you back at the beginning of chapter seven that I won't call a play on game day unless we've run it perfectly at least fifty times in practice. Thanks to the effort we've put into organizing our practice plans, and the detail-oriented way we've approached each practice, not only have we far exceeded that number with our offensive plays, but we've probably shown our *defense* some of the more common plays they'll have to face more than fifty times as well.

Almost more important, we've managed to run each of our special teams plays at least fifty times. Think about that when you're lining up for the opening kickoff. Your opposing coach probably installed his kickoff return two days ago and has only run it five or six times, total.

I recommend that you onside kick.

Game Week – Practice Five (Day 20), Segment 24: Chalk Talk – Game One *Tomorrow!*

Tomorrow is the big day. At this point in the season you simply cannot overemphasize how proud you must be of your players. I would venture to guess that there are a number of *high school* teams across the country that will not be as well-prepared as your players will be for their first game. Tell them that.

Make sure that everyone knows where to meet and what time to be there. If everyone is to meet at the field make sure that the team is there at least two hours early. You need to have time to change out as well as warm up before you take the field. If you're going to meet somewhere and caravan or carpool to the game field, plan for traffic.

One of the worst experiences of my life, on a number of levels, was fighting traffic to an away game that was located more than two hundred miles from our home field. We were supposed to get dinner on the way, but the traffic was so bad that we ended up not getting anything until about forty minutes before the kickoff, and of course it was junk food. We won the game, but we were flat and listless through most of it.

While we're on the subject of pre-game nutrition, the evening meal on the day *before* a game is actually more important to the player's energy level than the breakfast he eats that day, but that doesn't mean that breakfast should be overlooked.

The night before the game each player should have a balanced meal that goes slightly higher on complex carbohydrates than normal. I recommend about 75%

carbs, 15% proteins, and only 10% fats, not too different from what we've been recommending all along.

Pasta and whole grains are much better than white flour or sweets. For dessert, stick with fruits. For breakfast, stay away from "children's" cereals that have a massive amount of sugar and instead look for whole grains again. Juice is an excellent source of morning carbohydrates.

If your game is going to be played in the afternoon or evening, follow that same guideline. Above all, *avoid junk food* on the day of the game.

Game Week – Practice Five (Day 20), Post-Practice Meeting

The main topic of tonight's meeting is one of the awards you're going to give out at tomorrow's game. Every week our coaching staff selects a "Hardest Working Lineman of the Week." This player might be a third stringer that never seems to slow down or stop hustling, or he might be the starter that encourages everyone on the line to play better. Whoever it is, pick him tonight while your snappers get their reps.

For home games, we announce the hardest working lineman of the week over the intercom, and his parents are allowed a free trip to the snack bar. This is great, because the player not only feels like he accomplished something, but he feels that he earned something for his family as well. If it's an away game, we'll announce the player to the team during warm ups and allow him to take the field with this week's captains.

Your equipment should be ready to go. Your staff should be ready to go, and your *players* should be ready to go. Now, all that's left is to get some rest for yourself and start your journey to a championship tomorrow.

Game Day

Gather your team for warm-ups at least forty-five minutes before the opening kickoff. Long snappers, quarterbacks, centers, kickers, and returners should assemble at least ten minutes earlier.

Like you did at the scrimmage, have your players do their pushups and sit-ups and then do their speed work at half speed and half distance. After the speed work, split into offensive groups and continue the warm up with receivers' Drill A for the running backs and receivers, and blocking Drill B for the linemen.

At the end of five minutes, bring everyone together and run your offensive plays against the scout team defense at about half speed like you did yesterday at practice. Everything should be smooth. Take about ten minutes for this, and focus on the core plays, with a brief refresher of any plays that your players have had any problems with in the past.

When you're done, divide up into defensive groups and run basic drills like you did with the offense. Have everyone do their group's Drill A, and then move into a scout team period, running your opponent's plays. Go no faster than half speed during the plays.

When you're done it should be time to take the field. Like we did at the scrimmage, we take the field as a team, and that's usually where the team does their mascot jacks; nice and loud in front of the fans where they belong.

Referees

The referees should seek you out at some point during the pre-game. There are a couple of things I recommend you bring up with them. First off, if you run any unusual plays that take advantage of rarely used rules, make sure that you mention this to the refs. Try not to come across like you're trying to tell them their jobs, but make sure everyone is on the same page.

As an example, I run a wedge play in which all members of my offensive line push on the center and drive him forward. We do not interlock or grab each other's jerseys (both illegal), and we do not push on the ball carrier (also illegal). I always mention this play specifically to the referees to make sure that they know we have carefully taught this play the right way, and to ask them to please not call us for the illegal play unless they actually witness it. (You'd be surprised how often a referee makes a call based on what "must be happening in the pile.")

After you chat with the referees, they're probably going to ask for your captains for the coin toss.

You need to make sure that your captains understand which end of the field to defend if you end up receiving the kickoff. Take into account wind direction (make them kick into the wind), sun direction (try to keep your players from staring into late afternoon or early morning sun as much as possible), and the location of the scoreboard (its easier to run a two minute offense when your quarterback is looking at the scoreboard, so you might want it at the end of the half.)

Remember, if you win the coin toss, you may elect to kick, receive, or *defer*. If you choose to kick, your opponent gets the choice in the second half, and he can choose to make you kick again! If you want to receive the ball in the second half, have your captains defer the choice if you win the toss.

Last Words...

Another thing I like to do is shake the hand of each one of my players and whisper a little something in their ear. Maybe it's a reminder that I'm proud of them, or maybe it's a suggestion that we "Teach these city-folk how we play football out here in cow country." Whatever it is, it's something I try to do before every contest, typically while the captains are on the field for the coin toss.

Typically, my organizational system allows my team to be vastly better prepared than my opponents. Because of this, we tend to be very successful in our first game. I can almost guarantee to you that your team is going to be better prepared than your first opponent's team is, because you read this book, and hopefully will apply some of its thinking to your own preparation.

About the only thing you need to really worry about is if your opponent also bought this book, and is also preparing his team the same way. You should consider buying a second copy, just in case.

It's game time, Coach. Good luck.

AFTERWORDS
The Road Less Traveled

Final Thoughts

Well, we've done it. Three hundred pages later, and you've just started on the road to coaching football. Everything after this page is gravy. You'll find discussions of the drills used in chapter eight, an essay on the seriousness of concussions in football, information on the Black Lion Award, a glossary of football terminology, and of course, a crap load of charts that will hopefully make your coaching easier and more successful. (A crap load, by the way, is defined as slightly less than a metric butt-ton.)

I want to thank you for walking along this path with me. Coaching football is important. You'll have a number of battles ahead of you in your coaching career: parents that don't understand, assistant coaches that are clueless, administrations that don't believe in your program the way they should, and of course, the important one: the big game against your rival team. Just remember why you got into this in the first place. Come August, when the kids are taking a knee around you during segment one of day one, take a deep breath and look at them, really *look* at them. For most of us, nothing we ever do will be as important as standing right there with those young people gathered around us.

Very few people have the courage to do what you're doing and the sense of commitment it takes to do it right. I hope this book helps you, but more than anything I've written, what's *really* going to help you is that you're willing to read it; you're putting in the time and effort to make yourself a better coach. I salute you for that.

If you played football before, remember what it was like, and the way you respected your coaches. If you've never played, take it from me, for two hours a night throughout the fall those kids idolize you. Keep the faith with them.

I look forward to seeing you again in *Volume II: Coaching Youth Special Teams*. Until then, I wish you the very best of luck.

~D.

Derek A. "Coach" Wade
CoachWade@hotmail.com

APPENDIX ONE
Drills

Introduction

Probably the number one question I get asked by inexperienced coaches is "What drills should I run?" They ask this because, for most of us, all we really remember of football practice is running endless drills. *Why* we ran those drills is generally pretty vague, but we always remember banging helmets.

I have never been a large believer in drills. If you'll notice, the practice schedule in chapter eight spends very little time on drills. There's an important reason for that: teaching every vagary of your program is far more important than teaching a drill. Which would you rather your left guard be able to do: execute a West Point blocking drill properly, or pick up a blitzing defender in the "B" gap every time? Would you rather your linebackers know how to blitz, or *where* to blitz?

Drills are for teaching, practicing, and then perfecting specific skills that must be properly executed on game day. Unfortunately, great skill application with no direction tends to lead to teams that can hit like beasts—but lose every game because they don't know *who* to hit.

I remember a couple of things about my eighth grade year at Sumner Junior High. The second is the coach of the Edgemont Eagles that told me after the game, "I wish we had some hitters like you on our squad."

The first is my coach, yelling at me the entire game for not hitting the right guy.

Don't be that coach. Use the drills sparingly, and concentrate on two things: proper execution, and *speed*. Get as many reps as you can for each player. Most of the time I recommend breaking your team into groups. In a typical 30-player team, approximately fourteen players will be linemen and sixteen players will be receivers or running backs. Typically, this means about three quarterbacks, seven running backs, and six receiver types (tight ends and split ends). You might have a slightly different mix depending on your team.

Usually I break the players into sections by responsibility on the side of the ball we're working on. For example, one of my offensive linemen might be a linebacker on defense. When we work defense, he goes with the linebackers. When we work offense, he goes with the line. These groups are, offensively: backs, receivers, and offensive linemen. Defensively they are: backs, linebackers, and defensive linemen.

This chapter is designed to work in two manners. First, the drills are cross-referenced to the practice plan presented in chapter eight. Second, if you already have a good plan that you prefer to follow, you can simply use this chapter as a quick reference to gather new ideas. Either way, the format should be consistent and easy to follow.

You should do some form of blocking and tackling period every day, no matter what. I strongly recommend a four station tackling circuit and at least a two station blocking circuit. Keep the kids moving, and get them the reps they need to become safely proficient in the most dangerous parts of football.

Finally, make sure you teach to keep the kids safe. The helmet, whether mask, crown, or side, has no place in hitting. Teach the kids to protect themselves with their kinetic energy, and:

ALWAYS TEACH YOUR PLAYERS TO BLOCK AND TACKLE WITH THEIR HEADS UP!

READ THIS ⟶ Football is a rough sport. No amount of padding, protective equipment, or preparation can completely eliminate all dangers. The methods advocated within this book are designed to reduce danger to young athletes as much as possible. Use of these techniques, drills, and methods in any way constitutes acceptance of a certain amount of risk and is considered agreement that you indemnify and hold the author and publisher of this work not responsible for any injuries that may occur.

~D.

Tackling

<u>Drill A</u>: Slow Motion Form Tackling

<u>Object</u>: Teach proper form tackling fundamentals

<u>Procedure</u>: Align two rows of players facing each other at approximately two yards distance. Spread the coaches out so each coach is responsible for watching and correcting the form of 4-7 players. Demonstrate the proper steps to a form tackle and teach the players to yell out the correct procedure for the step after receiving a one-word cue from the tackling coach.

Steps for a proper tackle:

1) Coach yells, "Break it down."

    a. Players yell, "Eyes on the belt!"

2) Coach yells, "Hit."

    a. Players yell, "Numbers to numbers!"

3) Coach yells, "Wrap."

    a. Players yell, "Grab cloth behind the neck!"

4) Coach yells, "Lift."

    a. Players yell, "Take the hips with you!"

5) Coach yells, "Drive!"

    a. Players yell, "Short, choppy steps!"

After the proper technique has been demonstrated, the players will execute correct form tackles on one another, with one line tackling and the other line acting as the ball carrier, switching after every "tackle". Both lines remain immobile. This drill can be done with or without pads. Each tackler should get 5-10 reps before the end of the drill.

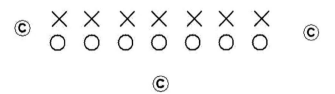

<u>Coaching Points</u>: Ensure that each player properly executes the five fundamental points of each tackle while repeating the tackling point goal aloud. This should be a nice and noisy drill.

1) <u>Breakdown</u> – Tacklers should take a good football position approximately one yard from the ball carrier. Weight should be balanced on the balls of the feet and the feet should be shoulder width apart. Hands should be in front of the hips or chest and the back straight. Eyes should be focused on the ball carrier's belt buckle.

2) <u>Hit</u> – Tacklers should step forward while rolling their heads backwards until they are in an "eyes to the sky" position. Their chest should be touching the chest of the ball carrier and they should have a slightly lower pad level.

3) <u>Wrap</u> – Tacklers should shoot the arms from hip level up and through the ball carrier's midsection, crossing wrists behind the shoulders. They should grab the jersey at the back of the ball carrier's neck.

4) <u>Lift</u> – Tacklers should drive the hips forward while lifting with the legs and arcing the back to slightly raise the ball carrier from the ground.

5) <u>Drive</u> – Tacklers need to maintain short, choppy drive steps with a wide base until they have driven the ball carrier back five yards.

<u>Drill B</u>: Head on Tackling

<u>Object</u>: Reinforce proper tackling form and teach tackling in motion.

<u>Procedure</u>: Place a ball carrier holding a protective shield in front of him in front of a series of landing mats, tackling dummies, or any other soft surface. A line of tacklers faces the ball carrier. At the coach's command the tacklers will move at 3/4 speed to the ball carrier and execute a proper five point tackle, lifting him up and over to land on the padded surface. The tackler will then take the shield and become the ball carrier for the next player.

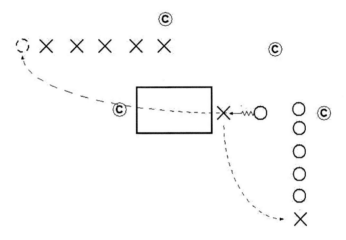

<u>Coaching Points</u>: Ensure that players execute all five points of the proper tackle as listed in <u>Drill A</u>.

<u>Variation 1</u>: Ball carriers charge forward and deliver a blow with the shield to the tackler.

Drill C: Eye Opener

Object: Teach/Reinforce mirroring the movement and attack angles of the ball carrier.

Procedure: Place a ball carrier holding a protective shield in front of him in front of a series of tackling dummies, cones, or other markers arranged to provide five gaps approximately four to five feet in width. The coach stands behind the tackler and points to a gap. The ball carrier then runs directly to that gap in a somewhat arcing path from his starting position on the side. The tackler should meet him in the hole and make a secure, five-point tackle. After rotating through the series, the tacklers should align to run the drill from the other side.

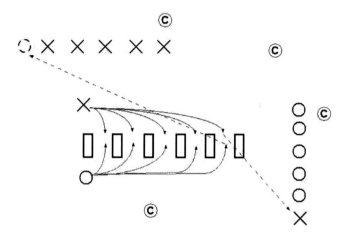

Coaching Points: Tacklers should scrape to the gap while keeping the shoulders square to the line of scrimmage and mirroring the ball carrier's movement. (He approaches the line = I approach the line. He moves away = I move away.) The tackler should get his head across the bow of the ball carrier while approaching for the breakdown and hit steps.

Ensure that players execute all five points of the proper tackle as listed in Drill A. Tacklers and ball carriers both should keep the legs driving and attempt to power one another over.

Variation 1: Ball carriers are allowed to fake, juke and cut before entering the gap.

<u>Drill D</u>: Box Drill

<u>Object</u>: Teach/Reinforce proper approach angles when pursuing the ball carrier.

<u>Procedure</u>: Place four cones at the corners of a five-yard by five-yard box. Arrange the players in two lines facing one another across one side of the box and standing at the cones. One line is ball carriers, and the other is tacklers. At the coach's signal, the ball carrier runs directly for the cone diagonally opposite him. He is not to deviate from a straight course to the cone. The tackler does *not* take the ball carrier to the ground.

The tackler should move laterally to get his "head across the bow" of the ball carrier, and execute a correct five point tackle that drives the ball carrier out of the square formed by the far cones.

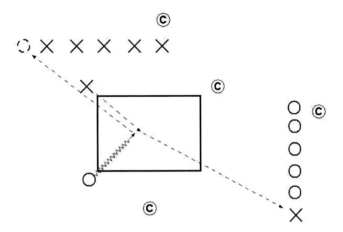

<u>Coaching Points</u>:

This is a <u>full speed</u> tackling drill. Both players should run at full speed towards their points. The tackler will have to adjust his angle to make sure that the head crosses the path of the ball carrier and impact is made with the near breastplate. The drill box must be kept small enough to keep the players from full acceleration.

Ensure that players execute all five points of the proper tackle as listed in <u>Drill A</u>. Tacklers and ball carriers should both keep the legs driving and attempt to power one another over.

<u>Variation 1</u>: Ball carriers are allowed to fake, juke and adjust speed as they approach the cones.

<u>Drill E</u>: Angled Pad Drill

<u>Object</u>: Teach/Reinforce proper angle tackling

<u>Procedure</u>: Place a ball carrier holding a protective shield in front of him in front of a series of landing mats, tackling dummies, or any other soft surface as described in <u>Drill A</u>. A line of tacklers faces the ball carrier, arranged at an angle that will intersect the ball carrier such that the ball carrier will fall onto the landing surface at the completion of the tackle.

At the coach's signal, the tackler charges forward and angles to drive through the near shoulder of the ball carrier, executing a proper five-point tackle.

The tackler should move laterally to get his "head across the bow" of the ball carrier, and execute a correct five-point tackle that drives the ball carrier out of the square formed by the far cones.

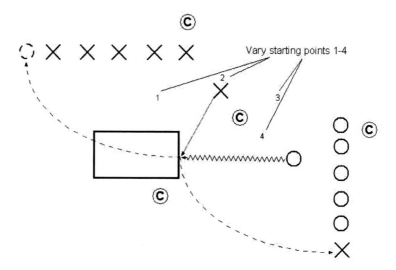

<u>Coaching Points</u>: This is a <u>full speed</u> tackling drill. The ball carrier must hold the shield to take the impact of the tackler. The tackler must adjust his approach angle to get his "head across the bow" of the ball carrier, and execute a correct five-point tackle that drives the ball carrier out of the square formed by the far cones.

<u>Variation 1</u>: Ball carriers jog across in front of the landing surface, with the tackler adjusting his approach angle as needed to maintain a proper head in front approach. Speed of the ball carrier may gradually be increased to a 3/4 speed run.

<u>Variation 2</u>: Tacklers make a secure wrap with the downfield arm while striking a blow down on the football with the upfield hand in an attempt to knock the ball loose.

<u>Drill F</u>: Bull in the Ring

<u>Object</u>: Teach/Reinforce aggression in tackling

<u>Procedure</u>: Place one player in the center of a circle of players that are fingertip to fingertip. On a coach's command this player chops his feet in place while the coach walks around the outside of the circle. The coach will select a player of approximate size, weight, and athleticism as the player in the circle and throw a football to him. This new player must catch the football and run directly across the circle of players in a straight line.

The player in the circle must attack the ball carrier and make a secure five point tackle to prevent him from reaching the other side of the circle.

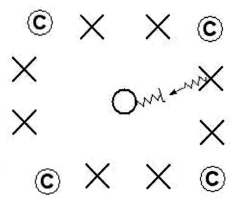

<u>Coaching Points</u>: This is a <u>full speed</u> tackling drill. Use a limited number of players (eight or fewer) to keep the circle less than six yards across. This puts the tackler approximately three yards from the ball carrier's starting point. Ensure that players execute all five points of the proper tackle as listed in <u>Drill A</u>. Tacklers and ball carriers both should keep the legs driving and attempt to power one another over.

<u>Drill G</u>: Head to Head

<u>Object</u>: Teach/Reinforce speed off the ball, proper tackling position, and tenacity

<u>Procedure</u>: Place two players on their backs with helmets touching in the middle of a five-yard by five-yard box formed by cones. Give a football to one player. At the coach's signal, both players scramble to their feet and the ball carrier attempts to run across the box while the tackler attempts to prevent this with a secure tackle. The players then swap lines.

The tackler should move laterally to get his "head across the bow" of the ball carrier, and execute a correct five-point tackle that drives the ball carrier out of the square formed by the far cones.

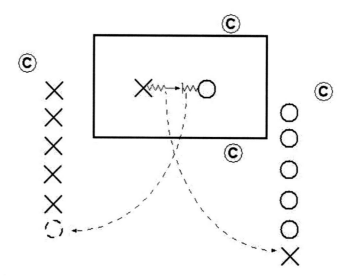

<u>Coaching Points</u>: This is a <u>full speed</u> tackling drill. Both players must get to their feet as quickly as possible. Speed is essential.

<u>Drill H</u>: Lane Tackling (Advanced Drill)

<u>Object</u>: Teach/Reinforce proper lane discipline, breakdown, and tackling form in the open field.

<u>Procedure</u>: Place a ball carrier holding a protective shield in front of him on the sideline facing inward to the field. He should stand on one yard line marker. Two lane tacklers face him from the hash marks. The ball carrier can run anywhere within the yard lines on either side of him (ten lateral yards). If he makes it to the hash marks he has scored a touchdown. The lane tacklers should secure their lanes as they move towards him, breaking down and closing to the ball only when the ball carrier is even with them. The tacklers do <u>not</u> take the ball carrier to the ground.

In the first weeks of practice, run this drill without contact. The defensive players should break down and trap the ball carrier without touching him. They need to be in a good breakdown position with their weight on the balls of their feet and their eyes pinned to the bottom of the ball carrier's numbers.

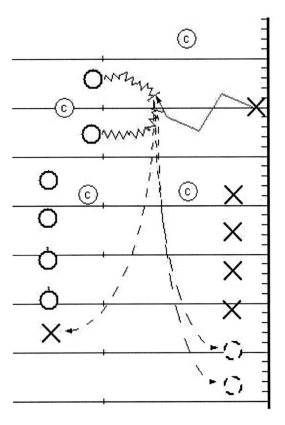

<u>Coaching Points</u>: This is a <u>full speed</u> tackling drill. The ball carrier must hold the shield to take the impact of the tackler. The tacklers must adjust their approach angle to get their "head across the bow" of the ball carrier, and execute a correct five-point tackle.

<u>Variation 1 (Extremely Advanced)</u>: The first tackler to the ball carrier makes a secure wrap of the ball carrier. The second tackler attempts to strip the ball from the ball carrier. The tacklers do <u>not</u> take the ball carrier to the ground.

Variation 2 (Extremely Advanced): A coach stands on the hash mark opposite the yard line the ball carrier is on. The ball carrier does not have a shield. The coach throws a football to the ball carrier while simultaneously telling the tacklers "Go!" The tacklers do not take the ball carrier to the ground.

Drill I: Scrape and Attack (Advanced Drill)

Object: Teach/Reinforce mirroring the movement and attack angles of the ball carrier.

Procedure: Similar to Drill C: Eye Opener, place a ball carrier holding a protective shield in front of him in front of a series of tackling dummies, cones, or other markers arranged to provide five gaps approximately four to five feet in width. The ball carrier should align in the middle of the gaps.

The coach stands behind the tackler and points to a gap. The ball carrier then runs to that gap. The tackler should meet him in the hole and make a secure, five-point tackle.

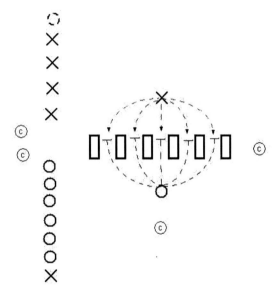

Coaching Points: Tacklers should scrape to the gap while keeping the shoulders square to the line of scrimmage and mirroring the ball carrier's movement. (He approaches the line = I approach the line. He moves away = I move away.) The tackler should get his head across the bow of the ball carrier while approaching for the breakdown and hit steps.

Ensure that players execute all five points of the proper tackle as listed in Drill A. Tacklers and ball carriers both should keep the legs driving and attempt to power one another over.

Variation 1: Ball carriers are allowed to fake, juke and cut before entering the gap.

Blocking

<u>Drill A</u>: Punch and Goes

<u>Object</u>: Teach/Reinforce initial explosion off the ball.

<u>Procedure</u>: Place a number of blockers in front of an equal number of defenders holding shields. The blockers should be in a proper three-point stance. A coach calls cadence. At the proper snap count, the blockers drive forward and deliver a blow with the forearms or heels of the hands into the shields. The blockers then immediately reset to proper stances. Repeat the drill five times before the blockers rotate to be bag holders and the bag holders go to the back of the blocking line.

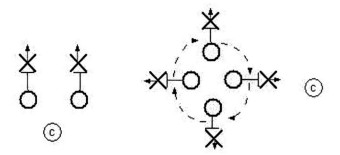

<u>Coaching Points</u>: This drill is extremely important for teaching proper burst from the ball. Ensure that the blockers deliver a quick, controlled blow and concentrate on getting two steps into the defender before resetting. The players must reset to a proper stance.

<u>Variation 1</u>: Pop and go circle: Divide the players into two teams. Team A makes a circle around Team B. Team A will have the shields. Team B takes proper three-point stances facing one of the Team A players. On a coach's cadence the players of Team B fire off and execute a pop and go into the bag held by the player of Team A. Instead of resetting in front of the same defender, Team B players rotate one player clockwise before resetting to a proper stance.

<u>Drill B</u>: Drive Blocking Form

<u>Object</u>: Teach/Reinforce finishing blocks after initial contact.

<u>Procedure</u>: Place a number of blockers in front of an equal number of defenders holding shields. The five blockers should be in a proper three-point stance. A coach calls cadence. At the proper snap count, the five blockers drive forward and deliver a blow with the forearms or heels of the hands into the shields. Unlike Blocking <u>Drill A</u>, the blockers do not then immediately reset to proper stances. Blockers must make contact and drive their opponent back a minimum of five yards. After the first step the defender should let go of the shield. If the shield drops to the ground the blocker is not maintaining proper contact.

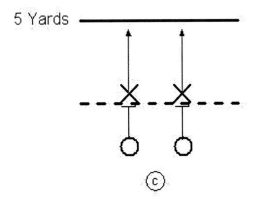

<u>Coaching Points</u>: Finishing blocks is a key component of offensive success.

1) Blockers must use an "icepicks to the chest" arm position during the block to minimize holds and prevent defensive separation.

2) Blockers must strive to make and maintain contact with the defender at bottom-of-the-numbers height. They should "climb down" the defender if they find themselves engaged too high to establish a push on the defender.

3) Blockers must maintain a wide base.

4) Blockers must use short, choppy steps to drive the opponent back.

<u>Variation 1</u>: Defensive players are allowed to spin or use other defensive techniques to avoid the block.

<u>Variation 2</u>: Drive blocking circle: As in <u>Drill A, Variation 1</u> arrange blockers in a circle with defenders outside. On cadence the blockers drive the defenders outward from the center of the circle. At the whistle the blockers then immediately shift one man clockwise and reset to a three-point stance.

<u>Variation 3</u>: Twelve step contact: On cadence the blockers drive the defenders as in the standard drill. After impact the defender should drop his pad. If the pad strikes the ground, the blocker is not maintaining proper push into the block and the blocker does ten pushups. The blocker should drive for twelve steps.

Drill C: "Splatter!"

Object: Teach/Reinforce delivering a blow and finishing blocks after initial contact.

Procedure: Similar to Tackling Drill B, place a set of mats or pads down to create a landing surface. In front of this surface station one player with a bag.

A second player charges the first from approximately six yards and delivers an upward-striking blow with the forearms. The object is to pancake the defender onto the mats.

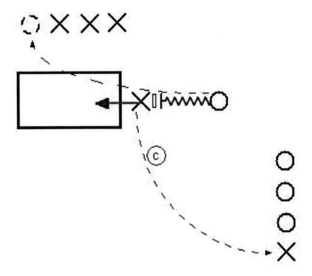

Coaching Points: Finishing blocks is a key component of offensive success.

1) Blockers must strive to make and maintain contact with the defender at numbers height.

2) Blockers must use an "icepicks to the chest" arm position during the block to minimize holds and prevent defensive separation.

3) Blockers must run through the defender, driving him to the mats

Variation 1: Defensive players are allowed to spin or use other defensive techniques to avoid the block. They may also charge the blocker and deliver a blow of their own with the shield.

<u>Drill D</u>: "Sumo"

<u>Object</u>: Competitive drill for teaching/reinforcing all aspects of drive blocking.

<u>Procedure</u>: Take a clothesline approximately 31 feet six inches in length and lay it on the field to make a circle ten feet across. Align two players of approximately equal weight within the circle and facing one another in three point stances.

On a coach's cadence, both players fire out and attempt to drive block one another from the circle. Play does not end until one player has been driven either to the ground, or out of the circle.

Sumo is an excellent drill for discovering offensive linemen. Set up three to five sumo circles and divide the team into as many brackets as you have circles and coaches to monitor. Each bracket competes until a final sumo challenger has successfully defeated all other members of their bracket. Then each bracket sends their challenger to the championship bracket. The winner of that bracket should receive some form of reward, such as no conditioning, or being allowed to carry the football in the next game.

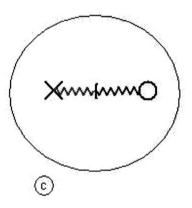

<u>Coaching Points</u>: Players should keep a low, wide base and engage their opponent with their feet moving and their heads up. Pure strength is not the only indicator of probable success; technique is vastly preferable.

Drill E: Double Team

Object: Teach/reinforce proper double team execution.

Procedure: Align a single defensive player with a blocking shield in a head up position over an offensive player with a teammate beside him. On coach's cadence, the first offensive player will execute a post block (identical to a correct drive block). As he works to neutralize the defender's charge he will receive assistance from the blocker next to him, who will slant sharply to make contact with the defender's side and drive him at an angle backwards.

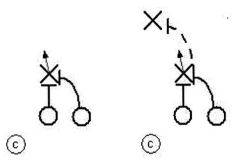

Coaching Points: Both blocking players must continually work to drive the defender upfield and keep their hips close together. They must maintain a low pad level.

Variation 1: The defender is now allowed to drop to all fours and "grab grass" like a well-coached defender. The post blocker should look to come off the double team and move upfield to block a linebacker while the drive blocker finishes the block and pushes the defender to the ground.

Offensive Line Drills

<u>Drill A</u>: Search and Destroy

<u>Object</u>: Teach/reinforce proper pulling technique and downfield blocking.

<u>Procedure</u>: Align two players (guard and tackle) side-by-side and foot-to-foot next to a blocking dummy laid lengthwise on the ground. On a coach's cadence, both players execute a proper pulling step without gaining backfield depth and with a downhill angle that crosses the line of scrimmage by the third step. At the end of the blocking dummy they should immediately turn up into the hole, with the guard looking to the inside to wall off inside pursuit from the linebackers and the tackle looking to the outside.

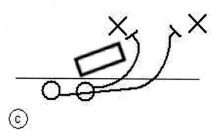

<u>Coaching Points</u>: The pullers should pull with their hips low to the ground and with a downhill angle that crosses the line of scrimmage as soon as possible. It is vital that they turn up into the hole as soon as they see daylight. The guard should make an exaggerated movement to snap his head around and look to the inside, and the tackle should do the same looking outside to inside.

<u>Variation 1</u>: Station one or two players with blocking shields in the defensive backfield at linebacker depth. As the pullers attack through the hole, these linebackers should scrape to flow from either side, giving the guard and tackle a moving target for blocking.

<u>Drill B</u>: Double Teams

<u>Object</u>: Teach/reinforce proper double team technique.

<u>Procedure</u>: Align two players (guard and tackle) side-by-side and foot-to-foot facing a defensive player that holds a shield. On a coach's cadence the blockers fire out and engage the defender. One player, the inside man, should post the defender and neutralize his charge. The second player should down block and move the defender out of the hole and backwards from the initial point of contact.

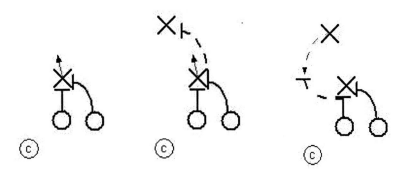

<u>Coaching Points</u>: A proper double team against a well-coached defender depends on the blockers marrying their hips together after initial contact and moving in unison to drive the defender back. Both offensive players should put a portion of their energy sideways into one another to maintain that contact while at the same time keeping a strong push.

<u>Variation 1</u>: Combo Blocking. Place a second defender behind the double team to act as a linebacker. Have the outermost player slide off the double team after driving the defender back approximately two yards. The blocker should look to the second level and attack the linebacker, seeking to place his head on the outer shoulder of the defender and steer his path downfield. A hard hit is not necessary; just interfere with his ability to scrape to the gap.

<u>Variation 2</u>: Blitz pickup. Similar to the combo block, but the innermost player slips off the double team immediately after neutralizing the charge of the defender. He should be alert to the blitzing linebacker and attack his playside shoulder, attempting to turn him perpendicular to the line of scrimmage.

<u>Variation 3 (Advanced)</u>: Give the linebacker a signal to blitz or scrape and allow the blockers to make their own decisions on whether to combo or cutoff.

<u>Drill C</u>: Pass Blocking

<u>Object</u>: Teach/reinforce proper pass blocking technique.

<u>Procedure</u>: Align two players facing one another from approximately one yard's distance and between two cones five yards apart. Behind one player place a cone at five yard's depth.

The player opposite the cone is the defender. On a coach's cadence, the defender tries to get through, over, or around the offensive lineman in front of him, who must pass block properly for six seconds.

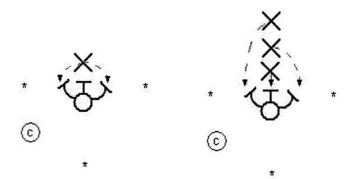

<u>Coaching Points</u>: Pass blocking requires that the offensive linemen aggressively deliver a blow to the defensive linemen to negate the defender's charge, and then keeps his body between the defender and the cone as long as possible. The defender may use any legal technique to get past the offensive lineman.

Offensive linemen that feel the defender starting to slip to the outside should steer the defender as far to the side as possible without holding.

<u>Variation 1</u>: Blitz pickup: Place two defenders side by side approximately two yards from the line of scrimmage. A coach stands behind the offensive lineman and points to one defender or another. At the snap, the selected defender rushes the passer.

The offensive lineman must correctly read which defender is blitzing, negate his charge by delivering a blow, and then steer the defender away from the passer for six seconds.

<u>Variation 2</u>: Blitz pickup. Place three defenders in a line facing towards the pass blocker and approximately three yards from the line of scrimmage. The defensive players should be stacked on top of each other so the offensive lineman can only see the one in front. Hold up one, two, or three fingers to tell the defenders which of them should blitz, and point to a side.

The offensive lineman must correctly determine the blitzing defender, deliver a proper blow to stop his approach, and then control the defender for six seconds to keep him away from the passer.

<u>Drill D</u>: Down Blocking

<u>Object</u>: Teach/reinforce proper down blocking technique.

<u>Procedure</u>: Align one defensive player at the end of a blocking dummy laid on the ground across the line of scrimmage. Give a shield to the defensive player. A blocker aligns across the line of scrimmage at the other end of the blocking dummy.

A coach calls cadence. At the snap the blocker takes a six-inch jab step with the near foot towards the man to be blocked. His second step should align him to a thirty-degree angle and he should be engaged with the defender at the correct blocking target (below the numbers.) The blocker drives with a wide base, along the bag, until the defender has been driven past the end of the dummy or to the whistle.

<u>Coaching Points</u>: Down blocking should take place using all blocking fundamentals of the standard drive block, but executed at a thirty-degree angle along the line of scrimmage away from the point of attack. The blocker should attempt to maintain leverage on the defender by placing his helmet to the upfield side of the block, i.e. in the hole.

Down blocks always begin with a short jab step towards the defender with the nearest foot, designed to engage and neutralize his charge. The blocker must bring his hips in line to the thirty-degree angle immediately after the first step and maintain a wide base.

<u>Variation 1</u>: Have the defender take a hard step forward to deliver a blow against the blocker. This is still a blocking drill, however, so the defender must allow his charge to be stopped and himself to be driven back.

Quarterback/ Running Back (Offensive Backfield) Drills

<u>Drill A</u>: Handoff Machine

<u>Object</u>: Teach/reinforce proper handoff technique.

<u>Procedure</u>: Place two lines of players in single file facing one another at approximately eight yards distance. One line starts with a football. On a signal, the first two players in line run towards each other and hand the ball off as they pass. The next players in line should move almost immediately after the initial players.

The ball should hover approximately in the middle of the eight-yard spacing and be handed from line to line. When a player has handed off the ball he immediately joins the line opposite the one he started in.

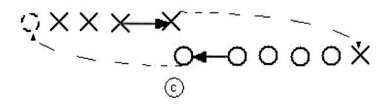

<u>Coaching Points</u>: One of the largest causes of fumbles on exchanges is players a) not looking the ball into the belly of the receiver, b) trying to make the handoff at too high a speed, and 3) the receiver using incorrect reception technique.

The receiver must take the handoff with his top elbow pointing at the player handing him the ball.

The coach must watch very carefully. The handoffs will be taking place rapidly. The players will also tend to creep towards one another, and they need to start their forward movement at the eight yard point every time.

For every fumbled handoff the entire group does five pushups.

<u>Drill B</u>: The Gauntlet

<u>Object</u>: Teach/reinforce proper football security.

<u>Procedure</u>: Place two lines of players in single file facing one another at approximately two yards distance. Give every other player a shield, and across from him should be a player that is empty handed.

Start a running back holding a football in each arm approximately three yards from the start of the gauntlet. At the cadence, the runner runs between the lines. The players with the shields hit him and try to knock him off balance while the players that are empty handed attempt to strip out the football.

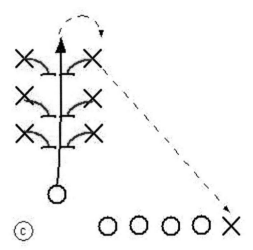

<u>Coaching Points</u>: The ball carrier should maintain four points of pressure on the football at all times, holding the ball with an "eagle claw" over the point, the bicep over the second point, and continuous pressure from the forearm that pushes the ball into the stomach.

If the ball is stripped out, the ball carrier does twenty pushups.

Receiver Drills

<u>Drill A</u>: One Thousand Hands

<u>Object</u>: Teach/Reinforce proper methods of catching the football and adjusting to the ball in flight.

<u>Procedure</u>: Align receivers on one yard line with a coach/quarterback standing approximately five yards from them (on the next yard line.) On the correct cadence the receiver runs in a straight line following the chalk and the coach/quarterback throws a ball to them. The pass may be accurate or inaccurate, and the receiver must accelerate, leap, gear down, or lay out to make the reception. After they catch the ball they sprint back and place it next to the coach/QB and then align to the opposite side of where they started.

When the receivers are competent at reacting to and successfully catching a thrown ball, use this same drill but require them to catch the ball with one hand.

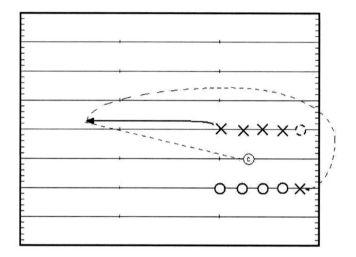

<u>Coaching Points</u>: Emphasize correct use of the hands. A thrown football should be caught with the hands and brought immediately to the body. The head and eyes must be down and looking the ball into the hands. A tennis ball, softball, or baseball may be used in place of a football to reinforce correct catching mechanics.

<u>Variation 1</u>: The next player in line plays bump-and-run defensive back and delivers a blow to the receiver as he tries to clear the line and get into his pass route. He does not cover downfield.

<u>Variation 2</u>: The receivers run specific pass routes from the offense, and the passers align in a position as close as possible to the spot from which the ball will be thrown.

<u>Drill B</u>: Concentration

<u>Object</u>: Teach/Reinforce proper concentration on the football.

<u>Procedure</u>: Align receivers in two lines facing one another, with one line approximately five yards from the coach/passer, and the second approximately ten yards distant. On cadence, the first player in each line runs directly forward.

The far line is the receiver. The near line is made up of distracters. The distracters may yell, jump, wave their hands, or do anything else to break the receiver's concentration. They may not touch the football or interfere with the receiver's path in any way.

After each player has run their route, have them join the opposite line.

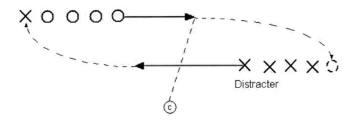

<u>Coaching Points</u>: Emphasize correct use of the hands. A thrown football should be caught with the hands and brought immediately to the body. The head and eyes must be down and looking the ball into the hands.

<u>Variation 1</u>: The next player in the receiver line plays bump-and-run defensive back and delivers a blow to the receiver as he tries to clear the line. He does not cover the receiver.

<u>Variation 2</u>: Have the last distracter in line bump the receiver just after he catches the ball. The receiver must carefully tuck the football away and maintain positive control with four points of pressure on the ball.

<u>Drill C</u>: Basketball Pass

<u>Object</u>: Teach/Reinforce proper methods of catching and securing the football.

<u>Procedure</u>: Align receivers in a circle facing inward with one football. For the duration of the drill period the receivers pitch the ball back and forth in a random pattern. The object is to make a secure catch with the hands and pull the ball in to the body on every touch.

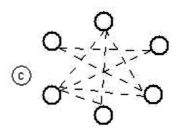

<u>Coaching Points</u>: Emphasize correct use of the hands. A thrown football should be caught with the hands and brought immediately to the body. The head and eyes must be down and looking the ball into the hands.

The players should be in good football stances with their weight on the balls of their feet and their eyes in constant motion, oriented towards the ball.

<u>Variation 1</u>: When the players are adept at catching and securing one football, add a second and third as needed.

<u>Variation 2</u>: All receivers must make catches one handed.

Defensive Drills

<u>Drill A</u>: Pursuit Angles

<u>Object</u>: Teach/Reinforce angles for pursuit and containment/trapping of the ball carrier.

<u>Procedure</u>: Place four bags on the ground to represent a pair of guards and tackles. Place a football at the center position, and use an extra player to represent a tight end who varies from side to side. Down each sideline place one cone every ten yards for forty yards.

The defense aligns against the bags and the coach calls a defensive stunt and coverage. When the ball is moved, the offensive linemen and linebackers should execute their stunts and attack their assigned gaps, while the defensive backs drop to their assigned coverage zones. The coach then either steps to the right, left, or straight ahead and the defense pursues using correct angles to trap the ball carrier. Alternately, the coach may choose to drop back and throw the ball, checking to make sure that the pass coverage defenders are dropping to their correct zones or mirroring their assigned men in man-to-man coverage. The coach may then throw the ball to an area between the zones and the defensive backs can intercept and practice a return with a proper bingo call.

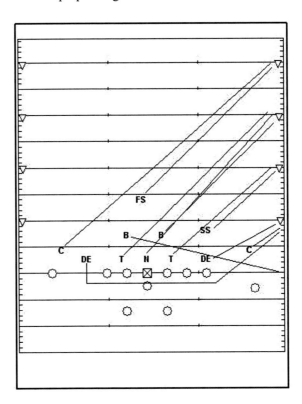

<u>Coaching Points</u>: Players must pursue at full speed, running towards the downfield side of their assigned cones. At least one linebacker should be assigned to pursue flat to the ball carrier in and "inside-out" relationship to prevent a cutback lane from opening up. Players must be coached to run "where the ball carrier is *about to be*" rather than where he is now.

<u>Variation 1</u>: Pick a defender at random and throw a hard pass towards him but slightly off target. The player should drive off, angle to intercept, and make a bingo call to alert teammates that the ball is now in his possession.

Defensive Line Drills

Drill A: Get Offs

Object: Teach/Reinforce defensive explosion at the snap.

Procedure: Place four or five defensive linemen in their typical front and techniques against five blocking shields laid on the ground to represent offensive linemen. A coach with a football stands at the center position and calls a cadence, trying to draw the players offsides. If the players cross the plane of the ball before the snap, they immediately do five pushups.

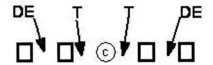

Coaching Points: Defensive linemen should keep an eye on the football and move the moment there is the slightest bit of daylight beneath the ball.

Variation 1: Have extra players hold the blocking shields and act as offensive linemen. The defensive rushers should execute a proper arm-over or arm-under technique to escape from the blocker and secure their gap.

<u>Drill B</u>: Defeating Trap Blocks

<u>Object</u>: Teach/Reinforce reading/reacting to offensive line keys.

<u>Procedure</u>: Place one shield on the ground as a center with one guard on either side of it. Align your defensive linemen against them in your normal front. A coach calls cadence. At the snap, one guard should attempt to cross the face of the defensive player without engaging him while the other pulls flat to the line and trap blocks him.

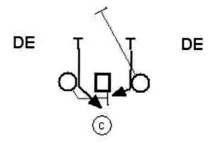

<u>Coaching Points</u>: As soon as the offensive lineman crosses his face the defensive player should immediately step to the inside and deliver a hard blow to the trapping guard with his inside shoulder, hopefully driving him back into the hole and creating a pile. He should keep a low hip and pad level, and make sure his eyes are up, scanning for the runner and keying the back farthest from him. His shoulders must be square to the line of scrimmage.

The defensive lineman aligned on the pulling guard should attempt to angle his path to get in the puller's "hip pocket" and follow him to the ball carrier. He, too, should have his eyes up and scanning for the runner while keeping his shoulders square to the line.

<u>Drill C</u>: Pass Rushing

<u>Object</u>: Teach/Reinforce proper pass rushing angles.

<u>Procedure</u>: Place five shields on the ground to indicate an offensive line and align defensive linemen in proper techniques across from them. A coach stands in the position of quarterback and holds a ball. At the snap (movement of the coach's foot) the defensive linemen execute a proper pass rush, staying in their lanes while the coach drops back, rolls out, or scrambles.

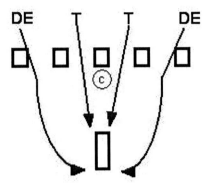

<u>Coaching Points</u>: All pass rushers must attack the upfield shoulder and hip of the coach/quarterback. For outside rushers this forces the quarterback into the inside rush and eliminates the scramble. For inside rushers, this provides the quickest path to the quarterback.

<u>Variation 1</u>: Arm over/under technique: At the snap the pass rushers execute an arm technique against air before rushing the passer.

<u>Variation 2</u>: Arm over/under technique against live opponent: have one or two extra defensive linemen hold the bag and provide pressure against the defensive lineman. The defensive lineman still executes the arm over/under technique before rushing the passer.

<u>Variation 3</u>: Place a tackling dummy at the approximate depth of the quarterback's drop back and have the defensive players swarm to make the sack.

<u>Drill D</u>: Splitting Double Teams

<u>Object</u>: Teach/Reinforce proper response to double team blocks.

<u>Procedure</u>: Place two offensive linemen across from one defensive lineman. One yard behind the defensive lineman place a shield or flat cone on the ground. A coach calls a cadence. At the snap the offensive linemen both attempt to engage the defender and drive him back. If the defensive lineman's feet move past the cone, he is considered blocked and must do five pushups.

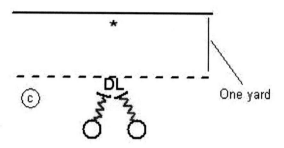

<u>Coaching Points</u>: To split the double team the defensive lineman must drop low as soon as he realizes two defenders are engaging him. At all times his pad level must be lower than that of both of his opponents. He should "grab grass" and make a pile on the spot.

<u>Variation 1</u>: Standing behind the defensive lineman, the coach points to one or the other offensive players. The player selected blocks the defensive lineman, who should use proper technique to escape the block. If the coach selects both offensive players, the defensive player should respond by grabbing grass and making a pile.

Linebacker Drills

<u>Drill A</u>: Crunch Time

<u>Object</u>: Teach/Reinforce proper angles and responsibilities when taking on a lead blocker.

<u>Procedure</u>: Place five blocking shields on the ground to represent offensive linemen. Two players with shields stand on the offensive side of the ball in either an I-Formation or twin backs backfield alignment. Align the linebackers in the standard defensive front facing the offense. A coach stands behind them and points to a gap in the offensive line. The player closest to the gap is the lead blocker, and should charge the gap looking to block the nearest linebacker. The back farthest from the selected gap becomes the ball carrier.

The linebacker being attacked should immediately attack the block, attempting to make contact with the blocker on the *offensive* side of the line of scrimmage and blow the blocker back into the ball carrier. His inside foot must be down, and his shoulders must be as square as possible to the line of scrimmage.

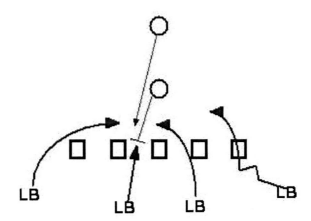

<u>Coaching Points</u>: Each linebacker has a specific assignment. The diagram shows the correct approach angles for each linebacker from a 4-4 Split. Loosely, the nearest linebacker eliminates the lead blocker. The closest outside linebacker slow plays from the outside to watch for the bounce-out. The nearest inside linebacker keys the ball carrier and watches for cutback. The far outside linebacker stays home and *does not move*. He must be alert to the counter.

<u>Variation 1</u>: Counters. Establish a hand signal for the ball carriers in which you can call a counter play in which the ball carrier takes one step to follow the lead blocker and then cuts sharply back against the grain to hit another hole.

<u>Variation 2</u>: Plays. Using scout team cards have the linebackers defend your opponents' plays without the line, taking proper pursuit angles and covering their assignments.

Variation 3: Reading the line. Using extra players to represent the offensive guards and center, have the linebacker read the offensive linemen's blocking pattern. When the guard to their side pulls inward, they should call, "Pull!" and slow-play to pursue. If the guard on their side charges, they should meet his charge, keeping the head up and "wrong-shouldering" to get his hips into the hole.

<u>Drill B</u>: Attacking Sweeps

<u>Object</u>: Teach/Reinforce proper angles and responsibilities when defending sweeps

<u>Procedure</u>: Place five blocking shields on the ground to represent offensive linemen. Two players stand on the offensive side of the ball in either an I-Formation or twin backs backfield alignment. Align the linebackers in the standard defensive front facing the offense. A coach lines up as the offensive quarterback. The coach will indicate sweep left or sweep right, and whether the play will be a pitch sweep or lead sweep.

At the snap the offensive players will execute a sweep to either sideline. The playside outside linebacker must string the play by attacking the upfield shoulder and hip of the ball carrier, always maneuvering to get his head across and in front of the runner.

Linebackers inside the sweep should attack the ball carrier using an inside-out path. The backside outside linebacker should trail the sweep flat along the line of scrimmage, looking to play counter/cutback.

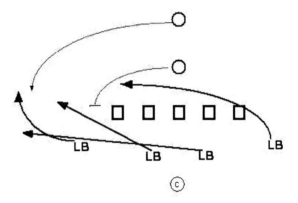

<u>Coaching Points</u>: Sweep defense is a matter of negating the speed of the ball carrier with the approach angles of the defense. The playside sweep defender absolutely must get his head "across the bow" of the ball carrier. If he at any time attacks the near shoulder and/or hip of the ball carrier, the runner will turn the corner and escape to the outside.

Inside linebackers must use the correct approach angles to place them in position to make the tackle if the runner stops and attempts to cut back against the grain. Shoulders should be kept as square as possible to the lie of scrimmage.

<u>Variation 1</u>: Counters. Have the offensive players execute a dive/sweep combination such as the buck sweep from the Wing-T. Inside linebackers must stay home to guard against the dive before taking inside-out pursuit angles to the ball.

Defensive Back Drills

<u>Drill A</u>: Punch and Go

<u>Object</u>: Teach/Reinforce proper bail technique for bump and run pass coverage.

<u>Procedure</u>: Place defensive backs into two lines facing one another across the line of scrimmage. Designate one line to be receivers and the other to be defensive backs. At the snap the receivers take one step as if to clear the line on a pass route. The defensive player should drive both hands hard into the breastplate of the receiver while taking a simultaneous drop step with the outside foot and opening to approximately 45-degrees. The impact of the bail should be hard enough to drive the receiver at an angle.

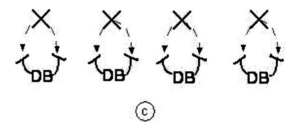

<u>Coaching Points</u>: The defensive backs cannot wind up before delivering a blow. Their hands should be held at chest level with their eyes focused on the bottom of the receiver's numbers.

<u>Variation 1</u>: No Cadence. Let the receivers move on their own, while the coach calls a random cadence. The defenders should react to the receiver's movement, regardless of the specific snap count.

<u>Drill B</u>: "W" Drill

<u>Object</u>: Teach/Reinforce proper footwork for breaking on the thrown football.

<u>Procedure</u>: Place defensive backs into one line facing the coach. When the coach raises the football to his shoulder the line backpedals. When he lifts his top hand from the ball they should break and charge forward. He should put his hand back on the ball and they should drop back to a backpedal. Repeat to each side at least three times.

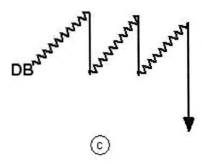

<u>Coaching Points</u>: Proper break on the football is a function of hip level. Players should compress their hips towards their knees and attempt to stop their rearward movement in one step before driving hard forward.

<u>Variation 1</u>: Pick a defender at random and throw a hard pass towards him but slightly off target. The player should drive off, angle to intercept, and make a bingo call to alert teammates that the ball is now in his possession.

Drill C: Man-To-Man Coverage

Object: Teach/Reinforce proper coverage technique for man-to-man pass coverage.

Procedure: Place one defensive back and one receiver across from each other on the line of scrimmage. At the snap the receiver runs a pass route called previously by the coach. The defensive back should maintain a cushion in basic man, or disrupt the receiver's route in bump and run. When the receiver makes his cut or closes the cushion the defender should plant and come up hard to the inside of the receiver's cut, getting to cutoff position. When the receiver looks back for the ball the defender should look back through the receiver (if possible) and shoot the far hand over the receiver's hands while wrapping the receiver's waist with the nearest hand.

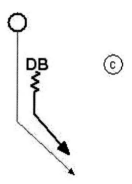

Coaching Points: The defensive backs must make every effort to maintain trail position before the cut, and cutoff position after the receiver makes his break. Flags must be thrown and the defender must be punished for pass interference. It is often useful to run this drill without a football to focus the defensive player on playing the opponent rather than the ball in flight.

The defensive back must look back for the ball or he runs the risk of being called for faceguarding.

Variation 1: Scout team. Using plays taken from the scouting report have extra players run pass patterns from the upcoming opponent's offense. All other aspects of the drill remain the same.

Variation 2: Run the drill without the football to concentrate on the man rather than the thrown ball. All other aspects of the drill remain the same.

Drill D: Zone

Object: Teach/Reinforce proper zone coverage technique.

Procedure: Align one defensive back in the middle of the zone facing two lines of receivers about fifteen yards apart. At the snap the receivers run directly down the field. The coach should drop, set up, and throw to one receiver.

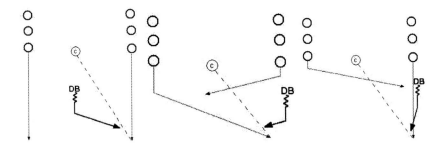

Coaching Points: The defensive backs must keep a close eye on the quarterback, breaking only when the ball is in the air and continuing to gain depth until the pass is thrown. At no point can the defender allow the receivers behind him.

Variation 1: Zone cross. Move the defender to a position across from one of the receivers. Have the receiver angle sharply across the field while the other angles over the top back into the defender's zone. The defender must gain depth and stay home in his zone. As soon as the receiver breaks across his face he should be calling "Slant!" or "In!" to notify the outside linebacker that the receiver is breaking into his zone.

Variation 2: Runoff. With the defender aligned across from one receiver, have that receiver run a deep route while the other receiver angles across into the zone underneath. The defender must stay as deep as the deepest man in his zone, break hard on the ball, and intercept or deny at the ball's highest point.

Variation 3: Scout team. Using plays taken from the scouting report have extra players run pass patterns from the upcoming opponent's offense. All other aspects of the drill remain the same.

Speed Drills   (Note: All speed drills are performed for at least twenty yards.)

<u>Drill A</u>: Butt Kickers

<u>Object</u>: Teach/Reinforce flexibility and arm follow through while running.

<u>Procedure</u>: Align a group of players in a single line horizontally across the field. On cadence, the players run forward taking as many steps as possible in a twenty-yard line. With each step they should bring their heels up to touch their buttock.

At the same time as the heels come up, the elbows should be driven back sharply until the shoulder and elbow are at the same distance from the ground. The opposite fist should come to just above eye level. The torso does not rotate.

<u>Coaching Points</u>: The player must keep his head up and elbows in motion. Speed of motion is unimportant, as this is a dynamic stretch.

<u>Drill B</u>: High Knees

<u>Object</u>: Teach/Reinforce flexibility and arm follow through while running.

<u>Procedure</u>: Align a group of players in a single line horizontally across the field. On cadence, the players run forward taking as many steps as possible in a twenty-yard line. With each step they should bring their knees to above waist level.

At the same time that the knees cross the plane of the hip, the elbows should be driven back sharply until the shoulder and elbow are at the same distance from the ground. The opposite fist should come to just above eye level. The torso does not rotate.

<u>Coaching Points</u>: The player must keep his head up and elbows in motion. Speed of motion is unimportant, as this is a dynamic stretch.

<u>Drill C</u>: Frog Hops

<u>Object</u>: Teach/Reinforce explosive movement in an upward direction.

<u>Procedure</u>: Align a group of players in a single line horizontally across the field. Each player takes one step, and then crouches until his thighs are just past parallel with the ground. With an explosive motion the player then leaps as high as possible, throwing his arms above his head as he does so, and trying to come down approximately one yard from his starting point. Roughly twenty frog hops should be necessary to cross the finish line.

<u>Coaching Points</u>: As fatigue sets in the players will not leap upward, but will instead leap forward. Caution the players that this is an upward-exploding exercise. The players must also make use of the arms, throwing them high overhead.

<u>Variation 1</u>: Double frog hops. The exercise is performed in precisely the same manner, except that the players execute two hops. The object is to make the hops as smoothly as possible, without pausing between them. This reinforces smooth muscle contraction during running.

<u>Variation 2</u>: Triple frog hops. Exactly the same as double hops, except with a third hop.

<u>Variation 3 (Advanced)</u>: Reverse frog hops. Same as original drill, except that the players leap backwards, focusing the exercise on the quads of the upper thigh more than the glutes.

<u>Drill D</u>: Forward Leap

<u>Object</u>: Teach/Reinforce explosive movement in a forward direction.

<u>Procedure</u>: Align a group of players in a single line horizontally across the field. The players leap forward as far as possible, in a standing broad jump. They should be able to cover at least two yards, so it should take approximately ten jumps to reach the twenty-yard mark.

<u>Coaching Points</u>: The player must use his arms, loading his elbows to a horizontal position even with his shoulders before throwing them forward during the jump.

<u>Drill E</u>: Form Running

<u>Object</u>: Teach/Reinforce proper sprinting form.

<u>Procedure</u>: Align a group of players in a single line horizontally across the field. The players run forward as slowly as possible while still staying in proper sprinting form.

1) All weight is on the balls of the feet.

2) Elbows return to a horizontal position, even with the shoulders behind the body.

3) Fists come to just above eye level on the forward movement.

4) The torso rotates with every arm thrust.

5) Each step moves smoothly into the next with no loss of kinetic energy.

<u>Coaching Points</u>: Watch for proper arm loading and follow through to eye level, as well as weight on the balls of the feet. Players should not "stomp" at the ground, instead gliding across it and using it to push themselves forward.

<u>Drill F</u>: Leaping run

<u>Object</u>: Teach/Reinforce proper sprinting form.

<u>Procedure</u>: Align a group of players in a single line horizontally across the field. The players bound forward in an extended step as if they were leaping from a boat to a dock. At the same time as the leap, the opposite hand punches forward as far as possible.

<u>Coaching Points</u>: Watch for proper arm loading with the elbows horizontal and even with the shoulders behind the body. Players should stretch and rotate the torso as they move forward.

APPENDIX TWO
Practice Plan

Introduction

In chapter eight I took you step-by-step through the first twenty days of practice leading up to your first game. This Appendix is a chart that is much more practical for use on the field. The chart matches up with the description in chapter eight.

Feel free to make copies of it as you need, and alter it as much as you like to suit your team and coaching staff.

Included in this Appendix is a blank practice planning form for you to use if you feel it necessary to completely rewrite the plan. I hope that won't be necessary.

Good luck

~D.

Appendix Two – Practice Plan

Week 1	Day 1			
Segment Number	**Time**	**Personnel**	**Activity**	**Notes**
1	6:00-6:05	All	Introduce Coaches	"Ready" Position, pushups and sit-ups requirement, teach three-point stance
2	6:05-6:10	All	Introduce Coaches	"Ready" Position, pushups and sit-ups requirement, teach three-point Stance
3	6:10-6:15	All	Speed/Warmups	Drill A, B, C, D, E
4	6:15-6:20	All	Speed/Warmups	Drill A, B, C, D, E
5	6:20-6:25	All	Tackling/Blocking	**Tackling**- Drill A **Blocking**- Drill A, B
6	6:25-6:30	All	Tackling/Blocking	**Tackling**- Drill A **Blocking**- Drill A, B
7	6:30-6:35	All	Tackling/Blocking	**Tackling**- Drill A **Blocking**- Drill A, B
8	6:35-6:40	All	Tackling/Blocking	**Tackling**- Drill A **Blocking**- Drill A, B
9	6:40-6:45	All	Agility Game	Deer Hunter
10	6:45-6:50	All	Agility Game	Deer Hunter
11	6:50-6:55	All	Agility Game	Deer Hunter
12	6:55-7:00	All	Agility Game	Deer Hunter
13	7:00-7:05	All	Time players	20, 10, Jingle-Jangle, Agility Four Corner (4-coaches, 1 segment per drill)
14	7:05-7:10	All	Time players	20, 10, Jingle-Jangle, Agility Four Corner (4-coaches, 1 segment per drill)
15	7:10-7:15	All	Time players	20, 10, Jingle-Jangle, Agility Four Corner (4-coaches, 1 segment per drill)
16	7:15-7:20	All	Time players	20, 10, Jingle-Jangle, Agility Four Corner (4-coaches, 1 segment per drill)
17	7:20-7:25	All	Skills Game	5 on 5 two-hand touch football (3 games, one coach per as referee)
18	7:25-7:30	All	Skills Game	5 on 5 two-hand touch football (3 games, one coach per as referee)
19	7:30-7:35	All	Skills Game	5 on 5 two-hand touch football (3 games, one coach per as referee)
20	7:35-7:40	All	Skills Game	5 on 5 two-hand touch football (3 games, one coach per as referee)
21	7:40-7:45	All	Punting/Kicking contest	Four groups, punt to kick, kick to punt, rotate.
22	7:45-7:50	All	Punting/Kicking contest	Four groups, punt to kick, kick to punt, rotate.
23	7:50-7:55	All	Chalk Talk	Down system, scoring, positions
24	7:55-8:00	All	Chalk Talk	Down system, scoring, positions

Appendix Two – Practice Plan

Week 1   Day 2

Segment Number	Time	Personnel	Activity	Notes
1	6:00-6:05	All	Speed/Warmups	Drill A, B, C, D, E
2	6:05-6:10	All	Speed/Warmups	Drill A, B, C, D, E
3	6:10-6:15	All	Tackling/Blocking	**Tackling**- Drill A **Blocking**- Drill A, B
4	6:15-6:20	All	Tackling/Blocking	**Tackling**- Drill A **Blocking**- Drill A, B
5	6:20-6:25	All	Tackling/Blocking	**Tackling**- Drill A **Blocking**- Drill A, B
6	6:25-6:30	All	Tackling/Blocking	**Tackling**- Drill A **Blocking**- Drill A, B
7	6:30-6:35	All	Demonstration Period	Handoffs, Carrying the Football, Receiving, "Scoop and Score"
8	6:35-6:40	All	Demonstration Period	Handoffs, Carrying the Football, Receiving, "Scoop and Score"
9	6:40-6:45	All	Drive Blocking	SUMO!!
10	6:45-6:50	All	Drive Blocking	SUMO!!
11	6:50-6:55	All	Drive Blocking	SUMO!!
12	6:55-7:00	All	Time players	Strength Four Corner 5x5, Agility 5x10x5 Ladder, Strength 5x10x5 Ladder
13	7:00-7:05	All	Time players	Strength Four Corner 5x5, Agility 5x10x5 Ladder, Strength 5x10x5 Ladder
14	7:05-7:10	All	Time players	Strength Four Corner 5x5, Agility 5x10x5 Ladder, Strength 5x10x5 Ladder
15	7:10-7:15	All	Time players	Get missing times for absent players
16	7:15-7:20	All	Skills Game	5 on 5 two-hand touch football (3 games, one coach per as referee)
17	7:20-7:25	All	Skills Game	5 on 5 two-hand touch football (3 games, one coach per as referee)
18	7:25-7:30	All	Skills Game	5 on 5 two-hand touch football (3 games, one coach per as referee)
19	7:30-7:35	All	Skills Game	5 on 5 two-hand touch football (3 games, one coach per as referee)
20	7:35-7:40	All	Punting/Kicking contest	Final Competition
21	7:40-7:45	All	Basic Offensive Alignment	Temporary starters based on computer scores
22	7:45-7:50	All	Walk Through First Play	Temporary starters based on computer scores
23	7:50-7:55	All	Basic Defensive Alignment	Temporary starters based on computer scores
24	7:55-8:00	All	Chalk Talk	Sportsmanship

Appendix Two – Practice Plan

Week 1   Day 3

Segment Number	Time	Personnel	Activity	Notes
1	6:00-6:05	All	Speed/Warmups	Drill A, B, C (Variation 1), D, E
2	6:05-6:10	All	Speed/Warmups	Drill A, B, C (Variation 1), D, E
3	6:10-6:15	All	Tackling/Blocking	**Tackling-** 4 Station: Drill A, B, C, D **Blocking-** 2 Station: Drill A, B
4	6:15-6:20	All	Tackling/Blocking	**Tackling-** 4 Station: Drill A, B, C, D **Blocking-** 2 Station: Drill A, B
5	6:20-6:25	All	Tackling/Blocking	Swap players from tackling to blocking. Repeat above.
6	6:25-6:30	All	Tackling/Blocking	Swap players from tackling to blocking. Repeat above.
7	6:30-6:35	All	Offensive Installation Period	Follow Installation Listing
8	6:35-6:40	All	Offensive Installation Period	Follow Installation Listing
9	6:40-6:45	All	Offensive Installation Period	Follow Installation Listing
10	6:45-6:50	All	Offensive Installation Period	Follow Installation Listing
11	6:50-6:55	All	Offensive Installation Period	Follow Installation Listing
12	6:55-7:00	All	Offensive Installation Period	Follow Installation Listing
13	7:00-7:05	All	Team Offense	Follow Installation Listing
14	7:05-7:10	All	Team Offense	Follow Installation Listing
15	7:10-7:15	All	Team Offense	Follow Installation Listing
16	7:15-7:20	All	Team Offense	Follow Installation Listing
17	7:20-7:25	All	Team Offense	Follow Installation Listing
18	7:25-7:30	All	Defensive Installation Period	Follow Installation Listing
19	7:30-7:35	All	Defensive Installation Period	Follow Installation Listing
20	7:35-7:40	All	Team Defense	Follow Installation Listing
21	7:40-7:45	All	Team Defense	Follow Installation Listing
22	7:45-7:50	All	Special Teams	Kickoff Walk Through
23	7:50-7:55	All	Special Teams	Kickoff Walk Through
24	7:55-8:00	All	Chalk Talk	Leadership

Appendix Two – Practice Plan

Week 1   Day 4

Segment Number	Time	Personnel	Activity	Notes
1	6:00-6:05	All	Speed/Warmups	Drill A, B, C (Variation 1), D, E
2	6:05-6:10	All	Speed/Warmups	Drill A, B, C (Variation 1), D, E
3	6:10-6:15	All	Tackling/Blocking	**Tackling**- 4 Station: Drill A, B, C, D **Blocking**- 2 Station: Drill A, B
4	6:15-6:20	All	Tackling/Blocking	**Tackling**- 4 Station: Drill A, B, C, D **Blocking**- 2 Station: Drill A, B
5	6:20-6:25	All	Tackling/Blocking	Swap players from tackling to blocking. Repeat above.
6	6:25-6:30	All	Tackling/Blocking	Swap players from tackling to blocking. Repeat above.
7	6:30-6:35	All	Drill Period	**Backs**- Drill A **Receivers**- Drill A **Oline**- Drill B
8	6:35-6:40	All	Offensive Installation Period	Follow Installation Listing
9	6:40-6:45	All	Offensive Installation Period	Follow Installation Listing
10	6:45-6:50	All	Offensive Installation Period	Follow Installation Listing
11	6:50-6:55	All	Offensive Installation Period	Follow Installation Listing
12	6:55-7:00	All	Offensive Installation Period	Follow Installation Listing
13	7:00-7:05	All	Offensive Installation Period	Follow Installation Listing
14	7:05-7:10	All	Team Offense	Follow Installation Listing
15	7:10-7:15	All	Team Offense	Follow Installation Listing
16	7:15-7:20	All	Team Offense	Follow Installation Listing
17	7:20-7:25	All	Team Offense	Follow Installation Listing
18	7:25-7:30	All	Drill Period	**All**- Defense Drill A
19	7:30-7:35	All	Defensive Installation Period	Follow Installation Listing
20	7:35-7:40	All	Team Defense	Follow Installation Listing
21	7:40-7:45	All	Team Defense	Follow Installation Listing
22	7:45-7:50	All	Special Teams	Punt Walk Through
23	7:50-7:55	All	Special Teams	Punt Walk Through
24	7:55-8:00	All	Chalk Talk	The Black Lion Award

Appendix Two – Practice Plan

Week 1   Day 5

Segment Number	Time	Personnel	Activity	Notes
1	6:00-6:05	All	Speed/Warmups	Drill A, B, C (Variation 2), D, E, F
2	6:05-6:10	All	Speed/Warmups	Drill A, B, C (Variation 2), D, E, F
3	6:10-6:15	All	Tackling/Blocking	**Tackling**- 4 Station: Drill A, B, C, D **Blocking**- 2 Station: Drill A, B
4	6:15-6:20	All	Tackling/Blocking	**Tackling**- 4 Station: Drill A, B, C, D **Blocking**- 2 Station: Drill A, B
5	6:20-6:25	All	Tackling/Blocking	Swap players from tackling to blocking. Repeat above.
6	6:25-6:30	All	Tackling/Blocking	Swap players from tackling to blocking. Repeat above.
7	6:30-6:35	All	Drill Period	**Backs**- Drill A **Receivers**- Drill A **Oline**- Drill C
8	6:35-6:40	All	Offensive Installation Period	Follow Installation Listing
9	6:40-6:45	All	Offensive Installation Period	Follow Installation Listing
10	6:45-6:50	All	Offensive Installation Period	Follow Installation Listing
11	6:50-6:55	All	Offensive Installation Period	Follow Installation Listing
12	6:55-7:00	All	Offensive Installation Period	Follow Installation Listing
13	7:00-7:05	All	Offensive Installation Period	Follow Installation Listing
14	7:05-7:10	All	Team Offense	Follow Installation Listing
15	7:10-7:15	All	Team Offense	Follow Installation Listing
16	7:15-7:20	All	Team Offense	Follow Installation Listing
17	7:20-7:25	All	Drill Period	**DBs**- Drill A **LBs**- Drill A **DL**- Drill A
18	7:25-7:30	All	Defensive Installation Period	Follow Installation Listing
19	7:30-7:35	All	Defensive Installation Period	Follow Installation Listing
20	7:35-7:40	All	Team Defense	Follow Installation Listing
21	7:40-7:45	All	Team Defense	Follow Installation Listing
22	7:45-7:50	All	Special Teams	Kickoff Return Walk Through
23	7:50-7:55	All	Special Teams	Kickoff Return Walk Through
24	7:55-8:00	All	Chalk Talk	Grades

Appendix Two – Practice Plan

Week 2 — Day 6

Segment Number	Time	Personnel	Activity	Notes
1	6:00-6:05	All	Speed/Warmups	Drill A, B, C (Variation 2), D, E, F
2	6:05-6:10	All	Speed/Warmups	Drill A, B, C (Variation 2), D, E, F
3	6:10-6:15	All	Tackling/Blocking	**Tackling-** 4 Station: Drill A, C, D, E **Blocking-** 2 Station: Drill A, C
4	6:15-6:20	All	Tackling/Blocking	**Tackling-** 4 Station: Drill A, C, D, E **Blocking-** 2 Station: Drill A, C
5	6:20-6:25	All	Tackling/Blocking	Swap players from tackling to blocking. Repeat above.
6	6:25-6:30	All	Tackling/Blocking	Swap players from tackling to blocking. Repeat above.
7	6:30-6:35	All	Drill Period	**Backs-** Drill A **Receivers-** Drill A **Oline-** Drill A
8	6:35-6:40	All	Offensive Installation Period	Follow Installation Listing
9	6:40-6:45	All	Offensive Installation Period	Follow Installation Listing
10	6:45-6:50	All	Offensive Installation Period	Follow Installation Listing
11	6:50-6:55	All	Offensive Installation Period	Follow Installation Listing
12	6:55-7:00	All	Offensive Installation Period	Follow Installation Listing
13	7:00-7:05	All	Offensive Installation Period	Follow Installation Listing
14	7:05-7:10	All	Team Offense	Follow Installation Listing
15	7:10-7:15	All	Team Offense	Follow Installation Listing
16	7:15-7:20	All	Team Offense	Follow Installation Listing
17	7:20-7:25	All	Drill Period	**DBs-** Drill A **LBs-** Drill A **DL-** Drill B
18	7:25-7:30	All	Defensive Installation Period	Follow Installation Listing
19	7:30-7:35	All	Defensive Installation Period	Follow Installation Listing
20	7:35-7:40	All	Team Defense	Scout Team - I-Formation
21	7:40-7:45	All	Team Defense	Scout Team - I-Formation
22	7:45-7:50	All	Special Teams	Punt Return Walk Through
23	7:50-7:55	All	Special Teams	Punt Return Walk Through
24	7:55-8:00	All	Chalk Talk	Nutrition

Appendix Two – Practice Plan

Week 2   Day 7

Segment Number	Time	Personnel	Activity	Notes
1	6:00-6:05	All	Speed/Warmups	Drill A, B, C (Variation 2), D, E, F
2	6:05-6:10	All	Speed/Warmups	Drill A, B, C (Variation 2), D, E, F
3	6:10-6:15	All	Tackling/Blocking	**Tackling-** 4 Station: Drill A, C, D, E **Blocking-** 2 Station: Drill A, C
4	6:15-6:20	All	Tackling/Blocking	**Tackling-** 4 Station: Drill A, C, D, E **Blocking-** 2 Station: Drill A, C
5	6:20-6:25	All	Tackling/Blocking	Swap players from tackling to blocking. Repeat above.
6	6:25-6:30	All	Tackling/Blocking	Swap players from tackling to blocking. Repeat above.
7	6:30-6:35	All	Drill Period	**Backs-** Drill A **Receivers-** Drill A **Oline-** Drill B
8	6:35-6:40	All	Offensive Installation Period	Follow Installation Listing
9	6:40-6:45	All	Offensive Installation Period	Follow Installation Listing
10	6:45-6:50	All	Offensive Installation Period	Follow Installation Listing
11	6:50-6:55	All	Offensive Installation Period	Follow Installation Listing
12	6:55-7:00	All	Offensive Installation Period	Follow Installation Listing
13	7:00-7:05	All	Offensive Installation Period	Follow Installation Listing
14	7:05-7:10	All	Team Offense	Follow Installation Listing
15	7:10-7:15	All	Team Offense	Follow Installation Listing
16	7:15-7:20	All	Team Offense	Follow Installation Listing
17	7:20-7:25	All	Drill Period	**DBs-** Drill B **LBs-** Drill A **DL-** Drill C
18	7:25-7:30	All	Defensive Installation Period	Follow Installation Listing
19	7:30-7:35	All	Defensive Installation Period	Follow Installation Listing
20	7:35-7:40	All	Team Defense	Scout Team - Wing-T
21	7:40-7:45	All	Team Defense	Scout Team - Wing-T
22	7:45-7:50	All	Special Teams	Field Goal Walk Through
23	7:50-7:55	All	Special Teams	Field Goal Walk Through
24	7:55-8:00	All	Chalk Talk	Weight Lifting/Supplements/Steriods

- 287 -

Appendix Two – Practice Plan

Week 2   Day 8

Segment Number	Time	Personnel	Activity	Notes
1	6:00-6:05	All	Speed/Warmups	Drill A, B, C (Variation 2), D, E, F
2	6:05-6:10	All	Speed/Warmups	Drill A, B, C (Variation 2), D, E, F
3	6:10-6:15	All	Tackling/Blocking	**Tackling**- 4 Station: Drill A, C, D, E **Blocking**- 2 Station: Drill A, B
4	6:15-6:20	All	Tackling/Blocking	**Tackling**- 4 Station: Drill A, C, D, E **Blocking**- 2 Station: Drill A, B
5	6:20-6:25	All	Tackling/Blocking	Swap players from tackling to blocking. Repeat above.
6	6:25-6:30	All	Tackling/Blocking	Swap players from tackling to blocking. Repeat above.
7	6:30-6:35	All	Drill Period	**Backs**- Drill A **Receivers**- Drill A **Oline**- Drill C
8	6:35-6:40	All	Offensive Installation Period	Follow Installation Listing
9	6:40-6:45	All	Offensive Installation Period	Follow Installation Listing
10	6:45-6:50	All	Offensive Installation Period	Follow Installation Listing
11	6:50-6:55	All	Offensive Installation Period	Follow Installation Listing
12	6:55-7:00	All	Offensive Installation Period	Follow Installation Listing
13	7:00-7:05	All	Offensive Installation Period	Follow Installation Listing
14	7:05-7:10	All	Team Offense	Follow Installation Listing
15	7:10-7:15	All	Team Offense	Follow Installation Listing
16	7:15-7:20	All	Team Offense	Follow Installation Listing
17	7:20-7:25	All	Drill Period	**DBs**- Drill D **LBs**- Drill A **DL**- Drill C
18	7:25-7:30	All	Defensive Installation Period	Follow Installation Listing
19	7:30-7:35	All	Defensive Installation Period	Follow Installation Listing
20	7:35-7:40	All	Team Defense	Scout Team - Double Wing
21	7:40-7:45	All	Team Defense	Scout Team - Double Wing
22	7:45-7:50	All	Special Teams	Field Goal Block
23	7:50-7:55	All	Special Teams	Field Goal Block
24	7:55-8:00	All	Chalk Talk	Drugs and Alcohol

Appendix Two – Practice Plan

Week 2   Day 9

Segment Number	Time	Personnel	Activity	Notes
1	6:00-6:05	All	Speed/Warmups	Drill A, B, C (Variation 2), D, E, F
2	6:05-6:10	All	Speed/Warmups	Drill A, B, C (Variation 2), D, E, F
3	6:10-6:15	All	Tackling/Blocking	**Tackling**- 4 Station: Drill A, C, D, E **Blocking**- 2 Station: Drill A, B
4	6:15-6:20	All	Tackling/Blocking	**Tackling**- 4 Station: Drill A, C, D, E **Blocking**- 2 Station: Drill A, B
5	6:20-6:25	All	Tackling/Blocking	Swap players from tackling to blocking. Repeat above.
6	6:25-6:30	All	Tackling/Blocking	Swap players from tackling to blocking. Repeat above.
7	6:30-6:35	All	Drill Period	**Backs**- Drill B **Receivers**- Drill A **Oline**- Drill D
8	6:35-6:40	All	Offensive Installation Period	Follow Installation Listing
9	6:40-6:45	All	Offensive Installation Period	Follow Installation Listing
10	6:45-6:50	All	Offensive Installation Period	Follow Installation Listing
11	6:50-6:55	All	Offensive Installation Period	Follow Installation Listing
12	6:55-7:00	All	Offensive Installation Period	Follow Installation Listing
13	7:00-7:05	All	Offensive Installation Period	Follow Installation Listing
14	7:05-7:10	All	Team Offense	Follow Installation Listing
15	7:10-7:15	All	Team Offense	Follow Installation Listing
16	7:15-7:20	All	Team Offense	Follow Installation Listing
17	7:20-7:25	All	Drill Period	**DBs**- Drill D **LBs**- Drill A **DL**- Drill B
18	7:25-7:30	All	Defensive Installation Period	Follow Installation Listing
19	7:30-7:35	All	Defensive Installation Period	Follow Installation Listing
20	7:35-7:40	All	Team Defense	Scout Team - Split Backs
21	7:40-7:45	All	Team Defense	Scout Team - Split Backs
22	7:45-7:50	All	Special Teams	Kickoff
23	7:50-7:55	All	Special Teams	Kickoff Return
24	7:55-8:00	All	Chalk Talk	Heroes

Appendix Two – Practice Plan

Week 2   Day 10

Segment Number	Time	Personnel	Activity	Notes
1	6:00-6:05	All	Speed/Warmups	Drill A, B, C (Variation 2), C (Variation 3), D, E
2	6:05-6:10	All	Speed/Warmups	Drill A, B, C (Variation 2), C (Variation 3), D, E
3	6:10-6:15	All	Tackling/Blocking	**Tackling**- 4 Station: Drill A, C, D, E **Blocking**- 2 Station: Drill A, B
4	6:15-6:20	All	Tackling/Blocking	**Tackling**- 4 Station: Drill A, C, D, E **Blocking**- 2 Station: Drill A, B
5	6:20-6:25	All	Tackling/Blocking	Swap players from tackling to blocking. Repeat above.
6	6:25-6:30	All	Tackling/Blocking	Swap players from tackling to blocking. Repeat above.
7	6:30-6:35	All	Drill Period	**Backs**- Drill B **Receivers**- Drill A **Oline**- Drill A
8	6:35-6:40	All	Offensive Installation Period	Follow Installation Listing
9	6:40-6:45	All	Offensive Installation Period	Follow Installation Listing
10	6:45-6:50	All	Offensive Installation Period	Follow Installation Listing
11	6:50-6:55	All	Team Offense	Follow Installation Listing
12	6:55-7:00	All	Team Offense	Follow Installation Listing
13	7:00-7:05	All	Team Offense	Follow Installation Listing
14	7:05-7:10	All	Team Offense	Follow Installation Listing
15	7:10-7:15	All	Team Offense	Follow Installation Listing
16	7:15-7:20	All	Team Offense	Follow Installation Listing
17	7:20-7:25	All	Drill Period	**DBs**- Drill C **LBs**- Drill A **DL**- Drill C
18	7:25-7:30	All	Defensive Installation Period	Follow Installation Listing
19	7:30-7:35	All	Defensive Installation Period	Follow Installation Listing
20	7:35-7:40	All	Team Defense	Scout Team - Single Wing
21	7:40-7:45	All	Team Defense	Scout Team - Single Wing
22	7:45-7:50	All	Special Teams	Punt
23	7:50-7:55	All	Special Teams	Punt Return
24	7:55-8:00	All	Chalk Talk	Congratulations on two weeks of hard work and effort/ Substitutions

Appendix Two – Practice Plan

Week 3   Day 11

Time	Personnel	Activity	Notes
6:00-6:05	All	Speed/Warmups	
6:05-6:10	All	Speed/Warmups	
6:10-6:15	All	Tackling/Blocking	Drill A, B, C (Variation 2), C (Variation 3), D, E
6:15-6:20	All	Tackling/Blocking	Drill A, B, C (Variation 2), C (Variation 3), D, E
6:20-6:25	All	Tackling/Blocking	**Tackling-** 4 Station: Drill H, C, D, E **Blocking-** 2 Station: Drill A, B
6:25-6:30	All	Tackling/Blocking	**Tackling-** 4 Station: Drill H, C, D, E **Blocking-** 2 Station: Drill A, B
			Swap players from tackling to blocking. Repeat above.
			Swap players from tackling to blocking. Repeat above.
6:30-6:35	All	Drill Period	**Backs-** Drill B **Receivers-** Drill B **Oline-** Drill C
6:35-6:40	All	Offensive Period	Speed reps as groups
6:40-6:45	All	Offensive Period	Speed reps as groups
6:45-6:50	All	Offensive Period	Speed reps as groups
6:50-6:55	All	Team Offense	Even, Odd, Covered
6:55-7:00	All	Team Offense	Even, Odd, Covered
7:00-7:05	All	Team Offense	Even, Odd, Covered
7:05-7:10	All	Team Offense	Goal Line Offense
7:10-7:15	All	Drill Period	**All -** Drill A
7:15-7:20	All	Drill Period	**DBs-** Drill A **LBs-** Drill B **DL-** Drill D
7:20-7:25	All	Defensive Period	**LBs/DL-**Blitz/Pass Rush Period **DBs-** Drill D
7:25-7:30	All	Defensive Period	**LBs/DBs-** 7on7 Period **DL-** Drill C
7:30-7:35	All	Team Defense	Scout Team - Multiple Offensive Sets
7:35-7:40	All	Team Defense	Scout Team - Multiple Offensive Sets
7:40-7:45	All	Team Defense	Goal Line Defense
7:45-7:50	All	Special Teams	Kickoff
7:50-7:55	All	Special Teams	Kickoff Return
7:55-8:00	All	Chalk Talk	Goal Cards - Scrimmage

Appendix Two – Practice Plan

Week 3   Day 12

Time	Personnel	Activity	Notes
6:00-6:05	All	Speed/Warmups	Drill A, B, C (Variation 2), C (Variation 3), D, E
6:05-6:10	All	Speed/Warmups	Drill A, B, C (Variation 2), C (Variation 3), D, E
6:10-6:15	All	Tackling/Blocking	**Tackling**- 4 Station: Drill H, C, D, E **Blocking**- 2 Station: Drill A, B
6:15-6:20	All	Tackling/Blocking	**Tackling**- 4 Station: Drill H, C, D, E **Blocking**- 2 Station: Drill A, B
6:20-6:25	All	Tackling/Blocking	Swap players from tackling to blocking. Repeat above.
6:25-6:30	All	Tackling/Blocking	Swap players from tackling to blocking. Repeat above.
6:30-6:35	All	Drill Period	**Backs**- Drill B **Receivers**- Drill A **Oline**- Drill D
6:35-6:40	All	Offensive Period	Speed reps as groups
6:40-6:45	All	Offensive Period	Speed reps as groups
6:45-6:50	All	Offensive Period	Speed reps as groups
6:50-6:55	All	Team Offense	Even, Odd, Covered
6:55-7:00	All	Team Offense	Even, Odd, Covered
7:00-7:05	All	Team Offense	Even, Odd, Covered
7:05-7:10	All	Team Offense	Panic Offense
7:10-7:15	All	Drill Period	**DBs**- Drill B **LBs**- Drill A **DL**- Drill B
7:15-7:20	All	Defensive Period	**LBs/DL**-Blitz/Pass Rush Period **DBs**- Drill D
7:20-7:25	All	Defensive Period	**LBs/DL**-Blitz/Pass Rush Period **DBs**- Drill C
7:25-7:30	All	Defensive Period	**LBs/DBs**- 7on7 Period **DL**- Drill C
7:30-7:35	All	Team Defense	Scout Team - Multiple Offensive Sets
7:35-7:40	All	Team Defense	Scout Team - Multiple Offensive Sets
7:40-7:45	All	Team Defense	Goal Line Defense
7:45-7:50	All	Special Teams	Punt
7:50-7:55	All	Special Teams	Punt Return
7:55-8:00	All	Chalk Talk	Read Goal Cards - Scrimmage

Appendix Two – Practice Plan

Week 3   Day 13

Time	Personnel	Activity	Notes
6:00-6:05	All	Speed/Warmups	Drill A, B, C (Variation 2), C (Variation 3), D, E
6:05-6:10	All	Speed/Warmups	Drill A, B, C (Variation 2), C (Variation 3), D, Ev
6:10-6:15	All	Tackling/Blocking	**Tackling-** 4 Station: Drill H, C, D, E **Blocking-** 2 Station: Drill A, C
6:15-6:20	All	Tackling/Blocking	**Tackling-** 4 Station: Drill H, C, D, E **Blocking-** 2 Station: Drill A, C
6:20-6:25	All	Tackling/Blocking	Swap players from tackling to blocking. Repeat above.
6:25-6:30	All	Tackling/Blocking	Swap players from tackling to blocking. Repeat above.
6:30-6:35	All	Drill Period	**Backs-** With receivers **Receivers-** Drill A **Oline-** Drill D
6:35-6:40	All	Offensive Period	Speed reps as groups
6:40-6:45	All	Offensive Period	Speed reps as groups
6:45-6:50	All	Offensive Period	Speed reps as groups
6:50-6:55	All	Team Offense	Even, Odd, Covered
6:55-7:00	All	Team Offense	Even, Odd, Covered
7:00-7:05	All	Team Offense	Even, Odd, Covered
7:05-7:10	All	Team Offense	Goal Line Offense
7:10-7:15	All	Drill Period	**DBs-** Drill C **LBs-** Drill B **DL-** Drill D
7:15-7:20	All	Defensive Period	**LBs/DL-**Blitz/Pass Rush Period **DBs-** Drill D
7:20-7:25	All	Defensive Period	**LBs/DL-**Blitz/Pass Rush Period **DBs-** Drill C
7:25-7:30	All	Defensive Period	**LBs/DBs-** 7on7 Period **DL-** Drill C
7:30-7:35	All	Team Defense	Scout Team - Multiple Offensive Sets
7:35-7:40	All	Team Defense	Scout Team - Multiple Offensive Sets
7:40-7:45	All	Team Defense	Goal Line Defense
7:45-7:50	All	Special Teams	Field Goal
7:50-7:55	All	Special Teams	Field Goal Block
7:55-8:00	All	Chalk Talk	Scrimmage Preview - Travel arrangments, Uniforms, Equipment, etc.

Appendix Two – Practice Plan

Week 3   Day 14

Time	Personnel	Activity	Notes
6:00-6:05	All	Speed/Warmups	Drill A, B, C (Variation 2), C (Variation 3), D, E
6:05-6:10	All	Speed/Warmups	Drill A, B, C (Variation 2), C (Variation 3), D, E
6:10-6:15	All	Tackling/Blocking	**Tackling**- 4 Station: Drill H, C, D, E **Blocking**- 2 Station: Drill A, B
6:15-6:20	All	Tackling/Blocking	**Tackling**- 4 Station: Drill H, C, D, E **Blocking**- 2 Station: Drill A, B
6:20-6:25	All	Tackling/Blocking	Swap players from tackling to blocking. Repeat above.
6:25-6:30	All	Tackling/Blocking	Swap players from tackling to blocking. Repeat above.
6:30-6:35	All	Drill Period	**Backs**- Drill B **Receivers**- Drill C **Oline**- Drill C
6:35-6:40	All	Offensive Period	Speed reps as groups
6:40-6:45	All	Offensive Period	Speed reps as groups
6:45-6:50	All	Offensive Period	Speed reps as groups
6:50-6:55	All	Team Offense	Even, Odd, Covered
6:55-7:00	All	Team Offense	Even, Odd, Covered
7:00-7:05	All	Team Offense	Even, Odd, Covered
7:05-7:10	All	Team Offense	Panic Offense
7:10-7:15	All	Drill Period	**All** - Drill A
7:15-7:20	All	Drill Period	**DBs**- Drill D **LBs**- Drill A **DL**- Drill D
7:20-7:25	All	Defensive Period	**LBs/DL**-Blitz/Pass Rush Period **DBs**- Drill C
7:25-7:30	All	Defensive Period	**LBs/DBs**- 7on7 Period **DL**- Drill C
7:30-7:35	All	Team Defense	Scout Team - Multiple Offensive Sets
7:35-7:40	All	Team Defense	Scout Team - Multiple Offensive Sets
7:40-7:45	All	Team Defense	Goal Line Defense
7:45-7:50	All	Special Teams	Kickoff
7:50-7:55	All	Special Teams	Punt
7:55-8:00	All	Chalk Talk	Atta-boys, Scrimmage Preview - Parents' Letter

Appendix Two – Practice Plan

Week 3   Day 15

Time	Personnel	Activity	Notes
6:00-6:05	All	Speed/Warmups	Drill A, B, C (Variation 2), C (Variation 3), D, E
6:05-6:10	All	Speed/Warmups	Drill A, B, C (Variation 2), C (Variation 3), D, E
6:10-6:15	All	Tackling/Blocking	**Tackling-** 4 Station: Drill H, C, D, E **Blocking-** 2 Station: Drill A, B
6:15-6:20	All	Tackling/Blocking	**Tackling-** 4 Station: Drill H, C, D, E **Blocking-** 2 Station: Drill A, B
6:20-6:25	All	Tackling/Blocking	Swap players from tackling to blocking. Repeat above.
6:25-6:30	All	Tackling/Blocking	Swap players from tackling to blocking. Repeat above.
6:30-6:35	All	Offensive Period	**Backs-** Drill B **Receivers-** Drill A **Oline-** Drill C
6:35-6:40	All	Offensive Period	Speed reps as groups
6:40-6:45	All	Offensive Period	Speed reps as groups
6:45-6:50	All	Offensive Period	Speed reps as groups
6:50-6:55	All	Team Offense	Even, Odd, Covered-- "Rehearsal"
6:55-7:00	All	Team Offense	Even, Odd, Covered-- "Rehearsal"
7:00-7:05	All	Team Offense	Even, Odd, Covered-- "Rehearsal"
7:05-7:10	All	Team Offense	Goal Line Offense
7:10-7:15	All	Drill Period	**DBs-** Drill B **LBs-** Drill B **DL-** Drill D
7:15-7:20	All	Defensive Period	**LBs/DL-**Blitz/Pass Rush Period **DBs-** Drill D
7:20-7:25	All	Defensive Period	**LBs/DL-**Blitz/Pass Rush Period **DBs-** Drill C
7:25-7:30	All	Defensive Period	**LBs/DBs-** 7on7 Period **DL-** Drill C
7:30-7:35	All	Team Defense	Scout Team - Multiple Offensive Sets
7:35-7:40	All	Team Defense	Scout Team - Multiple Offensive Sets
7:40-7:45	All	Team Defense	Goal Line Defense
7:45-7:50	All	Special Teams	Kickoff Return
7:50-7:55	All	Special Teams	Punt Return
7:55-8:00	All	Chalk Talk	Scrimmage information, Equipment, etc. Scrimmage Goals

Appendix Two – Practice Plan

Week 4   Day 16

Segment Number	Time	Personnel	Activity	Notes
1	6:00-6:05	All	Speed/Warmups	Drill A, B, C (Variation 2), C (Variation 3), D, E
2	6:05-6:10	All	Speed/Warmups	Drill A, B, C (Variation 2), C (Variation 3), D, E
3	6:10-6:15	All	Tackling/Blocking	**Tackling**- 4 Station: Drill H, A, B, E **Blocking**- 2 Station: Drill A, B
4	6:15-6:20	All	Tackling/Blocking	**Tackling**- 4 Station: Drill H, A, B, E **Blocking**- 2 Station: Drill A, B
5	6:20-6:25	All	Tackling/Blocking	Swap players from tackling to blocking. Repeat above.
6	6:25-6:30	All	Tackling/Blocking	Swap players from tackling to blocking. Repeat above.
7	6:30-6:35	All	Offensive Period	**Backs**- Drill B **Receivers**- Drill B **Oline**- Blocking Drill D
8	6:35-6:40	All	Offensive Period	**Backs**- Drill B **Receivers**- Drill B **Oline**- Blocking Drill D
9	6:40-6:45	All	Offensive Period	Speed reps as groups
10	6:45-6:50	All	Offensive Period	Speed reps as groups
11	6:50-6:55	All	Team Offense	Scout Team - Scouting Report
12	6:55-7:00	All	Team Offense	Scout Team - Scouting Report
13	7:00-7:05	All	Team Offense	Goal Line Offense - Scouting Report
14	7:05-7:10	All	Drill Period	**All** - Drill A
15	7:10-7:15	All	Defensive Period	**LBs/DL**-Blitz/Pass Rush Period **DBs**- Drill D
16	7:15-7:20	All	Defensive Period	**LBs/DL**-Blitz/Pass Rush Period **DBs**- Drill C
17	7:20-7:25	All	Defensive Period	**LBs/DBs**- 7on7 Period **DL**- Drill C
18	7:25-7:30	All	Team Defense	Scout Team - Scouting Report
19	7:30-7:35	All	Team Defense	Scout Team - Scouting Report
20	7:35-7:40	All	Team Defense	Goal Line Defense - Scouting Report
21	7:40-7:45	All	Special Teams	Kickoff, Kickoff Return
22	7:45-7:50	All	Special Teams	Kickoff, Kickoff Return
23	7:50-7:55	All	Special Teams	Kickoff, Kickoff Return
24	7:55-8:00	All	Chalk Talk	Return Goal Cards from Scrimmage - Goal Cards Game One, Captains

Appendix Two – Practice Plan

Week 4   Day 17

Segment Number	Time	Personnel	Activity	Notes
1	6:00-6:05	All	Speed/Warmups	Drill A, B, C (Variation 2), C (Variation 3), D, E
2	6:05-6:10	All	Speed/Warmups	Drill A, B, C (Variation 2), C (Variation 3), D, E
3	6:10-6:15	All	Tackling/Blocking	**Tackling-** 4 Station: Drill H, C, D, E **Blocking-** 2 Station: Drill A, B
4	6:15-6:20	All	Tackling/Blocking	**Tackling-** 4 Station: Drill H, C, D, E **Blocking-** 2 Station: Drill A, B
5	6:20-6:25	All	Tackling/Blocking	Swap players from tackling to blocking. Repeat above.
6	6:25-6:30	All	Tackling/Blocking	Swap players from tackling to blocking. Repeat above.
7	6:30-6:35	All	Offensive Period	**Backs-** Drill B **Receivers-** Drill A **Oline-** Drill D
8	6:35-6:40	All	Offensive Period	Speed reps as groups
9	6:40-6:45	All	Offensive Period	Speed reps as groups
10	6:45-6:50	All	Team Offense	Scout Team - Scouting Report
11	6:50-6:55	All	Team Offense	Scout Team - Scouting Report
12	6:55-7:00	All	Team Offense	Scout Team - Scouting Report
13	7:00-7:05	All	Team Offense	Goal Line Offense
14	7:05-7:10	All	Defensive Period	**DBs-** Drill A **LBs-** Drill A **DL-** Drill D
15	7:10-7:15	All	Defensive Period	**LBs/DL-**Blitz/Pass Rush Period **DBs-** Drill D
16	7:15-7:20	All	Defensive Period	**LBs/DL-**Blitz/Pass Rush Period **DBs-** Drill C
17	7:20-7:25	All	Defensive Period	**LBs/DBs-** 7on7 Period **DL-** Drill C
18	7:25-7:30	All	Team Defense	Scout Team - Scouting Report
19	7:30-7:35	All	Team Defense	Scout Team - Scouting Report
20	7:35-7:40	All	Team Defense	Goal Line Defense
21	7:40-7:45	All	Special Teams	Punt, Punt Return
22	7:45-7:50	All	Special Teams	Punt, Punt Return
23	7:50-7:55	All	Special Teams	Punt, Punt Return
24	7:55-8:00	All	Chalk Talk	Read Goal Cards for Game One

Appendix Two – Practice Plan

Week 4 Day 18

Segment Number	Time	Personnel	Activity	Notes
1	6:00-6:05	All	Speed/Warmups	Drill A, B, C (Variation 2), C (Variation 3), D, E
2	6:05-6:10	All	Speed/Warmups	Drill A, B, C (Variation 2), C (Variation 3), D, E
3	6:10-6:15	All	Tackling/Blocking	**Tackling-** 4 Station: Drill H, C, D, E **Blocking-** 2 Station: Drill B, C
4	6:15-6:20	All	Tackling/Blocking	**Tackling-** 4 Station: Drill H, C, D, E **Blocking-** 2 Station: Drill B, C
5	6:20-6:25	All	Tackling/Blocking	Swap players from tackling to blocking. Repeat above.
6	6:25-6:30	All	Tackling/Blocking	Swap players from tackling to blocking. Repeat above.
7	6:30-6:35	All	Offensive Period	**Backs-** Drill B **Receivers-** Drill A **Oline-** Drill B
8	6:35-6:40	All	Offensive Period	Speed reps as groups
9	6:40-6:45	All	Offensive Period	Speed reps as groups
10	6:45-6:50	All	Offensive Period	Scout Team - Scouting Report
11	6:50-6:55	All	Team Offense	Scout Team - Scouting Report
12	6:55-7:00	All	Team Offense	Scout Team - Scouting Report
13	7:00-7:05	All	Team Offense	Goal Line Offense
14	7:05-7:10	All	Defensive Period	**DBs-** Drill B **LBs-** Drill B **DL-** Drill B
15	7:10-7:15	All	Defensive Period	**LBs/DL-**Blitz/Pass Rush Period **DBs-** Drill D
16	7:15-7:20	All	Defensive Period	**LBs/DL-**Blitz/Pass Rush Period **DBs-** Drill C
17	7:20-7:25	All	Defensive Period	**LBs/DBs-** 7on7 Period **DL-** Drill C
18	7:25-7:30	All	Team Defense	Scout Team - Scouting Report
19	7:30-7:35	All	Team Defense	Scout Team - Scouting Report
20	7:35-7:40	All	Team Defense	Goal Line Defense
21	7:40-7:45	All	Special Teams	Field Goal, Field Goal Block
22	7:45-7:50	All	Special Teams	Field Goal, Field Goal Block
23	7:50-7:55	All	Special Teams	Field Goal, Field Goal Block
24	7:55-8:00	All	Chalk Talk	Game One Preview

Appendix Two – Practice Plan

Week 4   Day 19

Segment Number	Time	Personnel	Activity	Notes
1	6:00-6:05	All	Speed/Warmups	Drill A, B, C (Variation 2), C (Variation 3), D, E
2	6:05-6:10	All	Speed/Warmups	Drill A, B, C (Variation 2), C (Variation 3), D, E
3	6:10-6:15	All	Tackling/Blocking	**Tackling**- 4 Station: Drill I, H, G, E **Blocking**- 2 Station: Drill A, B
4	6:15-6:20	All	Tackling/Blocking	**Tackling**- 4 Station: Drill I, H, G, E **Blocking**- 2 Station: Drill A, B
5	6:20-6:25	All	Tackling/Blocking	Swap players from tackling to blocking. Repeat above.
6	6:25-6:30	All	Tackling/Blocking	Swap players from tackling to blocking. Repeat above.
7	6:30-6:35	All	Offensive Period	**Backs**- Drill B **Receivers**- Drill A **Oline**- Drill A
8	6:35-6:40	All	Offensive Period	Speed reps as groups
9	6:40-6:45	All	Offensive Period	Speed reps as groups
10	6:45-6:50	All	Offensive Period	Scout Team - Scouting Report
11	6:50-6:55	All	Team Offense	Scout Team - Scouting Report
12	6:55-7:00	All	Team Offense	Scout Team - Scouting Report
13	7:00-7:05	All	Team Offense	Goal Line Offense
14	7:05-7:10	All	Defensive Period	**DBs**- Drill C/D **LBs**- Drill A **DL**- Drill D
15	7:10-7:15	All	Defensive Period	**LBs/DL**-Blitz/Pass Rush Period **DBs**- Drill D
16	7:15-7:20	All	Defensive Period	**LBs/DL**-Blitz/Pass Rush Period **DBs**- Drill C
17	7:20-7:25	All	Defensive Period	**LBs/DBs**- 7on7 Period **DL**- Drill C
18	7:25-7:30	All	Team Defense	Scout Team - Scouting Report
19	7:30-7:35	All	Team Defense	Scout Team - Scouting Report
20	7:35-7:40	All	Team Defense	Goal Line Defense
21	7:40-7:45	All	Special Teams	Punt
22	7:45-7:50	All	Special Teams	Punt
23	7:50-7:55	All	Special Teams	Punt
24	7:55-8:00	All	Chalk Talk	Game One Preview, Parents' Letter

Appendix Two – Practice Plan

Week 4	Day 20			
Segment Number	Time	Personnel	Activity	Notes
1	6:00-6:05	All	Speed/Warmups	
2	6:05-6:10	All	Speed/Warmups	
3	6:10-6:15	All	Tackling/Blocking	Drill A, B, C (Variation 2), C (Variation 3), D, E
4	6:15-6:20	All	Tackling/Blocking	Drill A, B, C (Variation 2), C (Variation 3), D, E
5	6:20-6:25	All	Tackling/Blocking	**Tackling**- 4 Station: Drill H, A, B, E **Blocking**- 2 Station: Drill A, B
6	6:25-6:30	All	Tackling/Blocking	**Tackling**- 4 Station: Drill H, A, B, E **Blocking**- 2 Station: Drill A, B
7	6:30-6:35	All	Offensive Period	Swap players from tackling to blocking. Repeat above.
8	6:35-6:40	All	Offensive Period	Swap players from tackling to blocking. Repeat above.
9	6:40-6:45	All	Offensive Period	**Backs**- Drill A **Receivers**- Drill A **Oline**- Drill C
10	6:45-6:50	All	Offensive Period	Scout Team - Scouting Report
11	6:50-6:55	All	Team Offense	Scout Team - Scouting Report
12	6:55-7:00	All	Team Offense	Scout Team - Scouting Report
13	7:00-7:05	All	Team Offense	Scout Team - Scouting Report
14	7:05-7:10	All	Defensive Period	Scout Team - Scouting Report
15	7:10-7:15	All	Defensive Period	Goal Line Offense
16	7:15-7:20	All	Defensive Period	**All** - Drill A
17	7:20-7:25	All	Defensive Period	Scout Team - Scouting Report
18	7:25-7:30	All	Team Defense	Scout Team - Scouting Report
19	7:30-7:35	All	Team Defense	Scout Team - Scouting Report
20	7:35-7:40	All	Special Teams	Scout Team - Scouting Report
21	7:40-7:45	All	Special Teams	Goal Line Defense
22	7:45-7:50	All	Special Teams	All - Walkthrough
23	7:50-7:55	All	Special Teams	All - Walkthrough
24	7:55-8:00	All	Chalk Talk	All - Walkthrough

Game information, Equipment, etc.

Appendix Two – Practice Plan

Week: Day:

Segment Number	Time	Personnel	Activity	Notes
1				
2				
3				
4				
5				
6				
7				
8				
9				
10				
11				
12				
13				
14				
15				
16				
17				
18				
19				
20				
21				
22				
23				
24				

APPENDIX THREE
Helpful Charts

Introduction

As I've mentioned before, football is such a complex sport to coach that it is nearly impossible to keep track of every tiny detail in your head. Anything that I can write down, I do.

Charts are extremely useful. One of the more effective ones I've developed is the Offensive Repetition Checklist. By using this chart and marking off each play you have in your offense when you run it successfully in practice, you'll be able to keep track of the number of reps you're getting. This can not only help you plan out your practices, but it also helps a great deal when you're faced with a 4th and one on game day. By being able to check and immediately tell which plays you've gotten the greatest numbers of repetitions at, you can call a play with confidence that should get you the first down.

This appendix contains the following charts:

- Film Study Chart/Stats form

- Offensive Repetition Checklist

- Player Improvement Charts (Offensive backs, Offensive line, Receivers, Linebackers, Defensive linemen, Defensive backs.)

Use the heck out of them. I do.

~D.

Game Day Statistics Form

	Formation	Play	Ball Carrier	Result (+/-)	Comments
Ex:	*Double Wing*	*24 Toss*	*#34*	*+4*	*Fumble, Recovered by #64*
1					
2					
3					
4					
5					
6					
7					
8					
9					
10					
11					
12					
13					
14					
15					
16					
17					
19					
19					
20					
21					
22					
23					
24					
25					

Offensive Repetition Checklist

Week One

Series 1		Day 1	Day 2	Day 3	Day 4	Day 5

Series 2		Day 1	Day 2	Day 3	Day 4	Day 5

Series 3		Day 1	Day 2	Day 3	Day 4	Day 5

Week Two

Series 1		Day 1	Day 2	Day 3	Day 4	Day 5

Series 2		Day 1	Day 2	Day 3	Day 4	Day 5

Series 3		Day 1	Day 2	Day 3	Day 4	Day 5

Week Three

Series 1		Day 1	Day 2	Day 3	Day 4	Day 5

Series 2		Day 1	Day 2	Day 3	Day 4	Day 5

Series 3		Day 1	Day 2	Day 3	Day 4	Day 5

Week Four

Series 1

	Day 1	Day 2	Day 3	Day 4	Day 5

Series 2

	Day 1	Day 2	Day 3	Day 4	Day 5

Series 3

	Day 1	Day 2	Day 3	Day 4	Day 5

Player Improvements: Offensive Backfield

	Name	Done Well	Needs Work
ex.	*Bobby*	*Kickout Blocks*	*Securing the ball*
1			
2			
3			
4			
5			
6			
7			
8			
9			
10			
11			
12			
13			
14			
15			
16			
17			
18			
19			
20			

Player Improvements: Offensive Line

	Name	Done Well	Needs Work
ex.	Mark	Trap blocks	Reach Blocks
1			
2			
3			
4			
5			
6			
7			
8			
9			
10			
11			
12			
13			
14			
15			
16			
17			
18			
19			
20			

Player Improvements: Receivers

	Name	Done Well	Needs Work
ex.	*Jesse*	*Downfield blocks*	*Crack blocks*
1			
2			
3			
4			
5			
6			
7			
8			
9			
10			
11			
12			
13			
14			
15			
16			
17			
18			
19			
20			

Player Improvements: Linebackers

	Name	Done Well	Needs Work
ex.	*Justin*	*Tackling*	*Reading plays*
1			
2			
3			
4			
5			
6			
7			
8			
9			
10			
11			
12			
13			
14			
15			
16			
17			
18			
19			
20			

Player Improvements: Defensive Line

	Name	Done Well	Needs Work
ex.	*Dave*	*Pursuit*	*Tackling*
1			
2			
3			
4			
5			
6			
7			
8			
9			
10			
11			
12			
13			
14			
15			
16			
17			
18			
19			
20			

Player Improvements: Defensive Backs

	Name	Done Well	Needs Work
ex.	*Gordon*	*Man-To-Man*	*Zone*
1			
2			
3			
4			
5			
6			
7			
8			
9			
10			
11			
12			
13			
14			
15			
16			
17			
18			
19			
20			

APPENDIX FOUR
Letter to Parents

Introduction

Good communications with the parents of your players is vital for avoiding major conflicts. I won't try to pretend that annoying parents and players aren't out there, because they are, but if you make your expectations and rules clear from the outset, it goes a long way towards keeping them in their place.

I encourage you to remember that you are the coach. Your word is law on the football field. By the time you've gotten to this appendix you've read more than three hundred pages of material about coaching football. You've decided on an offense, a defense, and a special teams program. You've created practice schedules, and assigned responsibilities to your assistants.

If this is the only book you've ever read on coaching football, then you're still way ahead of the average parent, that hasn't read *anything*. Don't let them try to intimidate or sway you from the things you know are best for your team. Watching NFL football doesn't give them any special knowledge or understanding of youth football, and while the First Amendment gives them the privilege of speaking their mind, their freedom of expression *ends* where your right not to hear it begins.

Parents tend to have some tunnel vision, which is only natural, I suppose. They're inclined to think that their little Johnny is the best athlete on the team, and they forget that there are twenty other players out there. By meeting with them during the preseason, you can make sure they understand that you are there for *all* the kids, not just theirs, and that your commitment is to the team, rather than to specific players on it.

Feel free to make copies of this letter and distribute it to the parents within your program.

~D.

We are happy to welcome all players and parents to the _____ Youth Football program. We are hopeful that this will be the most exciting and rewarding football season you've ever experienced. Our goal is to develop well-rounded young men and women who learn not only the fundamentals of football, but also the importance of education and teamwork, in an atmosphere conductive to developing sound mind, body and character, and to have a good time along the way. We practice the ideals of sportsmanship, scholarship and physical fitness. Our program stresses learning lessons of value far beyond the playing days, such as self-discipline, teamwork, concentration, friendship, leadership, and, good sportsmanship.

We, as coaches, will do our very best to ensure that each player is utilized to his utmost potential and their talents are used for the team's best advantage. The team comes before individuals. Safety is our top concern. Many of the exercises, drills, and team rules are there to ensure your child is physically and mentally fit for football. Each child is unique and will develop at his own pace. We will exercise their bodies and minds in an effort to develop the skills needed to execute the game of football.

TRAITS OF A GOOD FOOTBALL PLAYER

DESIRE: Desire is the determination to overcome an opponent, whether by delivering a solid block or by shaking off the block attempt of an opponent and going on to make the tackle. Desire is a state of mind, an abandonment of self, a form of courage, the joy of mixing it up. It is doing one's best, calling up whatever reserve power is available and never quitting. It is playing both for oneself and for the team's interest. It is the exercise of a determined will. It flows from your competitive spirit and drives you to achieve your goal. Desire is available to all kids, not just to a gifted few. We, as coaches, firmly believe that the size of the heart is more important than the size of the body. Desire is 100% effort, 100% of the time.

CONFIDENCE: The belief that he can do what he has been asked to do. Football is a sport that builds it. The coaches will yell and bark a lot, kind of like the military, but the idea is not to humiliate or hurt the players, it's to get the kids to wake up, to realize that they are part of a team, and their actions affect their teammates. Most kids will get yelled at and be upset by it. Parents will be worried by it and begin to feel protective. The coach is just trying to motivate the player, to toughen him up, to prepare him, and to get him excited enough to put forth the effort needed to play football. Sometimes the coaches will need to bark at a player who is not paying attention. We don't do it because we like to yell, and we certainly don't do it to make the player feel bad. We do it because all team sports, football especially, require team effort. A player who is doing his own thing, talking, or not paying attention while the coaches are teaching is risking possible injury to himself or a teammate, and is setting himself up for failure. Remember, as the great Woody Hayes once said, "Discipline is something you do *for* someone, not *to* them."

THE LOVE OF THE GAME: This is an important part of any football player. A good football player enjoys the competition of a depth chart, and is willing to work his way up the ladder to starter. They have the willingness to play any position. They have the motivation to study the playbook and be responsible to their teammates.

TEAM RULES

- Keep up with your schoolwork. Poor grades in school and not completing homework will result in disciplinary actions by the coaches.

- If you don't practice, you don't play. All excused absences must be coordinated with the coaches. We have a minimum play rule. However, if you don't make an effort to attend practices, we as coaches are not required to play you. Generally a missed practice will result in a missed quarter of that week's game unless the absence is excused.

- What the coaches say goes. Back talking, profanity, or any form of disrespect will result in disciplinary actions. With the high quality of kids we have on this team, this is not expected to be a problem.

- Respect other players. Remember your teammates are working with you, not against you. Any unnecessary aggression or violence towards another player will result in disciplinary actions. This also goes for our opponents. Without them, there would be no football game, so treat them with respect.

- Take care of your equipment. Let the coaches know if your equipment needs repair. This is the key to safety.

- Wear your mouthpiece when required and keep a spare. On game day, if a player draws a safety penalty for not having a mouthpiece in, he will sit out the remainder of that quarter.

- Come to practice prepared to work and play.

- Learn the rules of the game. Remember especially the safety rules. Players who draw flags for unsportsmanlike conduct, clipping, late hits, or other serious safety violations will be removed for the remainder of the game.

- Know the name of each position.

- Arrive on time for practices and games. Six pm means you are *on the field and in position* at six pm, so you must be a few minutes early. A six pm practice begins at 5:55pm.

- Bring your playbook and a pencil to each practice

- Study your playbook daily. The shortened season at the youth level makes it all the more important for each player to learn his responsibilities early and well. This can only be accomplished by studying the playbook outside of practice.

REWARDS

Rewards can come in two forms: verbal and material. Many of the rewards a player receives are positive reinforcement from coaches and parents. Often the coaches will not require individuals to run sprints at the end of practices if the player has showed some exceptional behavior. However, the best reward is always a smile and a pat on the back by a parent. Game captains will be used to honor our hardest workers. A game captain has shown, through considerable effort that week, that he deserves the honor of representing our team to the officials. Typically game captains will be drawn from the ranks of offensive and defensive linemen, because it is their hard work and determination that will make us successful this season.

DISCIPLINARY ACTIONS

Running is an everyday part of practice. On those few occasions when it is necessary to discipline a player for a minor infraction, like failing to pay attention, or talking while the coaches are talking, the player may be asked to run additional laps around the practice field, do pushups, or perform another exercise. Normally that will be the end of disciplinary action. A player will be asked to leave practices early for more severe incidents (i.e. fighting or profanity). If a parent is not present the player will be supervised until the child is picked up. The last resort is to use game suspensions. Coaches will use each of these sparingly. With such a high caliber of players, severe disciplinary problems are not expected to be a problem on this team.

FIELD POSITIONS

During the first few weeks of practice the coaches will decide the best position for each player. In general, the fastest kids play in the backfield on both offense and defense. The biggest most heavily built kids play on the line. Aggressive kids who combine speed, strength, and agility play linebacker. Taller kids who have some quickness play end, offensive end if they can catch and block, or defensive end if they have the discipline required for that position. The quarterback is the one who has it all: he must know every position, and have agility, good hands, and a strong arm. He must be able to receive snaps, remember plays, and hand off the ball securely. Throwing the football is secondary when compared to the player's ability to lead the offensive unit and earn the respect of his teammates. The quarterback must know every position, every play for the entire offense. He is the field general of the team, and the coach on the field.

A key thing to remember is the importance of the offensive line. Without a strong, motivated, and disciplined offensive line our offense will go backwards more often than forwards. Without dominating linemen to block for them our backs cannot run for touchdowns. Therefore, it is important to understand that lineman is a coveted position on this team. Although you cannot carry the ball, you, more than any other person, are responsible for the success of this team. A player is never *condemned* to play offensive line; they *earn* the right through hard work and effort. To be an offensive lineman on this team is to be one of the elite: you will be stronger, faster, and better trained than any other player in this league. That is our coaches' promise to you.

Defense is the key to winning football. Vince Lombardi once said, "A good offense will win you games, but a good defense will win you *championships*." Playing defense requires a more aggressive mentality and a desire to make an *impact*. The coaches have put in literally hundreds of hours of research in order to find and develop the most effective defense for this level of play. The cornerstones of defensive play are *discipline* and *aggressiveness*, so our defensive players must be ready to do the right thing, first time, and every time, and do it at full speed as well.

The defensive unit also uses a quarterback, called Sam, who is the strong side linebacker. Sam must be the most "football smart" player on the team, and a strong leader as well. He must also know every player's position and responsibility for the defense. In the defensive huddle, Sam is the only player who talks.

A player's attitude plays a large role in the position they play. The player with a bad attitude, who is oversensitive, or who demonstrates any sort of problem with a position will be passed over. A negative attitude is costly. When selecting starting players, attitude and desire wins over ability every time. *Can't* has no place on this football team.

If you wish to play a particular position, then make an effort to study the playbook for that position's responsibilities. We will give you the chance to earn any position on the team. Make certain you do not neglect your assigned position while you are learning the new one though! Your coaches will consider you for the new position based largely on how well you played the assigned one.

WINNING

Nothing in life, including football, is worthwhile unless you enjoy it and gain something from the experience. Sure, we're trying to win football games and we are going to set our goals high, but it shouldn't ruin our lives if we lose. Our football team should not believe that a football loss is a tragedy. All you can ask of our kids is to do their best. If we win, Great! If we lose, it's not the end of the world. There will be another game along in a few days. Coaches that think only of winning don't belong in football. Try this: Ask your child if he had a good time instead of whether he won or lost.

By the same token, we feel that we owe it to the players to do everything we can to make them winners. We plan to win every game, because if you don't, then you need to ask yourself which game you plan to lose, and if you're planning to lose, why show up, or practice the week before?

We're going to practice hard, we're going to play hard, and our scores will reflect this.

COACHES

We can only do our best. We view coaching as an awesome responsibility. Your coaches will:

- Get the players in physical condition to play football safely

- Understand each player's potential

- Work on individual skills for each position

- Work on team execution of plays

- Motivate, communicate, lead

- Perform the "behind the scenes work" that will give the players the maximum chance of success; like researching our opponents and doing necessary scouting.

- Teach the players the skills they need to play football safely

Coaches must have the freedom to develop three things in their athletes: pride, poise, and self-confidence. We use the following steps to instruct the game of football.

- Explain what is required

- Demonstrate the technique

- Have the player perform the technique

- Explain the consequences of not performing the technique properly

- If necessary, execute the consequences of not performing the technique properly

If you have any problems with the coaching staff please contact the league commissioner.

Your Head Coach: _____ ###-####

Assistant Coaches: _____ ###-####

_____ ###-####

_____ ###-####

Your League Commissioner: _____ ###-####

PLAYERS EQUIPMENT

Each player is required to supply the following equipment in order to play football.

- Mouth piece

- Athletic supporter with protective cup

- Socks of calf or knee length

- Custom mouth guards, if preferred, (Made by dentists) must attach to helmet face guard

- Water jug containing only water or a sport drink such as Gatorade

- A practice jersey (one of Dad's old tee shirts or sweat shirts will do just fine.)

- Shoes, must not have detachable cleats.

Players will be issued the following equipment:

- Helmet with face mask and chin straps

- Mouth guard

- Shoulder pads

- Hip pads

- Thigh pads

- Knee pads

- Jersey and pants

This equipment must be returned to the _____ Football Program at the season's end or parents will be billed for replacement equipment.

PARENTS

Parents are as important to the success of the team as the players. Coaches and parents must work together. Please keep the coaches informed about problems that may be going on with your child. If the child has been sick, taking medication, or going through some emotional trauma please make sure the coaches are made aware of the problem as soon as possible. Parents and coaches must communicate with mutual respect. Parents and coaches reserve the right to postpone conversations that are getting out of hand. Heated discussions have no place in front of the players.

Although many parents have coaching experience, and may have played on a higher level then the current coaches of this team, the coaches must ask that you refrain from coaching your kids at home. These kids are being taught to play as a team, each player performing a set function that his teammates can rely on. A player who abandons his teammates to do something his parents coached him to do is letting down his team, his coaches, and himself. At best he may open up the door for the opponent to win the game, at worst he may cause himself or a teammate to be injured.

If you have suggestions or ideas, please do not hesitate to present them to the coaching staff after any practice, or call Coach _____ at home at ###-####.

PRACTICES

Every week practices are different. New skills are learned, problem areas are corrected, and new plays are taught. Your child will be at a disadvantage by not making practice on time and regularly. Practices are held _____ through _____, from 6pm to 8:00pm until the games begin. Practices will be held at _____ field.

HOME CONDITIONING

Proper nutrition and hydration is very important to a young football player. Players need to drink as much water as possible every day; at least four to six glasses. Heat stroke is always a danger, despite cooler weather during fall, so it is very important to stay hydrated at all times. It is also recommended that players wear a tee shirt under their pads and jersey to help keep them warm during the colder practices and games.

Players need a high-carbohydrate diet, with plenty of fruits and vegetables and few fats and sugars. We will not be teaching any form of weight lifting other than standard calisthenics like pushups and sit-ups. If your child wishes to lift weights during the off-season he is encouraged to do so, *provided* he obtains a doctor's permission to do so and has his workout designed by a specialist in youth fitness. Improper weight lifting can cause irreparable damage to young joints and bones. We will be discussing proper nutrition and fitness throughout the season in our nightly "Chalk Talks", but we will not at any time be engaging in weight lifting.

WATER BOTTLES

Players are required to have one 20oz water bottle, filled with water or a 50/50 mixture of a sport drink at every practice. Water breaks will not be given. Instead, the players will have the water bottle with them during each drill period and when they are waiting in line. The bottle should be empty by the time practice ends. The player should also drink water when he arrives home. Sodas have no place on the football field, and the player should limit their consumption as much as possible before and after practice.

CHALK TALKS

Chalk Talks are a five to ten-minute period near the end of every practice where the coaches will teach or discuss a wide variety of topics with the players. Sometimes we will tell old "war" stories of our days in football to motivate the players. Sometimes we'll discuss athletic role models. Sometimes we'll discuss nutrition and fitness. Chalk Talks are an important part of playing football. They give the coaches a chance to teach concepts that may otherwise be left out of a regular practice due to time constraints or other reasons. Practice is not over until the Chalk Talk ends.

NECESSARY SKILLS OF FOOTBALL

The following skills will be taught during the preseason, and will be honed by daily practice. They are highly important to a successful football team.

OFFENSIVE SKILLS: BLOCKING

DRIVE BLOCK:

- Explode from your stance, taking your first step with the foot closest to the opponent, and drive your hips forward on the third and fourth steps, through the block.

- Start with short, choppy steps, and keep your feet moving.

- Deliver the block from a wide base, and keep your head up and shoulders square. Make sure your hips are slightly forward from your feet, and your shoulders forward from your hips. (If you're sitting on air, you'll fall over backwards. If anything, you want to be falling *forwards*, into your opponent.)

- Punch hands or forearms into the opponent to establish momentum, and deliver the blow on impact with the forearms, ***not the head***.

- Keep your head on the side of the opponent toward the hole, and follow through with short, choppy steps, turning the opponent away from the hole.

REACH BLOCKING:

- Like the drive block, the reach block is all about the first step. Take the first step with an explosive motion using the foot closest to the hole (outside foot.) Ideally you should step just past the defender's outermost foot.

- Engage the defender with your forearms, getting into his body as much as possible. You cannot allow separation because the defender will shed your block, maintaining outside leverage, and be pushed into the hole.

- Bring your hips hard towards the foot you stepped with, keeping a low pad level and a forward lean. Keep your feet moving

- Work your hips around to the outside until your body is between the ball carrier and the defender.

PASS BLOCKING:

- Explode from your stance as if you were attempting to execute a drive block. Step first with the foot closest to the opponent you are going to block.

- Keep your back straight and your *EYES UP!*

- Engage the defender and reroute his charge by turning his closest hip in the direction you want him to go. (Avoid grabbing him, just steer him with pressure.)

- Keep your weight over your toes, with a slight forward lean. If the Starship *Enterprise* beamed up your defender, you should fall through where he was.

- Keep a wide base and your feet moving at all times.

CRAB BLOCKING:

- Explode from your stance as low to the ground as possible, throwing your arms in front of his path as if you were diving.

- As soon as your hands hit the ground, scramble forward with your knees and head up, keeping constant pressure into the defender's legs.

- Turn your body until you are parallel to the line of scrimmage and occupying the greatest amount of space across the hole.

- Keep scrambling into the defender until the whistle.

DEFENSIVE SKILLS: TACKLING

Tackling is the single most important skill in football. Every player will be taught to tackle correctly, and the coaches will be insisting on a proper five point tackle at all times. The five points are:

- Break down (Assume a good football position with the eyes focused on the ball carrier's belt/lower numbers. Be prepared to move in any direction.)

- Hit (Place breastplate into lower numbers of ball carrier)

- Wrap (Throw arms around ball carrier with upward motion and grip his jersey with both hands, aiming to grab cloth at the back of the runner's neck)

- Lift (Using the legs and *not* the back raise the ball carrier 1-2 inches from the ground)

- Drive (Using short choppy steps drive into the ball carrier to break his momentum and push him off balance)

At *all times* these tackling points will be adhered to, for the safety of the tackler and the ball carrier, and the good of the team. Players who fail to execute one or all of the four points will be sent to "remedial tackling" and given extra training. This is not a punishment; it is a reinforcement of the correct tackling technique.

HEAD-ON TACKLE:

- Make sure that you are under control so as not to overrun the ball carrier or dive and miss a tackle.

- Watch the ball carrier's hips. They will tell you where he is going.

- Maintain a wide, balanced stance; keep the feet moving with choppy steps.

- Extend your arms and head in front of your body.

- Keep your head up, your back arched, and your knees slightly bent.

- Slide your head to the outside, putting your face to the side the ball is on just before making contact.

- Drive your shoulder into the "bull's eye."

- With your arms, grasp cloth behind the neck of the ball carrier and pull him toward you.

- Lift and pull the ball carrier toward you as you take him off his feet.

- Drive with short choppy steps to push the ball carrier off balance.

ANGLE TACKLE:

- Keep under control and be ready to move in any direction.

- It's important to maintain a good balanced stance in a good hitting position.

- Drive your head in front of the ball carrier's number, across the line of his run.

- Drive your shoulder upward on the runner in the "bull's eye."

- With your arms, grasp cloth behind the neck of the ball carrier and pull him toward you.

- Arch your back to lift and drive through the ball carrier.

- Keep the feet moving with short choppy steps as you finish the tackle.

OPEN-FIELD TACKLE:

- Keep under control with your legs bent.

- Use the sideline to your advantage, penning in or getting an angle on the runner.

- Your number one priority is to grasp the runner.

- Once you have a hold on the runner, help should be soon to arrive. But, if possible, try to drive him out of bounds or pull him to the turf.

- Don't worry about driving through the man or delivering a hard blow. Your sole responsibility is to get a hold of the player and prevent the score.

ALWAYS KEEP YOUR <u>HEAD UP</u> WHEN YOU BLOCK OR TACKLE!

APPENDIX FIVE
The Black Lion Award

Introduction

In 2000 one of my mentors, Hugh Wyatt, received permission from the 28th Infantry to begin awarding a decoration in honor of one of their fallen comrades. Since that time, thousands of youth and high school programs have begun giving out the Black Lion Award to the one player on their squads with the heart that most resembles Don Holledar's.

In 2004, the Army Military Academy at West Point became the first Division I college team to begin giving the award.

What follows is a description of the award and what it means in Hugh Wyatt's own words, reprinted by permission of the original author.

This is the only individual award I give out. It's also one of the most important awards I've ever seen. Take a moment and consider awarding it to someone on your team.

~D.

For young American football players of all ages

BLACK LION AWARD BOARD OF ADVISORS

Colonel Ed Burke - Executive Director, 28th Infantry Regiment Association, The Black Lions, Vietnam Veteran

Tom Hinger- Black Lion Combat Medic, recipient of the Silver Star for Gallantry, Vietnam Veteran

David Maraniss - Author, "When Pride Still Mattered," "They Marched into Sunlight"

Colonel Robert Novogratz, USA(Ret.) - West Point All-American Guard/Linebacker, Vietnam Veteran

Bobby Ross - Army veteran and head coach, United States Military Academy

Brigadier General James Shelton, USA (Ret) - Former Delaware Guard/Linebacker, Vietnam veteran, Honorary Colonel - Black Lions

Hugh Wyatt - Founder and Administrator, Black Lion Award

At last! An award a lineman has as good a chance of winning as a back! An award that a non-starter has as good a chance of winning as a star!

Tired of the greed for individual recognition that threatens our sport? Want to do something to recognize the unselfishness that really makes a football team great? The Black Lion Award is one that <u>all</u> young football players across America, whatever their talents, can aspire to winning.

The Black Lion Award is one that you'd like to be able to give to <u>all</u> your players.

The Black Lion Award is not intended to recognize great talent - although the winner may be very talented. It is not intended to go to the Most Valuable Player, or the Highest Scorer, or the Leading Tackler - although such individuals certainly might qualify. It might not even go to a starter. It is meant simply go to the sort of person America needs more of, the sort of person all coaches wish they had more of - the player who leads, who inspires others with his courage and effort, who puts the team ahead of himself.

It is given in memory of Major Don Holleder, former West Point All-American who died in combat in Vietnam on October 17, 1967 and the men of the Black Lions - the 28th Infantry Regiment - who died with him that day. Don Holleder is a symbol of everything that football can and should represent.

The award is intended to go to the person on his team "who best exemplifies the character of Don Holleder: leadership, courage, devotion to duty, self-sacrifice, and - above all - an unselfish concern for the team ahead of himself."

As coaches, there is no better way for us to keep the memory of a brave man alive than by encouraging our young people to be like him.

The Black Lion Award was first established in 2001, the 100th anniversary of the forming of the 28th Infantry Regiment - the famed Black Lions of Cantigny, who were the first Americans to see combat duty overseas, in World War I.

The award is given with the approval of the 28th Infantry Association, and with the permission and approval of Major Holleder's former wife.

> *"Black Lions are made, not born - by their parents, and by their friends, and by their coaches. When they learn that their buddies are depending on them, then they become Black Lions." Jim Shelton (General James Shelton, USA (Ret.) Honorary Colonel of the 28th Infantry Association)*

A testimonial from a Black Lion Award coach...

> *"We had our banquet last Friday and like always the Black Lion award was a huge hit. I hope to always have that award with the patch to give out at each of my banquets, the players really look forward to seeing who gets it."* **Greg Gibson, Head Coach, Orange HS, Orange, California**

And one from a Black Lion dad...

> *"My son Austin has a room full of trophies, medals and awards from wrestling, track, baseball and football, but I guarantee there is only one that he really cares anything about -- and that's his Black Lion award. I think the real "meaning" of that award struck a chord with him, and he really values it. He quietly talks about becoming a Navy Seal, and I guarantee that all stems from his Black Lion award. Who knows what he'll do with his future, but that award made a difference in his life. I underestimated its effect."* Scott Barnes, Rockwall, Texas

Should you choose to participate in the Black Lion Award program, you will need to *enroll your team*: send Coach Wyatt (coachwyatt@aol.com) your team's name and the name and address of the person (preferably, but not necessarily the head coach) to be contacted.

There is no cost to you whatsoever. The Black Lion Award program is funded by anonymous donors. There are no strings attached. There is nothing to buy. There is no connection whatsoever with recruiting. You do not have to run the Double-Wing offense. The requirements are very few...please take a few minutes to read them...

You are asked, as a matter of coaches' honor, to help keep alive the memory of Don Holleder and the brave men he served with by (1) informing your players before the season of the award and its meaning, then (2) by selecting the recipient "who best exemplifies the character of Don Holleder: leadership, courage, devotion to duty, self-sacrifice, and - above all - an unselfish concern for the team ahead of himself," and finally (3) by explaining the significance of the award once again when presenting it at your awards ceremony.

You will be required to select a player (just one) from your team who best represents the spirit of the award, which reads: *"This award is given to that football player who best exemplifies the character of Don Holleder: leadership, courage, devotion to duty, self-sacrifice, and - above all - an unselfish concern for his team ahead of himself."*

You will receive a certificate, like the one shown at the top, suitable for framing or mounting, signed by General Jim Shelton, the Honorary Colonel of the Black Lions, and himself a former All-America mention at the University of Delaware. Your player's name will be inscribed on it. In addition, you will receive a Black Lions patch, such as the one worn on the player's jersey on the left. All you will need to do before presentation will be to sign the certificate and prepare your speech.

You will be required to submit a written nomination of your player, explaining why you believe he represents the spirit of the award – leadership, courage, devotion to duty, self-sacrifice, and an unselfish placing of the team ahead of himself. Please elaborate - more than just a sentence or two ("Timmy is a great kid. He is very deserving" isn't enough.) Explain why your player represents the spirit of the award – *leadership, courage, devotion to duty, self-sacrifice, and an unselfish concern for the team.* This is not meant to be a "nice try" prize, a "good-conduct award" for the kid who trails the pack and barely makes a lap around the field - it is meant for the kid who is out in front, inspiring others. Give examples and be specific. But please leave out personal details that others don't need to read ("his parents are both drunks") because all letters of nomination will be shared with members of the Black Lions (the 28th Infantry Association) and with Major Holleder's family, and may be posted on this Web site. (Be sure to include your address - the certificate will be mailed to you, and not directly to your player.)

(You might consider having a local veteran or active serviceman present the award. (See the photos at the top of the page.) Not only does it add something special to your awards program, but it serves the dual purpose of allowing us to honor the people who serve and have served us.)

You are encouraged to have the award recipient write (e-mail will work) a few sentences to my attention, explaining what Don Holleder's example has meant to him. Letters may be posted along with the recipient's name, and may be shared with Don Holleder's former comrades and his family. (Major Holleder's former wife wrote to tell me that his family would be thrilled to learn of this "living tribute to his memory.")

You are also encouraged to inform your local news media of your team's winner and of the significance of the award. This is wonderful PR for your program. You are free to use any information on this page in preparing your news release.

Read about the kind of men the Black Lion Award honors at www.coachwyatt.com.

ARMY GREAT DON HOLLEDER (Number 16, above, in the West Point team photo, his senior year)

AUGUST, 2004 - ARMY ITSELF IS A BLACK LIONS TEAM!

Excerpted from a letter dated August 2, 2004

Dear Coach Wyatt,

As a high school AD, I appreciate your efforts in beginning the tradition of the Black Lion Award. As a graduate of West Point and former Army Football Player, I am deeply touched that you would do this. As the President of the Army Football Club, you have earned my respect and admiration for life. The Board of the Army Football Club met last Friday and decided that we would sponsor the award for an Army football player annually. I request permission from you to do so. I know that this is for high school players, but it only makes sense that the one college that presents the award is to be West Point. I met with Coach Bobby Ross, and he is very much in favor of it.

Don Holleder is one of the most highly thought of persons that West Point has produced. A field house is named for him, but more importantly, he is in all our hearts. We of the Long Gray Line "grip hands" with those who have gone before us and are strengthened by them. We will never forget or be without our Don Holleder.

Many of Don's teammates were in attendance this past weekend at the annual Army Football Club golf outing at West Point. The outgoing President, General Dick Stephenson, recounted with difficulty the fact that Don was killed on his birthday in October '67.

Looking forward to hearing from you, Coach Wyatt. Once again, thank you for honoring the memory of Don Holleder. I wish you all the best. God bless you and God Bless America. And... Beat Navy!

Respectfully yours,

John Simar, West Point, Class of 1972

Excerpted from a letter sent to members of the Army Football Club (which consists of all former Army Football players, managers and coaches):

Dear Members of the Army Football Family,

Outgoing President of the AFC, MG (Ret.) Dick Stephenson '57, spoke to us. He stated that the AFC Board has voted to fund an annual Black Lion Award for the Army Football Team. More than 300 schools have already presented this award, so it is most appropriate that the Army Football team honor one of its own each year with such a meaningful recognition. Details about this wonderful award that honors the memory of Don Holleder '56 can be found below. This award goes to the young man that all coaches wish they had more of, the kid who leads, who inspires others with his courage and effort, who puts the team ahead of himself..... just like Don Holleder did! This award is extra special because both Coach Bobby Ross and 1958 Knute Rockne Award recipient (college football's best lineman), Bob Novogratz '59, serve on its Board of Advisors. I would encourage you to start this award at your local school.

Army - West Point - The United States Military Academy - one of the truly classy college football programs in America and the college of my boyhood dreams, will be presenting the Black Lion Award annually to an Army football player!

Not only that, but the award will be sponsored by the Army Football Club, men who have played Army football.

What it means to you, as a youth coach, a middle-school coach or a high school coach is that all of you who have chosen to enroll your teams as Black Lion Award teams, and all of you who are about to do so, are joined by one of the most storied of all American college football teams. You can tell your kids that there will be a player at Army working hard to earn the same award that they can earn. That he's going to be a Black Lion just like them. That he's going to be given an Black Lions patch and a Black Lions Award certificate just like them. (His award will be presented at the annual football awards banquet at West Point on January 5.

In practical terms, what it means for the Award is that it becomes more meaningful than ever, but even more important, it has now acquired a permanence that - let's face it - it could never have had so long as it depended for its existence on the efforts of one coach in the Pacific Northwest.

To those of you who have already participated in this great program - my extreme gratitude for recognizing its value to your team and to young Americans. And to those who are about to join us - welcome aboard! Black Lions! Hugh Wyatt, Camas, Washington

HOW TO ENROLL YOUR TEAM...

E-mail Coach Wyatt at coachwyatt@aol.com with the name of the team, and the name, mailing address and e-mail address of the person who will be serving as your team's contact (preferably, but not necessarily, the head coach)

For example: East End Falcons - Staten Island, New York - Vince Wilson - 555 East 14th St, Staten Island, NY 15055 - vwilson@aol.com

> WHEN YOUR SEASON IS OVER AND YOU HAVE SELECTED YOUR BLACK LION (ONE PLAYER PER TEAM) E-MAIL ME YOUR LETTER OF NOMINATION
> AS SOON AS POSSIBLE AFTER YOUR LETTER OF NOMINATION IS RECEIVED, YOUR AWARD CERTIFICATE WILL BE MAILED TO YOU.
> THE CERTIFICATE WILL BE MAILED TO YOU, AND NOT TO YOUR PLAYER. *BE SURE TO INCLUDE YOUR MAILING ADDRESS*.
> BE SURE TO ALLOW ENOUGH TIME FOR MAILING. THERE IS NO MONEY IN THE PROGRAM'S BUDGET TO OVERNIGHT AWARDS.
> CERTIFICATES WILL BE READY FOR MAILING SOME TIME IN MID-NOVEMBER.

---FAQ ABOUT THE BLACK LION AWARD---

Q. Can I e-mail my letter of nomination or do I have to mail it?

A. E-Mail will be fine.

Q. How elaborate does the letter have to be?

A. More than just a sentence or two ("Timmy is a great kid. He is very deserving" isn't enough.) Explain why your nominee represents the spirit of the award - *leadership, courage, devotion to duty, self-sacrifice, and an unselfish concern for the team.* Give examples and be specific, but please leave out details that you might not want others to read ("his parents are both drunks") because the letters will be shared with the Black Lions (28th Infantry Association) and with members of Major Holleder's family. It is a small effort on a coach's part to bring a prestigious honor to one of his players.

Q. Is the award meant to go to the best player? Could it go to someone who never plays at all?

A. Doubtful, unless we're talking about an injured starter. "Strong Leadership" is the first of the Black Lion Award criteria, and - except for an inability to play due to an injury - it is normally necessary to be a fairly good player in order to be a strong leader - in order to be one that the other players look up to and respond to. The Black Lion Award <u>definitely</u> is not meant to be a "consolation" prize, to go to a player who didn't win any other award. It is NOT a "hardest worker" or "Most Improved" or "Best Citizen" or "Best Student" award, either, although your winner certainly could be all of those things. It is NOT designed to be a "feel good" award for a youngster who surprised everybody by making it through drills or coming to all the practices, or one who never complained even though he never got to play. The Black Lion Award is not intended to be a "Most Valuable Player" award, either (although your MVP could also be your winner if he fits the criteria of the award). It is quite possible that the recipient could be a guard, or a center, or a defensive lineman. Wherever he plays, though, whatever his role may be, he is *"that football player who best exemplifies the character of Don Holleder: strong leadership, courage, devotion to duty, self-sacrifice, and a demonstrated concern for his team ahead of himself."*

Q. I just found out that our school is having its awards day next Friday. We won't have another one until after Christmas. I would like to give my Black Lion Award at this ceremony if possible. I realize that you are 3 hours behind us, but I need to know if I can get the award by the 24th of October.

A. I am sorry, but we do work on a high school schedule, and since most high schools are still playing in mid-October, the awards will not be ready to be sent out until mid-November.

Q. I hope I understand this correctly. It's not just one person in the country that gets the award, right? It's one person from any school that puts in a nomination, right? Let me know if I am not correct, please.

A. It is one person from each team, and we must receive a letter of nomination from his coach, explaining why this player fits the criteria of the award leadership, courage, devotion to duty, self-sacrifice, and an unselfish devotion to the team. Notice that talent or stats have nothing to do with it. We would like to be able to give out Black Lion Awards to 1,000 different players on 1,000 different teams.

Q. But we have two players on our team who are both deserving...

A. The stipulation of the award is that it will go to that (one) player who... The fear of our board is that very soon, this award will go the way of the valedictorian. The vote to select one was unanimous. I am coaching a group of kids right now from whom we could easily select two or three. But we can select only one.

Q. I am leaning toward letting our team choose the recipient

A. I think that would be a big mistake. Popularity is what wins most elections, and this is not about popularity. It is about things that the other kids don't always see or appreciate. The beauty of this is that it allows coaches to use their mature judgment and recognize kids for the things coaches see that kids aren't yet wise enough to see.

Q. I'm having some issues here. This award should go to the most deserving player on the team. The problem, he's my son. Parents and players would really get a perception, real or not, that I'm way out of line. Fifth and sixth grade parents are a different breed. Got any advice?

A. Ultimately, it's your son and you have to be honest and fair with him. I know you're in a spot. I think the main issue is validating your choice. Maybe you should consider having the kids - and coaches, too, of course - vote for it. But one way or another, if he is the most deserving, I don't think he should be deprived of it because his dad is the coach.

Q. How is the award funded? Do you need additional funding for it? Can I help in any way?

Up to this point, the award has been funded by the 28th Infantry Association (think of it as an alumni group) and by a Friend of the Black Lions who chooses to remain anonymous. I donate the labor as my way of trying to repay people I can never fully repay. Your offer is most kind, and perhaps at some point we will need help, but frankly, I am not savvy enough tax-wise to know how I would handle donations. (I might add that one of the concerns of the Black Lions and of Major Holleder's family when the idea of the award was submitted to them for their approval was that it would never be tinged by commercialism.)

Q. Where should I have my player send his thank-you letter?

A. You can e-mail it to me and I'll see that it gets into the right hands!

Q. How will I find out any further information about the award?

A. Any further information that Black Lion teams will need to know will be printed on this page, and also on my news page, which is updated twice weekly.

Q. I would like to have tee-shirts made saying that we are a Black Lions team.

A. Great idea. You have our permission to do so, and to use the Black Lion insignia. (You may not, however, imply any connection between the Black Lion Award and any commercial message or endorsement.)

Q. I'm pushing for the Black Lion Award at our school Our system is very slow to change - how would you recommend approaching them?

A. Just show them the this page and say that you'd like to be able to present the award to one of your kids. Unless the person in charge has some serious issues, it should sell itself!

DON HOLLEDER, ALL-AMERICAN

(Collage of photos and memorabilia lovingly provided courtesy of Dave Berry and Tom "Doc" Hinger)

(Clockwise from Upper Left: Don Holleder, All-American end; The 1st Infantry Division patch; Major Donald W. Holleder; Combat Infantryman's Badge; A photo taken on the morning of the Battle of Ong Thanh and printed from film recovered after the combat photographer, Verland Gilbertson, was killed - Don Holleder is in the center; The symbol of the Black Lions; Army's Colonel Earl "Red" Blaik and the man he chose to become his quarterback; Don Holleder in the front row of Army's 1955 team picture; MIDDLE: The Holleder Center at West Point)

By Hugh Wyatt ©1998, Hugh Wyatt (reprinted by permission of the author.)

Led by senior quarterback Pete Vann and junior All-America end Don Holleder, and four outstanding runners in Tommy Bell, Bob Kyasky, Pat Uebel and Mike Ziegler, the Cadets of West Point led the nation in total offense in 1954, finished 7-2 and ranked seventh in the nation in the AP poll.

But with Vann graduating, Army's Coach Earl Blaik found himself facing the 1955 season without a quarterback. His solution, after considerable deliberation, was to approach Holleder, the returning All-America end, about making the switch to quarterback. Holleder, though a gifted athlete, had never played a down in the backfield.

Blaik was well aware of Holleder's limitations, but felt that he had other qualities that more than compensated for them. "I knew," the coach recalled in his autobiography, "that in the one season of eligibility he had left, he never could possibly develop into a superior passer, but he might do well enough to get by. On the plus side, Holleder was a natural athlete, big, strong, quick, smart, aggressive, a competitor. I knew he could learn to handle the ball well and to call the plays properly. Most important, I knew he would provide bright, aggressive, inspirational leadership."

After proposing the plan to an astonished Holleder, Blaik told him to go back to his room, think it over, and come back the next day with his answer.

After his first morning class, Holleder met with Blaik as agreed on. (He later told Blaik that he hadn't slept much that night.)

But then and there, Don Holleder, the All-American for whom Blaik had predicted brilliance had he remained at end, announced his willingness to make a personal sacrifice for the good of his team—a sacrifice almost unthinkable to the athlete of today. As Blaik remembered, "He said that if I thought he could do the job, he was willing to make a try at it."

In his 15 years at West Point, Blaik had made important personnel moves, but none so highly publicized; none so controversial, as this one. In the past, it was generally accepted that Blaik knew what he was doing and that results would prove him correct; but this move was greeted with skepticism in all quarters. In 1955, Army was still a very high-profile national football power, and once Blaik's decision was announced, his judgment was questioned on the radio, in the newspapers, and at West Point itself. Some even suggested that, at the age of 58, Colonel Blaik might be losing his senses.

And almost from the start, when Holleder broke his ankle a week into spring practice, the skeptics appeared correct.

Injuries and graduation had required other personnel switches as well - so many, in fact, that only one Cadet started the 1955 season at the same position he had played in 1954. And the running back corps, originally expected to be a strong point, was depleted when Kyasky broke his collarbone in the opening game, and Ziegler was sidelined by disciplinary infractions.

Although suspect at several spots, the Cadets nevertheless opened the season with a pair of victories, one of them a 35-6 win over Penn State. Next , though, came two very good teams, Michigan and Syracuse. And when Army suffered back-to-back defeats, Holleder received much of the blame.

Michigan, whom the Cadets had defeated 26-7 the year before, turned the tables in 1955 by shellacking the Cadets, 26-2. Anyone looking for a reason for the loss needed to look no further than the turnover statistics: Army fumbled 11 times, and lost the ball seven times.

But when a team fails to score offensively, it is easy and convenient to point a finger at the losing quarterback, and Holleder hadn't helped his own cause, completing only one pass in eight attempts for just 15 yards. And even the one completion resulted in a turnover, with the receiver fumbling at the end of the play.

On the Monday morning following the Michigan game, the Academy Superintendent stopped by Blaik's office to convey his concerns about the quarterback situation. At a place acutely aware of the importance of leadership, a great many of West Point's officers and cadets were critical of Holleder's leadership, and much of their criticism had made its way to the Superintendent.

Blaik heard him out, then tossed the ball right back to the Superintendent, asking him to suggest someone else. "You tell me," he challenged. "If not Holleder, then who?"

When the Superintendent confessed that he couldn't think of anyone else, Blaik then asked him to voice his support of Holleder - publicly. Blaik, a West Point graduate himself, knew quite well that once others knew where the Superintendent stood on the matter, criticism of Holleder would be less open.

Shortly after the Superintendent left the office, Holleder arrived for his regular Monday meeting with the coach. And Blaik learned just how destructive the criticism of his quarterback was becoming.

Holleder told Blaik that on his way to the meeting, he had overheard a conversation between two other Cadets walking closely behind him. Unaware of who he was, they were discussing Holleder's play at quarterback; they were in agreement that Holleder had been an excellent end, but that either one of them would make a better quarterback.

Putting an arm around his quarterback's shoulder, Blaik told him that he still had his coach's confidence. "It doesn't matter what anybody else thinks or says around this place, "Blaik told young Holleder. "I am coaching this Army team. And you are my quarterback!"

Blaik recalled seeing Holleder's eyes start to fill with tears. He told Blaik that he had given thought to what he had just heard the two cadets saying about him, and that as he climbed the stairs to the coach's office, he was prepared to offer to go back to end. But in spite of the criticism, he told the coach, he really wanted to play quarterback - because he wanted to lead the team. "I was praying you would say just what you have said," he told the coach. "I'll show everybody around here that I can do more for the team at quarterback than I could anyplace else."

But Syracuse was next, and combined with a lifeless Army offense and the running of future NFL Hall-of-Famer Jim Brown, the Orangemen won, 13-0. After a second straight offensive shutout, the criticism of Holleder mounted. It subsided somewhat as the Cadets soundly defeated Columbia and, with Holleder throwing for three scores and running for the fourth, downed a good Colgate team 27-7, but it resumed in full force the next week, as the Cadets lost to Yale 14-12 before 70,000 in the rain and mud of the Yale Bowl.

A 40-0 win over a dismal Penn team did little to silence the critics, as the Cadets prepared to meet powerful Navy.

The Midshipmen, 6-1-1 going into the Army-Navy game, were led by quarterback George Welsh (now head coach at Virginia). Welsh, had been the hero of the previous New Year's Day Sugar Bowl win over powerful Ole Miss, and was the nation's leading passer.

The night before the game, traditionally played in Philadelphia, the Army team gathered for a few pre-bedtime words from Coach Blaik.

"I've grown weary, " he told his players, "of walking across the field to offer congratulations this year to Bennie Oosterbaan of Michigan, Ben Schwartzwalder of Syracuse, and Jordan Olivar of Yale. Now, I'm not as young as I used to be, and that walk tomorrow, before one hundred thousand people, to congratulate Eddie Erdelatz (Navy coach) would be the longest walk I've ever taken in my coaching life."

Blaik recalled a few moments of absolute silence. Finally, Don Holleder spoke up. "Colonel," he said, "you are not going to take that walk tomorrow!"

Once the game was under way, though, Holleder's words seemed an empty promise, as Navy took the opening kickoff and drove 76 yards for a score.

Controlling the ball for most of the first half, Navy threatened to put the game away with two more long drives, but the Cadets' defense stopped both of them at the Army 20. Holleder , playing both ways under the rules of that time, had a hand in both stops, first when he hit the receiver so hard he dropped a fourth-down pass, then when he fell on a Navy fumble.

Frustrated offensively for most of the first half, the Cadets finally managed to put together a drive of their own in the closing minutes, but stalled at the Navy one-yard line as time ran out.

Rather than discouragement, though, the Cadets seemed to gain confidence from the abortive scoring effort, coming out and driving 41 yards for a third period touchdown and, with the conversion, a 7-6 lead.

But led by Welsh, the Midshipmen roared back, driving 72 yards to the Army 20, but once again lost the ball on a fumble.

From that point, as if to demonstrate that wars are still fought on the ground, Army's running game took over, marching 80 yards to a score, and then holding on tenaciously for the 14-6 upset win.

Despite the aerial heroics of Navy's Welsh, who threw 29 times and completed 18 for 179 yards and a touchdown, the contest was won by the infantry. Army finished with 283 yards total offense—all of it on the ground. Of the two passes the Cadets attempted, one was intercepted and the other fell incomplete.

"There hasn't been anything like it since the ancient days of the flying wedge," marveled the <u>New York Times</u>' Arthur Daley.

General Douglas MacArthur, a long-time supporter of Army football and of its coach, sent Blaik the following telegram, indicating that he was well aware of the problems Blaik and Holleder had overcome:

NO VICTORY THE ARMY HAS WON IN ITS LONG YEARS OF FIERCE FOOTBALL STRUGGLES HAS EVER REFLECTED A GREATER SPIRIT OF RAW COURAGE, OF INVINCIBLE DETERMINATION, OF MASTERFUL STRATEGIC PLANNING AND RESOLUTE PRACTICAL EXECUTION. TO COME FROM BEHIND IN THE FACE OF APPARENT INSUPERABLE

ODDS IS THE TRUE STAMP OF A CHAMPION. YOU AND YOUR TREMENDOUS TEAM HAVE RESTORED FAITH AND BROUGHT JOY AND GRATIFICATION TO MILLIONS OF LOYAL ARMY FANS.

Jesse Abramson, in the New York Herald-Tribune , had the last word on the move of Holleder to quarterback: "Never were a coach and a player subjected to so much criticism on a matter which involves a basic item of coaching: proper appraisal of an individual's ability to handle the job assigned to him."

For Holleder, who passed up a sure repeat spot as an All-America end because his team needed him elsewhere, the win over Navy was his final vindication. As he had promised, his coach did not have to make the loser's walk across the field to offer congratulations to the Navy coach.

The consummate team player, he received the ultimate individual recognition by making the cover of that week's Sports Illustrated.

But now he had a military career ahead of him. After graduation from West Point, Holleder went on to become an outstanding officer. Following Infantry Officers School and Paratroopers School, he spent two years in Hawaii, before spending a 3-year tour of duty as an assistant coach at West Point.

Speaking for both the Superintendent and himself, Coach Blaik stated in 1960 that it would not surprise either of them if Don Holleder were to go as far as a military leader as his "selflessness, courage and inspiration" had taken the Army football team.

Who will ever know? On October 17, 1967, as the West Point team prepared to meet Rutgers, Major Donald W. Holleder, the personification of the selfless leader and team player, a man who sacrificed personal glory for the good of his team, a man who persevered and ultimately prevailed despite the odds, a man who represented the very best America has to offer, was caught in an ambush 40 miles from Saigon, and killed by a sniper's bullet as he hurled himself into enemy fire attempting to rescue wounded comrades. He was 33 years old, father of four. (Newsweek Magazine, October 30, 1967)

Michael Robert Patterson, in his personal eulogy, wrote, "Major Holleder overflew the area (under attack) and saw a whole lot of Viet Cong and many American soldiers, most wounded, trying to make their way our of the ambush area. He landed and headed straight into the jungle, gathering a few soldiers to help him go get the wounded. A sniper's shot killed him before he could get very far. *He was a risk-taker who put the common good ahead of himself, whether it was giving up a position in which he had excelled or putting himself in harm's way in an attempt to save the lives of his men.* My contact with Major Holleder was very brief and occured just before he was killed, but I have never forgotten him and the sacrifice he made. *On a day when acts of heroism were the rule, rather than the exception, his stood out.*"

In 1985, Don Holleder was installed in the National Football Foundation Hall of Fame. That same year, West Point's indoor sports facility was dedicated and named the Donald W. Holleder Center in his honor.

Author's note: As a football coach, it was a highly emotional moment for me when I visited The Wall in Washington, D.C. a few years ago. Undoubtedly feeling the same emotion thousands before me had felt, I hoped that somehow the name I was looking for wouldn't be there - that it was all a mistake. But, dear God, there it was—panel 28E, row 25—Donald W. Holleder.

Further note: I have been privileged as a result of my research into the life of Don Holleder to have made the acquaintance of two men who were on the scene on that fateful day, Tom Hinger and Jim Shelton.

December 18, 1998

Sir,

While surfing the net I came across your page, and the tribute to Major Holleder. I am a survivor of the battle in which he lost his life, in fact he died in my arms. A visit to West Point would not be complete without a visit to the Holleder Center. For those of us that were lucky enough to survive the Battle of Ong Thanh, the Center is a tribute to all our fallen comrades.

Thank you,

Tom Hinger

December 21, 1998

Dear Coach Wyatt:

A friend of mine , Tom Hinger, who held Don Holleder as he died in the jungle in Vietnam on 17 Oct 1967, introduced me to your web site. In 1953 I went to the University of Delaware as a center and linebacker. I played for Dave Nelson for 4 years. Mike Lude was our line coach. Mike later went on to become AD at UW with Don James, and you must know Mike. I was a guest of his at the Waldorf when Don Holleder was inducted into the College Football Hall of Fame. In 1955 we went up to West Point and scrimmaged Army. Don Holleder was the quarterback, and was a load to bring down. He couldn't throw, but he loved to belly to the fullback then keep the ball. Our defense was lousy (I was defensive captain) but prior to that scrimmage we hadn't worked a day on defense. Riding up the New Jersey turnpike in a bus to West Point Mike was telling me to call the defenses we had worked on in spring practice. None of our guys remembered any of those stunts. We sat in an Eagles 550. Army was taking big splits and we ended up using a goal line defense to shoot the gaps. Needless to say, a Dave Nelson (and Tubby Raymond) football team will always be an offensive minded ball club. We did score about 6 TDS in the scrimmage. It was a great experience for us. Twelve years later I found myself in an infantry battalion in Vietnam as S3(Operations officer) and Don Holleder was our brigade operations officer. I spent many hours laughing with Don over that football scrimmage. He was an indomitable man--courageous and bullheaded. When he saw those wounded men on the ground he dived into the middle of the fray and was immediately cut down by a sniper. I was later one of the guys who helped to identify his body, along with too many others. I couldn't believe that he could be dead--how a guy as powerful and full of strength could be so lifeless. It was a very sad day--unforgettable. Each year a small group of us trek up to West Point on a date near to 17 Oct to remember Don and our other comrades that were lost that day. In spite of the sadness we always have a good time. Tom Hinger and I are very close--with a mutual experience which transcends most everything else. I want to wish you continued success with your Double Wing system.

God bless America.

Jim Shelton

APPENDIX SIX
Concussions in Football

Introduction

No book on coaching football would be complete without a discussion of one of the most common injuries in the sport—the concussion. Typically ignored or understated by NFL and college players, coaches, and doctors, this life-threatening injury simply cannot be disregarded by the youth football coach.

Carrying with it the danger of permanent disability, the first concussion tends to lead to a second and third, each caused by a lesser blow than the last. This condition is called *Second Impact Syndrome*, and it can result in *permanent* brain damage.

At the pro level, concussions tend to be ignored until it's far too late. Former Cowboys quarterback Troy Aikman, and former 49ers quarterback Steve Young are two prime examples of this mode of thinking. Both of them disregarded concussions as severe as grade three, returning to play within the week instead of giving their bodies time to heal. The result: early retirements for both of them, ending careers that could have continued for a few more years. Anyone that has seen Muhammad Ali lately should be well aware of the dangers posed by concussions.

As youth football coaches, it is our responsibility to prevent concussions on our practice and game fields by educating ourselves on correct tackling and blocking form. In Chapter Two I discussed the worst football coaching materials I've ever seen. In Chapter Three I discussed the best educational material for teaching tackling; Hugh Wyatt's *Safer and Surer Tackling* video. We must be always attentive to the danger that concussions present to our players.

I strongly encourage you to educate yourself and your staff on concussion safety, using the guidelines proposed in the paper below. I wrote this paper for an Introduction to Anatomy class at the American Military University. My professor was Doctor Larry Forness, author of *Don't Get Duped!*, and holder of doctorates in sports medicine and sports law. Doctor Forness advised me that this was one of the best-researched papers he'd seen, and the technical advice for the coach is letter-perfect for reducing concussion likelihood at all levels of football.

Keep your players safe.

~D.

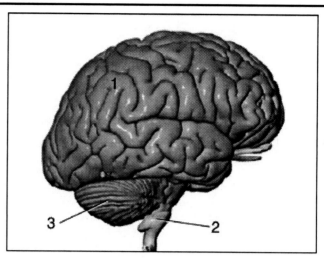

(Image courtesy of http://www.healthopedia.com/head-injury/brain-structures.html)

CONCUSSIONS IN FOOTBALL, WHAT THEY ARE, HOW THEY CAN BE PREVENTED, AND WHEN IT'S SAFE TO PLAY AGAIN

Submitted in partial fulfillment for the requirements for

SC102 – Introduction to Human Anatomy

Derek A. Wade

American Military University

July 25, 2004

TABLE OF CONTENTS

CHAPTER 1

Football, by its very nature, is a rough sport. The human body was not really constructed for collision and impact, and yet this fall, every week from mid-August until at least mid-November, young men (and the occasional young woman) will hurl themselves together in that frantic time between the snap of the football and the shriek of the whistle.

Most of them will take an impact to the skull at some point in the season. Almost all of them will leap to their feet and run back to the huddle. Some of them will not even realize that they were hit hard enough to jar their brains into the bones of their cranium. Brain injuries are so difficult to diagnose and treat that few coaches and fewer parents are prepared to cope with the enormous risk to the player that they present. In football, the most prevalent of these injuries is the concussion.

In his article for the Mom's Team website, Dr. Robert C. Cantu, MD, presents one of the major issues facing coaches, athletes, parents, and medical personnel alike. Dr. Cantu phrases the problem very eloquently, "No consensus has developed in the medical community on either the definition and grading of concussions or when it is safe for an athlete to return to play, as evidenced by the different guidelines that have been proposed." (2) If the medical community cannot come to accord on the proper treatment of a concussion, we cannot reasonably expect an untrained youth football coach and his staff to do so.

This paper will attempt to provide a set of clear-cut guidelines for concussion safety at the youth level, and will focus on three specific issues for the youth football coach: 1. Preventing concussions, 2. Recognizing the symptoms of a concussion, and 3. Returning an athlete to the field after concussion recovery.

CHAPTER 2

"A concussion is a violent jarring or shaking of the head that results in a disturbance of brain function." (6)

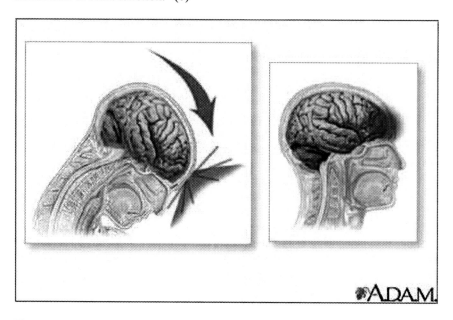

Figure 1: "A concussion occurs when a violent impact causes a disturbance of brain function. Most concussions do not cause loss of consciousness."(4)

I discovered the true meaning of a concussion for the first time as a third grader on the playground of Brigadoon Elementary, in Federal Way, Washington in 1982. While leaping from the monkey bars, my foot got caught, and the last thing I remember was the ground coming towards my face at rapid speed. I returned to class at the end of recess, thanks largely to the assistance provided by one of my friends, but I have only the most vague memories of the next hour or so.

My teacher finally sent me to the office, where the school secretary called my grandmother. My next recollection is of the hospital emergency room, and an orderly holding a pan under my jaw so I could heave the contents of my stomach into it. While I presented this charming spectacle, he calmly explained to my mother that the nausea was a common symptom of concussions.

This was the first concussion I suffered; indeed, it was the first time I ever heard the word in that context. Unfortunately, it wasn't to be the last. I endured a second severe concussion in 1985, as a seventh grade wrestler at Sumner Junior High School, and additional ones in 1988 and 1992 in competition martial arts.

According to Dr. Mark Graber, MD, Concussions are normally graded on a three-point scale, with one being the mildest, and three being the most severe. (5) Figure 2 shows this scale.

Grade 1	Transient confusion, no loss of consciousness, and a duration of mental status abnormalities of <15 minutes.
Grade 2	Transient confusion, no loss of consciousness, and a duration of mental status abnormalities of >15 minutes.
Grade 3	Loss of consciousness, either brief (seconds) or prolonged (minutes or longer).

Figure 2 Concussion Grading

"The acute symptoms of concussion have been examined in prospective studies. The only validated symptoms are amnesia, loss of consciousness, headache, dizziness, blurred vision, attentional deficit, and nausea. Headache, of course, is not confined to concussion--up to 50% of athletes report exercise-related headaches." (7)

Judging by the lack of awareness, loss of consciousness, vision problems, and other symptoms of the concussions I suffered, it is likely that at least three, and probably all four of the concussions I endured through school were grade three.

I walked a football field as a player from 1985 through 1990. As a seventh grader, my physical size was not a detriment. I stood five foot two inches tall, and weighed in at 90 pounds. Unfortunately, by my junior year in high school I had gained merely two inches in height and twenty pounds in mass. It did not take me long to discover that being that small on a football field isn't a lot of fun. My sophomore year alone I knocked myself unconscious three times making tackles, twice in one practice. According to Doctor Graber's scale, those are also classified as grade three concussions, although I awoke with no further ill effects other than a headache.

Recognizing concussions in your players is a vital and necessary part of treating them effectively. It must start with the players themselves, who must have at least a basic understanding of concussion symptoms and be able to recognize them in their teammates as well as themselves. "Most serious head injuries in college football are never reported to team trainers or coaches because the players don't think their symptoms are severe enough to indicate a concussion, according to a new Indiana State University study." (10)

Each coach on your staff should also be properly trained in both First Aid and CPR. The National Safety Council's *First Aid Handbook* gives excellent advice on treating concussions that have been graded using the scale above:

> *Grade One: Remove from activity. Examine immediately and every 5 minutes for dizziness, ringing sound in ears, and loss of memory. Can return to activity if amnesia does not appear and no other symptoms appear for at least 20 minutes.*
>
> *Grade Two: Remove from activity and do not allow to return. Physician should examine frequently. Physician should*

reexamine the following day. Return to activity after one full week without symptoms.

Grade Three*: Transport to nearest hospital by ambulance (with spine stabilized). Physician performs thorough neurological evaluation. May be admitted to hospital. If findings are normal, physician will instruct family or friend about overnight observation. Return to activity only after two full weeks without symptoms.* (8)

On my team, *all* suspected concussions are assumed to be Grade Two until determined otherwise. To the distress of my players, this means the sufferer is immediately removed from contact, and will not return until asymptomatic for one full week. I also recommend following the advice of *The Merck Manual*: "Patients with concussion should be closely followed for [twenty-four hours]. If a CT scan shows no evidence of intracranial bleeding or displaced fractures and the patient is neurologically intact, hospitalization is not needed. Skull x-rays are useless for making this decision."(11)

Any player diagnosed with a confirmed Grade Three concussion is finished for the season. I love football, but I love my players more. Taking a season's games from them is an almost physical pain to me, but it is nothing compared to the guilt I would experience if I allowed them to return to the field before they were fully healed and they were badly injured as a result.

Concussions, and the corresponding permanent and semi-permanent damage they force the victim to endure, are simply too risky to handle in any other manner. All competent football coaches should have a specific concussion policy in place that follows the guidelines listed above, and this policy should never, under any circumstances, be deviated from.

CHAPTER 3   In the years since the end of my playing days, I have been fortunate to coach football at both the youth and high school levels. Luckily, I have never had a severe or life-threatening injury on the practice field as a coach, and only one ankle dislocation on the game field. There have been no significant head injuries on my football fields, and I attribute a large part of this extraordinary success to the training tips I have received from such stellar coaches as John T. Reed and Hugh Wyatt.

Coach Wyatt, in particular, has been a force for proper tackling and following the American Football Coaches' Association guidelines to keep the head out of football. His videotape, *Safer and Surer Tackling*, is a must have for any competent football coach. His tackling system advocates the following crucial steps for proper tackling:

- Hit

- Fit

- Lock

- Lift

- Drive (12)

In short form, *Hit* is the initial contact position, which is an eyes-up, chest-to-chest impact with the ball carrier. *Fit* is the continuation of the first step, striking upward through the ball carrier's body and keeping the head up in a position called "Eyes to the Sky." *Lock* is the wrap up, throwing the arms around the ball carrier in an upward motion from the tackler's hips to the ball carrier's shoulders. I call this movement "gunslinging" because it looks like a Wild West gunfighter drawing his pistols. This aids in the fourth step, *Lift*, which is the driving, upward force of the arm motion added to the inward and rising hip movement designed to break the ball carrier's balance and contact with the ground.

The tackle is finished by execution of the fifth step, *Drive*, which is the rapid footwork necessary to maintain forward momentum against the ball carrier's progress. (12)

The most important portion of this tackling procedure is the initial step, which, when coached correctly, places primary contact on the tackler's chest, and completely eliminates any form of collision with the helmet. In fact, Wyatt advocates an "our numbers to their numbers" body position. (12)

All coaches must remember that the helmet is not a weapon. The Encyclopedia of Sports Science has this to say on the subject:

> *Because football is a collision sport that requires a player to keep a low center of gravity, his head is usually extended in front of his body. Players and coaches have long understood the vulnerability of the head and neck to injury and the vital need for headgear. The first headgear was the lightweight leather skullcap developed in 1896. Like the headgear used in boxing today, skullcaps provided only modest head protection.*

Consequently, a player avoided using his head to tackle unless absolutely necessary.

Because the advanced, hard-shell helmets of the 1990's give players a sense of security (perhaps false), some players may risk leading their tackles with the head. (13)

The text goes on to state that the number one step that should be taken to prevent head injuries is to use a properly fitting helmet that does not have stress points, which are areas of tightness. (13)

This is a significant problem at the very lowest levels of youth football, mitigated solely by the low speeds and lack of collision mass in the players themselves. Many children in the 6-7 or even 8-9 year-old age groups are outfitted every year in helmets and shoulder pads that are far too large for them. Parents are sometimes to blame when they purchase their child's own equipment. Young children grow so fast that parents may want to buy a helmet their child can "grow into." This is an unsafe practice. A far better decision would be to purchase a helmet with an adjustable, inflatable liner that can fit a range of sizes, or simply use gear provided by the team or organization that has been properly inspected and sized to the player.

Inspecting for size and damage should be done on a weekly basis to make certain that the players are still adequately protected by their gear. Never allow a player to participate in contact with incorrectly fitting or damaged equipment.

Properly outfitting the player is only the beginning of concussion safety. A player can reduce his risk of injury by spending a significant amount of his training time during the season and off-season strengthening the neck muscles and improving their flexibility. This allows the neck to flex without straining and ablate the impact of a blow to the cranium.

Finally, a player absolutely must practice using proper technique in both tackling and blocking, *at all times*. He must *never* lower his head at the moment of impact. New York Jets defensive lineman Dennis Byrd made this crucial error during the 1992 season, and received a crippling spinal injury that he has still not recovered from. (13)

Above all it is absolutely imperative to follow the AFCA recommendation to "Keep the helmet out of hitting." (1)

No helmet can completely eliminate all cranial injuries, unfortunately, so it is up to the competent coach to make absolutely certain that football players never, *ever* make contact with any portion of the helmet, which includes the facemask, whether blocking or tackling.

Helmet collisions exert two forces upon the brain. The initial impact force occurs when the brain slams forward against the skull, toward the collision point, and a whiplash effect follows as the brain ricochets to the opposite side of the skull, slamming against the skull's ridges and bone boundaries. While the helmet absorbs impact blows, it can do little to prevent the brain from accelerating within the skull.

The acceleration of the brain within the skull can cause extremely dangerous concussions. In the middle of the 1992 season, Al Toon, an All Pro New York Jets receiver, retired after suffering his ninth and most severe concussion. Each new concussion came from a lesser blow than the previous one, and recovery time successively increased. Likewise, each new trauma was more debilitating than the last. (13)

This is the hidden danger of the concussion, and it is a fearful one. Each successive concussion is worse than the one before, more easily caused, and more dangerous to the player's health. This condition is referred to as *Second-Impact-Syndrome*, or SIS. "The second blow may be unremarkable, perhaps only involving a blow to the chest rather than the athlete's head, but it sends accelerating forces to the brain." (3)

It should be obvious that the number one way to prevent SIS is to avoid the first concussion. Tackling and blocking, bar none, are the most dangerous techniques in the sport of football because they involve what is usually a high-speed collision with an opponent. Teaching safe and effective contact methods to players that are properly outfitted in the correct, well fitting equipment is absolutely *vital* to protecting players from injuries in general, and concussions in specific.

CHAPTER 4

The nature of football being what it is, at some point in the career of every coach it will be necessary to deal with a concussion received by one of your players. Perhaps worse than the initial fears of permanent disability is the knowledge that you may have to face your player and deny them the privilege of taking the field with their teammates as a result of their injury, even though they may seem perfectly all right.

It is vital to the safety of your players that you be firm in your concussion policy. *The Gale Encyclopedia of Medicine* states that, "Studies show that approximately 1 in 5 players suffer concussion or more serious brain injury during their brief high-school careers." (9)

To put this into perspective, that means that on a team of twenty-five freshman players, approximately five of them are at significant risk of permanent or semi-permanent disability from brain injury. Reducing or eliminating the number of first impacts at the youth and high school levels of football can considerably lessen the risk of Second-Impact-Syndrome, and the subsequent risk of death or permanent impairment. "Head injury causes more deaths and disability than any other neurologic condition before age 50 and occurs in > 70% of accidents, which are the leading cause of death in men and boys < 35 yr old. Mortality from severe injury approaches 50% and is only modestly reduced by treatment."(11)

I strongly encourage the following procedures for any football coach at any level of football. Even as high as the semi-professional level, competent medical professionals that are capable of immediately diagnosing and responding to concussion symptoms attend few practices. At the youth levels, it is not uncommon to even see games being played without any form of medical staff present. Therefore it falls to the coach, as always, to protect his players from harm.

1. Research and decide upon a tackling and blocking system that does not involve the use of the helmet in any way as a contact surface—this includes the facemask.

2. Commit to the use of this system—train your staff, managers, assistants, and players in how to teach it and spot potential mistakes.

3. No matter what specific tackling and blocking system you select, teach your players to do so with the head up at all times.

4. Avoid using full-speed tackling drills in practice. (John Gagliardi of St. John's College in Minnesota has never done a full-speed hitting drill in his 52 years of coaching, and recently passed Grambling legend Eddie Robinson as the most successful college coach of all time, with 409 lifetime wins. Full-speed drills are not necessary to teach proper tackling or blocking form.)

5. Learn the proper ways to fit protective padding and helmets to your players. Contact helmet manufacturers like Riddell and Schutt for information on proper helmet fit.

6. Establish weekly equipment checks for your players in which you and your staff examine pads and helmets for any incorrectly fitting items or damages that might prove hazardous.

7. Understand the grading system for concussions provided by the National Safety Council's *First Aid and CPR Handbook*. Use this system any time you suspect one of your players has received a blow to the helmet, or shows any of the signs of concussion, no matter how minor.

8. Always assume a concussion to be Grade Two or worse. Never send a player back into the game or practice after a concussion, and don't let him return to the field until a competent physician has examined him. Treat even the most minor concussions as life threatening.

9. Keep all players with confirmed Grade Two or Grade One concussions out of action for at least one week. Sideline all confirmed Grade Threes for the season.

It must be fully understood that the minimum recovery time allowed for by this policy is one week, *regardless of the apparent insignificance of the wound*. Brain injuries are simply too dangerous to be treated in any other manner. Speak with the parents and players before the season begins so they understand your policy and can help distinguish the warning signs of any potential concussions.

CHAPTER 5

Football is a rough sport. Some people call it a contact sport, but I would disagree. Contact is made in basketball. Contact is made in wrestling. Football is a sport of collisions, a sport of *impact*. In that frozen, perfect moment between the snap of the ball and the whistle's cry young men and women across this country will learn and display a truly astonishing amount of selflessness, courage, and dedication as they walk the grass of our nation's gridirons this fall.

It is the responsibility of the competent football coach to do his utmost to protect these players from harm. One of the most significant and potentially life threatening injuries consistently received on the football field is the concussion, the violent jarring of the brain into the skull. This hazardous injury can never be completely eliminated from impact-driven sports such as football, hockey, and rugby, but the likelihood of receiving one can be drastically reduced by preventative measures that are the cornerstone of good coaching.

Outfit your players properly in a well-fitting helmet that has been inspected and certified by a helmet refitting company. Be certain that the helmet does not have any tight spots that can chafe or cause impact zones on the head. Make sure the player keeps the helmet's air pockets, if equipped, fully inflated until the helmet is tight upon the skull. Check your players' gear weekly and inspect for damaged or poorly fitting equipment. Youth players grow very rapidly, so this is extremely important.

Teach proper blocking and tackling with an eye towards the safety of your players and their opponents. Keep the head out of football, and make sure that the contact points you teach are not the helmet or facemask. Run your drills at 1/2 to 3/4 speed, and never let the players reach full acceleration prior to impact during practice.

Learn the symptoms of a concussion, and the grades of severity. Remember, every concussion is a Grade Two until diagnosed otherwise by a physician, and the physician can only revise the diagnosis *upwards*, never downwards. Keeping a kid out of contact for one full week sounds like an eternity to the player that thinks he isn't badly hurt, but it is far preferable to a permanent disability. Never gamble with your player's health and safety. We need look no further than Muhammad Ali to see the result of multiple concussions.

Above all, once you establish a concussion treatment policy, never deviate from it. You set it up for a reason: the health and safety of your players, and that never changed.

BIBLIOGRAPHY

1. *AFCA Proceedings Manual 2003*. Accessed on July 2nd, 2004 at www.AFCA.com/Proceed_2003.htm

2. Cantu, Robert "Concussions: Advice for Parents of Youth Athletes." *Mom's Team – Youth Sports Parenting Information*. Accessed on July 1st, 2004 at: http://www.momsteam.com/alpha/features/health_safety/concussion_advice.s html

3. Cantu, Robert "Second-Impact Syndrome: What is it?" *Mom's Team – Youth Sports Parenting Information*. Accessed on July 1st, 2004 at: http://www.momsteam.com/alpha/features/health_safety/second_impact_synd rome.shtml

4. "Concussion" *The Why Files*. Accessed on July 1st, 2004 at: http://whyfiles.org/190sport_injury/3.html

5. Graber, Mark "Emergency Medicine: Box 2-2 Returning to Normal Activities After Concussion." *University of Iowa Family Practice Handbook, Fourth Edition Chapter 2*. Accessed June 8th, 2004 at: http://www.vh.org/adult/provider/familymedicine/FPHandbook/Chapter02/Bo x2-2.html

6. Lambert, J. G., "Concussions." *Medline Plus Medical Encyclopedia*. Accessed on June 8, 2004 at: http://www.nlm.nih.gov/medlineplus/ency/imagepages/17143.htm

7. McCrory, Paul R.; Johnston, Karen M. "Acute Clinical Symptoms of Concussion." *The Physician and Sports Medicine*. Accessed on July 1st, 2004 at: http://www.physsportsmed.com/issues/2002/08_02/mccrory.htm

8. National Safety Council. *First Aid and CPR Handbook; 3rd Edition*. (Massachusetts: Jones and Bartlett Publishers, 1997)

9. Olendorf, Donna. *The Gale Encyclopedia of Medicine, vol 2*. (Michigan: Gale Research and Publishing, 1999

10. "Researchers Find Most Football Concussions Go Unreported." *Sportsline Wire Reports*. Accessed on June 8th, 2004 at: http://www.cbs.sportsline.com/collegefootball/story/7423419

11. "Trauma of the Head." *The Merck Manual Sec. 14, Ch. 175*. Accessed on June 8th, 2004 at: http://www.merck.com/mrkshared/mmanual/section14/chapter175/175a.jsp

12. Wyatt, Hugh. *Safer and Surer Tackling*. Video, 1999

13. Zumerchik, John. *Encyclopedia of Sports Science*. (New York: Simon & Schuster Macmillan, 1997)

APPENDIX SEVEN
Glossary of Football Terms

Introduction

Football, unfortunately, is a complex sport. One of the things that makes it so difficult to coach is the jargon that is used. An experienced coach might comment on how the opposing defense was "aligned in a split-6 with the tackles in a four technique, with a cover-three behind it. They rotated the zone to force frontside, and dropped the backside defensive end off into intermediate third on initial flow away. Sam dogged in pure passing situations, and Will drifted to the hook, giving a landmark coverage that took away our drag, but we were able to pop the split open on a smash by using a play-action off our twenty series."

Is your head spinning yet?

I have a book written by one of the greatest football minds in history, defensive genius Bill Arnsparger. Coach Arnsparger's text, *Coaching Defensive Football* (ISBN 1574441620) may well be the definitive document on the subject.

I say, "may well be," because I don't know for sure. I've read the book from cover to cover three times and I still can't figure out much more than basic alignments. The jargon is so thick I can only translate about every third word of coach-speak into a human tongue.

This chapter is nothing more than a dictionary of football terms that will hopefully make your life easier as you work your way through the library of books and videos you're gradually going to accumulate as you continue coaching. I wish I'd had something like this a few years ago.

~D.

"A" Gap

Name given to the gaps between the offensive *center* and *guards* in an offensive *formation*.

Alignment

1) Specific formation of an *offense* or *defense*.

2) Location of one player in relationship to another (Ex. "The tight end's <u>alignment</u> is next to the tackle.")

"B" Gap

Name given to the gap between the offensive *guards* and the *tackles* in an offensive *formation*.

Backfield

1) The area on either side of the *line of scrimmage*. May be the offensive or defensive backfield.

2) The men aligned on either side of the line of scrimmage. For example, the *halfbacks*, *fullback*, and *quarterback* are all aligned in the offensive backfield, while the *linebackers*, *defensive backs*, and *safeties* are all members of the defensive backfield.

Backs

Any member of the offensive or defensive *backfield*.

Bail (Defensive Back Technique)

Defensive *backfield* disruption technique designed to knock the *receiver* off his *pass route* upon his first movement. Typically an open step coupled with a fast punching movement into the receiver's breastplate with one or two hands.

Bear

(See *Forty-Six*)

Black Lion Award

Annual award given to one member of a football team that most represents the ideals and courage exemplified in Don Holledar, a former cadet at the United States Military Academy at West Point who was killed in action in the Battle of Ong Than on October 17th, 1967. The award was initiated in 2000 by Coach *Hugh Wyatt*, who received permission from General Jim Shelton (*USA, Ret.*) the former commanding officer of the 28th Infantry, Holledar's former unit, whose operational emblem is a black lion on a field of white. Further information about the Black Lion can be found in appendix five or at <u>www.coachwyatt.com</u>.

Blast

(See *Lead*)

Blitz

Defensive tactic designed to overwhelm the pass blocking or confuse run blocking assignments. Performed when a *linebacker* or *defensive back* charges through his assigned gap and pressures the *passer* or disrupts the running lane.

Blocking

Any one of a series of movements designed to impede the path of a defensive player or move him out of the path of the ball carrier.

Bump

(See *Bail*)

Bump-and-Run

Man-to-man pass coverage in which the defensive player assigned to cover a *receiver* executes a *bail* technique on the receiver's first movement and attempts to either prevent him from releasing from the line of scrimmage, or interfere with the timing of the pass route. The defender covers the receiver if the bail technique fails.

"C" Gap

C

Name given to the gap between the offensive *tackles* and *ends*, whether split or tight, in an offensive *formation*.

Center

In a seven man offensive line, the middle player. Typically the player responsible for *snapping* the ball to the *quarterback*. (Note: colloquial usage has lead to the snapper being titled "center" regardless of his position on the *line of scrimmage*.)

Chair

A pass *route* in which the *receiver* heads directly upfield and then makes a sharp cut to the outside after three to five steps. On his third step the receiver cuts back upfield and executes a *streak*. Very effective pattern for breaking coverage, but requires exceptional *pass blocking* from the *offensive line*.

Chip

Type of brush *block*, usually executed by an eligible *receiver* as he moves to his actual blocking assignment. The receiver lightly bumps the outer shoulder of the *defender*, turning his torso and distracting him. Usually performed in concert with a *kickout* block.

Cloud

Defensive pass coverage system designed to confuse opposing *quarterbacks*. Typical zone coverage has the *second level* defenders dropping to levels about eight to twelve yards deep, while the *third level* is responsible for the deepest levels of coverage, from twelve yards to the *end zone*. In cloud coverage, *linebackers* take a deeper zone while the *cornerbacks* maintain a shallow depth and flow to the ball. (Note: This coverage is not suitable for *youth football*.)

Comeback

A *pass route* in which the *receiver* breaks hard from the *line of scrimmage* and runs ten to twelve yards straight downfield, drawing the coverage deep. At the moment when the coverage has committed to stopping the *streak*, the receiver gears down and curls his hips inward, coming back to the football, which is usually thrown just before he breaks.

Corner; Cornerback (Defensive halfback)

Defensive player primarily assigned to coverage of individual *receivers* or passing areas on the field. In a normal defensive *alignment*, the corners are typically aligned on the widest eligible receivers in the offensive *formation*.

Corner (Pass Route)

Receiver path that angles towards the corner of the field where the boundary markers intersect. (See *Flag*.)

Combo

Run *blocking* scheme in which two offensive players engage one *defender* at the same time, attempting to drive him back from the *hole* with a *double team* block. As soon as the defender's charge has been neutralized, the outermost blocker slips off the double team and attacks the nearest inside *second level* defender. Can be very effective when properly coached.

Counter

A type of offensive *play* designed to confuse the defense by presenting them with the initial *backfield* flow of a certain play, and then using a countering movement to attack a different point. Typically used with some form of *trap* blocking.

Coverage

Act of either defending an eligible *receiver* from catching a thrown forward *pass* or of preventing the *punt* or *kickoff* returner from advancing the ball.

Crab Block

(See *Scramble Block*)

Crack

Blocking technique usually performed by a *wide receiver* in which he releases straight down the *line of scrimmage* and attempts to hit a *linebacker* or *defensive end*. Typically performed when the offense is running a *sweep*.

Curl

1) Pass route similar to the *comeback* route, but shorter in depth. Curls are typically five to nine yard routes designed to hit underneath the *linebacker* coverage. Curls also usually turn away from the initial ball placement to put the *receiver*'s body between the ball and the linebacker.

2) The area of the field in which the curl route is usually run; a ten-yard by ten-yard box immediately downfield from the tight end. Inside *linebackers* are typically assigned hook-to-curl *zone* pass coverage responsibility.

Cut

(See *Trap*)

Cut block

Any *block* that occurs below the waist. Illegal downfield, but legal inside the *free blocking zone*. Similar in execution to the *scramble block*, but executed in one movement rather than with continuous pressure.

"D" Gap

Name given to the gap between the offensive *ends* and the *sideline*.

DC-46

Name given to a version of the *"46" defense* that was developed by Internet author and *youth football* coach Clark Wilkins, who goes by the nickname "Dum Coach." Extremely effective defensive system that puts horrendous pressure on the *passer* and still prevents the run.

Dead Ball Foul

Rule infraction incurred when the ball is not in play. The awarded team typically cannot refuse dead ball fouls.

Defender

Any one of the eleven members of the defensive unit charged with stopping the ball carrier and preventing him from making it to the *end zone* with the football.

Defense

Name given to the unit charged with preventing the opposing *offense* from moving the ball downfield and across the *goal line*.

Defensive Back

(See *Cornerback*)

Defensive Halfback

(See *Cornerback*)

Dig

A pass *route* in which the *receiver* runs directly upfield for three to five steps and then angles inward towards the goalposts (approximately 45-degrees). On his second step after the initial cut he makes a second cut of 45-degrees that sends him flat across the field and parallel to the *line of scrimmage.*

Dime

A further evolution of the *nickel* defense. The nickel is named for the five *defensive backs.* A "dime" removes one of the remaining two *linebackers* from the field and substitutes a sixth defensive back. Like the nickel, the dime is a professional and college level defense with extremely limited usefulness at the *youth football* level.

Direct Snap

Any *exchange* in which the ball is *snapped* directly to the offensive player that will run with it. Offensive *systems* using the direct snap have fallen out of use in favor of the *indirect snap* in which the *quarterback* receives the snap and then performs a *handoff* to another player or *passes* the football.

Double Team

Very similar to the *combo* block, a double team uses two offensive blockers to engage one defender. Instead of the outermost defender slipping off to block *second level,* the object of the double team is to drive the hapless defensive player into the second level and interfering with their ability to *scrape* to a gap.

Double Wing

1) Offensive system developed by *Don Markham* and popularized by *Hugh Wyatt* and *Jerry Vallotton.* The *system* features an interlocking *series* of offensive *plays* designed to maximize both power and *misdirection.*

2) Primary offensive *formation* of the Double Wing offense. Features two *tight ends,* two *wingbacks,* and a *fullback* that is aligned directly behind the *quarterback* and extremely close to the line of scrimmage. *Line splits* are particularly tight across the line to prevent

leakage and allow the backside *guards* and *tackles* to *pull* and be used as *lead blockers*.

Dog Blitz

Delayed *blitz* designed to confuse offensive *blocking* on *passing downs*. The *linebacker* hesitates briefly to allow each offensive blocker to engage a defender, and then attempts to blitz through any available opening in the line. Has limited usefulness in youth football because of the emphasis on the running attack.

Down

1) A single offensive play. The team with possession of the ball is given four attempts, called downs, to move the football ten yards.

2) An action by a *receiver* catching a *punt* or *kickoff* who chooses not to advance the ball. Usually performed in the *end zone*, this results in a *touchback*.

3) Type of *block* in which the blocker moves towards the initial placement of the ball at a sharp angle instead of engaging the defender aligned directly across from him. This provides excellent leverage.

Down, First

If the *offense* is able to move the ball ten yards in four attempts, they are given a new set of *downs*. This resetting of the down markers is called "gaining a first down." There is no limit to the number of first downs a team may gain in a game or *possession*.

Downhill

Towards the goal line. (Ex. On this play, the *halfback* needs to run parallel to the *line of scrimmage* and then break <u>downhill</u> after he gets the ball.)

Draw

Offensive *play* designed to fool the *defense* into thinking that the play is a *pass* attempt. This causes the *linebackers* and *defensive backs* to drop into pass coverage, and frees up running lanes for the ball carrier. A typical draw involves the *quarterback* dropping back to show pass, and handing off to a *running back* that has delayed in the *backfield*. The draw can be used to beat a *blitz* attempt unless the linebackers are very well coached.

Drive Block

Standard one-on-one block used in most football running *plays*. The offensive blocker fires out from his *three-point stance*, places his helmet on the side of the defender that the ball carrier will be approaching, and attempts to use leverage and physical strength to drive the defender out of the *hole*. Drive blocking is generally effective only when the offensive personnel are clearly superior to the defending personnel. Regardless, drive blocking is a key fundamental skill in all levels of football.

Encroachment

Dead ball defensive foul incurred when a defending player jumps across the *line of scrimmage* after the *offense* has been set for one second. Similar to *offsides*, encroachment occurs only when the defender makes physical contact with an offensive player. The penalty is five yards.

End, Defensive

Term given to a *defensive lineman* aligned near the edges of the formation and usually assigned responsibility for defending *sweeps* or *off-tackle* plays.

End Line

Line at either end of a football field marking the ultimate boundary between the playing surface of the *end zone* and out of bounds.

End, Offensive

Eligible *receiver* located on the *line of scrimmage*. Only the last two members of the offensive line are eligible to catch a forward *pass*. (See *Tight End* and *Split End*)

End, Split

Nomenclature used to describe a *receiver* that is located on the *line of scrimmage* and split more than three yards from the offensive *tackle*.

End, Tight

Eligible *receiver* aligned on the *line of scrimmage* just outside the offensive *tackle*. Usually more heavily built than a *split end*, the tight end is more often than not thought of as a blocking *lineman* that happens to be eligible to catch passes.

End Zone

Ten yard deep zone that extends across the field. This is the scoring area for football. A *touchdown* is scored when any player legally possesses the football in this area, which is behind the *goal line*.

Exchange

The act of giving the football to another player. This may occur through *handoff*, *pitch*, *pass*, or by any other legal means.

Extra Point

(See *Point After Touchdown*)

Facemask

1) Protective shield placed on the front of the helmet to protect the eyes and face from impact.

2) Rules infraction committed by grabbing the shield. Divided into two penalties: a five-yard penalty for unintentional grabbing of the facemask, and a *personal foul* fifteen-yard penalty for intentionally seizing the mask.

Fair Catch

When receiving any kicking play, such as a *punt* or *kickoff*, the *receiver* may make a fair catch call by waving his hand above his head with the arm fully extended. The coverage team may not touch him or interfere with his ability to catch the kick. The kick returner may not advance the ball beyond the point at which it is caught. If he *muffs* the ball, it is still *live* and may be recovered by the kicking team.

False Start

A *dead ball foul* in which an offensive player, usually a lineman, has set himself for one second, and then jumps with a rapid movement that simulates the snap. This incurs a five-yard penalty.

Field Goal

A *scrimmage kick* in which the ball is *snapped* to a *holder* who places it either on the ground or on a tee. A *kicker* then kicks the ball with the intent for it to pass between the uprights and over the crossbar of the *goalposts*. A field goal is worth three points. A field goal that does not enter the *end zone* is treated as a *punt*, and may be advanced by the defense or *downed* by the kicking team.

Five Step Drop

A passing play in which the *passer*, usually the *quarterback*, takes five quick steps backwards to avoid the *pass rush* while searching through his receivers looking for the open man. Typically five and *seven step drops* are used in conjunction with deeper *pass patterns* that allow the receivers to get further downfield.

Five-Two, Five-Three, or "Fifty"

A commonly used defensive *formation* that features five *defensive linemen* and two or three *linebackers*.

Flag

1) Style of football in which body contact is minimized. Players are "*tackled*" by having a Velcro™ flag torn from a belt.

2) *Pass route* in which the *receiver* runs straight down the field for a predetermined distance before breaking at a 30 to 45-degree angle

towards the sideline, roughly towards the flags that mark the boundary lines. (See *Corner*.)

Flanker

A *wide receiver* aligned outside the offensive *tight end* by three yards or more and also in the offensive *backfield*. May be on the same side as the *split end*, in which case the flanker is usually referred to as lining up in the *slot*.

Flare

A *pass route* usually run by *running backs* just behind the *line of scrimmage* in the offensive *backfield*. The running back runs a banana-shaped route that looks like the arcing path of a flare as shot from a flare gun.

Flat

1) *Pass route* in which the *receiver* angles to the outside perimeter underneath the *cornerback* at between twelve and zero yards in depth.

2) The passing *zone* into which the flat route is designed to attack. The outside *linebacker*, or *cornerback* is typically responsible for the curl-to-flat area.

Fly

1) *Pass route* in which the *receiver* runs directly down the field in a straight line. The ball is thrown in a high arcing path to allow the receiver to run under it.

2) Offensive system characterized by a sprint-style *motion* across the *offensive backfield*. This motion is designed to get the potential *ball carrier* to full speed before handing him the ball. His high-speed movement provides for an immediate threat to the perimeter.

3) Nickname for the type of sprint motion typically used in the fly offense.

Formation

An arrangement of offensive players in some prescribed manner for a particular purpose. Formations may be designed to isolate defensive players in space, place *running backs* close enough together to execute fakes and *blocks*, or force the defense into an unsound *alignment*. A formation is not an offensive *system*, but coaches have taken to referring to their style of offense with the name of their primary formation, thus terminology such as *Double Wing*, *Wing-T*, and *Wishbone* have become common usage when referring to a complete offense.

Formationing

Term used for the offensive technique of aligning in a particular formation to force the defense to counter you. An example is the unbalanced *offensive line*, with four linemen on one side of *center* and two on the other. If the defense fails to adjust to the imbalance, the *offense* is free to exploit the strong side.

Forty-Six

Defensive alignment developed in the 1980s by Buddy Ryan while coaching with the Chicago Bears. Traditionally defenses have been named for the number of players in the first two levels (Ex: 4-3, 5-2). The 46 was named for the *strong safety* who wore jersey number 46 when the system was introduced, Doug Plank. Featuring a four man *defensive line* with Mr. Plank aligned just outside the *tight end* and a *linebacker* aligned just inside the end, the defense allowed the Bears to completely dominate in the NFL by providing immediate pressure on the *quarterback* at the *snap*, and also clogged the running lanes. A simplified version of this defense is ideal for *youth football*, but requires competent coaching to be successful.

Forward Pass

(See *Pass*.)

Four-Point Stance

A basic football stance similar to the *three-point stance* but with both hands on the ground. Weight should be approximately 60% on the hands and 40% on the toes. This stance is usually used on the defensive side of the ball by *linemen* desiring a low, powerful line charge.

Four-Three, Four-Four, "Forty"

Commonly used at the college and NFL levels, the 4-3 is the predominant seven-man front featuring four *defensive linemen* and three *linebackers*. The 4-4 removes a *safety* and adds another linebacker to put eight players close to the *line of scrimmage* to prevent the run. Featuring astonishing flexibility, the 4-4 is a very effective defense, even at the youth level.

Free Blocking Zone

An imaginary box that extends from the ball. This box is three yards to either side of the ball along the *line of scrimmage* and extends four yards into the defensive *backfield* and two yards into the offensive backfield. Within this zone it is legal to *cut* block within certain parameters as long as the football has not left the zone.

Free Kick

Any kick with which an opponent may not interfere. The ball is placed upon a tee and all defending personnel are required to remain ten yards from it until the kick.

Free Safety

Defensive Back typically assigned a *zone* rather than a *man-to-man* assignment, and used as a backstop for the defense. Almost always aligned as the deepest man in a defensive *formation*.

Front

Typically used to refer to the front half (*linemen* and *linebackers*) of a defensive *alignment*. (Ex: "The Bears were in a sixty front.")

Fullback

An offensive position that usually lines up in or near the middle or *strong side* of the offensive *formation*. Fullbacks are usually stronger and more powerful blockers than *halfbacks*, and are usually placed in a position to be able to *lead block* for the halfbacks. Fullbacks are eligible receivers.

Full House

Any offensive *formation* in which all four backfield eligible receivers are inside the offensive *tackles*. Examples include the *wishbone, T-formation,* and *Power-I*.

Fumble

To lose hold of the football while handling or running. Fumbles may be recovered and advanced by either team. Fumbles occur most often on *handoffs* and other *exchanges*.

Gap-8, Gap-Air-Mirror, GAM

G

Defensive system developed in the early days of football that stops the run with eight defensive players aligned on the *line of scrimmage*, each in a pre-selected *gap*. Behind this formidable defensive front is a *bump-and-run* pass coverage scheme in which one player plays a deep *zone*. Developed for the youth level in 1991 through 2005 by Coach *Jack Reed*.

Goal Line

1) A line at either end of the field across which it is the objective of the offensive unit to carry the football. It is the innermost boundary of the *end zone* as the *end line* is the outermost boundary.

2) A defensive alignment used primarily in short yardage situations when the opposing offense is close to scoring a touchdown or achieving a first down. Goal line defenses are typically designed to favor run stopping and pressure the pass with blitzes. Examples of typical goal line defenses used in NFL, college, and high school levels are the 6-3 and 6-4, and 7-1. At the *youth football level* a goal line defense may be used successfully anywhere on the field.

Goal Posts

Set of posts or bars arranged at both ends of the field and placed even with the *end line* consisting of a 10-ft vertical pole topped by a horizontal crossbar from which two vertical upright posts extend. In college and professional football, the posts are 18 ft 6 in apart. At the high school and *youth level* the goal posts are 23 ft 5 in wide. It is the object of a *field goal* to kick the ball over the crossbar and between the uprights.

Guard, Defensive

Name sometimes given to the innermost defensive linemen in a six-man defensive front. Usually responsible for defending running plays to the *"A" Gaps* or *"B" Gaps*, depending on defensive assignment.

Guard, Offensive

Positions directly on each side of the *center* and located on the offensive line. Typically larger and heavier than the offensive *backs*, guards are responsible for most of the *pulling* and *trapping* in an offensive system, so they are usually faster and more agile than the offensive *tackles*.

Halfback

1) Offensive player located in the *backfield* and primarily used as a ball carrier. (See *Running Back*.) Halfbacks are eligible receivers.

2) Defensive player located in the backfield and primarily used in pass coverage. (See *Cornerback*.)

Handoff

Basic football skill in which one offensive player hands the ball to another. Although seemingly simple, it requires some practice and teaching. The inside elbow of the receiving player must be up and pointed at the person handing them the ball, and the giver must push the ball into the taker's belly with some force to prevent a *fumble*.

Hash Mark

A series of short marker lines that runs parallel to the *sidelines*. The hash marks are 53 ft 4 in from each sideline in college and high school football, and 70 ft 9 in from each sideline in the National Football League (NFL). Youth teams typically use the high school sized hash marks. The ball is brought to between these two sets of lines to start each offensive *play*. Thus, a running play that goes out of the left sideline will be spotted (placed) on the closest hash mark in preparation for the next play.

Hi-Lo

1) Illegal *blocking* technique. One blocker engages a defender high, and then a second *cut blocks* the defender's legs. While cut blocking is legal in the *Free Blocking Zone*, Hi-Lo blocking is not.

2) A pass *pattern* developed by Andrew Coverdale and Dan Robinson in which two *receivers* brush closely with one another, one being the "High" route (further downfield) and the second being the "Low" route (closer to the *quarterback*). The pattern disrupts the timing of defenders trying to maintain trail position on the receivers.

Hit Position

Basic football stance similar to the *four-point* and *three-point* stances, but upright with only the feet in contact with the ground. The back should be straight and head up, with the feet parallel at just past shoulder width. This stance is fundamental to all movement on the field, and is the basic starting point for all instruction in proper *tackling*.

Holder

Player in a *scrimmage kick formation* that is located seven yards from the *snapper*. The holder catches the snap and places the ball on a tee for kicking by the kicker. Usually used only in *field goal* attempts, but may be used for *kickoffs* in inclement weather.

Holding

Rules infraction committed by offensive personnel that have either allowed their arms to wrap around the defender, or grabbed the defender's jersey or equipment. May also be committed by a defensive player grabbing the jersey or equipment of a player not actively engaged in blocking that defender. Offensive holding is a ten-yard infraction enforced from the spot of the foul and repeating the *down*. Defensive holding is a five-yard penalty and an automatic *first down* for the defense.

Hole

Offensive term for point of attack on running plays. *Blocking* schemes are structured to lever an opening, or hole, in the defensive team and allow the ball carrier through.

Hook

1) Pass route similar to *comeback* routes, but shorter in depth. Hooks are typically five to nine yard routes designed to hit underneath the *linebacker* coverage. Hooks turn to the inside of the formation to give the *quarterback* the best possible target for his pass.

2) The area of the field in which the hook route is usually run; a ten-yard by ten-yard box immediately downfield from the tight end. Inside *linebackers* are typically assigned hook-to-curl *zone* pass coverage responsibility.

Horizontal Stretch

Offensive tactic typically performed by *alignment* or with *receivers* in which the *defense* is forced to spread themselves across the field along a broad front, thereby weakening downfield coverage and pursuit to the ball within the tactical center of the defense. (See *Vertical Stretch*.)

Hot Read

Any short *pass route* used as an outlet *receiver* for a *passer* under pressure from the *pass rush*. Typically a *running back* or *tight end* that releases into the *flat* underneath the pass coverage. Most *pass patterns* developed by competent coaches have a hot read built in.

Intermediate

Term given to the *passing zone* just behind the *linebackers* and just in front of the *safeties*. Approximately twelve to eighteen yards from the *line of scrimmage*.

Indirect Snap

Form of *exchange* between the *center* and *quarterback* in which the ball is *snapped* between the snapper's legs. Sometimes called the "T-Formation Snap" because of its introduction at the inception of the *T-Formation* offense. Given the title "indirect" because the ball does not go directly to the eventual ball carrier.

Isolation ("Ice")

"The most common play in football." Typically run from an I-formation offensive *formation*, the isolation uses basic *drive* or *zone blocking* across the *point of attack*. The *fullback* is used as a *lead* blocker and it is his job to 'isolate' the *linebacker*. The *tailback* takes the *handoff* from the *quarterback* and follows the fullback. The tailback reads the fullback's block and angles his path to keep it between him and the linebacker as long as possible. The isolation is also referred to as a "blast," or "lead."

I-Formation

"The most common *formation* in football." Offensive football formation in which the *running backs* line up in a line directly behind the *quarterback*. There are several different versions of the I-formation *set*, but the most common is usually preferred to as the "*Pro-I*" because of its prevalence at the professional level. In this version, the *flanker* is split wide on the same side as the *tight end* and the opposite end is split out. This provides three potential deep *receivers* spread across the field in any *pass pattern*, while still keeping the running backs available inside the formation to protect the quarterback and provide a strong inside running game. The I-formation is extremely versatile, as simple shifts of the flanker's *alignment* and *motion* can force the *defense* into unsound responses. The formation's usefulness at the *youth level* is impaired by the lack of comprehension in both players and coaches.

Illegal Forward Pass

The ball may be *passed* forward (towards the end zone) only from the *offensive backfield*. If the passer crosses the *line of scrimmage* before throwing the ball the pass is judged to be illegal. The penalty for this infraction is five yards and loss of *down*.

Illegal Procedure

Dead ball offensive foul caused when a) a set player moves prior to the *snap*, or b) the *offense* lines up in violation of the *seven-man rule*. The penalty is five yards without loss of *down*.

Illegal Shift

Offensive players are required to be still for one full second before the snap. Only one player may be in *motion* at a time, and not towards the *line of scrimmage*. Illegal shift is a *dead ball* foul if either or both of these rules are violated. The penalty is five yards without loss of *down*. (Note: *False Start* and Illegal Shift are very closely interchangeable, and occasionally even officials make the incorrect call. The penalty is the same, so it doesn't really matter.)

Illegal Touching

The five *offensive linemen* are not eligible to catch forward passes. If any offensive player throws a pass and the first person to touch it before it hits the ground is an offensive lineman, the action is judged to be illegal touching of the ball. This penalty may also be enforced if a kickoff fails to go ten yards and is touched by any member of the kicking team. The penalty is five yards and loss of *down*.

Illegal Use of the Hands

Any time a player's hands strike the face or head of an opposing player this penalty is enforced. The penalty is five yards and loss of *down* if the offending player was on the offense. If the defense performs this infraction, the penalty is ten yards and an automatic first down for the offense.

Ineligible Receiver Downfield

On *passing plays* offensive *linemen* are allowed to be three yards or less downfield from the *line of scrimmage*. If an offensive lineman moves beyond this point he is judged to be an ineligible receiver. The penalty is five yards and loss of *down*.

Intentional Grounding

If a *passer* is under pressure from the *pass rush* and throws the ball away rather than take a *sack*, he may be called for intentional grounding. To avoid this penalty, an eligible *receiver* from the offense must be near the flight of the ball, or the passer must be outside the *tackles*. The penalty for intentional grounding is five yards from the spot the foul occurred and loss of *down*.

Judge (Field, Side, or Line)

J

Any one of the officials responsible for enforcing the code of conduct, sportsmanship, and rules of football on the field. Each judge is responsible for a different area of the field, section of the offensive/defensive *formation*, and game play.

K

Kicker

Offensive player responsible for *scrimmage kicking* the football on *field goal* attempts or *punts*. Typically, field goal and *placekick* kickers are referred to as kickers and the player who punts the ball away is the *punter*.

Kickoff

Placekick involving change of *possession*. The ball is placed on a tee on the thirty-yard line (NFL), thirty-five yard line (College) or forty-yard line (High School and most *youth football*). A *kicker* kicks the ball from the tee towards the opposing team. Once the ball has traveled ten yards and touched the ground, or been touched by any member of the receiving team it is *live* and may be recovered by any member of either team. Kickoffs are performed whenever a team scores a *touchdown* or *field goal*, and when a team earns a *safety*.

Kickout

Inside-out angled *block* typically performed by a *running back* or *pulling* offensive *lineman* attempting to drive a defender, usually a *defensive end* outward so the ball carrier may pass inside him.

L

Landmark Zone

Standard *zone pass coverage* in which the linebackers are responsible for defending passes to the underneath locations on the field, and the *safeties* are responsible for defending deep threats. Typically, this form of pass coverage results in every member of the *defensive secondary* dropping almost straight back from their assigned position the instant they read pass. Landmark zones are the most common form of pass defense from *youth football* to college, and they are relatively easy to attack for a coach with an understanding of how they work.

Landry, Tom

Head football coach of the Dallas Cowboys from 1960-1988. Developer of the professional *4-3* defense while an assistant coach with the New York Giants from 1956-1960. Landry developed the "flex defense," in which one tackle plays slightly off the *line of scrimmage* in order to read and react to the offensive play. Landry compiled a 250-162-6 record in regular season play and won 20 of 36 in playoff competition. He guided the Cowboys to five Super Bowls, a record, and won two of them. During his 29 years, Dallas won 14 division championships and had 21 consecutive winning seasons.

Lateral

A thrown ball that moves backwards, towards the possessing team's *end zone*. Any player of the possessing team may lateral to any other player. The *pitch* and *toss* are examples of the lateral.

Lead

(See *Isolation*)

Lead Blocker

Any member of the offensive unit that leads the ball carrier to the *point of attack* and is assigned to *block* the first defender to cross his path. Lead blockers may be used on virtually any play in football, from *kickoff* and *punt* returns, to specific plays like the *isolation* and *power*.

Linebacker, Inside

Defensive player usually aligned between the *center* and *tackles* of the *offensive line* and in the defensive *backfield*. His usual responsibility is to defend and prevent running plays up the middle, and to cover and stop *passes* thrown in the *hook* and *curl* zones. In *man-to-man* pass coverage the inside linebackers are usually responsible for covering the number three eligible *receiver* counting from the outside of the formation to the inside. Typically, this is a *running back*.

Linebacker, Middle

Defensive player usually aligned in the middle of the offensive *formation* and in the defensive *backfield*. His assigned responsibility is to defend and prevent running plays that attack the *"A" gaps* and to cover and stop *passes* thrown into the *hook* zones to either side of the *center*. In *man-to-man* coverage the middle linebacker is usually responsible for covering the centermost eligible *receiver* (almost always a *running back*).

Linebacker, Outside

Defensive player usually aligned towards the outside of the offensive *formation* and in the defensive *backfield*. Outside linebackers are usually charged with defending running plays that attack the *"C" gaps* and *"D" gaps*, and with covering and preventing passes thrown to the *curl* and *flat* zones. In *man-to-man* coverage, the outside linebacker's responsibility is usually the second eligible *receiver* from the outside. Against most offensive *formations* this is either a *flanker*, *tight end*, or *running back*.

Linebacker Stance

(See *Hit position.*)

Line, Defensive

Group of defensive players charged with aligning close to the *line of scrimmage* and with the dual responsibility of stopping the run and providing a *pass rush* to pressure the *quarterback* into making a poor throw. The defensive line usually consists of *tackles* and *ends*, but may also include *outside linebackers* that are aligned closely to the line. Certain coaches will also refer to the innermost defenders of the defensive line as *guards*.

Lineman

Any offensive or defensive player that plays on the *line of scrimmage.*

Line, Offensive

Group of offensive players that are ineligible to receive *passes*. Their primary responsibility is to block the defensive players and attempt to open *holes* at the *point of attack*, and to impede the *pass rush* of the *defensive line* and *linebackers*. The offensive line consists of the *center*, usually the most centrally located lineman and the one most commonly used to *snap* the football, the *guards* to either side of him, and the *tackles* to the outside of the guards. Some coaches consider the *tight end* to be a part of the offensive line as well, although he is an eligible *receiver.*

Line of Scrimmage

An imaginary line drawn parallel to the *goal lines* and running the width of the field through the football. This line divides the field into the offensive and defensive sides.

Line Splits

Distance between *offensive linemen* in an offensive formation. Certain formations may have extremely wide splits, like the *spread*, which uses typical splits of four to five feet at the high school level, or extremely close splits, like the *Double Wing*, which places the linemen foot-to-foot.

Live Ball

A loose football that may be recovered by either the *offense* or the *defense* during a scrimmage play, or the kicking or receiving teams during a *placekick* or *scrimmage kick*, and gain that team possession at the spot of the recovery. If the offensive unit recovers the ball before the *first down* marker, they waste a down. If the ball has been advanced beyond the first down marker, a new set of downs is awarded. The defensive unit will gain their team possession and a set of downs no matter where they recover the ball. A ball does not become live during a scrimmage kick unless touched by a member of the receiving team. *Fumbles* may always be advanced by either team.

Load

Block usually performed by a *fullback* on a *defensive end* in which the fullback attacks the end's inside shoulder. After engaging, the fullback then maneuvers for outside leverage. The *ball carrier* usually runs outside of a load block.

Log

Similar to a *load* block, except that the *fullback* attacks the outside shoulder of the *defensive end* and attempts to seal him to the inside without turning him.

Markham, Don

"Father of the Double Wing" High school football coach Don Markham has coached for 34 high school seasons using the *Double Wing* offense. In that period he has achieved a record of 289-96-1 and won five California Interscholastic Federation titles. Characterized by a power running game and a relentless, detail-oriented attack that tailors the *point of attack* for each individual play to weaknesses in the *defense*, Coach Markham's systems are highly effective for the youth game as well. Don Markham was a clinic speaker at the 2004 Double Wing Symposium in Dallas, TX. His website is www.coachmarkham.com.

Maryland-I

(See *Stack-I*)

Max or Max Pro

Pass protection call that assigns secondary pass blocking responsibilities to the *running backs* rather than assigning them to run a *pass route* as part of the overall *pattern*. Used with much success at the youth level to give inexperienced *quarterbacks* more time to find the open *receiver* and deliver an accurate throw.

Man-To-Man

Pass *coverage* in which the pass defenders are assigned a specific eligible *receiver* to cover. Man-to-man coverage has many advantages at the youth level, including simplicity, but loses its effectiveness in the face of highly superior talent.

Mesh (Option)

Triple Option technique typically involving the *quarterback* and *fullback*. When the ball is *snapped* the quarterback places the football in the fullback's belly where the fullback grips it lightly. Both players make an either/or read of a *defensive* player (typically a *defensive tackle*). If the defensive player attacks the fullback to make the *tackle* the quarterback will pull the ball out and attack another *gap*. If the defensive player does not attack the fullback, the quarterback will release the ball and let the fullback carry it. This technique takes some careful coaching, but can be highly effective at the *youth football* level. Offenses such as the *Veer* and *Wishbone* are famous for the triple option play that requires this technique.

Mesh (Passing)

Any *pass pattern* that requires two or more eligible receivers to cross paths in a very close relationship to one another. The most common of these is the *hi-low*. This combination of pass *routes* is very difficult for the *defensive backfield* to cover. The mesh can be difficult to teach to *youth football* players in limited practice time because of the precise timing necessary.

Mike

Nickname traditionally given to the *middle linebacker* in a defense. Systems with even numbered linebackers such as the *4-4* and *6-2* do not have a Mike linebacker. (See *Sam, Will.*)

Minimum-Play

Many *youth football* leagues have a rule requiring a certain minimum amount of playing time that each player has to have in each game. Typically this is divided up into plays per game, half, or quarter. A normal minimum-play-rule is six plays per game. All youth coaches should have some form of minimum-play rule of their own to govern substitutions and insure that each player gains as much experience as possible. Minimum play players are often called MPPs.

Misdirection

Any *offensive play* in which the main purpose of the play is to simulate an attack in one direction before assailing the true *point of attack*. Highly effective at the *youth football* level, misdirection is one of the best possible ways to move the ball in large chunks of yardage.

Monster

Nickname given to a defensive player in a *strong safety* or *outside linebacker* position. Certain variations of the *5-4* use one of the *safeties* in a dual role of *run support* and *pass defense*. This player is sometimes referred to as the monster.

Motion

Offensive technique for altering the *formation* before the ball is *snapped*. Motion can only be performed by an *eligible receiver*, who moves from one position on the field to another. A motioning player cannot simulate the snap (by jumping and freezing) or be in motion towards the line of scrimmage at the snap. In American Football only one player may be in motion at any one time. Offenses like the *Fly, Double Wing*, and *Wing-T* make extensive use of motion for various reasons.

Muff

Any *scrimmage kick* may be returned for yardage or score by the *defense*, provided it does not enter the opposing end zone. A muff occurs when a defensive player attempts to catch or recover such a kick and fails, but touches it in the process. This touching creates a *live ball* situation in which either team may recover, but not advance, the muffed ball to secure *possession*.

N

Nasty Split

Offensive alignment of the *tight end* in relationship to the *offensive tackle*. Typically a "normal" *split* at the youth level is from zero to eighteen inches. A "nasty" split extends this to anywhere from three to five feet. This formation technique is usually used to widen the area of responsibility for a *defensive end* or *outside linebacker*. The technique is extremely effective in *youth football*.

Neutral Zone

An area of the field the width of the football's length and stretching from sideline to sideline. No player may be aligned in the neutral zone prior to the snap with the exception of the *snapper*, usually the *center*, but not always.

Nickel

Defensive formation adjustment developed at the professional level and used in passing situations. A natural evolution from the pro *4-3* defense expanded by *Tom Landry* in the late 1950's, the nickel removes one of the three *linebackers* and substitutes a fifth *defensive back*, thus leading to the nickname "nickel." The defensive system is totally unsuitable for *youth football*.

Nickel Back

Name given to the *defensive back* subbed into the game in place of the removed *linebacker* in the *nickel* defense.

Noseguard/Nosetackle

Defensive lineman typically aligned over the center man in the *offensive line*. So named because his alignment places him "nose-to-nose" with the offensive center.

Onside Kick

Type of *kickoff* in which the kicking team attempts to recover the ball and retain *possession*. According to the rules of football, an onside kick is treated as a *live ball* once it has gone ten yards and touched the ground. Onside kicks typically involve an unbalanced kicking team, with most of the players stacked to the side the ball will be kicked to.

Offense

The team that has *possession* of the ball. The offense is given four attempts (See *Downs*) in which to gain ten yards of field position or score. At any time they may elect to attempt a *scrimmage kick*. The offense attempts the move the ball by running or *passing*.

Offensive line

Term used to describe the five members of the offense that are required by the rules to play on the *line of scrimmage*. Typically heavier-built than the *backfield*, the offensive line is charged with *blocking* the *defense* and opening holes for the ball carrier to run through as well as protecting the *quarterback* on passing plays.

Official

(See *referee*.)

Offsides

Infraction committed by a member of the *defense* that crosses the *neutral zone* before the ball is snapped. Offside is punished with a five yard penalty. Since it is a *dead ball* foul there is no loss of *down*. The *offense* would move immediately from a first down and ten yards to go, to a first down and five yards to go.

Off Tackle

1) Descriptive term given to any play whose point of attack is the "C" gaps, or between the *tight end* and the *offensive tackle*.

2) Area of the field in which an off tackle play attacks. (Ex: "We gained 52 yards off tackle in that game.")

Oklahoma 5-4

Defensive system developed by Bud Wilkinson in the late 1950s through the early 1960s while coaching at the University of Oklahoma. Designed primarily to combat the *triple option*, the "Okie 5-4" uses *zone* pass coverage and requires the *secondary* to assist in run support. The defense can be effective at the youth level, but requires exceptional talent and coaching.

Out

Pass route in which the *receiver* heads downfield and makes a sharp cut towards the sideline. The out is usually very difficult to utilize successfully at the *youth football* level due to the relative weakness of youth *quarterbacks'* arms.

Option

Offensive attack in which at least one defensive player is left unblocked. The *quarterback* will make a determination of the defensive player's attack angle and either keep, *pitch*, or *hand off* the football, depending on the specific option play called. The option is highly effective in *youth football*, but takes careful and precise coaching, and a certain amount of talent to be successful. It is extremely difficult to prepare more than one quarterback per team in this system, so most option teams suffer a drastic drop in output after the loss of a quarterback for any reason.

Pass (Backward)

(See *Lateral)*

Pass (Forward pass)

Offensive method of advancing the ball by throwing it forward (towards the opposing *end zone*). The pass is generally thrown by the *quarterback*, although

P

by definition any member of the *offense* may throw the pass (although the *center*, *guards*, and *tackles* must face their own goal line before taking the ball and running with it or throwing it.) Any member of the *offensive backfield* and the two *ends* are eligible to receive the pass.

Pass Blocking

Blocking skill or technique used to protect the *passer* long enough for him to find an open *receiver* and throw the football. Typically pass blocking involves giving ground while steering the charge of the defensive player.

Pass Coverage

Any technique or tactic designed to cover offensive *receivers* and prevent the completed *forward pass*.

Passer

Any member of the *offense* charged with throwing the ball to an eligible receiver. Typically the *quarterback*.

Passer Efficiency Rating

Mathematical formula that supposedly calculates the competence of a quarterback at throwing the ball. The NCAA and NFL levels use different formulae that are weighted in different directions. Since most high school and thereby *youth football* teams use the NCAA formula, this is the only formula that will be shown. (Thanks to http://www.4malamute.com/zl4.html for providing the formula and example.)

At the NCAA level this formula is:

$$ER = TY/PA*8.4+PC/PA*100+TD/PA*330-I/PA*200$$

(Where TY=total yards; PC=pass completions; PA=pass attempts; TD=touchdowns; I=Interceptions; ER=Efficiency Rating.)

Factoring out 1/PA leaves:

$$ER = (TY*8.4+PC*100+TD*330-I*200)/PA$$

For example: Cody Pickett's stats as of 20 October 2003.

256 attempts, 148 completions, 8 interceptions, 1913 yards, 10 TDs

$$1913/256*8.4 + 148/256*100 + 10/256*330 - 8/256*200=127.21$$

Pickett's passer efficiency rating at that time was 127.2

Passing Down

Term used to describe a long yardage situation. This expression applies more to the professional and college levels than to high school or *youth football*.

In second and more than seven, third and more than five, or any such circumstances the professional teams usually resort to *passing* the football, leading to the term.

Pass Interference

The act of interfering with an eligible *receiver* during his *pass route*. NCAA and NFSHSA rules allow contact with a receiver until the ball is in the air. This is to give the defender time to determine whether the receiver is blocking or attempting to run a pass route. The NFL only allows contact during the first five yards of the route. Most levels punish pass interference with a fifteen-yard penalty, but the NFL enforces this penalty from the spot of the foul, which may be many yards downfield. An *offensive* player may interfere with a defender as well. The penalty is the same, except all levels apply the consequence to the original *line of scrimmage*.

Pattern

A combination of *pass routes* designed to get a *receiver* or number of receivers open (in the clear and away from pass *coverage*). Some coaches use the terms "pattern" and "*route*" interchangeably. This is inaccurate. Patterns are composed of routes.

Pass Route

Path of an eligible *receiver* that is designed to attack the defensive *coverage* and get the receiver into the clear, or "open." (See Pass *Pattern*.)

Pass Rush

Performed by the *defense*, the pass rush is an attempt to get to the *quarterback* or *passer* before he can throw the football. Any defensive player may rush the *passer*.

Personal Foul

Any of a number serious infractions that violate the rules of safety or sportsmanship. *Spearing, unsportsmanlike conduct*, and an intentional *facemask* infraction are all examples of a personal foul. Flagrant fouls may result in ejection of the player from the game. All personal fouls are punished by a fifteen-yard penalty.

Placekick

Kicking play in which the ball is placed on a tee and kicked from the ground rather than held and dropped to be kicked in the air, as in a *punt*. The *kickoff* is a placekick.

Placekicker

Any player that kicks a *placekick*.

Play

A set of prescribed, pre-planned movements performed by the *offense* for the purpose of advancing the ball towards or across the opposing *goal line*. Plays may involve running with or *passing* the ball.

Play Action

Term used to describe the *misdirection* technique of faking a running play before throwing a downfield *pass* to an eligible *receiver*. Play action has some success in *youth football* when the *offensive line* is capable of *pass blocking*.

Pattern

A combination of *pass routes* designed to get a *receiver* or number of receivers open (in the clear and away from pass *coverage*). Some coaches use the terms "pattern" and "*route*" interchangeably. This is inaccurate. Patterns are composed of routes.

Pick

Illegal Pass pattern in which two *receivers* cross paths with the intention of running one of them into the defender covering the other and interfering with his path. Patterns that force two defenders to run into each other are not illegal. (See *Rub*.)

Pitch

A short *lateral* to the ball carrier.

Point After Touchdown (PAT)

After a team advances the ball across their *goal line*, they are given an opportunity to gain one or two additional points. From the professional level to the high school level this may take the form of a *scrimmage kick* like a *field goal*, which will earn one point, or a run or *pass play*, which will earn two points. Some *youth football* leagues and levels reverse this to advance teaching of the kicking game. At the youth levels the ball is placed on the three yard line for this try.

Point of Attack

The place on the *line of scrimmage* at which a particular play is directed.

Pop Warner (Little Scholars)

Most successful and well-known *youth football* governing body in the United States. Pop Warner Little Scholars is named for legendary football coach *Glenn "Pop" Warner*. Pop Warner football is used as a "catch all" phrase to describe all football programs below the high school level, although this is not truly accurate. There are more independent teams than Pop Warner ones. Further information about the Pop Warner Little Scholars can be obtained from their website, www.popwarner.com. (See *Warner, Glenn*.)

Possession

Series of *downs*. The object of football is to cross the *goal line* with the football, thus one cannot score without the ball. A team maintains possession of the ball as long as they continue to travel a minimum of ten yards in four attempts (*downs*). A team may lose possession on a *fumble*, *interception*, or by failing to move the ball the required distance in four attempts.

Possession, Time of

The longer one team has *possession* of the football, the more likely they are to score, and the less likely their opponents are to do so. Time of possession is the total amount of time in the game that one team has held onto the football.

Post

Pass route in which the *receiver* runs downfield for a predetermined distance before angling sharply to the middle of the field at approximately a 45-degree angle. Before the goalposts were moved to the back of the *end zone* in 1974, this route was often used by teams in the red zone to run the defender into the goalposts, thus leading to the name of the path.

Post-Corner

A *pass route* in which the receiver runs a *post* before breaking back towards the *sideline* at an angle towards the corner of the field where the boundaries intersect. Highly effective route at the *youth level*, but takes successful *pass blocking* to allow the *play* to develop.

Power

An offensive *play* in which all or nearly all members of the *offensive backfield* move in the same direction towards the *point of attack*. The ball is usually carried by the *offensive back* farthest from the hole, thus allowing all other members of the backfield to *lead block* for him. Very effective play at the *youth level* when competently taught.

Power-I

Full house backfield offensive *formation* in which a *flanker* is removed from the field and a second *fullback* is substituted. The power-I can be very effective at the *youth level*, but the compressed backfield leads to difficulty in getting to the perimeter and making use of the passing game.

Pro-I

Offensive *formation* characterized by a *fullback*, *tailback*, and *quarterback* lined up in a straight line behind the *center*, looking like the letter "I." One *end* is split wide, and the other is tight. The final player on the offense is the *flanker* who is placed on the same side as the *tight end* and split wide as well. Unmatched for its versatility, the Pro-I is difficult to use at the *youth level* because of its lack of perimeter *misdirection* and the reliance on the three potential deep *receivers* to be utilized in the passing game, something few youth teams are capable of. Requiring superior talent, the offense designed around the Pro-I is at the same time the most ineffective and yet most successful offensive system in history.

Progression

(See *Receiver Progression.*)

Pull

Typically performed by an *offensive lineman*, a pull is a technique used to get the player out in front of the play. The lineman "pulls" out of his position and travels laterally across the field to get in front of the ball carrier. Misdirection offenses such as the *Double Wing* and *Wing-T* make extensive use of this technique.

Punt

Scrimmage kick in which the ball is snapped to the punter (kicker), who drops it from approximately chest height and kicks it before it touches the ground. Punts are usually performed on fourth *down* when the offense is unlikely to score or reach their ten yard goal were they to go for it.

Quarterback

Offensive player who usually lines up behind the *center*, calls the signals, and directs the offensive play of the team. In most offenses the quarterback is the primary *passer* for the team.

Quarterback Efficiency Rating

(See *Passer Efficiency Rating.*)

Raymond, Harold "Tubby"

Developer of the *Wing-T* offense to the modern, flexible system known as the "Delaware Wing-T," and currently in use (mostly at the high school level) across the country. Coach Raymond's books can be located on www.amazon.com.

Harold Rupert "Tubby" Raymond was born in Flint, Michigan in November of 1926, and is one of only four coaches to achieve three hundred wins at one school. During Coach Raymond's years as head coach of the Fighting Blue Hens, the University of Delaware football team won three national titles, 16 NCAA playoff appearances, 14 Lambert Cup trophies, nine ECAC Team of the Year awards, and nine conference titles.

Read Progression

(See *Receiver Progression.*)

Receiver

Term used to describe any member of the offensive unit that is eligible to catch a forward *pass*.

Receiver Progression

In any competently designed *pass pattern* the *passer* should look through a series of his *receivers* in a certain order. This categorization is referred to as the "progression." Typically, the order of the receivers is designed to take into account the depth of the pattern, timing of the *offensive backfield* movements, and pressure on the passer.

Reed, John T. "Jack"

John T. Reed coached freshman, junior varsity, and varsity high school football for six years. He also coached *youth football* for eight years (ages 8 through 15). He coached youth baseball from tee ball to age 18 and was player/manager of two semi-pro teams. Counting baseball, high school volleyball, and soccer, he has coached over thirty teams ranging from five-year olds in tee ball to high school. He is a member of the American Football Coaches Association, the American Baseball Coaches Association, the California Coaches Association, the National Federation of Interscholastic Coaches Association, the Football Writers Association of America, and the Professional Football Researchers Association. He is a West Point graduate and a Harvard M.B.A.

Reed is the author of six books on coaching football, predominately at the youth level, one book on coaching youth baseball, and several books on business, real estate investing and success. His website is www.johntreed.com.

Referee

1) Generic term used to describe any member of a football officiating crew.

2) Member of a football officiating crew charged with overall supervision of the officiating and responsibility for ensuring that the game is played safely and by the rules of whatever governing body applies to the participants. The referee is denoted by a white hat.

Reverse

Trick *play* in which one ball carrier carries the football and appears to be heading for the perimeter on a *sweep*. Instead, however, the ball carrier *hands off* to another offensive player, typically a *wide receiver*, who carries it in the opposite direction. Simple to execute, the reverse usually results in a large gain for the *offense*. However, the depth of the play in the *offensive backfield* usually adds an amount of risk disproportionate to the reward of the play.

Robber

Defensive technique in which a *blitzing linebacker* is replaced by a *safety* that moves into his position on the field. The goal is to pressure the *passer* with the blitz while making him think that the area of field the linebacker came from has been abandoned and that any *receiver* entering the area will be uncovered. If the passer doesn't see the safety, he should throw the ball into *coverage* and the result could be an interception. Robbers are advanced coverage techniques that are, for the most part, unsuitable for the *youth level* of football. A defensive safety engaged in the act of playing a robber technique may also be referred to as the robber.

Rollout

Pass play designed to use the *passer* as a running threat to force the *defense* to react horizontally across the field while the *receivers* add a *vertical stretch* with their pass routes. Typically, the passer (usually the *quarterback*) takes the snap or handoff and sprints towards the sideline after executing a *play action* fake. Well-designed rollouts will make use of receivers at multiple levels along the same side of the field to allow the passer to make a natural read *progression*. Rollouts are highly effective at the *youth level* where *pass blocking* competence is less than ideal.

Route

(See *Pass Route*)

Rub

A *pass pattern* similar in nature to the *pick* in which two receivers come close enough to one another to "rub." The purpose of a rub is to force man-to-man defenders to run into one another. This action makes the rub legal where the pick is not. Rubs can be extremely effective in *youth football*, provided they are coached and executed competently.

Run and Shoot

Offensive system developed by Glenn "Tiger" Ellison and Darrel "Mouse" Davis in the 1960s through 1980s. The system relies on a passing attack in which everything is based on reads of the *defense*, and no matter what the defense does, something is wrong. The modern version has incorporated a *triple option* attack that adds enormous flexibility to the system. Highly effective, the run and shoot has evolved into the *West Coast* and *Spread* offenses of today. Unfortunately, the coaching-intensive nature of the system makes it difficult to use at the *youth football* level.

Running Back

Any offensive player that aligns in the backfield and is primarily charged with carrying the football on running plays. *Halfbacks, fullbacks,* and *upbacks* are all considered running backs, although the prevalence of the *Pro-I* has resulted in the term gradually coming to be used interchangeably with *tailback.*

Run Support

Act of providing additional defense against a running play. Typically performed by the members of the *defensive secondary*, run support may be by design, as in a run *blitz* from a *strong safety*, or it may be as the result of necessity, as in a *free safety* coming up to make the touchdown-saving tackle.

S

Sack

The act of *tackling* a *passer* in the offensive *backfield* before he can throw a forward pass.

Safety, 2 pt.

If any member of the team with *possession* of the ball is *tackled* while carrying the ball in his own *end zone*, the tackling team is awarded a safety. A safety gives the tackling team two points, and the team that suffered the safety is forced to *free kick* from their twenty yard line. (Note: the kicking team is given the option to use a punt-style kick rather than kick from a tee.)

Safety , Free

(See *Free Safety*.)

Safety, Strong

(See *Strong Safety*.)

Sam

Nickname sometimes given to the strong side *linebacker* (See *Mike*, *Will*.)

Shula, Don

Famous for coaching the only undefeated team in National Football League History, Don Shula retired in 1995 with more wins than any other coach in pro football history. Among his many accomplishments Shula lists:

- Coached only undefeated team in NFL history - 1972 Miami Dolphins

- Lead his teams to more wins than any other coach in the history of the NFL

- Appeared in more Super Bowls than any other coach

- Unanimous election to the Pro Football Hall of Fame

- Youngest head coach in the history of the NFL

- 4-time Coach of Year

- Shula's teams reached the playoffs 20 times in 33 seasons

- Took six teams to the Super Bowl

- Won 4 Super Bowls - twice with Baltimore (1964, 1968) and twice with Miami (1970-71)

- Served from 1975 through 1995 on the league's influential Competition Committee

Scramble (Crab) block

Low *block* against the legs of a defender. Legal only in the *free blocking zone*, the blocker puts his hands on the ground and scrambles sideways, attempting to pin the defender between his hips and the inside of the upper arm without *holding*.

Scrape (Linebacker Technique)

Slightly arcing path used by a *linebacker* to reach his assigned *gap* without being blocked. The shoulders should remain parallel to the *line of scrimmage*, and the player should keep his hips and feet under him.

Screen

Pass play designed to take advantage of a *blitzing* or pressuring defense. The *passer* drops back as if to throw downfield and allows the rush to come to him. Behind the rush, a *running back* or other eligible *receiver* loops out behind a screen of blockers. The passer loops the ball to him, and the receiver follows the blockers downfield. Screens have limited usefulness in *youth football* largely due to the lack of patience in the players and the inability to handle the stress of the pass rush.

Scrimmage Kick

Kicking play from scrimmage. Scrimmage kicks belong to the receiving team unless touched by a member of that team, in which case the ball may be recovered, but not advanced, by either team. (See *Live Ball*.) The *punt* and *field goal* are examples of scrimmage kicks.

Scrimmage Kick Formation

Any *offensive formation* in which the recipient of the *snap* is at least seven yards deep in the *offensive backfield*. During a scrimmage kick the snapper is protected by rule, and may not be touched until he brings his head up following the snap or a "reasonable" time to do so has elapsed.

Seam

Pass route, usually performed by the *tight end*, in which the receiver runs directly down the field into the "seam" between the *zones* of a *landmark pass coverage*.

Second Level

Term used to describe the *linebackers*, typically by offensive coaches. Ex: "Billy, your assignment is to go 'second level' after the *Sam Linebacker*."

Series

A group of interconnected *plays* that offer similar backfield movements designed to confuse the *defense* and allow the offense to attack a number of different points in the defense.

Series-Based

Any offensive system such as the *Wing-T*, *Double Wing*, or *Wishbone* in which the primary methods of attack are divided into groups of plays designed to look identical at the *snap*. Series-based offensive football is possibly the most effective method for attacking a defense at the *youth level*, and does not require the extensive training time of the *triple option* or passing-based attacks.

Set

(See *Alignment*)

Seven-Man Rule

Rule 2, Section 14, Article 1 of the National Federation of State High School Athletics 2005 Football Rule Book, which states that "A scrimmage formation requires a minimum of seven A players on their line at the snap." Note that there is no <u>maximum</u> number of players.

Seven Step Drop

Footwork typically performed by a *passer*, usually the *quarterback* immediately after taking the *snap*. The passer takes seven quick steps backwards to avoid the *pass rush* while looking downfield and going through his receiver *progression*. (See *Five Step Drop, Three Step Drop*.)

Short Punt

Offensive system developed by Lou Howard during the 1940s and 1950s that featured a *shotgun snap* to a deep back. The resulting formation looked like a compressed version of the formation use to *punt* the ball at that time.

The major premise of the short punt offense is that the *offensive linemen* are typically not the athletes that the *backfield* players are, therefore crucial *blocking* assignments are given to the *running backs* rather than the offensive line. The system can be highly effective at the *youth football* level, especially when used as a standard punting formation and punt fake *series*, or as a surprise offense.

Shotgun Snap

A deep *snap* to a member of the *offensive backfield* that is less than seven yards from the snapper.

Sideline

Out of bounds marker for the edges of the field. Typically a three to six inch wide strip of white chalk or paint. Each team in the contest occupies one sideline.

Single Wing

Extremely effective offense system developed originally at the turn of the century by *Glenn "Pop" Warner* and expanded considerably from then until now.

Still in use today, the system usually features an unbalanced *offensive line* and an advanced misdirection attack. The most notable difference between the single wing and other offenses is the use of a *direct snap* to the ball carrier rather than an exchange to the *quarterback* as has become the norm. The single wing is an excellent offense for the *youth football* level, and many high schools continue to use it today. Even the NFL occasionally uses principles taken from this system.

Six-Two, Six-Three, Six-Five, or "Sixty"

Defensive system used at the high school and college levels mostly as a *goal line front*. The sixty has some effectiveness at the *youth football* level, but is typically weak against the pass in the *flats*.

Sky

Defensive pass coverage system designed to provide *run support* or bolster *pass coverage* in a specific area of the field by rotating the *zones*. Instead of dropping straight back to their *landmark zones*, coverage men rotate, thus a sky coverage to the right would result in the right *cornerback* playing up tight to the *line of scrimmage*, while the *free safety* drifts over to take the cornerback's original position. The left cornerback would drift to cover the free safety's empty zone, and the left *outside linebacker* would move to fill in for the left cornerback. Sky coverage has its uses, especially against the *sweep*, at the *youth football* level, but overall the ineffectiveness of zone coverage and the difficulties in execution make this highly difficult to use.

Slot

Any *receiver* aligned approximately midway between the widest eligible receiver on the side of the formation and the nearest *offensive lineman*.

Smash

A *pass pattern* using two receivers. One receiver typically runs a *post* or *post corner* route while the other one runs a *hook* or other short pattern. Highly effective against certain pro-style defenses, the pattern has potential for the youth level, but it is difficult to execute due to the length of time the *pass blockers* must protect the *passer* to allow the play to develop. Use of a *rollout* to give the passer extra time drastically increases the effectiveness of this play.

Snap

Act of passing the ball from one player to another to start the play. A snap is almost always performed between the legs of the snapper. There are two variants of snaps, the *direct* and the *indirect*. The *center* is usually the offensive lineman responsible for snapping the ball, but he does not necessarily have to be the center man in the formation.

Snapper

Any player assigned the responsibility of executing a snap.

Spearing

Personal foul in which the offender uses the top of the helmet as the hitting surface, both illegal and dangerous.

Split (Gap)

Distance between *offensive linemen* in a *formation*. Splits are an important part of the timing of many plays.

Split-T

The Split-T of Faurot, Wilkinson and Jim Tatum of Maryland was a Chicago Bear-style full house *T-formation*, but with much bigger *line splits*, up to one yard, depending on the play called, and featured the dive and *double option* as the foundation of its attack.

Split-6

Defensive system in which the *outside linebackers* of the *4-4* are walked up to the *line of scrimmage*. The *defensive ends* play more of an interior *tackle* role, and are usually assigned responsibility for the *"C" gaps*. The interior *linemen* are assigned to defend the *"A" gaps*, leaving the *"B" gaps* for the *inside linebackers*. The system has limited effectiveness for the youth level for the same reasons as the standard sixty front.

Spread

Offensive system that evolved from Mouse Davis's *Run and Shoot* system of the early eighties. The modern spread features a route-switching concept that assigns *pass routes* to the *receivers* based on receiver alignment, and uses motion to change these alignments at will, placing defenses always at a disadvantage in determining which defender is responsible for which receiver. The spread has the potential to be a highly effective *youth football* offense, but the level of coaching required makes it extremely difficult for the average youth football coach to run successfully. It normally takes years to master the intricacies of a spread offense, and receivers and *passers* must work for many hours to become proficient, time that most youth coaches cannot devote to one aspect of their offense.

Sprint Out

Very similar to the *rollout* in nature, the sprint out typically involves the *passer* taking the snap and immediately sprinting to the *sideline* without executing any form of running fake or *play action*.

Stack

Method of "hiding" members of the *defensive backfield* by placing them immediately behind *defensive linemen*. A stacked defender can charge to either side of the lineman in front of him, executing a *blitz* that will interfere with the *blocking* assignments of the *offensive line*.

Stack-I

Offensive *formation* in which the *quarterback, fullback, upback,* and *tailback* are arranged in a single line behind the *center.* Popularized by the University of Maryland in the 1960s, where it gained the nickname "Maryland-I," the system is powerful between the *tackles,* but offers a severely limited passing and perimeter game. The offense can be used at the *youth football* level, but in modern programs at the high school level it is usually used as a change-of-pace formation.

Streak

(**See** *Fly, Pass route.*)

Strong Safety

In any two *safety* defense, the *defensive back* responsible for aligning to the *strong side* of the offensive *formation.* A strong safety is usually a player midway between a *linebacker* and a safety. He will provide *run support* to the strong side, as well as being primarily responsible for *pass coverage.* Most *youth football* defenses avoid the use of a strong safety by using eight players in some combination (*5-3, 4-4, 6-2*) to stop the run, and leaving pass defense largely in the hands of two *cornerbacks* and a single safety.

Strong Side

The strongest potential side of an offensive *formation.* Typically the side where a *tight end* aligns, assuming that the other end is split wide.

Stunt

Similar in nature to a *blitz,* stunting is an anti-passing tactic used to confuse the *offensive line* blocking. Usually performed by two or more linemen, stunts include such tactics as a *defensive tackle* aligning in one *gap* and looping through another, or crossing behind another tackle or *end.* Stunting is difficult to be successful with at the *youth football* level because it takes the defensive tackles away from their primary responsibility and asks them to travel to a gap. The term 'stunt' is often used interchangeably with the term 'blitz,' although this is not really accurate.

Super Power

An offensive football blocking call in which the *quarterback* is used as a *lead blocker* on the play. To make this happen, the player takes the ball in a *snap* from the *center,* and *pitches* it back to the *running back* while pivoting through 270-degrees.

Sweep

An offensive *play* that is designed to strike outside the perimeter of the *defense.* At the *snap* the ball is *handed off* or *pitched* to a *running back* that then sprints towards the *sideline* in an effort to outflank the defense. Referred to often as the most feared play in *youth football.* Many youth teams are successful

T

because of this play and in spite of poor coaching, although the play is not particularly difficult to stop with adequate preparation.

Tackle

1) Act of seizing and throwing to the ground the ball carrier. A player is considered "tackled" when his knee, shoulder, or helmet touches the ground.

2) Any player on the *offensive line* located outside the *guards* but inside the *ends*.

3) *Defensive linemen* located between the *nosetackle* and the *defensive ends*.

Tailback

Generally the deepest member of the *offensive backfield* and the player primarily responsible for carrying the football on running *plays*.

Technique, Defensive Alignment

Location of a *defensive player* in relation to his offensive counterpart, usually a member of the *offensive line*. The techniques are given numbers, counting from the middle of the *center* outward. Thus, a "3-technique" is aligned in an outside shade position on the *guard*; while a "0-tech" is aligned head up on the center.

T-Formation

Offensive Football *formation* and system from the dawn of football. Developed and expanded at the University of Notre Dame by legendary coach Frank Leahy. The system features a *full house* offensive backfield and is famous for being the first system to place a *quarterback* under *center* and dividing the labor of running and passing the ball between the *running backs* and the quarterback. The T-formation eventually evolved into such notable systems as the *Wing-T*, *Split T*, and other programs.

Third Level

Term used to describe the *defensive backs*, typically by offensive coaches. Ex: "Johnny, your assignment is to run a *fly* pass *route* and then block 'third level' on the *strong safety*."

Three-Point Stance

Most common body position in football. The stance features three points of contact with the ground: feet and one hand. Weight should be evenly divided, and the back should be close to flat. Incorrect instruction in this most basic stance may be the number one reason why many *youth football* teams are unsuccessful.

Three Step Drop

Similar in nature to the *seven step drop* and the *five step drop*, the three step drop is designed to allow the *passer* to gain depth in the *offensive backfield* to get away from the *pass rush* long enough for the *receivers* to get open. Typically this technique is used for short yardage *passes* without the use of *play action*.

Timing Route/Timing Pattern

Any *pass route* or *pattern* in which the *passer* does not make a read to determine the defensive *coverage*. The ball is simply thrown at a certain time in the play, typically to an area of the field and at an angle that the defender cannot hope to intercept. It is the *receiver*'s responsibility to get to the thrown ball and make a catch.

Toss

1) A short *lateral* to the ball carrier. Usually performed immediately after the *snap*.

2) Nickname for the most basic and fundamentally important *play* in the *Double Wing* offense: 24 Toss (Also referred to as the "*Super Power.*")

Touchback

The act of downing a ball intentionally in one's own *end zone* after a *placekick, scrimmage kick,* or other turnover of *possession*. The team with possession is awarded the ball at their own twenty-yard line.

Touchdown

Act of *possessing* the ball and crossing the *goal line* into the opponent's *end zone*. A touchdown may be scored by running with the ball across the line, or by throwing the ball (passing) to a teammate inside the end zone. A touchdown is worth six points.

Trail Position

Defensive halfback position in relation to a *receiver*. Trail position is defined as "directly behind the receiver and able to reach out and touch his back pocket."

Trap

Blocking technique in which a *defensive lineman* is allowed to penetrate the *offensive line* untouched by the players in front of him. An *offensive lineman* (usually a *guard*) executes a *pull* and blindsides the defender. Used in conjunction with *misdirection*, trap blocking is highly effective in *youth football*, and is responsible for a large part of the continued success of the *Wing-T, Double Wing,* and other misdirection offenses.

Triple Option

Offensive *play* in which the *fullback* dives to the *"A"* gap. The *quarterback* places the ball into the fullback's belly and moves with him to the hole. If the *defensive lineman* in the hole moves to *tackle* the fullback, then the quarterback pulls the ball back and moves on to the outside while the fullback fakes the dive as if he still had the ball. As the quarterback moves outside the *guards*, the *halfback* takes up a position approximately three yards deep and three yards outside him. At least one defensive player at the point of attack is left unblocked. This allows a double team on another player. As the unblocked defender approaches the quarterback, the quarterback executes a second "option". If the defender attacks him, the quarterback will pitch to the halfback trailing him. If the defender hesitates, the quarterback will keep the football and turn up field.

The triple option is highly effective in *youth football*, but it requires a level of coaching expertise difficult to obtain in most youth coaches.

Unsportsmanlike Conduct

Personal Foul used to punish excessively aggressive or harmful actions such as taunting/trash-talking, fighting, and coaches arguing with the officials. Unsportsmanlike conduct may result in a player's or coach's ejection from the game. The penalty is fifteen yards from the current spot of the ball.

Upback

Offensive backfield position. Generally thought of and used as a second fullback in systems such as the *Maryland-I* and *Power-I*.

Vallotton, Jerry

Author of <u>The Toss: A New Offensive Attack for High Scoring Football</u>, one of the premier works of instruction in running the *Double Wing* offense. Coach Vallotton was a part of the staff that took the 1990 Foothill High School in California from an 0-9 season to an 11-0 record. Information on ordering <u>The Toss</u> can be obtained from Coach Vallotton's website, <u>www.doublewing.org</u>.

Veer

Developed by Bill Yeoman at the University of Houston, the Veer is an astounding *triple option* offense. Primarily using a *formation* similar to the *Split-T*, the Veer relies on a relatively small number of offensive plays executed in a precise fashion. The system can be overwhelming for a *youth football* defense, but few offensive coordinators at the youth level are capable of coaching the myriad of details necessary to be successful with it.

Vertical Stretch

Offensive tactic typically performed by *receivers* in which the *defense* is forced to defend a deep *passing* threat, and thereby weakens themselves in the shorter areas of the field. Can be used to open up the short *zones* for passes or to weaken the *run support*.

Warner, Glenn "Pop"

Legendary coach of the Carlisle Indians at the turn of the 20th century, Glenn "Pop" Warner coached such amazing football players as Jim Thorpe and Ernie Nevers. Credited with many of the innovations that make modern football what it is today, such as men in *motion*, the development of the *forward pass*, and others, "Pop" Warner has been immortalized in the College Football Hall of Fame and by the creation of the *Pop Warner Little Scholars*, a *youth football* and cheerleading system that has achieved nationwide recognition. Glenn Warner was also the original inventor of the *Single Wing* offense.

Wide Receiver

Any eligible *receiver* split more than three yards from the nearest *offensive lineman*. *Split ends*, *flankers*, and receivers in the *slot* could all be considered wide receivers.

Will or Willie

Nickname given to the weak side linebacker. Will is typically a smaller, faster linebacker than *Mike* or *Sam* linebackers. (See *Mike*, *Sam*.)

Wingback

A *running back* aligned in a "wing" position, which is generally one yard in the *offensive backfield* and one yard outside the nearest *offensive lineman*.

Wing-T

One of the more common offenses in football from the high school levels on down, no one is completely certain where the *Wing-T* was developed originally. The system obviously evolved from the *T-formation* that was in widespread use in the 1930s and 1940s. University of Delaware coach *Harold Raymond* is credited with many of the numerous alterations that resulted in the modern Wing-T.

Currently, the Wing-T is a misdirection system that has evolved into a complex shifting *formation* attack based on the *triple option* and a highly progressive *passing* game. At the *youth football* level, the effectiveness of the system is largely impaired by the ability of the coaches. Due to the widespread popularity of the Wing-T in the 1980s and 1990s, many current coaches vaguely remember playing in such a system, and faded memories are not adequate preparation for the use of this intricate system.

Wishbone

Name given to the offensive *formation* developed by Emery Bellard of Ingleside and Breckinridge High Schools in Texas in 1968. The offensive system developed by Bellard was given to University of Texas head coach Darryl Royal, who used it with the *triple option* to win thirty straight games and two national championships.

Wheel

Pass route in which a *running back* or *slot receiver* runs towards the *sideline* before "wheeling" downfield and running a *streak*. Used in conjunction with other, inward-breaking pass routes, the resulting pattern can be very effective. Unfortunately, the length of time required to get the pass off requires extensive *pass blocking* capability.

Wyatt, Hugh

Promoter of the modern *Double Wing* offense. Hugh Wyatt was coaching American Football in Finland when his team ran into a team coached by *Don Markham* and was destroyed, 77-0. Coach Wyatt liked what he saw in the power potential of the offense, and began to couple it with the *misdirection* of the *Wing-T* system he was currently using. The result is a highly effective offense that is currently winning games on numerous levels, from professional down to *youth football*. Coach Wyatt used his extensive background in video broadcasting and production to produce the <u>Dynamics of the Double Wing</u> series of instructional videotapes on coaching the offense. From there he moved on to production of <u>Safer and Surer Tackling</u>, reviewed in chapter two.

Hugh Wyatt is also the developer of the *Black Lion Award* discussed in appendix five. Information about ordering his coaching materials or the Black Lion Award can be located at www.coachwyatt.com.

X

Letter designation traditionally given to the *split end* in a three *receiver* offensive *set*.

Y

Letter designation traditionally given to the *tight end* or *receiver* in the *slot* in a three receiver offensive *set*.

Youth Football

The exact definition of youth football varies widely depending on your location, but for the purposes of this text it is taken to mean all levels of American football from high school junior varsity (typically freshman and sophomore players from ages fourteen to sixteen) down to junior pee wee (typically six to eight years of age) and even younger on occasion.

This distinction in age is important because many of the techniques, tactics, and systems discussed in books, video, and other instructional methods about coaching football are designed for the high school, college/junior college, and semi-pro or professional levels. This results in confused coaches trying to assimilate material with no frame of reference, and confused players that are given programs not tailored to their maturity level.

Z

Z

Letter designation traditionally given to the *flanker* in a three *receiver* offensive *set*.

Zone

1) Area of the field

2) Shortened form of "zone *pass coverage*," a coverage method in which defensive players are assigned to cover areas of the field instead of being assigned to a particular eligible receiver.

3) *Blocking* scheme currently in vogue at the professional levels and trickling down to college, high school, and *youth football*. In its simplest form, zone blocking is a track blocking scheme that assigns an area of the *line of scrimmage* to a particular *offensive lineman*. If there is no one to block in his zone, he continues along his path until a defender crosses his face.

In the youth level zone blocking has little merit, since it usually forces the offensive lineman into a one-on-one match up with a defensive player that may be his physical superior. Its one great strength is that the *running back* is usually not assigned a specific hole, but rather a general *point of attack*. This allows the running back to use his greater talent to find the seam and escape from the defense.

Zone Blitz

Anti-passing tactic used at the higher levels of football to confuse *passers*. A *defensive lineman* drops back from his normal position on the *line of scrimmage* and acts as a *zone* defender. His position on the line is occupied by a *linebacker*, who *blitzes*. The object is to confuse the passer, usually a *quarterback*, by making him think that there is an open area in the *pass coverage*. The zone blitz is practically worthless in *youth football* because few youth passers are capable of discerning coverages in the first place, much less isolating a blitz.

INDEX

Q

R

S

Who the Heck is Coach Wade?

Derek Wade is a youth football coach that happens to coach at the high school level. He has been active as an Internet coach and author since 1999. His coaching experience includes two years at the 10-11 and 11-12 age groups in non-Pop-Warner affiliated programs. Since 2001 he has coached with the Tomales High School Braves where he has functioned on both the Varsity and Junior Varsity levels as head scout, position coach, tackling coach, and special teams coordinator.

Coach Wade is the author of *The Gap-8: Positions and Responsibilities*, a PowerPoint presentation widely disseminated on the Internet, and is also the Webmaster and editor of *Football for Youth!*. He has been a regular clinic speaker at the Double Wing Symposiums, and his well-received presentations have covered such topics as "Reading and Attacking Defensive Keys," "Advanced Misdirection with the Double Wing Offense," and "Installing a Successful Double Wing in Limited Practice Time."

He is an active duty enlisted member of the United States Coast Guard stationed at USCG Training Center Petaluma in Northern California, where he works as a training design specialist and electronics instructor. He holds an Associate's level degree in Electronics Technology from the University of Phoenix, and is pursuing a Bachelor's level degree in Sports and Health Science with a focus in Coaching Studies from the American Military University.

He is married, with three dogs, and lives in Santa Rosa, California, where he divides his time between complaining about local politics and teaching young people to play football.

Printed in the United States
95930LV00001B/123-128/A

9 781420 892109